LAW AND REPRESENTATION IN EARLY MODERN DRAMA

This examination of the relation between law and drama in Renaissance England establishes the diversity of their dialogue, encompassing critique and complicity, comment and analogy, but argues that the way in which drama addresses legal problems and dilemmas is nevertheless distinctive. As the resemblance between law and theatre concerns their formal structures rather than their methods and aims, an interdisciplinary approach must be alive to distinctions as well as affinities. Alert to issues of representation without losing sight of a lived culture of litigation, this study primarily focuses on early modern implications of the connection between legal and dramatic evidence, but expands to address a wider range of issues which stretch the representational capacities of both courtroom and theatre. The book does not shy away from drama's composite vision of legal realities but engages with the fictionality itself as significant, and negotiates the methodological challenges it posits.

SUBHA MUKHERJI is Lecturer in English at the University of Cambridge, and Fellow and Director of Studies in English at Fitzwilliam College. She has contributed to *Shakespeare Survey 49* (Cambridge, 1996), *Shakespeare and Sexuality*, edited by Catherine Alexander and Stanley Wells (Cambridge, 2001) and *Literature, Politics and the Law in Renaissance England*, edited by Erica Sheen and Lorna Hutson (2004). Her work has also appeared in the journals *English Literary Renaissance* and *Essays in Criticism*.

LAW AND REPRESENTATION IN EARLY MODERN DRAMA

SUBHA MUKHERJI

CAMBRIDGE
UNIVERSITY PRESS

CAMBRIDGE UNIVERSITY PRESS
Cambridge, New York, Melbourne, Madrid, Cape Town, Singapore, São Paulo

Cambridge University Press
The Edinburgh Building, Cambridge CB2 2RU, UK

Published in the United States of America by Cambridge University Press, New York

www.cambridge.org
Information on this title: www.cambridge.org/9780521850353

First published 2006

Printed in the United Kingdom at the University Press, Cambridge

A catalogue record for this book is available from the British Library

ISBN-13 978-0-521-85035-3 hardback
ISBN-10 0-521-85035-5 hardback

In memory of 'Dada'
Tarapada Mukherji (1902–1987)

Contents

Illustrations

Maps

Acknowledgements

My most profound debt is to Anne Barton. She sustained her faith in me, and in the thesis that forms the basis of this book, quite literally in sickness and in health, and through great gaps of time. Without her support, both academic and personal, this piece of work might have languished.

Two others to whom I owe much are John Kerrigan and Tony Nuttall. John supervised the M.Phil dissertation from which this research developed, and has continued to offer a degree of support that goes beyond the call of his duty or my claim. He has sustained me with practical advice and general encouragement, read early drafts of chapters and provided incisive criticism. I feel the deepest gratitude for all this. My debt to Tony is for his intellectual bounty, for 'there was no winter in't'. I have learnt more from him than I have been able to use in the book, and my thanks to him are for immeasurably more than this specific venture.

I am grateful to John Baker for entertaining ignorant questions about legal procedure with humour and largesse; and to Neil Jones for clarification on specific legal terms. My thanks to Jim Sharpe for a clarifying conversation about law courts at an early stage of this work; to Marie Axton and the late Jeremy Maule for their active encouragement of my archival research; and to Ian Donaldson and Emrys Jones for their help as examiners of my Ph.D. thesis. Many thanks to Marina Kiprianou and Jen Pollard for their help with maps.

Lorna Hutson and Luke Wilson provided invaluable constructive criticism and advice for revision. So did Colin Burrow at an earlier stage. Thanks to Terence Cave and Jan Schramm for illuminating conversations at crucial junctures, and to Peter Goodrich for inspiration and encouragement. Sarah Stanton has been an admirably patient and supportive editor.

The manifold inadequacies that remain, I acknowledge mine.

Many friends, in their different ways, have supported me, and my research, over the years. My thanks go to Moitrayee Basu, Yota Batsaki,

Pippa Berry, Supriya and Sukanta Chaudhuri, Nadina Christopoulou, Eleanor Coghill, Santanu Das, Tania Demetriou, Dan Dombey, Pietro del Favero, Christine Garabedian, Bahi Ghubril, Nick Hammond, Juan José Herrera de la Muela, Andreas Janousch, Gabriel Josipovici, Aptin Khanbaghi, Mary Laven, Supriyo Mitra, Katy Mullin, Ralph and Clèmence O'Connor, Debdulal Roy, Ray Ryan, Jason Scott-Warren and Hugh Stevens. Katy, Tania, Yota, Ralph, Santanu, Supriya and Jason read parts of the text with care, and offered suggestions for editing and refining. Dan's characteristic and constructive ruthlessness has no doubt made the Introduction a little more readable than it might have been. Thanks to Mike Hallsworth for his help with the Bibliography. Special thanks to Yota and Tania for making the much-interrupted period of revision bearable, even fun. Two unique debts demand mention: to Katy, for endless sloe gins and stimulating distraction which it is now her turn to acknowledge; and to Santanu, for unfailing comic relief.

I owe gratitude to the Fellows of Fitzwilliam College, Cambridge, for providing a stimulating environment for work. In particular, I would like to acknowledge the kindness and support of Nicky Padfield, John Cleaver, Amy Goymour, Brian Johnson and John Leigh. Thanks also to my students past and present, who made my arrival in Fitzwilliam joyful, have kept me mentally agile, and provided remarkable support and affection through the years.

Last, but by no means least, I am grateful to my parents, Indrani and Asoke Mukherji, for their unconditional love, their long-distance support and their patience.

My most far-reaching debt – at once personal and intellectual – is to my late grandfather, as acknowledged in the dedication.

Glossary

Common law   The body of laws that emerged in England in the middle ages, developed from arguments and rulings used in actual cases and based on the practice of 'the law of the land' rather than written and codified in textual form; taught at the Inns of Courts (professional law schools – and more) until the middle of the seventeenth century, and then left largely to self-help; administered mainly through the central courts of common law, but also through assizes in the counties. So the term also referred to a professional structure, independent of the university law faculties.

Canon law   The law of the Church of Rome, initially systematised in Gratian's *Decretum* (c.1140), expanded by the fourteenth century into the *Corpus Juris Canonici*. It continued to be in force in England, even after the Reformation, in ecclesiastical jurisdictions, and was administered through church courts. From 1857 the jurisdiction of church courts was confined to Church matters, but in the sixteenth and seventeenth centuries it was expansive, and covered marriage, bastardy, personal property, sexual morality and spiritual matters, defamation, wills and probate, and church governance. Canon law was taught in the English universities until 1535, the year which marked the formal closure of the separate canon law faculties (and degrees) at Oxbridge. But some study of it seems to have informally survived at the universities under the wider auspices of Civil law. It was in any case heavily influenced by Roman law method and to some extent by Roman law content.

Civil law   Roman Civil law, codified in the *Corpus Juris Civilis* established by Emperor Justinian in the sixth century. In the Renaissance, this text-based system was still authoritative on the Continent, but England had evolved its own 'common law', which was unwritten. Students of jurisprudence at Oxford and Cambridge studied the literature of Civil law, while law students at the Inns of Courts studied the practice of common law. Doctors of Civil law from the universities went on to become practitioners or judges at the English ecclesiastical and admiralty courts till 1857. Civil law could also be occasionally relevant to Council arbitration, and to prerogative and equity court action; but the bulk of secular legal action in England was under common law which rendered Civil law largely academic. Note that in some contexts, the term 'civil law' could also be used, in an entirely separate sense, to describe civil as opposed to criminal action: a law that dealt with disputes between private individuals and organisations.

Dower and jointure   Dower was a widow's entitlement, for her lifetime, to a third of the real property held by her husband during the marriage. But the law was asymmetrical, for a widower was entitled to all of his wife's real property for the rest of his life, provided a child had been born, not simply a third. A jointure, on the other hand, was joint tenancy of land, usually agreed upon in the marriage settlement, from which a widow could receive income for her life.

Depositions   The responses of witnesses and deponents to official court interrogatories; usually written down by clerks of court before a trial and thereafter presented during the trial.

Elenchus   A maxim or precept, in rhetoric, that contradicts a given 'colour' and offers the opposite case. Plural: *elenches.*

Fact   Alleged deed, usually assumed to be of a criminal nature; but a conjectural entity rather than an established or objective truth.

Feoffment A grant in fee simple, made by 'feoffor' (or 'feoffer' or 'feeoffer') to a 'feoffee'. This could be an 'ordinary feoffment', i.e. a feoffment not involving uses but made upon sale or gift where the feoffor retained the whole interest; in such a case, the trustee would be the legal owner of the property only on the understanding that he would hold it not for his own benefit but for the benefit of beneficiaries. The other kind of feoffment was a feoffment to uses – a product of the arrangement whereby a feudal tenant was bound, by contract or trust, to allow another person – the landowner, or, often, his heirs – to have the beneficial enjoyment of land vested in himself. Yet law could only grant one right – that of the tenant – so there was a conflict between legal right and actual ownership. This practice of granting 'use' of land inevitably led to discontents and misuse. So it had to be a matter of mere trust, since the only person entitled to enter on breach after the feoffor's death was the heir. If the feoffee failed to perform the conditions specified by the feoffor, the land reverted back automatically to the feoffer or his heirs. But it also allowed a feoffor to defer selection of successors to the land until he approached death, since the land would be meanwhile invested in others, while he himself still enjoyed absolute ownership and profits ensuing from the land. Or he could sell it off before such time by simply commanding his feoffees to convey it to his purchaser. Note that by the sixteenth century, feudal land law, originally the province of local civil law and manorial custom, had effectively passed into the jurisdiction of royal justice, and tenancy had become a function of English common law.

Inns of Chancery Lesser Inns – *hospicia minora* – which, by 1600, were attached to particular Inns of Court. They gave instruction, provided by barristers sent from the Inns of Court as 'readers', and moots were held there. Ideally, one was supposed to spend a couple of years in one before proceeding to an Inn of Court – witness

Justice Shallow in Shakespeare's *2 Henry IV*, who was at Clement's Inn. Their ruling members were not barristers, but attorneys who had not joined the Inns of Court. A member of an Inn of Chancery could be considered a lawyer if he practised law as an attorney (as many of them did). But most members of the Inns of Chancery, and indeed of the Inns of Court, never studied or practised law, so membership by itself does not indicate a lawyer.

Inns of Court Professional law-schools of England, established in the fourteenth century, situated in London: Gray's Inn, Lincoln's Inn, Middle Temple and Inner Temple. English common law was not taught at the universities but at the Inns – the reason why they were informally termed the 'Third University of England'. They were also a residential society of lawyers, with their own customs and entertainments, and indeed often used as a finishing school for young men not necessarily intending to join the legal profession.

Interrogatories A set of questions prepared by the court and put to the witnesses and defendants in a case.

Inventio or Invention Rhetorical term meaning the finding or amassing of matter, or the matter or idea itself; it was the first 'part' of rhetoric, which was then to be arranged, memorised and delivered to the greatest effect. As the anonymous writer of *Ad Herennium* says of classical rhetoric: 'among the five tasks of the orator, the mastery of invention is both the most important and most difficult of all' (*Ad C. Herennium* 1954, II. I.I, 58).

Paraphernalia A wife's linen, jewellery and plate, and in some cases her bed – property originally part of her husband's estate which she could claim as a widow.

Pin-money Early modern equivalent of pocket-money for trinkets so that a woman did not constantly have to pester her husband; held by a married woman as a personal annual income.

Plus quam satis 'More than enough'; a phrase typically applied to charges of incontinency in adultery cases, and possibly linked to impotence in annulment cases.

Seisin   The situation of being in possession in one's capacity of a feudal tenant was called 'seisin', linked often to an act of homage to the lord. 'Disseisin' is the act of divesting him of this possession by the lord through judgement because of some lapse of contractual performance on the part of the tenant. Though seisin was originally a question of the relationship between lord and tenant, over time, and certainly by the sixteeth century, the role of the feudal lord was much reduced: seisin could be roughly equated with possession of freehold land and disseisin with putting someone out of possession, but not necessarily or exclusively by a lord. 'Novel disseisin' was a variation on, and extension of, the action of disseisin.

Separate estate   A specified property belonging to the wife, and at her disposal, during coverture, and held by means of a trust.

A note on the text

Notes give author and short title. Full title and publication information is provided in the Bibliography.

In transcribing original manuscript sources, old spellings and punctuation have been retained except where there are obvious mistakes that obscure the meaning. Superscripts and contractions have been italicised and expanded.

In the appendix – Swinburne's *Matrimony* – portions included within angular brackets (< >) indicate text written between the lines with omission marks; folio numbers have been indicated in the margin. Conjectural reconstructions where the ink has faded or the paper is torn have been put inside square brackets ([ ]), and preceded by a question mark. Marginal annotations in Latin have been omitted as they are not immediately relevant to the present purpose; they are of a similar nature to the Latin marginalia to *A Treatise of Spousals* which has an inclusive modern edition – consisting mostly of summaries of arguments or abbreviated references which are dealt with more fully in the body of the text next to them. References to the appendix in the book are to the original folio numbers, not the page numbers of the book.

Abbreviations

APC	*Acts of the Privy Council*
BL	British Library, London
Bod.	Bodleian Library, Oxford
BRO	Bedfordshire Record Office
Bullough	G. Bullough, ed., *Narrative and Dramatic Sources of Shakespeare*, 8 vols. (London, 1957–75)
CCA	Canterbury Cathedral Archives
CJC	Justinian I, *Corpus Juris Civilis*, ed. Paul Kruger and Theodor Mommsen (Frankfurt, 1968–70)
CRO	Cheshire Record Office
CSPD	*Calendar of State Papers, Domestic Series*
CUL	Cambridge University Library
	Comm. Ct.: Commissary Court Records
	V.C.Ct.: Vice-Chancellor's Court Records
EDR	Ely Diocesan Records
First Folio	The First Folio of Shakespeare (1623): The Norton Facsimile, prep. Charlton Hinman (New York, 1968)
Q	Quarto edition of Shakespeare's plays
Hawarde	John Hawarde, *Les Reportes del Cases in Camera Stellata 1593 to 1609*
HL	Huntington Library
Institutio	Quintilian, *Institutio Oratoria*, ed. Donald A. Russell (Cambridge Mass./Harvard, 2001), Loeb Classics.
LRB	*The London Review of Books*
LTS	London Topographical Society Publication
Matrimony	Henry Swinburne, *Of the signification of diverse woordes importing Matrymonye, and whye yt is <rather> named matrimonie than Patrymony*
MG	Middlesex Guildhall

Murthers	*Two Most Unnaturall and Bloodie Murthers* (1605), Appendix A, *A Yorkshire Tragedy*, ed. A. C. Cawley and Barry Gaines (Manchester, 1986)
NNRO	Norfolk and Norwich Record Office Diocesan Records
	DN/DEP: Deposition books of the Consistory Court
	DN/ACT: Act books of the Consistory Court
OED	*The Oxford English Dictionary*
OUA	Oxford University Archives, Bodleian Library, Oxford
PRO	Public Record Office, Kew, London
	ASSI: Assize records
	STAC: Court of Star Chamber Proceedings
	Req.: Proceedings and Act Books of the Court of Requests
Shakespeare	The Riverside Shakespeare (Boston, 1974)
Spousals	Henry Swinburne, *A Treatise of Spousals, or Matrimonial Contracts*
Testaments	Henry Swinburne, *A Briefe Treatise of Testaments and Last Willes*
t.p.	title-page

PLAYS

Arden	Anon., *Arden of Faversham*
AW	Shakespeare, *All's Well That Ends Well*
AYLI	Shakespeare, *As You Like It*
DLC	John Webster, *The Devil's Law Case*
DM	John Webster, *The Duchess of Malfi*
LLL	Shakespeare, *Love's Labours Lost*
Lear F	*The Tragedy of King Lear* 1623 (in parallel text edition by René Weis)
Lear Q	*The History of King Lear* 1608 (in parallel text edition by René Weis)
Leir	*The True Chronicle Historie of King Leir*
MfM	Shakespeare, *Measure for Measure*
Miseries	George Wilkins, *The Miseries of Enforced Marriage*
MSND	Shakespeare, *A Midsummer Night's Dream*
Much Ado	Shakespeare, *Much Ado About Nothing*
MV	Shakespeare, *The Merchant of Venice*
RA	Lording Barry, *Ram Alley*
R&J	Shakespeare, *Romeo and Juliet*

Shrew	Shakespeare, *The Taming of the Shrew*
Warning	Anon., *A Warning for Fair Women*
WD	John Webster, *The White Devil*
WKK	Thomas Heywood, *A Woman Killed with Kindness*
WT	Shakespeare, *The Winter's Tale*

Introduction

'The law *is* theatre', said Sartre, in an interview with Kenneth Tynan in 1961; 'for at the roots of theatre is not merely a religious ceremony, there is also eloquence . . . The stage is a courtroom in which the case is tried.'[1] But dramatic works in different periods and places spring from different roots. Sartre was commenting on Greek tragedy, and his remark might even be equally applicable to the televised drama of American courts in our own times. However, in early modern England – the focus of this book – the roots, as well as forms, of drama were more mixed, as were the institutional forms of litigation. While the Athenian trial was a public spectacle with a clearly adversarial structure where both litigants presented their own case,[2] trials in sixteenth- and seventeenth-century England were jurisdictionally varied, mediated by counsel except in criminal cases, and consequently less starkly agonistic events. Yet the theatre-as-court metaphor is pervasive in Renaissance drama, sometimes suggesting the theatricality of trials, at other times the judicial structure of drama. Francis Beaumont, in his commendatory verses to *The Faithful Shepherdess* (1610), describes the Blackfriars playhouse as a court 'where a thousand men in judgement sit'.[3] Dramatists such as Kyd, Marlowe, Shakespeare, Jonson and Webster repeatedly open up the action of their plays, explicitly or implicitly, to the judgement, even 'sentence', of the theatre audience. Did the analogy between the two in English Renaissance drama amount to a substantive connection rather than a mere literary commonplace? Were there culturally specific affinities and investments driving the playwrights'

---

[1] Sartre, 'Interview', 126–7.
[2] See Eden, *Poetic and Legal Fiction*, 13–14; Todd, *Shaping of Athenian Law*; and MacDowell, *Law in Classical Athens*, Ch. 7.
[3] Beaumont and Fletcher, *Dramatic Works*, Vol. III, 490.

I

preoccupation with the law? And where does the drama of trial scenes in these plays come from?

Curiously, such plays often anticipate current phenomena in law and life. Vittoria Corombona in Webster's *The White Devil,* and Anne Sanders in *A Warning for Fair Women* (anon.), accused of adultery and murder, self-consciously project their protested innocence through symbolic modes of speech and action, stepping into court with a white rose or fashioning a densely metaphorical rhetoric of moral whiteness. How different are such modes of self-representation from, say, Michael Jackson (accused of child molestation) and his entire family turning up dressed in white in the Superior Court of California in 2004? Or from Al Qaeda terrorists releasing videos of hostages in orange jumpsuits pointedly reminiscent of Guantanamo Bay prisoners' jackets, and related by the same token to the fantasy of symmetry and justice that has informed revenge in imaginative literature? Such gestures seem to speak to some human need to conceptualise and almost symbolise the experience of law, justice and injustice. They express the need for representation, not just in art or in law, but in life, suggesting a connection between the symbolic imagination and moments of crisis. Mary Wragg appeared in court in Lewes on 2 March 2005, wearing a blue ribbon and a lock of her son Jacob's hair on the lapel of her coat, claiming innocence and non-complicity in his killing by his father.[4] Is there something about the legal situation itself – functioning centrally through figuration – that calls up a commensurate representational impulse? The need for justice, the need for credibility, and the need for representation – all attributes of legal procedure – are common to people and texts engaging with the law in all ages. So is the question of how congruent the procedures of institutional law are with the laws that govern our emotional and moral lives. But their expressions take distinct forms, and in different social contexts, produce different alchemies with the dramatic imagination. One of the particular characteristics of legal plots is indeed the inflection of such inherent and abiding issues by historically specific conditions.

The aim of this book is to illuminate the nature and the extent of the engagement between the disciplines and cultural practices of the stage and the court in early modern England. Few periods or kinds of literature show such a deep and comprehensive engagement with the subject. A majority of English Renaissance dramatists had studied law at the Inns of Court, and the theatre audience itself contained lawyers and

---

[4] Jacob was a sufferer of Hunter's syndrome.

law-students.[5] Beaumont himself, the son of a common law judge, attended the Inner Temple Inn, and the private theatre audience whom he describes in terms of judicial spectatorship is likely to have included students of law, Blackfriars having been practically next door to the Middle Temple.[6] Besides, the Inns themselves were, among other things, a site of theatrical playing – the best-known example being the first staging of *Twelfth Night* at the Middle Temple on Candlemas Day in 1602.[7] So there was an immediate proximity between the professional worlds of theatre and law in the cultural geography of London.

At the same time, the conceptual link between legal and dramatic structures in ancient Athens, formulated most clearly in the Aristotelian tradition, was mediated to the English Renaissance primarily through the adaptations by Latin rhetoricians and commentators on Terentian comedy.[8] This transmission created a parallel culture in the northern European Renaissance where proofs became integral to dramatic analysis – a phenomenon familiar to most of our English dramatists. The perception of structural affinity between theatrical and legal practice allowed playwrights to address actual legal issues of evidence, interpretation and judgement – the commonest preoccupations of plays interested in the law. Evidence, of course, entails representation, and this immediately links courtroom practice to theatrical mimesis. Representation is indeed one of the features that reconnects the ancient Greek legal arena with the apparently different early modern English courtroom. When Sartre talked about 'eloquence', he was registering the rhetorical aspect of judicial procedure: the presenting of a case involves the staging of truth, and the verbal representation of litigants by lawyers – what Quintilian calls 'prosopopœiae' or 'fictitious speeches of other persons'.[9] In that sense, as well as in the more specifically rhetorical sense of arguing both sides of a case and constructing as well as assessing probability, the Renaissance English courts were as much engaged with eloquence as the Athenian ones. But also, like the people's courts of ancient Attica,[10] the jury system that replaced older forms of trial in England reinforced, in this period, the

---

[5] On the Inns, see glossary; Prest, *Inns of Court*; and Baker, *Legal Profession*, 3–98.
[6] On the children's companies' satirical drama and 'private-theater audiences of law students, lawyers, and litigants', see Shapiro, *Children of the Revels*, 53–8 (55).
[7] The earliest reference to the play is indeed a note on this performance in the diary of the barrister John Manningham: see Manningham, *Diary*, 48. On theatre at the Inns, and the 'continuum between the court and Inns revels', see Axton, *Queen's Two Bodies*, 1–10 (8).
[8] For a discussion of this transmission trajectory, see Ch. 1, pp. 45–7 and n. 96.
[9] Quintilian, *Institutio*, 6.1.26.
[10] See Humphreys, 'Evolution'; Bullen, 'Lawmakers and Ordinary People'.

role of the people's representatives in independently evaluating evidence, including witness testimony, especially in the functions of the 'trial jury' (as opposed to the 'grand jury' who could only decide if bills of indictment were actionable or not).[11] The notion of the audience as an equitable jury that underlies so much of Renaissance drama, often providing a provocative basis for alternative criteria of judgement, is surely related to this. What Joel Altman calls 'the equity of tragedy' is a version of precisely such an investment of judicial authority in audience response to the theatrical representation of a 'case'.[12]

The use of drama to create an alternative framework of judgement, however, points to a complexity inherent in the relationship between rhetoric and the theatre since classical times, which goes beyond straightforward affinity. The prohibition against acting on stage in Justinian's *Digest of Roman Law* (seventh century AD) on pain of *infamia* (loss of citizenship or civil death)[13] is located by Peter Goodrich in the paradoxical combination of proximity and rivalry between law and rhetoric.[14] Both practices were determined by forms and conditions of representation. Rhetoric, a discipline that originated in the legal context of persuasion – often called *theatrum veritatis et iustitiae* (the theatre of truth and justice) – was 'the medium through which the drama of law was . . . played out' (418); it focused the performative and argumentative aspects of legal procedure. But the legal tradition itself developed a resistance to acknowledging the fundamentally rhetorical character of legality, going back to Plato's distinction between performance and law, or rather, between verbal performance and the theatre of justice which was meant to persuade to a truth beyond artifice. Traces of such a denial of the affective and social function of legal oratory find their way into later periods, including the Renaissance, when interpretation and passionate persuasion were not always perceived by the law as legitimate roles for the legal orator whose aim should be to arrive at an incontestable 'science or truth that exceeds the realms of contingency' (422). Admittedly, this is a residue of the Roman glossatorial tradition which revered the authority of the text

---

[11] See Green, *Verdict according to Conscience* and *Twelve Good Men*; Stone, *Evidence*; Shapiro, *Culture of Facts*, 11–13, on the commensurate importance of witness testimony and jurors' assessment of 'facts'. See also Hutson, 'Rethinking "the Spectacle of the Scaffold"', on the implications of jury trial and the participatory nature of the common law for Renaissance revenge tragedy, meant to be a corrective to Hanson's reading of the investigative methods of English common law in terms of the French inquisitorial system in *Discovering the Subject*.

[12] See Altman, *Tudor Play*, esp. 283; cf. 394.

[13] Justinian, *Digest*, Vol. I, 3.2.1.

[14] Goodrich, 'Law'.

whereas common law was based on precedence, and therefore implicitly on the logic of probability.[15] But as we shall see, these traditions were less segregated in English legal thinking than they might seem to have been. Ironically, the parodic, esoteric figure of the term-spewing, hair-splitting lawyer, common in comic drama,[16] is at least partly a result of the reduction of the role of the legal rhetorician and the displacement of rhetoric from law to literature. At her trial, Webster's Vittoria is described by the Latin-speaking lawyer as a woman 'who knows not her tropes or figures' (III.ii.40).[17] But by making fun of the lawyer and exposing the rhetorical strategies of her prosecutor Monticelso, Vittoria at once re-locates legal procedure in artifice and turns the traditional hierarchy upside down by claiming the superior order of rhetoric for her own affective defence plea.

The relation between law and rhetoric, then, is one of the vital clues to the double-strand of similarity and critical distance in drama's relation to law. Rhetoric is at once what aids recognition of the probable nature of the arguments and enthymemes of law, and what allows plays to address it more clearly than legal practice or theory could. It is what aligns the theatrical and the legal through a shared exercise in staging narrative and enargeically representing truths. But if, as Goodrich puts it, 'forensic rhetoric encodes and formalizes the affective and performative dimensions of legal practice' (417), drama decodes it by a more untroubled deployment of rhetorical principles.

But the rhetoricity of legal representation is no more knotty than the business of representing invisible intentions and secret actions – a difficulty that the theatrical medium not only comments on, but enacts, and shares with courtroom investigations of evidence. In the process, the incertitudes of law allow dramatists to create carefully defined areas of uncertainty around the motivation and action of characters onstage. Thus, drama not only addresses but also exploits uncertainties and conflicts within legal procedure and discourse. Its focus on intractable

---

[15] The glossatorial method characterised the twelfth-century reception of Roman law, which prohibited commentary and interpretation to preserve the inviolable text of the law. See Goodrich, 'Law', 423; Maclean, *Interpretation*, esp. 12–66; and 39–40 on the inbuilt checks to infinite interpretive proliferation in the *CJC* itself.

[16] Tangle in Middleton's *The Phoenix*, Throat in Barry's *Ram Alley*, Lurdo in Day's *Law-Tricks* and Otter and Cutbeard in Jonson's *Epicne* are only a few examples. Voltore in Jonson's *Volpone* is a well-known comic treatment of a corrupt lawyer. See Tucker, *Intruder*, on dramatic representations of the common lawyer, and Johansson, *Law and Lawyers*, on legal figures in Jonson and Middleton.

[17] Webster, *White Devil*. For satire on legal obscurantism, see also Day, *Law-Tricks*, Ruggles, *Ignoramus*, and Jonson, *Epicne* and *The Staple of News*.

intentions, however, also conveys its understanding of a simpler, but urgent, often fierce, human impulse. As Edgar says in *King Lear*, we 'rip . . . hearts' to know minds (*Lear* F, IV.v.254); Lear himself seeks to 'anatomise Regan' to 'see what breeds about her heart' straight after the mock trial in the Quarto (III.vi.33); Bracciano in *The White Devil* vents his hermeneutic frustration on Vittoria's supposed love-letter to another – 'I'll open't, were't her heart' – and swears to 'discover' her cabinet (IV. i.22, 76). The urge to uncover the inward is not simply a concern of representation but of finding out truths that we do not understand, though the two are not unrelated, as representation presupposes a degree of knowledge and control over material. It is a desire driven by the sense of the inscrutable at the core of the psyche, a mystery that can entice or horrify, tempt as well as resist 'plucking [out]'.[18] Consequently, its literary expressions become inseparable from legal as well as epistemological ideas of discovery; at any rate, from legally inflected language, if not frameworks such as trial or inquisition.[19] Indeed, they symptomise the way in which drama addresses what happens when legal process provides structures of feeling and articulation. When Othello raves, 'It is the cause, it is the cause, my soul',[20] he is expressing his innermost compulsion in terms that are specifically legal: William West, writing in 1590 about contracts in law, defines 'cause' as 'a business, which being approued by law, maketh the Obligation rise by the contract, & the action vpon the obligation'.[21] In other words, 'cause' does not only mean the nature of offence, i.e. adultery, as modern editors seem to assume,[22] but is also the property

---

[18] Shakespeare, *Hamlet*, III.ii.365. References to Shakespeare's plays are to *The Riverside Shakespeare*, unless specified otherwise.

[19] See Hanson, *Discovering the Subject*, on the inquisitorial context for the contemporary discourse of discovery.

[20] Shakespeare, *Othello*, V.ii.1.

[21] West, *Symbolaeography*, A3[b]; the 1597 edn. cites St. German's *Doctor and Student*, Bk II, Ch. 24, as the authority: A3[a]. See also Sacks, 'Slade's Case', 30, which recounts the entire intertextual conversation.

[22] Cf. Riverside, New Cambridge and New Penguin editions. When Lear asks, 'What was thy cause? Adultery?' (*Lear* F, IV.v.106), he echoes lawyers who spoke of 'cause of action' loosely to mean the abstract nature of the offence involved in a case (e.g. defamation, breach of contract, etc.), and litigation itself as a 'cause' in an even looser sense. But in *Othello*, the word resonates with more technical and specific legal meanings: harking back to the Roman *causa*, it could mean either that in return of which a promise is made; or the reason why a promise is made (*causa promissionis*), defined in a broader sense than common law did; or, finally, the classic English sense of consideration, or why a promise is actionable (*causa actionis*, closely related to the question of *quid pro quo* in the first of these three senses). It is this last sense that is most significant in Othello's use, leading to his putting the case to legal action and referring Desdemona to 'each article' (54), i.e. each item in a formal indictment. On the association between cause and obligation, see Baker, 'Origins of the "Doctrine" of Consideration', 385–7. On the use of *causa* in Quintilian as a case worthy of being

that lends a bare agreement the weight of lawful 'consideration'. 'Consideration' in turn was defined by judges in a landmark case from 1574 as 'a cause or meritorious occasion, requiring a mutual recompence in fact or law'.[23] The perceived breach of marital contract by Desdemona gives rise to a 'consideration' which provides Othello his 'cause': a solemn and rightful covenant with himself, an actionable case requiring and justifying legal satisfaction, which finds the language of technical legitimation. From meaning Desdemona's crime, through the route of legal signification, 'cause' almost comes to mean a moral purpose, a mission. When Tomazo, in Middleton and Rowley's *The Changeling*, complains, 'How is my cause bandied through your delays!/'Tis urgent in blood, and calls for haste', he is, similarly, pressing his case, demanding justice or 'recompence' for murder and adultery committed by others, not suggesting the nature of any crime perpetrated by him.[24]

Overall, legal plots in drama communicate a sense of law as a tentative and contingent measure, made human and less-than-apodeictic by the same token; enabling and manipulable at the same time. They are alive at once to the detrimental consequence of the exploitation of loopholes by individuals, and the range of human and emotional possibilities often opened up by precisely such cunning use; to the merely probable end of legal logic as well as to the miraculous probabilities created by mobilising law. Sometimes the inflexibility of certain laws is seized upon to create gaps and errors in experience that are tragic in content, but formally conducive to comic resolutions; in such cases, the law becomes analogous to the rules of comedy, and each becomes the other's tool. Thus, dramatic explorations of legal issues not only illuminate the workings of literary form in relation to the matter of experience, but in the same act communicate an apprehension of law as social action and communication. This perception is confirmed and sometimes modified by the archival research in which this project is grounded.

METHOD

Integrating the methods of social history, intellectual history and literary criticism, this study constructs a history of law as lived experience from a

---

legally pleaded, see *Institutio Oratoria*, ed. Russell (hereafter, *Institutio*), 10.7.21. The only modern editor to gloss Othello's 'cause', albeit cryptically, as 'ground for action' or 'the case of one party in a law suit' is Honigman, in the Arden Shakespeare edition (1997).
[23] Calthorpe's Case, as cited in Simpson, *Common Law of Contract*, 323.
[24] Middleton and Rowley, *Changeling*, V.iii.134–8.

research of three principal classes of primary material: play-texts; theoretical legal treatises such as Henry Swinburne's *A Treatise of Spousals* and *Of Matrimony* and Christopher St. German's *Doctor and Student*; and legal documents surviving from court cases, such as depositions, interrogatories, personal responses and exhibits. It also considers pamphlet literature generated by law cases.[25] A comparative enquiry is especially productive since each of these groups of texts is particular in its narratorial investments and strategies. Institutionally produced and often accidentally preserved, legal records give us essential facts, but tend to leave out details that would interest the cultural historian – often elusive and non-quantifiable. For these, I turn to literary texts, which translate historically specific perceptions through fictional devices that are distinct from the 'fictions' shaping court papers. But to map this larger interrelated field, I also look at legal theory – to be found, in this period, not only in the obviously legal texts but also in philosophical writing more generally. The book aims to recover, from these distinct sources, a sense of law as a site of changing notions of privacy, certainty and contingency in terms of custom and use; it posits, in the process, a nuanced way of writing the history of emotions and perceptions by drawing upon literature as substantive evidence. To quote Goodrich, 'a critically adequate reading of law should take account of the various levels of law as a social discourse, as a series of institutional functions and rhetorical effects.'[26] The present study offers precisely such a reading, showing especially how legal plots in drama bring together the affective and the discursive, concerns that can easily suffer an unfortunate separation in critical studies. Ideas such as probability and uncertainty, emerging in the legal and philosophical traditions of the period, are given a human face in plays.[27]

Attempting to recover the perceptions of individual and communal experience of law through drama has made it necessary to consider the subject across several jurisdictions. It has also meant being alive to gender-specific experiences. As a literary critic, I do not offer statistical analysis;

[25] The term 'law' is used in the widest sense to include law-texts, institutions, legal procedure and courtroom practice. Textually, however, statutes are less revealing for my purposes than legal treatises, commentaries and court papers. See Baker, 'Editing the Sources', 207–8, on how Acts of Parliament, though theoretically above the common law, never took the form of a comprehensive code and remained, until the nineteenth century, an appendix to the main body of English law.

[26] Goodrich, *Legal Discourse*, 205–6.

[27] On the emergence and development of probability in legal philosophy, see Shapiro, *Probability and Certainty* and *Culture of Facts*; Franklin, *Science of Conjecture*; and Hacking, *Emergence*, against which both Shapiro and Franklin react. Patey, *Probability*, is an exemplary study linking philosophic theory to literary form in a later period.

but then, the objects of my study are, emphatically, qualitative rather than quantitative, perceptions rather than records, a *sense* of things rather than figures. Indeed, in some cases, as with the often quasi-legal role of women in court procedures, statistics could be positively misleading.

Some of the larger ideas about law intimated in this book would bear consideration over a longer period of change and development. The evolution of the notion of probability, for instance, calls for observation across the Civil War period and well into the first decade or so of the Royal Society's activities. This study points the way to this and other hinterlands, and has implications for the larger, possibly collective research that the subject merits.

The choice of literary material, though necessarily selective, is deliberately various, to indicate the generic determination of dramatic treatments of law. Similarly, well-known plays by dramatists such as Shakespeare and Webster are addressed alongside neglected plays such as the anonymous *Warning* or John Day's *Law-Tricks*, to indicate the range of early modern drama's preoccupation with law, and the diversity of literary texts that shared in this conversation. The archival research has been inevitably determined in part by practical considerations. The Cambridgeshire documents preserved in the University Library (including Ely diocesan records) have been an obvious treasure-trove. But in using canon law depositions I have tried to ensure a balance between disputed spousal litigation or adultery cases from northern dioceses like Durham and those from southern locations like Canterbury and Norwich, as older Catholic customs and practices died harder in the North than in the more Puritan-influenced South.[28] For common law sources, I have relied heavily on the archives of the Public Record Office. The research of social and legal historians has provided valuable pointers and facilitated my archival investigations. I have also looked at cases from Chancellor's courts of both Oxford and Cambridge, indicative of practices in the less clearly defined and lesser-known jurisdictions.

CONTENTS

In the last Act of Jonson's *The New Inn*, when Fly declares that Beaufort and Frank are married in the stable, the 'Host' – Lord Frampul in disguise – exclaims, 'I have known many a church been made a stable,/But not a

---

[28] But see chapter 1, p. 34 on overriding similarities of attitudes and social practices.

stable made a church till now'.[29] Contrary to his feigned disbelief, many a stable and backyard was 'made a church' in early modern England, where a simple verbal pledge in the present tense could make a canonically valid marriage, no matter how much the Church and the State, not to speak of the Reformers, discouraged or denounced it.[30] Confusions were inevitable, and it was at times fiendishly difficult to ascertain the validity of marriages and indeed of spousals, from the assemblage of reports and evidences cited and refuted. The dramatic engagement with contemporary marriage law and sexual litigation provides a point of entry, in my opening chapter, into the larger issue of uncertainty that the law of evidence had to negotiate in trying to determine truths of motive and intention, and raises questions about the relation of the concept of probability to the dramatic form. The dramatic corpus is understood not only with close reference to legal records from the period, but also in relation to Swinburne's *Spousals* (c. 1600). This three-pronged approach demonstrates the need for subjecting legal texts themselves to a judiciously deconstructive attention where appropriate. Swinburne is singularly vexed by the potential of dissonance between positive law and the law of conscience:[31] this awareness opens his text up to the precise hermeneutic possibilities that are deliberately made visible by the fictional lens of legally preoccupied plays.

Chapter 2 focuses on the treatment of adultery in 'domestic' tragedies, concentrating on Heywood's *A Woman Killed With Kindness*. Rather than discussing critiques of legal evidence, it explores the implications of the social process of investigation and evidence-collection, especially in cases involving sexual conduct, and how the drama addresses the nature and limits of this procedure through a self-conscious, indeed self-critical,

---

[29] Jonson, *New Inn*, V.ii.13–14.

[30] Such a contract was known as spousal *per verba de praesenti*, to be distinguished from spousals *per verba de futuro* – contracts made in the words of the future tense, denoting a promise to marry in the future. Private chambers and bedrooms were also 'made a church', as testified by Webster's Duchess who has 'heard lawyers say, a contract in a chamber/ *Per verba de praesenti* is absolute marriage', even as she marries Antonio in her bedroom, kneeling, and proclaiming that the church cannot 'bind faster' (*Duchess of Malfi*, I.i.477–9, 491). As a rough and ready distinction, then, 'spousal' could be either an engagement (when *de futuro*), or a present contract of marriage (when *de praesenti*), while 'marriage' usually referred to solemnised unions, though the confusion over contracts made that definition slippery.

[31] 'Positive law' refers to human, institutional law, as distinct from (but ideally reflective of) natural law – a moral standard deriving from the nature of the world and the nature of humanity. So, in theory, natural laws may be authoritative by value of their intrinsic morality, independent of social or institutional conventions. On natural law and the drama, see White, *Natural Law*; McCabe, *Incest*. See also Kahn and Hutson, *Rhetoric and Law*, Introduction.

application of its own representational devices to the inscribed situation. The play is shown to illuminate the way in which the ascertainment of adultery as a legal fact provides a historical basis to the metaphor of public spectatorship that such a situation calls up, and helps us understand key aspects of early modern mental life, such as privacy, intimacy and experience of domestic space.

Some of the 'domestic tragedies', however, draw from a distinct background of Protestant judgement books and moral tracts on the one hand, and popular news pamphlets, broadsides and ballads on the other, both genres exploiting the impact of the spectacular for their particular moral and commercial ends. Chapter 3 examines the exploration of evidence within a different set of generic parameters in these texts, where the legal scepticism of the plays of Chapter 1 is replaced by a preoccupation with legitimate representation. Likewise, the communal practices of investigation in the adultery plays of Chapter 2 are absorbed into a different order of discovery staged in the 'theatre of God's judgements',[32] even as the status of proof alters drastically. Consequently, the gap between the law of conscience and the law of courts is rhetorically written out of the configurations of legal justice in the providentialist theatre – a world apart from Jonson's Venetian law court where Bonario and Celia are mocked for citing their 'consciences' as 'testimonies' (*Volpone*, IV.ii.197–9). The anonymous *A Warning for Fair Women* is the central play-text here, but is examined alongside Yarrington's *Two Lamentable Tragedies* as well as the better known *Arden of Faversham* (anon.), which share selectively in *Warning*'s providentialism. Illustrating how genre can decide drama's attitude to evidential issues, this chapter is a corrective to the literary-critical tendency to regard all drama as being suspicious of legal procedures.

Chapter 4 approaches the issue of dramatic evidence and judgement in *The White Devil* through a discussion of 'colour' in its interrelated senses, played off against one another by Webster. The concept of 'colour' belonged simultaneously to several discourses, and the contemporary theatrical phenomenon implicated these diverse traditions of rhetoric, physiognomy, theology and law. I attempt to recover the transactional economy existing among these disciplines, which the play deploys and comes out of, rather than offer a posterior 'critical' synthesis of disparate fields. If Chapter 2 explores the social implications of judicial attitudes, this chapter shows how Webster's drama addresses its relation to the representational motives of law itself.

---

[32] Beard, *Theatre*, title.

The first four chapters, then, mainly focus on the vexed issue of evidence as a way into the drama's engagement with law. But alongside the difficulty of reading intention or making it evident, there are other issues which also stretch the representational capacities of both law and theatre, and challenge the epistemological constraints of the courtroom – issues such as informal legal operations, women's use of the law, the fluid boundaries between official legal agency and popular participation and intervention, and indeed at times custom itself. The final sections of the book expand the discussion to address this larger interface between representation and legal experience more fully. They also complement my earlier method of studying plays in their social and legal contexts, by reconstructing legal realities and perceptions through using drama as historical evidence – an approach that implies a larger argument about historical method and the place of literary evidence in it. Not only does Chapter 5 move from the question of what the drama does with the law to look at what the law does with drama; it also marks a transition from a more theoretical approach to an exploration of the actual, physical overlap between the legal and theatrical cultures in early modern London through a discussion of Barry's *Ram Alley* and a Star Chamber case. Chapter 6 focuses on gender and law, mainly through Webster's *The Devil's Law Case*. By looking at agents who are often absent, or wholly disregarded, in official texts – such as court audience or women litigants – the last two chapters deepen our understanding of certain intangible aspects of legal experience, and indicate the relation between dramatic fiction, and the realities and fictions of law.

CRITICAL CONTEXT

Writing in 1992 about fictional narratives, Richard Weisberg asserted that

in each period, law has drawn the attention of the literary artist because of its similarities to narrative art, not its differences. Law's manner of recreating and discussing reality strikes the artist as close . . . to what story-tellers themselves are in the business of doing.[33]

The same could be said of the procedural affinities between drama and law. Weisberg was of course reacting against such critics as Richard Posner who saw the 'legal matter in most literature on legal themes' as 'peripheral

---

[33] Weisberg, *Poethics*, x.

to the meaning . . . of the literature'.[34] Indeed, a study of the plays as a form of social practice comparable to, and interactive with, legal processes rapidly uncovers the special interest these situations have for drama. But if recognising the similarities and overlaps is the first step towards an interdisciplinary enquiry, a nuanced discrimination is the second. Crucially, there remains a distinction between a discipline that seeks actively to arrive at verdict and another that complicates it, though they may share traditions, the need to engage with an audience, and strategies of representation; and in spite of the fact that literary forms have their own drive towards resolution. If it had not been for a fundamental difference, there would be no distinction about the way in which the dramatists are equipped to address complexities and illuminate dilemmas that legal writers seek to either resolve or conceal. This distance has been increasingly elided in law-literature studies, albeit, understandably, in cumulative reaction to extreme scepticism about any affinity between the disciplines. Luke Wilson's *Theaters of Intention*, published in 2000, makes the timely point that 'despite deep and abiding dissimilarities', early modern theatre and law show a common preoccupation in their engagement with the way intention was expressed, articulated and represented.[35] He acknowledges the relatively hermetic nature of common law discourse and qualifies the glib reciprocal argument of the 1980s about the comparable influence of the two disciplines upon each other. But he goes on to emphasise that it was the developments in common law thinking about intentional action that provided sophisticated tools to the theatre to express aspects of human action and agency (4). While

---

[34] Posner, *Law and Literature*, 15. For an excellent summary of the debate, see Schramm, *Testimony and Advocacy*, 7–17. A splendid example of the potential of such analogical thinking is Welsh, *Strong Representations*, addressing the use of the rhetoric of circumstantial evidence to create convincing narrative in eighteenth- and nineteenth-century fiction.

[35] Wilson, *Theaters of Intention*, 4. Wilson focuses on contract law to suggest patterns of transition in the conceptualisation of intentional action, and how these are registered, articulated and paralleled in the theatre. So, despite fruitful points of intersection, my book has a different set of concerns. I primarily consider canon law cases to examine intention and evidence; when I widen out and look at common law, it is less with a jurisdictionally specific quarry than with the purpose of arriving at perceptions about litigation *across* jurisdictions. Rather than re-examine intentional action vis-à-vis the anterior position of intending, I focus on representation, and not solely on representing intention either, though my identification of evidence as a vital interest that drew dramatists to the law necessarily brings intention centre-stage, and provides a useful supplement to Wilson's more tightly focused study. But while Wilson privileges his 'historical and theoretical work' over his 'readings of [plays]' (Preface), readings of plays in my book are often the most productive approach to the perceptions that I seek to understand and clarify. Also, my book is preoccupied with epistemological problems and challenges, which Wilson is less interested in than in 'action itself' (14).

Wilson's argument is by no means a simple one about straightforward derivation, I suggest that the drama had its own distinct devices which made possible a unique, and uniquely human, focus on aspects of legal practice and experience.

While not claiming that literature necessarily gives a more profoundly truthful account than formal court records, this book does show that drama gives a more well-rounded view that cannot be ignored. What often appears to be legal imprecision by the dramatist should not obscure the validity of ordinary people's experience of the workings of law in everyday life. It is necessary, for example, to correct the historicist literalism of attempting to find exact correspondence between dramatised representations of legal events, and actual procedures and trials in the period. Instances in which the relation between dramatic fiction and real events is direct and intended are rare.[36] So this study attempts to understand the composite vision of legal realities that the plays offer; to address the fictionality itself as significant; and to negotiate the methodological challenges its relation with law posits, both for the dramatist and for the cultural historian or literary critic.

Related to the debate engaged in affirming or denying the fundamental affinity between law and drama is the tension between criticism that suggests that the drama is necessarily critical of the law and the opposite, resistant view. This, too, is a sterile polarity that needs to be gone beyond. While Civil lawyers such as Swinburne struggled with the subtext of positivistic legal discourse, and tried to negotiate, as it were, the repressed matter in the legal consciousness,[37] common lawyers grappled with emergent notions of flexibility and probability, based in the evolving practices of English law. Legal education in the universities centred on Roman

---

[36] On the perils of trying to establish a one-to-one correspondence between historical events and play-scenes, see Ian Donaldson's salutary discussion of the scene between Otter and Cutbeard in Jonson's *Epicœne*, and its relation to the Essex divorce trial: *Jonson's Magic Houses*, 132–7. The impotence trial and virginity test involved in establishing non-consummation in this notorious legal case would no doubt be brought to mind by Morose's disclosure, in Act V, that he is impotent, in the hope that he can get a divorce from the woman he has married (who turns out in the end to be a boy). Frances Howard had claimed that her marriage was never consummated, in order to procure a divorce from the Earl of Essex. But the dates and facts about *Epicœne* contradict any notion that Jonson was deliberately representing the Essex trial, as indeed does the deeper thematic resonance of the idea of impotence through the play. The connection lies, rather, in social structures, cultural practices, and modes of perceiving and self-fashioning. The same could be said of attempts to connect the virginity test of Middleton and Rowley's *The Changeling* with the Essex trial.

[37] For a theoretical formulation of the 'unconscious' of the law, and of the 'legal imaginary', see Goodrich, *Oedipux Lex.*

Civil law whereas students at the Inns were training in the law of the land. The full range of creative contradictions that ensued in general legal thinking must be the subject of another book. But this study does indicate how this double legal inheritance (which may be crudely mapped on to the gap between theory and practice in the English context),[38] combined with legacies inherent to the dramatic tradition, resulted in the complexity of the drama's attitude towards law's methods of knowing. While certain dramatic situations offer a critique of legal certainty, other situations and structures share in the more circumspect philosophical-cum-legal thinking in the English tradition to question, through analogy, not only law's straight lines towards assured knowledge but also drama's own tendencies towards determinacy; its mechanisms for obfuscating the uncertainties created and left unresolved by plot elements that drive towards a satisfactory closure – emotional, juridical or epistemological. Even some of the plays of Chapter 1 – most clearly sceptical of law's resolutions – implicitly interrogate the status of their own adjudicatory apparatus. Though evidence is shown to be an issue on which drama often hinges its critique of law, Chapters 5 and 6 demonstrate that drama's exploration of the tentativeness of evidence is not invariably a criticism. It can be part of a humane and pragmatic vision of likelihood and contingency as positive epistemological functions. The false trial, a motif briefly touched upon in the Epilogue, is an instance of how plays use formal devices that can at once embody and undercut the supposedly felicitous ends and means of both positivistic law and veridical plots of literature.

Thus, this book's resistance to determinacy on the matter of drama's attitude to law says more about the nature of the interaction than about either of the two disciplines *per se*. Pulling away from the understandable tendency, in law-and-literature studies, of hinging the entire argument on whether or not the theatre is critical of the law, and whether the law is culpably positivistic or not, it establishes that the dialogue between law and drama is more various than usually supposed. In exploring a range of dramatic engagements with legal representation, it tries to be receptive to critique, comment or analogy, complicity or interconnection, as demanded by the particular emphases and investments of individual plays.

The last two decades have seen exciting research on law and literature. Katharine Maus's marvellous study, *Inwardness and Theater in the English Renaissance* (1995), addresses one of the significant issues I look at – the

---

[38] But note that civilians went on to practise canon law in church courts, and Civil law could be relevant to some areas of secular law not covered by common law: see Glossary.

elusiveness of intention – in the specific context of the history of subject-ivity. The emphasis and scope of my book are different, as is its interdis-ciplinary range, combining literary material with broadsides, records of actual court proceedings as well as legal and, where necessary, rhetorical treatises. My work shares with Victoria Kahn and Lorna Hutson's invigor-ating collection of essays on *Rhetoric and Law in Early Modern Europe* (2001) an understanding of English and Continental law as a double heritage that English philosophical thinking drew on; and a belief in rhetorical textuality and legal practice as overlapping and interactive discourses. But its focus is specifically on how dramatic texts insert themselves into this cross-disciplinary dialogue. Ian Ward's pioneering work, *Law and Literature*, helpfully surveys the field across the periods and indeed across cultures. In his introduction, he provides two useful categories of analysis: 'Law *in* Literature' and 'Law *as* Literature'.[39] I examine the former, and read the texts of law as narratives too where appropriate, as with Swinburne's treatises. But I also propose a further category of 'Literature in Law'. Where legal documentation is insufficient or non-existent, there is a case to be made for using literary material to reconstruct certain aspects of the experience of law. For instance, this will be the first book of literary criticism or interdisciplinary enquiry that attempts to reconstruct the physical realities of courtroom interaction and experience – admittedly a hazardous venture, but a necessary one. Nor have legal historians attempted it, for the obvious reasons of a shortage of documentary evidence and the impossibility of a statistical study. These, I argue, are precisely the reasons why literary studies should have a say in the matter. In the end, what my book hopes to contribute to this stimulating field is a study that is alert to issues of representation without losing sight of a lived culture of litigation; and one that pays close attention to literary texts' engagement with legal facts and perceptions without occluding the diversity of this relation, or trying to make it fit into an overarching theory about any one aspect of law. It shows that this interrelation is premised on a combination of similarity and difference: because the resemblances between law and theatre primarily concern the form and representational structures of the two media, not their methods and aims, comparison reveals much about both of these fundamental arenas of early modern life, whose relationship continues to this day.

---

[39] Ward, *Law and Literature*, 3–27. See also his *Shakespeare and the Legal Imagination*, more concerned than my book with implications of legal change for the political order or for the royal prerogative; my argument runs somewhat counter to Ward's model of Shakespeare as a 'literary supplement' to 'illustrate legal texts'.

CHAPTER I

'Of rings, and things, and fine array': marriage law, evidence and uncertainty

Renaissance drama is full of men and women with an uncertain and indeterminate marital status. Their numerous articulations of bewilderment or loss convey a sense of complex overlap between this specific indeterminacy and their personal identities. Katherine is, to William Scarborrow, in *The Miseries of Enforced Marriage* (1607), 'She that I am married to, but not my wife';[1] to herself, 'tho married', she is 'reputed not a wife' (1004); Clare Harcop, meanwhile, occupies that peculiar position common to unlucky women in Renaissance England – 'a Troth-plight-Virgin' (785), wife enough to 'be made a strumpet gainst [her] will' (827) if she marries anyone but Scarborrow, yet not wife enough to be a legal impediment to his later, arranged marriage to Katherine. In Shakespeare's *Measure for Measure*, Mariana is 'neither maid, widow, nor wife' (V.i.177–8); Juliet is, as Claudio claims, 'fast [his] wife' (I.ii.128), but equally, the 'fornicatress' (II.ii.24) of Angelo's rigorous legal description.

The historical counterparts of figures such as these are to be met in surviving records of spousal litigation conducted in English church courts in the sixteenth and early seventeenth centuries. In May 1622 at Stratford, 'Michael Palmer and his wife' – acknowledged as a married couple even in the citation – are required to obtain 'dismission . . . for . . . unlawful marriage and . . . enioyned penance . . . for incontinency before marriage'.[2] Mawde Price of Chester, legally but forcibly married to Henry Price, was also married to Randle Gregorie by a 'full precontract'; by having 'carnall dole' with Randle and not Henry, she commits adultery as well as resolutely avoids it.[3]

Such inconsistencies arise from contradictions and fluidities in contemporary marriage laws. No text can be a better point of entry into these

---

[1] Wilkins, *Miseries*, 652.
[2] Brinkworth, *Shakespeare and the Bawdy Court*, 151.
[3] Furnivall, *Child-Marriages*, 76–9; see also 56; and Raine, *Depositions*, 52.

laws and their complexities than *A Treatise of Spousals*, published in 1686 but written c.1600 by Henry Swinburne, civil lawyer of York, 'to expound the ecclesiastical laws for the benefit of English readers'[4] and to assimilate the inherited corpus of canonical treatises and commentaries to the changing needs and practices of post-Reformation England. It is particularly revealing because it does not simply enumerate existent laws but confronts their ambiguities. It is indeed a deeply anxious text, attempting to determine certain fixed points by which to chart the uncertainties at the interface between marriage laws and human participants or litigants. An unfinished and unpublished sequel to *Spousals*, entitled 'Of the signification of divers woordes importing Matrimonye', extends this engagement but focuses more specifically on marriage.[5] Swinburne's treatment of the ambiguities of marriage law often raises more fundamental issues – principally those related to the problem of uncertainty which law must find a way to grapple with and work through in order to establish certainties. The contemporary dramatic preoccupation with legal problems also engages centrally, if variously, with these larger issues. Marriage laws cast a particularly sharp light on some of these, while their confusions provide ideal dramatic scenarios, inextricably linked as they are with emotional, psychological and moral complexities, and with the legally unresolvable but dramatically alluring issues of motive and intention. For drama, as well as for Swinburne, they provide an extraordinarily dense example of the problems at the heart of law. My route is through Swinburne's treatises, mainly *Spousals*, a work uniquely qualified to provide legal and literary pointers simultaneously. Acts and depositions of the late sixteenth and early seventeenth centuries are also examined, mainly from the ecclesiastical courts of Durham, Chester, Norwich and Canterbury. These complement the insights derived from Swinburne's theoretical text. Together, these two sets of legal material provide a comprehensive picture of law as human action – precisely the object of dramatisation in the plays considered in the second part of my argument in this chapter.

But it is necessary, first, to establish the meanings of certain basic legal terms and categories. Marriage law in early modern England was something of an anomaly in the European context, in that it still retained, in

---

[4] Houlbrooke, *Church Courts*, 19. On Swinburne, see Derrett, 'Henry Swinburne', and Ingram, *Church Courts*, 42.

[5] Appendix 1 is a transcript. I am grateful to Sheila Doyle for alerting me to this document. See also her 'Research Notes', 2, 162–72.

spite of the Reformation, the rule of canon law.[6] In a sense it remained more Roman than Roman law itself which had modified the inherited canons after the Council of Trent, while England persisted with pre-Tridentine rules way into the middle of the seventeenth century.[7] In Elizabethan and early Stuart England, this ecclesiastical form of law was administered by church courts across the country, arranged hierarchically at the levels of province, diocese and archdeaconry. Marriage law (including annulment and separation), sexual litigation, slander trials and testamentary disputes were among the principal kinds of suits covered by this jurisdiction, apart from moral and financial matters relating to Church governance. As such, it was involved with some of the daily and intimate affairs of men and women, and played a central role in local communities.[8]

There was canonical provision for two kinds of spousal contracts in the period. The first was a *de praesenti* contract which could be made by two people using a given set of words in the present tense, expressing mutual and present consent to take each other as husband and wife. Canonically, this was sufficient to make a marriage valid, though the Church and the State discouraged people from making such informal contracts and urged them to solemnise contracts in church, in the presence of a priest and witnesses. A *de futuro* contract, on the other hand, was like an engagement, a promise made by two parties in the words of the future tense, to take each other as husband and wife. Such a contract could be turned into indissoluble matrimony by solemnisation or consummation, and rescinded on the lapsing of any conditions if conditions were attached to the promise in the first place.

Swinburne, as a civil lawyer, would have been well versed in Roman law, both civil and canon. Ecclesiastical law, after all, derived from two main sources: the shared body of the canon law of the Church across Europe, known as the *Corpus Juris Canonici*, and the code of Roman law, *Corpus Juris Civilis*, which was a partial foundation for testamentary law

---

[6] On the failure to implement the Reforming of Ecclesiastical Laws between the 1530s and 1571, see Carlson, *Marriage*, 74–9.

[7] See, Carlson, *Marriage*, 7–8. The Council of Trent, held between 1545 and 1563, was the nineteenth ecumenical Council of the Roman Catholic Church. Its main purpose was to forge an integrated response to the challenge of the Protestant Reformation and readjust its own tenets to address the needs of the historical moment.

[8] Often enough, though, cases from these courts could drift into the appellate ecclesiastical Court of Arches, or, more cross-jurisdictionally, into the central courts of common law or equity, or into the Star Chamber, the highest Court of Appeal. So there was more jurisdictional overlap in practice than official categories would suggest.

and also fed into matrimonial law, if less centrally. In England, the legal curriculum at the universities was based on Civil law, while the Inns of Courts, London's own legal universities, taught the practice of English common law. While the two jurisdictions were broadly in contest, and English common law resisted, to some extent, the influence of Civil law reinforced by the humanist education of the Renaissance, recent historiography suggests more of an overlap in legal thinking, in some cases even legal practice, than was earlier supposed.[9]

HENRY SWINBURNE AND UNCERTAINTY

In each section of *Spousals*, Swinburne states the basic code of law regarding the matter at hand. He then tackles varying opinions on the issue, in an effort to eliminate objections to his own view which is supposed merely to be an echo of the law's opinion, rescued from a maze of contradictory views. This 'orthodoxy' is then asserted more strongly. Then follows a series of 'ampliations' or 'limitations' which are alternative possibilities or exceptions to the general rule, after which comes a restatement of the author's overall view, a 'conclusion'. However, the statement of law, the author's considered opinion and his conclusion are tiny sections sandwiched between long discussions of objections and elaborate accounts of 'ampliations'. These substantial portions of the text often cast long shadows of doubt on the truth that is ostensibly asserted.

Let us take the sections on the 'form of words' in *de futuro* and *de praesenti* spousals[10] which illustrate the problems central to matrimonial law in Renaissance England. The 'two distinctions' on which the definitions of these kinds of spousals are based are stated at the beginning of Section X (p. 55); they are to do with whether the words of espousal refer to a present or a future time, and whether they 'harp of the *entrance*

---

[9] See Glossary. There are several excellent historical studies of church courts and canon law in the period. The most useful for the non-specialist are Ingram, *Church Courts*, and Houlbrooke, *Church Courts*. On the medieval background, see Helmholz, *Marriage Litigation*. For a study of the Reformation context of marriage, see Carlson, *Marriage*. A recent literary-historical exposition of marriage law is Sokol and Sokol, *Shakespeare, Law and Marriage*. For an overview of secular law in the period, especially common law, see Baker, *Introduction*. On the overlap and connections between civil and common law, see Shapiro, 'Classical Rhetoric and the English Law of Evidence', in Hutson and Kahn, eds., *Rhetoric and Law*, 54–72; Martin, *Francis Bacon*, esp. 118, 128–9, 212 n. 49; Helmholz, *Roman Canon Law*, forcefully argues the substantial survival of canon law, and by extension, civil legal thought, after the Protestant Reformation in England. For the alternative view, stressing the 'prophylactic' isolation of common law from civil legal traditions, see Baker, *Introduction*, esp. 33–5.

[10] *Spousals*, 55–73, Sections X and XI.

or *beginning* of Marriages' or of 'the *end* and *execution*'.[11] The difference is vital, since *de praesenti* spousals were tantamount to valid matrimony, though solemnisation was required for property rights to be secured. Once the sense of the spoken formula was determined, one would seem to have a clear guideline to define the nature of the contract. Yet the ampliations indicate the manifold variations possible, even where Swinburne evokes them apparently with the sole purpose of eliminating them. The Parties may, for instance, 'instead of the Verb [*volo*, I will]' use some other form of words, such as 'I promise' (67). They may use a combination of two phrases, one of which imports spousal *de praesenti*, the other *de futuro* (68). The two parties may not use the same words (86). Since by Swinburne's own admission, 'Divers words are sufficient to prove a perfect contract of Matrimony' (93), the sufficiency of verbal formulae becomes suspect. Words having a certain legal weight may, moreover, mean much less when spoken in 'Jest or Sport' (105). Then again, there is the factor of the 'Common Use of Speech and Custom of the place' to which 'the propriety of words ought to give place' (83, 72). An 'ampliation' like this instantly questions the legal formula. The argument of the 'seventh Limitation' in Section X (72) is a virtual admission of the incapacity of words, in the context of marriage, to be stable signifiers: 'When it is doubtful whether the words uttered by the Parties import Spousals *de futuro* or *Matrimony*, being apt and indifferent, by reason of the double sense thereof, to signifie either the one or the other. In which Case, that Sense is to be received which maketh for *Matrimony*, unless . . .' – and here he adds further qualifications. There is already an awareness that words can offer only an approximate 'sense'. As the examples, exceptions and opinions pile up, a bewildering collage emerges of disparate acts and utterances constituting marriage as social practice. How far, one wonders, is it possible to locate its legalities? Swinburne, menwhile, opens up his discourse and allows alternatives to the position that he aims to affirm. '[An] accumulation of some Act' over and above the words, such as the man delivering a ring to the woman, may impart matrimonial significance (71). Even silence may suffice if consent can be indicated 'by Signs' (72, 86, 203–12). This crossing of legality with semiotics makes language an even more slippery ethical index. Drama is specially qualified to point up this inadequacy by filling verbal gaps with gestures, signs and facial expressions, but Swinburne apprehends it

---

[11] This discussion extends into a consideration of the difference between 'matrimony begunne' and 'matrimony consummated' in *Matrimony*, 120–1.

already, albeit against the thrust of the argument, addressing even the possibility of outright deception (84). Special provisions are suggested in instances where 'the words be so general and uncertain that the meaning of the Parties cannot appear' (105).

This uncertainty is clearly what prompts Swinburne's anxious warnings against too strict an adherence to the letter of the law. He rejects a certain 'Distinction' regarding spousals between absent Parties 'as consisting rather upon a *Quiddity* than *Equity*, and stuffed with rigour instead of favour' (165).[12] He defines himself as a practical lawyer, in contrast to theorists – writers, sophists or dialecticians. As a member of a variety of courts,[13] he is aware of the interfaces demanding negotiation in the practice of marriage laws; his project includes mediating between theory and practice, written word and spoken word, word and sign – all these being, like marriage itself, forms of social practice. Further, he takes the unprecedented step of attempting to domesticate a Latin legal/textual tradition for an English-speaking people, leaving Latin marginalia for the Justinians, as he explains in the preface to his other completed work, *A Briefe Treatise of Testaments and Last Willes* (1590).[14]

Translation, of course, can itself be an interpretation: witness Swinburne's struggle to determine what senses the Latin verb *volo* can convey (*Spousals*, 57–61). Paradoxically, however, Swinburne's conclusion here is reached through an intricate argument about the indeterminate status of a verb of Infinitive Mood. The question that inevitably raises its head is whether 'translation' in this case has fulfilled its stated purpose of '[serving] the majority' and 'may be understood by all' (*Testaments*, 'B2v). William Sidall's testimony in the Chester trothplight case of Strete v. Jepson (1561–2) is revealing. Having described the words and gestures through which Katherine Strete and Nicholas Jepson contracted themselves in what is clearly in Sidall's perception a valid marriage, he is asked

'how hit chauncid that he (Nicholas) spake not the word*es* of marriage de presenti'; he sais 'he is vnlernid, and knewe not thos word*es*; but, he said, yf he had knowne any other word*es* of more effecte then the above written were, he said at that tyme he wold have spoken them; for this depone*nt* sais, his mynd was to have made them as sure as he cold.'[15]

---

[12] A contemporary sense of 'rigorous' was 'in literal sense' (*OED*).
[13] Derrett, 'Henry Swinburne', 8–9.
[14] *Testaments*, 'B2–'B3. Signatures B–C4 are repeated, so that there are two gatherings of both B and C.
[15] Furnivall, *Child-Marriages*, 184–6.

The question that troubles us is also, significantly, the precise objection Swinburne cites and tackles immediately after he has stated the legal distinction between *de futuro* and *de praesenti* spousals in grammatical terms: the argument 'drawn from the Simplicity of the Vulgar sort' who may get the words wrong, but 'mean uprightly'. Should we not regard their 'Intents' rather than 'the formality of the Phrase' (62)? The exponents of this view end up emphatically rejecting the carefully worked out distinction of '*I will* and *I do*' 'lest . . . any Man's conscience (through ignorance of Terms) might be entangled in the Snares of this subtle and captious Distinction' (63).[16]

Swinburne argues back just as emphatically that exactly these distinctions are needed to steer through a maze of uncertainty. Curiously, the very perception of multiplicity and potential bewilderment prompting the disregard of a 'distinction' as being too rigorous in Section XIII, is also what presses the need for a mooring in 'distinctions' and categories.[17] Law needs to be codified as well as equitably applied, and this is Swinburne's double bind. It is interesting, however, to see where Swinburne locates the uncertainty, and at this point his encomium on distinctions will bear quotation at some length:

> . . . these Distinctions . . . are so far from the nature and property of Snares and Gynns, whereby to catch or entrap any Man at advantage against his meaning, or to incumber his Conscience with subtilty, that on the contrary, They may . . . be compared unto the Thred which Ariadne gave unto Theseus; for as without that Thred he could never have escaped out of that endless Labyrinth, wherein were so many difficult Turnings . . . and but one only Out-gate; so without Distinctions it is impossible to escape out of the confused Maze of such intricate Questions and Infinite Errors, amongst the which there is but one only Truth: by Distinctions we discern the Scent and Footsteps . . . of each Man's purpose . . . and hunt out the very Center of each Man's thought . . . By Distinctions are ambiguous questions resolved . . . and dark and obscure Enigma's cleared and made bright. By Distinctions we apprehend the true meaning, not of Men only, but of God himself, as without the which the time meaning and sense of Scriptures cannot be attained: . . . neither the law, neither the Gospel, can stand . . . from Contrariety. Hence . . . Distinctions are . . . the next Neighbours of Truth . . . thereby we are directed to each Man's meaning . . . (65–6)

Swinburne's metaphor contains the ambiguity inherent in the interpenetration of text and subject. The Minotaur, it would seem from some of

---

[16] This relates to the older Christian idea of 'consent' validating marriage, regardless of formulae.
[17] See *OED* definitions.

his statements, is human intention – the 'Center of each Man's thought'. But these statements are interwoven with others which suggest that the 'labyrinth' is the legal discourse itself,[18] or rather, the chaotic interface between text and interpretation, with its proliferating possibilities; through this maze, the interpreting individual works out his path with the thread provided by the ordering, heuristic device of *distinctio*.[19] In legal practice, the centre of the labyrinth is a dual centre, where the law's intention and the agent's intention come together. Swinburne's truth encompasses both the 'enigma' of law and the mystery of 'each Man's meaning'. This is what his rather mixed metaphors try to grasp. But can 'distinction' illuminate the infinite particulars of human situations, as it clarifies textual ambiguities?[20] Indeed, can textual legality stand at all as a sufficient expression of the legislator's meaning, without being supplemented by the intention of 'each man'?[21]

This brings us straight to the two-fold interpretative difficulty in the operation of law: understanding the accused's intention is a condition for an appropriate translation of the legislator's purpose. These two intentions have to fit. Marriage laws in Renaissance England give this fusion a peculiar focus, since the legal determination of truth here depends on fixing the meaning of certain words as they conjoin in a legal formulation and as they are used by individuals in particular situations to express their intentions. 'I hereby take thee to my wife' is the set legal formula by which a *de praesenti* spousal is contracted; it is also a statement expressive of the agent's 'intent' and has, in this case, the status of the agent's action, the object of judgement in the event of an uncertain union.[22] The words

---

[18] Cf. the terms used to describe the bewildering 'multitude' of texts forming the inherited corpus of Romano-canonical law in *Testaments*, 'B.

[19] On *divisio* or *distinctio* as a dialectical device used by jurists, see Maclean, *Interpretation*, 72–4. It is ironic that Swinburne should be pushed to uphold a dialectical tool as being essential to his legal method when he repeatedly differentiates himself, as a practising lawyer, from sophists and dialecticians (*Spousals*, 95–6, 165).

[20] See Montaigne, *Essays*, trans. Screech, Bk III, 1208, for a sceptical view of *divisio* in jurisprudence. Ironically, Swinburne's attack on hair-splitting distinctions is directed at jurists, those men 'at Consistories and places of judgement' whom Swinburne privileges over the theoreticians he criticises in *Spousals*, 95–6. The contradiction between Swinburne's argument in favour of 'intent' there, and the advocacy of verbal 'signification' and distinctions in the present passage, points to the central tussle in his manual.

[21] On 'the logic of the supplement' in law, see Derrida, *Of Grammatology*, 141 ff., and *Writing and Difference*, 289 ff.

[22] Thus, the *de praesenti* formula, which could actually make the marriage happen in the act of utterance, is a perfect example of what J. L. Austin calls 'performative utterances': 'in these examples . . . to utter the sentence . . . is to do it . . . The uttering of the words is, indeed, usually a, or even *the*, leading incident in the performance of the act'. Austin goes on, however, to stress

'I will hold thee for my lawful husband', because they 'do savour the execution of marriage' (73), induce matrimony 'by interpretation of law'. Suppose the same words are used by an 'vnlearnid' person to mean a spousal *de futuro*; alternatively, suppose that they are uttered by someone in jest; both common occurrences in the period. Here the two sets of intention come together almost schematically, but in an imperfect fit. Where the two intentions are thus in conflict and are yet to be negotiated by a common factor, what happens in moral terms is precisely the 'catching' or 'trapping' of conscience, of which Swinburne vehemently clears the legal method (63). What happens in legal terms is an adoption of the law of presumption in case of doubt: despite the uncertainty of intention because of the relative inviolability of the legal formulation, 'law presumes' in favour of matrimony, given it is 'such a favourable matter' (88, 103, 149). Inevitably there arises a tension between moral law and institutional law – a tension fleshed out by drama which allows us to see into the hearts of characters, as jurists with all their 'distinctions' may not.

Representations of the precontract are a common dramatic situation that highlights this conflict. In Fletcher's *Love's Pilgrimage* (1616), Marc Antonio makes 'jests of oaths' (IV.iii.215), with the result that Leocadia, 'contracted by seal and oath' to him, has to give him up to his precontracted spouse Theodosia.[23] This is all very well legally, but Leocadia who had made no jest of the contract is, in conscience, his wife: 'Am I not his? his wife? Though he dispense/With his faith given, I cannot with mine' (V.iv.82–8). This circumstance points up the full complexity of the marriage contract: it involves not only two intentions but three, since the agency in spousals is double. Though, as Philippo says to Leocadia, 'his precontract/Doth annul [hers]' (89–90), her difficulty in accepting this indicates that truth in such disputes is neither simple nor single; the 'one only Truth' (*Spousals*, 65) that Swinburne would discern through 'distinctions' is reductive and partial, no matter how handy for the jurist.[24] For in principle, as Swinburne himself concedes in *Matrimony*,

---

that the circumstances of the utterance must be 'appropriate' and the speaker 'should also perform certain other actions, whether physical or mental', and this leads to the concession that 'for many purposes outward utterance is a description, *true or false*, of the occurrence of the inward performance': Austin, *How to Do Things with Words*, 6–9. This brings us very close, as we shall see, to Swinburne territory.

[23] Beaumont and Fletcher, *Dramatic Works*, I.

[24] Interestingly, one of the categories of *divisio* described by Boethius is that which reduces 'polysemic words or propositions into words or propositions with single senses'. See Boethius, *De divisione*, § I, cited in Maclean, *Interpretation*, 111.

'the single consent of thone partie alone is not sufficient to constitute matrimonie for oneles the Consent be mutuall yt is . . . no Coniunction' (122). In Rowley, Dekker and Ford's *The Witch of Edmonton* (1608), Frank Thorney contracts a private verbal spousal with Winnifride, after getting her with child, and then leaves at his father's summons; Winnifride, with a misgiving heart, implores him to remember his child if not her: after all, the sole basis of her claim on him is an unwitnessed contract.[25] But Thorney protests the sanctity of his 'bridal oath' (I.i.62): 'we are man and wife', he admits to Clarington (111). But he then goes on to marry Susan Carter for fear of disinheritance. This leads to the anomaly of what Winnifride calls '[his] second adulterous marriage' (III.ii.10). This second marriage to Susan, of course, has been confirmed through various recognised and witnessed ceremonies, and apparently duly consummated too (II.ii.36–8). For Susan, the ceremony constitutes a lawful marriage – she has entered it in good faith. Yet Thorney is technically correct when he spurns her as 'my whore./No wife of mine' (III.iii.30–1), before stabbing her. Nor is Winnifride lying when she discloses her identity to the Carter household: no page of Frank's, but 'his first, only wife, his lawful wife' (IV.176–7). Here, then, is a contradiction within law, between formal legality and conscience. Thorney, sentenced to death for wife-murder, finds it much the easier sentence to bear, because 'a court hath been kept' in his heart – 'here where I am found/ Guilty' (V.iii.87–8).

A contingency that would most easily lead to such a conflict is enforcement. If 'mutual consent' is the essence of matrimony (*Spousals*, 4, 70, 131, 197), is Annabella (in John Ford's *'Tis Pity She's a Whore*) the 'adulterous' 'whore' of Soranzo's description in having known her brother sexually, or is she, as Giovanni says, 'greedy of variety of lust' in getting married (IV.iii.1–2; II.v.41–2)?[26] Several orders of legitimacy are played off against one another, leading to a fundamental reassessment of the very notion of lawfulness. In Chester in 1562, Mawde Gregorie's firm conviction of the superior legitimacy of a willing precontract sees her through a somewhat similar situation, though of course the absence of the further complication of incest makes it easier for her.[27] As we have seen, 'Compellid . . . to marie . . . Henrie Price', she refuses to let him have 'his pleasure apon her' and, still more, continues a full-fledged relationship with her troth-plighted spouse Randle Gregorie, having two children by him. Randle

[25] Rowley, Dekker and Ford, &c., *The Witch of Edmonton.*
[26] Ford, *'Tis Pity.* Cf. *Matrimony*, 120.
[27] Furnivall, *Child-Marriages*, 76–9.

shares her faith in the validity of the 'full precontract, by God*des* lawe'. Finally, Price himself has his solemnised marriage annulled, and Mawde and Randle marry. Such situations, however, do not always lead to such happy ends. There was many a real-life equivalent to Mawde's dramatic counterpart Penthea in Ford's *The Broken Heart*, who, bound 'by . . . the laws of ceremonious wedlock' to Bassanes, considers the consummation of her marriage 'a rape', for she was Orgilus' 'by promise': 'cruelty enforced/ Divorce betwixt my body and my heart' (II.iii.54, 79, 100; 77; 57). This is an important distinction in a period when the concept of *mens rea*[28] or mental guilt was increasingly central in common law procedure and contributed to the ethical climate of a society which had to grapple, at the same time, with the determination of intention in spousal proceedings at the church courts.

The anomalous illegitimacies that law itself can force finds a focus in the contemporary legal institution of wardship in *The Miseries of Enforced Marriage*.[29] Minor offspring of deceased tenants largely forfeited the right to choose their marital partners to their lords or guardians – in return, of course, for a degree of financial security.[30] So it happened with Master Calverley of Yorkshire, 'warde to a . . . noble and worthy gentleman' – as we learn from *Two Most Unnaturall and Bloodie Murthers* (1605) (hereafter, *Murthers*), the pamphlet source of both *A Yorkshire Tragedy* and of *Miseries*.[31] When he made a private contract 'in the country' to seal an 'interchangeable affection' he had to wait for a 'fit howre' for solemnisation as 'Maister Caverleys yeeres could not discharge the charge his honourable gardian had over him' (*Murthers*, 1). Back in London, however, he 'knit a new marriage knot' 'by all matrimoniall rites' to a niece of his guardian (2–3) whom he loathed 'from the first houre' (8). The marriage ended disastrously, with Calverley first dragging his family into poverty and then killing his children whom he called bastards, nearly killing his wife whom he always considered a whore, and being at last apprehended for murder. There is, however, some ambiguity regarding his motive in concealing his first match,[32] as there is about the reason for

---

[28] See Herrup, *The Common Peace*, 2, 191.

[29] On the socio-economic and political implications of wardship, see Hurstfield, *Queen's Wards*, and Baker, *Introduction*, 275–6. On the history of resistance to wardship, see Croft, 'Wardship', 39–48.

[30] On patterns of exchange and obligation in the operations of wardship, see, Fumerton, *Cultural Aesthetics*, 29–60.

[31] *Murthers*, App. A to *A Yorkshire Tragedy*.

[32] *Murthers*, 2: 'whether concealing his late contract from his honorable gardian, or forgetting his private and publicke vowes, or both I know not'.

his hating his wife (8) in the pamphlet.[33] *Miseries* replaces the ambiguities of the pamphlet account by a consistent pinning down of the 'miseries' to the fact of enforcement. Scarborrow, unlike the generic 'husband' of the other play, is an individual whose conscience is ensnared by the formalities of law, and his naming Katherine 'an adulteress in [his] married arms' and his children 'bastards' clearly reflects a perception of the problematic legality of an enforced marriage, not a suspicion of the wife's virtue (I3v). Significantly, despite Clare's belief that her suicide will release him from the sin of adultery (D–Dv), her death makes no difference to Scarborrow's perception of his marriage. There is a sense of a widening gulf between formal legality and the law of conscience, designated gestures and intention, entities which marriage has to straddle. Yet both the Doctor and Scarborrow, advocates of the former and the latter respectively, claim divine law for their own positions. The Doctor accuses Scarborrow of breach of consent as he sees his church wedding as a 'deed' 'God himselfe . . . seald' and 'Angels are made the Iurors' to (K2). Yet Scarborrow describes this very event in opposition to 'thats deuine': mere 'words of Ceremonie,/ . . . hands knit as fellows that weare fetters,' while he stood 'all water' (I3). It is significant, too, that 'the unnatural tragedies' (*Tragedy*, x, 23) of history and of the anonymous play are turned into a social tragicomedy by Wilkins. While the decline of Calverley is seen to fit into a providential pattern of God's revenge in *Murthers* (4, 16), in *Miseries* there is a conspicuous displacement of the providential turnabout common in tragicomedy. Instead, the news comes that the guardian has dropped dead and left an abundance of riches to all parties concerned (K4). All is immediately well, and both Scarborrow and his sister settle down to their erstwhile unhappy marriages. This clinches, all over again, the location of the sufferings in social, economic and legal factors, and disallows a dissociation of genre from the operations of social and legal control.

Yet another play where enforcement due to the power relations of wardship plunges marriage into a grey area is Shakespeare's *All's Well that Ends Well*. Let us, however, briefly revisit Swinburne before assessing the proprieties of Bertram's marriage. 'The verb *spondeo*', says Swinburne, while expounding the term *sponsalia*,

is as much as *sponte do*, i.e., to give freely or without constraint . . . how great soever the Authority of Parents is in that behalf . . . yet the children or Parties . . . espoused, are to give their consent freely and voluntarily; or at least . . . they are

---

[33] In *Calverley's Examination*, App. B, *Yorkshire Tragedy*, Calverley claims that his wife 'had . . . given signes and tokens . . . whereby he might . . . perceive her adultery'.

not to be constrained thereunto against their Wills, . . . otherwise the Contract of Spousal or Matrimony, made through fear, is utterly void *ipso jure*. (*Spousals*, 4)[34]

Elsewhere he says that 'if the Parents of the Children Contract Matrimony in behalf of the Children, though the Children say nothing, yet being present and hearing the same, their silence is a sufficient proof of their Consent' (86–7). The unacknowledged gap between these two statements of law is filled in and pointed up in a performance of *All's Well* by signs, gestures, facial expressions, and the language of silence – all areas that Swinburne himself has admitted into his discourse at various points. Theatre, we shall see, can provide proofs that legal distinctions cannot.

In *All's Well*, the King invites Helena to 'peruse . . . well' and take her pick from 'a youthful parcel/Of noble bachelors' (II.iii.52–3). 'These boys', as Lafew calls them, are a collection of wards on display for Helena's 'election', in a reversal of the usual gender roles in the marriage market: she has 'power to choose, and they none to forsake' (II.iii.55). Here is a clear statement of the power relation that Bertram articulated on his very first appearance: 'I must attend his majesty's command, to whom I am now in ward, evermore in subjection' (I.i.4–5). The 1993 Stratford production of *All's Well* by Peter Hall infused this scene with tense anticipation and fear as Helena was set loose on the young men; their movements were stiff and staccato as they danced paces to the theme music of the 'election', and each time she declined one of them, there would be instant relief on the part of the man rejected, and a corresponding mounting of tension among those still in the ring. The cue for this body language is there in the text – most succinctly in Lafew's comment, 'These boys are boys of ice; they'll none have her' (II.iii.92), and his remark, earlier, that for all the interest the men are showing in this eminently desirable woman, they ought to be sent 'to th'Turk to make eunuchs of' (II.iii.85–7). It is after he has expressly and repeatedly stated his unwillingness in vain, and the King has threatened him and commanded him thrice to 'take her' by the hand and 'tell her she is thine', that Bertram reticently says, 'I take her hand' (II.iii.175). Pointedly, he does not in our hearing utter the marriage vow and tell her she is his. We witness the 'favour of the King' smiling upon the contract; we hear too that Bertram has had to swear before the priest. By Swinburne's definitions, then, it is a marriage, for Bertram's presence itself is presumed

---

[34] Cf. *Matrimony*, 121; see *Testaments*, 240v, on wills, also documents of intention: 'Nothing is more contrary to free consent than Fear'.

to be 'proof' of 'consent', no matter what we hear him say; at the same time, it is 'void *ipso jure* since we have seen enough and heard his tone clearly enough to perceive the lack of consent. Everyone in the play, including Bertram himself, acknowledges him and Helena to be married. Yet, at another level, Bertram almost does not believe it; he has wedded her, but will never bed her (II.iii.268–71; III.ii.21), as if by resisting consummation he will somehow prevent the 'wedding' from materialising into marriage. The caution, the non-committal precision and the element of riddling in Bertram's two letters even while he is technically committing himself – swearing 'to make the "not" eternal' (III.ii.19–24 and III.ii.56–74) – translates the sense of a lacuna written into the language of the marriage ritual itself, a possibility of the coexistence of opposite polarities of meaning in a single act or formulation.

The discrepancy emerging from these examples suggests a rift between natural law and institutional legality. Rather than mirroring an instinctive sense of moral justice, formal law seems to be at variance with it. This discordance also raises its dark head in Swinburne. Yet why should it, if Swinburne upholds the centrality of mutual consent in marriage law? It is in trying to answer this question that we realise where Swinburne stumbles. When consent is the particular intention required for valid matrimony, it becomes difficult to ascertain validity. For how can intention be proved in law? Swinburne, defending the expressive function of the set words, asks rhetorically, 'For how can we *know* a Man's meaning but by his words?' (63). Yet, as we have already seen, the word cannot be trusted. In theoretically confronting endless situations that make this apparent, he has to concede that 'albeit the words of the Contract' neither intrinsically nor by custom 'conclude Matrimony; Yet whereas the Parties do thereby intend to contract Matrimony, they are inseparable Man and Wife, not only before God, but also before Man; in case their meaning may lawfully appear' (87). The proviso gives a lie to the foregoing claim. In the very process of asserting 'the natural propriety' of the words of matrimony 'albeit he or she had no meaning . . . to Contract Matrimony (. . . perhaps the Mans purpose was . . . to deceive)', Swinburne is suddenly brought to admit the limitations of law as a means of reading men's hearts and to state its necessity, notwithstanding, as dictated by human imperfection. The turn in his argument is signalled by 'although' which separates what is evident to man and what to God:

. . . the parties shall be adjudged . . . to have contracted Matrimony, *although* (before God) they be not Man and Wife, for he which is the searcher of the heart doth well know their deceit and defect of Mutual Consent . . . But mortal Man cannot otherwise judge of Mens meanings, than by their sayings for the Tongue is the Messenger of the heart; and although it sometimes deliver a false message, yet doth the Law accept it for true, when as the Contrary doth not lawfully appear. (84–5) (italics mine)

Thus a secretly contracted person remarrying commits 'adultery in the infallible sight of God's . . . Judgement', though 'the Church' – falling under 'man's law', not 'God's' – 'doth not judge of secret and hidden things, whereof there is no appearance' (196). 'For proof is not of the Essence of Matrimony; and if it were, yet their Consciences shall be as a thousand Witnesses before the Tribunal of . . . God' (87).[35] Can there, then, be any way of judging intention, if 'Not to be, and not to appear, is all one in Construction of Law' (181)?

But the mortal judge must perform his duty. The extent of uncertainty in the constitution of marriage made the need for proof the more acute. However, the contracting parties were the least likely, especially at the moment of spousal, to be verbally precise, and not sure to be conversant with legal formulae, while witnesses were often uneducated and reliant on memory. To make matters worse, spousal disputes often involved secret contracts, with no witnesses. Here, other forms of proof, usually material, were required.[36] Hence, phrases to the effect of 'unless it doth otherwise lawfully appear' follow upon every consideration of an eventuality that may indicate either the inadequacy or the unavailability of the 'word' as evidence. The object of 'lawful appearance', after all, is an invisible intention.[37]

---

[35] Cf. *Spousals*, 124.

[36] Ibid., Sections XIII–XV; Rushton, 'Testaments', 25–31. See also O'Hara, *Courtship*, esp. Ch. 2 – an excellent account of token-exchange and courtship in early modern society. O'Hara discusses some of the Canterbury cases I looked at independently before her book was published. Her historical findings about courtship tokens and their social and economic implications on the whole corroborate my reading of these records. Her principal concerns, however, are 'not with the significance of such gifts and tokens for the legal probity of marriage, but rather with the social importance of those practices' (63); not with the 'legal validity of a union' but the 'popular perception and social practice of marriage formation' (10). In fact, her 'perspective . . . does not interest itself unduly with matters of marriage law' (7). My study of tokens in drama addresses precisely the indistinguishable interface between law and social practice or attitudes.

[37] Revealingly, the central preoccupation of *Testaments* is with determining the validity of a 'testament' which is 'a testifying or witnessing of the minde', 'a iust sentence of our will' (²B3–v). As with marriage, so with last wills, the centre is the human will – witness the importance of *volo* in marriage vows. Cf. ²C2–²C2v. In the seventh part, a list 'shewing by what means Testaments [. . .] become voide' include 'Of feare' (no. 5), 'Of errour' (no. 8), 'Of uncertaintie' (no. 9) and the defect of intention (no. 11) – categories familiar from *Spousals*.

'THAT RING'S A THOUSAND PROOFS'[38]

Among the non-verbal signs that take on a demonstrative or validating function, Swinburne talks of rings: '*Subarration*, that is the giving and receiving of a *Ring*, is a Sign of all others, most usual in Spousals and Matrimonial Contracts' (207). It can even suffice when 'the one party use no words at all' (86).[39] This particular class of evidence focuses several problems and implications of proof simultaneously, both in the specific context of marital evidence and also, more variously, in the legal process itself. This is spotted by a significant number of dramatists. The ring straddles the world of legal evidence and that of tokens of promises, acts or identity in fictional, especially anagnoristic plots. What makes it a connective between the two worlds is its role of supposedly embodying an internal truth. Particularly suggestive among tokens that possess this function, the ring is exploited by dramatists dealing with sexual behaviour and contracts because of its metaphoric and metonymic associations with female genitalia. An examination of rings as tokens in law, social transactions and plays suggests that drama's techniques of addressing the legal problem of evidence are generically determined. Romance and comedy, of course, thrived on tokens. At the same time, a number of depositions from Renaissance England show that the dramatic treatments of proof are not a purely imaginative preoccupation conducive to fictional plots or genres; they address uncertainties already present in the legal procedure but not so clearly and frankly articulated. By virtue of its distance from law, and its own distinctive modes, drama can probe some of the problems of law better than law can afford to do. In a period as highly litigious as it was theatrical, where courtrooms were as much a public stage as the theatre was an open court, such connections would be as easy for the playgoer to understand as they would be felicitous for legally informed playwrights to make.[40] I hope to recapture some of these unmistakable resonances for the modern reader and playgoer by stating what is often only suggested in the plays: the real connections between legal problems and their metamorphosed counterparts in drama. In some plays, of course, they are less 'metamorphosed' than in others; what

---

[38] *AW*, V.iii.198.

[39] Cf. *Spousals*, 71, 101, 206–12.

[40] This is not to suggest that a court proceeding, in all its chaotic details (see Herrup, *Common Peace*, 141, 144), was identical to its dramatic representation, but to note the performative and structural similarities often shared by events on stage and in the courtroom.

is required is an understanding of the nature of the relevant phenomena in legal practice and thought, and an analysis of why, how and to what effect a playwright dramatises a specific selection from these; and what literary-analytical devices they employ in doing so.

The ring is a prominent presence in church court action. The determining factor in the case of Thomas Allen v. Alice Howling of Norfolk (1562) is a 'Ring of gould'.[41] Alice's personal response to Thomas's charge chiefly consists of a denial of her alleged receipt of this ring 'in the waye of matrimony' on a certain 'Satturdaye . . . night' at Rushford. However, both John Smith and William Walker, whose depositions are built, equally, around the event of that night, testify in vivid and almost identical terms that Thomas gave and Alice accepted the ring as an acknowledged token of present matrimony. In Smith's words, Thomas,

havinge hir by thande hear Alice I give the [heere?] my Ringe as my wiff yf thowe wilte take yt vppon this condicion and weare yt yf not, take yt not, who toke and receyved the same and then the sayd Thomas Allen toke a bottell of wyne and saye Alice I drink to the as my wyff who did thank him and did pledg him saying I do pledg yow as my husbend.

From the frustratingly cryptic act book entry, one gathers that Alice appealed to the Court of Arches, and so the case was deferred. Evidently the verdict of this particular proceeding went against her. By establishing her receipt of the ring in an expressly marital context, Thomas seems to have established, at least for the time being, his marital claim on her.

The conclusive role of rings in determining judgements has been dismissed by some historians on statistical grounds.[42] But the number of surviving depositions from the years 1570–1640[43] is not necessarily a proportional indication of the number of uncertain marriages being contracted, given that the Church was trying to regularise and formalise marriage during exactly this period.[44] Out-of-court settlements were common, and certainly the plays of this period abound with disputed contracts.[45] Besides, law can only misleadingly be separated from social attitudes and customs.[46] The deposition narratives unite the social and the

---

[41] NNRO, DN/DEP 9, Bk VIII, 158v, 162–163v; DN/ACT 9, Bk. X.
[42] See Houlbrooke, 'Making of Marriage', 339–52 (344); also Houlbrooke, *Church Courts*, 60–1.
[43] See Ingram, *Church Courts*, 192; Houlbrooke, 'Making of Marriage', 349.
[44] Ingram, *Church Courts*, 193.
[45] It is usually difficult to trace Act book entries corresponding to the depositions, and judgements are often abbreviated or cryptic.
[46] See Gillis, *For Better, For Worse*, 6–7; also 16–17 on Swinburne's use of the word 'rite'.

legal: the terms in which the validity of marriage is popularly configured determine the course of the interrogation and the criteria by which a contract is sought to be proved, no less than the testimonies are shaped by set articles of interrogatories. About the contested runaway match between Thomas and Margaret Sothworth of Chester (1565), George Haydock deposes that he secretly followed the parties on the night concerned to the house of an 'old and sicklie', bedridden priest; 'what wordes were spoken [there] betwene the parties, he certenlie cannot declare, biecause he did not marke them well'; what he does remember, however, is that 'gold and silver was put on the boke and a ringe put on her finger . . .'[47] The general perception of ring-giving as an integral ceremony in a matrimonial context derives, paradoxically, from its public association with solemnised weddings in *facie ecclesiae*, though its legal significance is greatest in cases of clandestine marriage to which it almost lends a semblance of formality. The conjunction of the ring and the 'boke' – the Book of Common Prayer – abounds not only in the northern and north-western dioceses of Durham and Chester,[48] but also, down south, in Canterbury, where one might have expected Catholic marriage rituals to be losing importance, given that Puritan writers were already, in these parts, beginning to challenge the ritual of the ring.[49] In a Canterbury case of 1582, Wanderton v. Wild,[50] the ring clinches a contract – in pre-Reformation manner – and gives a *de futuro* spousal the sanctity of a present marriage, at least in the eyes of the deponents.[51] Michael Haell, witness, 'remembreth not' the words of pledge, but recalls urging the parties to 'conclude the matter as it myght to be done' (175v). Then 'Wanderton gaue her a Ring gelt saying to her take this as a token that you have confessed and I the like to you, you to be my wyf and I to be your husband . . . and she receaued the same Ring thankfully' (176). It was only then that the witnesses felt free to 'depart'. Note that the deponent's claim is that the parties are well and truly married. The spousal 'ring' had become assimilated from its original Catholic wedding location into popular and collective associations of love and marriage.

[47] Furnivall, *Child-Marriages*, 65–6.
[48] Raine, *Depositions*, passim, esp. 239–40, 243, 254, 283; Furnivall, *Child-Marriages*, 65–7, 69, 140–1, 187.
[49] Gilby, *Pleasaunte dialogue*, M5r; Fenner, *Certain Learned and Godly Treatises*, 96; Kingsmill, *Viewe of Mans Estate*, K2r; McGinn, *Admonition Controversy*, 218–19; Greaves, *Society and Religion*, 184–5.
[50] CCA, MS. X.10.20, 173–6.
[51] *Sarum Missal*, 552–9; 'The Form of Solemnization of Matrimony' as given in *Book of Common Prayer 1559*, 290–3.

A suggestive enactment of the constant shift between public ceremony and the reclaiming of ritual for a private binding occurs in Chapman's *The Gentleman Usher*, where Vincentio and Margaret 'marie before heaven' by improvising their own ritual (IV.ii.120–98).[52] They tie a scarf about each other's arms which functions, in its 'circumferent flexure', as a ring. Vowing by it, Vincentio is satisfied that 'It is enough and binds as much as marriage' (179). The ritual space they create around themselves invokes 'the lawes of God and Nature' and internal solemnisation, as opposed to 'the formall lawes of man' and 'outward rites' (131–4).[53] The paradox of this repudiation is that the ritual exchange is 'deuise(d)' (146) as much as a contingency measure to claim some formal value, as to give the nuptial a private and deeper legitimacy. The duality persists in the symbolic consummation of the marriage through the removal of Margaret's 'snowie vaile' (191–3); what is performed as an internal 'token' (190) derives its weight from the legal power of consummation to clinch a private contract and to frustrate others' attempts at enforcing a different, public spousal. Webster's *The Duchess of Malfi* provides another remarkable instance of the use of public gestures and ceremonial tokens to reinforce a private contract. The Duchess asserts the autonomy of the lovers' 'circumference' (I.i.469) and their freedom from institutions: 'How can the church bind faster'? (491). Yet the autonomy remains dialectically defined, as she weds Antonio by using the legal formula of spousals *per verba de praesenti*' (479) and '[putting] her ring upon his finger' – her wedding ring, which she 'did vow never to part with' 'but to [her] second husband' (404–15).

Several strands fed into the well-recognised symbolism of the ring.[54] Among those related to marriage, the associations of eternity, constancy and continuity with its circular shape were most prominent.[55] 'The first Ring was . . . of Iron, adorned with an adamant'[56] – the metal signifying durability. In time, the symbolism accumulated other kinds of value, as iron was replaced by gold. That ephemeral rings made of rushes were thought suitable for temporary liaisons corroborates the symbolic

---

[52] In Chapman, *Plays*.

[53] On custom, see Schochet, ed., *Law, literature*, 131–72.

[54] For the various symbolisms of the ring, see *Spousals*, 207–9; Cirlot, *Dictionary of Symbols*, 273; de Vries, *Dictionary*, 386–7; Cooper, *Encyclopaedia*; Kunz, *Rings*, 193–248; Bury, *Introduction*, 15–17; Thompson, *Motif-Index*, E321.1, H86.3, J1171.1.1, J1243. See Heywood, *Curtaine Lecture*, 122, 102–3: a contemporary comment on the currency of the Roman spousal ceremony of ring-giving in Stuart England.

[55] E.g. Bullen, *English Garner*, 296, posy no. 15.

[56] *Spousals*, 208.

importance of the metal.[57] The ring-finger was supposed to be connected to the heart through the *Vena amoris*: 'because to that finger alone (as the best anatomists tell us) proceeds a veine that hath its originall from the heart'.[58] The ring was also a binding symbol,[59] deriving from the meaning of the first ever ring (worn by Prometheus), the only remaining link of a chain. In the depositions, it is the context of giving that determines how binding a ring, or indeed any other token, can be.[60] There are often three distinct viewpoints: the giver's, the receiver's and the observer's. Sometimes, even more bewilderingly, there is no observer.

Edmund Hodgson of Cokerton insists that any gift he may have sent to Margaree Wormeley was 'upon frenshipe, but as no token'.[61] John Smith protests he gave Christian a ring 'not for that he wold mary her' but because he 'wold have to do with her'.[62] Alice Cotton says she received Thomas Baxter's gifts as 'mere gift' and not 'in . . . waie of marriage' (1574).[63] The problem, as ever, is of correctly assessing the intention of the giver, vis-à-vis the perception of the receiver and/or others. The pains taken by the parties to prove or disprove matrimonial intentions emphasise the obligation created by the receipt of a demonstrably marital token. So Alice Berry refused to take Simon Marketman's 'angell' since 'if she should receaue it, it wold be thought and said that she receaued the same vp*p*on condic*i*on to marry with Marketman' (1581).[64] That associations had consolidated through custom into legally legitimate grounds for expectation is attested by numerous court orders like the one given to Jane Bredford in 1558 for the restitution of the gold ring and the bracelet she had received from Oliver Symons when her father refused to let her appear at a 'naughty corte' to settle matters.[65] The several instances of forced or 'planted' gifts indicate conscious manipulation of the proof

---

[57] In Shakespeare and Fletcher's *The Two Noble Kinsmen*, IV.i.88–91, rings of rushes are a poignantly appropriate token of the distracted 'Jailers daughter's' illusory love-pledge with Palamon.

[58] Heywood, *Curtaine Lecture*, 103.

[59] Cf. *Cymbeline*, I.i.121–2: though a bracelet, Posthumus' 'manacle of love' – like Vincentio's scarf – is analogous to the ring.

[60] See Kunz, *Rings*, 205, on the uncertainty about when 'the betrothal ring became the wedding ring, but this change seems to have taken place in England about the time of the Reformation'. He adds, however, that this change was not a replacement. The confusion over betrothal and nuptial rings mirrors the difficulty in fixing the distinction between spousal and marriage: see *Spousals*, 2.

[61] Raine, *Depositions*, 285.

[62] Furnivall, *Child-Marriages*, 57.

[63] CCA, X.10.17, 152v. See also ibid., X.10.12, 182–v.

[64] Ibid., X.10.21, 81v.

[65] Ibid., X.10.6, 200v–1.

value of tokens.[66] These specific givings and receivings, of course, partook of the general social implications of the act of giving in the period.[67]

In drama, the idea of obligation is tellingly dealt with. In Shakespeare's *Richard III*, despite Anne's protestation, 'To take is not to give', she is in fact both 'woo'd' and 'won' through her acceptance of Richard's ring (I.ii.201–28). For the audience, too, the ring visually makes this scene embody the ritual of courtship and spousal; the next time we see Anne, Richard 'is [her] husband' (IV.i.65). Nor is this symbolic value confined to the drama. When the 'fickle maid' in Shakespeare's *A Lover's Complaint* is 'espied' 'tearing of papers, breaking rings a-twain', she is destroying precisely such tokens. Significantly, she presents herself as a defendant right through her confessional 'complaint', and is surely being prudent when she tears 'folded schedules' and cracks 'posied' rings, as well as expressing her heart break over 'what unapprovèd witness' these testaments have borne.[69]

Several functions of the ring are intricately combined in the ring-episodes in *The Merchant of Venice*. Portia's ring is initially the object 'with' which Portia makes '[herself] and what is [hers]' over to Bassanio (III.ii.166–71); it is, thus, a symbol of her love and submission to him. However, it is also a token of the transfer of property, subtly reversing gender roles. It was not uncommon in the sixteenth century for a signet to be set in the betrothal ring, signifying a bestowal on the woman – the recipient – the right to seal up the household goods, in token of which a small key was sometimes attached.[70] The verbal counterpart is found in these words of the marriage ceremony: 'With all my worldly goods I thee

---

[66] Ibid., X.10.6, 200v–1; X.10.18, 154v–5; NNRO DEP/6, Book 5b, 212. See CCA, Y.3.15, 270v for a defendant's use of 'token' to mean evidence ('tokens that she is my wife').

[67] See Fumerton, *Cultural Aesthetics*, passim. On the credit economy of early modern English society, see Muldrew, *Economy*.

[68] *MV*, IV.i.434.

[69] *Lover's Complaint*, esp. stanzas 1–8. See Kerrigan, ed., *Motives of Woe*, 45–6, on the legal language of the poem. Cf. John Donne's 'The Token', which lists the traditional tokens of love he does not want from his beloved, in an attempt to define the token that he seeks. Among these negative evocations, the ring is prominent. This poem not only testifies to the conventionality of the ring as a love-token but also indicates its familiar symbolic meaning. The significance of comparable circular tokens is similarly mocked in 'Elegy II The Bracelet': its negative evocations at once suggest – and reject – the similetic, synecdochic and symbolic associations of bracelets, chains and rings as conventional amorous tokens.

[70] Kunz, *Rings*, 193.

endow' – a transformed version of which is discernible in Portia's speech. The signet, significantly, was also a traditional symbol of authority.[71] Portia's ring here functions like one, except that the husband is the recipient. Even while using the language of surrender, Portia retains her power as the giver, proleptically indicated in her final claim that if Bassanio should 'lose, or give away' the ring, 'Let it . . ./ . . . be my vantage to exclaim on you' (III.ii.173–4). The extent to which Bassanio's lordship over her is her gift, an implicit ground for expecting returns, is driven home in V.i. Bassanio's 'return' is a relinquishing of his freedom to her; the act of bestowal brings love and ownership together in a slightly dubious compound. With respect to Antonio, however, the implications of Portia's generosity are more sinister, and the same ring has a suggestive role to play. The combination of overt giving and covert reclaiming with interest in the ring incident of III.ii anticipates the exaction of an exchange under cover of bounty that Portia conducts with Antonio in V.i. The model there, more unambiguously than in the betrothal scene, is that of a nexus of transactions and investments projected as an act of donation, not, as Karen Newman concludes, that of the Maussian Big Man binding one by giving one more than one can repay. Portia does not 'short circuit' the system of exchange[72] but in fact instals it in a relationship founded on non-transactional giving, a relationship to which she herself was – and is no more content to be – an outsider.[73] In the course of these carefully engineered processes, the ring is made to evoke several of its disparate associations according to the needs of particular stages of Portia's operations, so that it is hard to fix its signification in any one economy.

Antonio, at the outset, agrees to act as a surety for Bassanio, and ends up risking his life for him. For this, Bassanio is 'infinitely bound' (V.i.135). However, Antonio considers himself 'well acquitted' (138), since his end was never a repayment from Bassanio but his release; there were even perhaps elements of a desire to prove or show his love by staking his 'purse', 'person' and 'extremest means' (I.i.138), and a happiness in forever giving, but this proceeds rather from his own sublimated self-abasement than a desire to put Bassanio under obligation. He seems to genuinely feel what Portia claims to feel at IV.i.415–17: 'He is well paid that is well satisfied;/And I in delivering you am satisfied/And therein do account

---

[71] See Cooper, *Encyclopaedia*, 138–9; de Vries, *Dictionary*, 386.

[72] Newman, 'Portia's Ring', 26.

[73] See the suggestive distinction between investment and expense in Barthes, *Lover's Discourse*, 77: 'To speak of the gift is to place it in an exchange economy (of sacrifice, competition, etc.); which stands opposed to silent expenditure.'

myself well paid'. But Portia, who has righteously dissociated herself – albeit as Balthazar – from the 'mercenary' nature of exchange (IV.i.418), is quick to state the need for reciprocal obligation in the situation, the moment Bassanio says he is bound: 'You should in all sense be much bound to him,/For as I hear he was much bound for you' (V.i.136–7). Thus, she draws Antonio into a nexus of exchange in relation to Bassanio. Meanwhile, the hue and cry over the giving away of the rings reduces Antonio to a feeling of guilty obligation: 'I am th'unhappy subject of these quarrels' (238). He is already the embarrassed outsider who is 'welcome notwithstanding' (239). Portia, by generating a 'salutary anxiety'[74] pushes him to offer, finally, to 'be bound again', and then seizes upon his metaphor: 'Then you shall be his surety. Give him this/And bid him keep it better than the other' (254–5). Here is the completion of a barter begun with Portia's releasing of Antonio by cavillation,[75] for this time the 'creditor' is Portia, and Antonio – as 'surety' for Bassanio's faith – is bound to her.[76] Portia, on behalf of Bassanio, gave Antonio his life. Now it is Antonio's turn to reciprocate in kind by returning the ring and making Bassanio swear to keep it, thereby relinquishing his emotional claims on Bassanio, since it was for him that the ring was relinquished. Yet, if Portia manipulated the trial on Bassanio's behalf, this acquittal is redundant because she, standing for Bassanio, has repaid *his* debt to Antonio by releasing the latter. Thus, the pretence of a barter further conceals an opening out of a settled deal – if one must look at it through Portia's eyes – into a new extortion; for Antonio, if anyone, is the giver here. But he never seems so, and this is due to Portia's projecting her moves as being bounteous, culminating in her mystification of the return of Antonio's ships; we almost do not notice that 'the strange accident' pertains merely to her chancing on the letter, not to the restoration of the argosies, no matter how 'sudden' (275–9). She successfully makes Antonio feel indebted to her for both 'life and living' (286), yet we know that his living matters as little to him as his 'body' which he 'once did lend' for Bassanio and which he also now owes to Portia (III.iii.35–6; IV.i.266–81). This time, it is his 'soul' that is 'upon the forfeit', for Portia is playing at higher stakes than Shylock, as far as Antonio's priorities are concerned. The gift of life and living to Antonio – partly real, partly pretended – is in a sense as useless as sparing Shylock his life while robbing him of

---

[74] See Greenblatt, *Shakespearean Negotiations*, 133–6.
[75] On 'cavillation', see Maclean, *Interpretation*, 135–7.
[76] Sonnet 134 offers verbal and situational parallels.

his living, for to Shylock, 'the means whereby [he lives]' *is* his life (IV.i.376–7). The connection between the two scenes begins to emerge, as we discern in both the same pattern of cheese-paring justice, or equality of exchange – dubious enough already in a professedly Christian space – giving over to something like a civil revenge, in excess of the settling of scores, but in the guise of generosity.

Within this circuit, the ring, accepted 'as tribute/Not as a fee' by Portia/Balthazar (IV.i.422–3), is used by her as an instrument in creating a network of transactions. The furore over the missing ring hinges on the sanctity of the associations surrounding a betrothal ring – '. . . the virtue of the ring,/Or half her worthiness that gave the ring,/Or your own honour to contain the ring' (V.i.100–201). Bassanio's (and Gratiano's) offence has been to let go of 'the thing held as a ceremony' (206). 'Virtue' also suggests the magical associations of the ring.[77] Magic objects are traditionally believed to have the property of making synecdochic or symbolic connections real, a notion that complements the sentimental and representational value of tokens – consider posies like 'Not the gift but the giver'.[78] They are also objects that must not be lost or sold, or ruin will befall, thus again feeding into the sense of sacrilege in giving away a betrothal ring – 'Which when you part from, lose, or give away,/Let it presage the ruin of your love'(III.ii.172–3).[79] Portia and Nerissa's lectures on the right valuation of the ring hold the men guilty of letting it enter improper economies (V.i.151–8, 166–76, 199–206). Yet Portia herself has been the driving force behind the numerous trips it makes from one economy to another. In the betrothal scene it was a token of love and faith, and of a transfer of power and property. At the end of the trial scene it is a 'tribute' of gratitude from Bassanio who rightly considers himself as 'bound' to Balthazar as Antonio is; to Portia, however, it betokens Bassanio's affection for Antonio and is thus a love-token in a different circuit from the one within which it was first given.[80] In the last scene, the

---

[77] See Thompson, *Motif-Index*, D800–899, D1076, D1406, P510 on powers, ownership and loss of magic objects.

[78] Kunz, *Rings*, 240, 243, 245; Cooper, *Encyclopaedia*, 139; Bullen, *English Garner*, 296/no.14, 299/35,303/58, 305/67; also *Loues Garland*, no.45; Evans, *English Posies*, 1, 3.

[79] Posies like the one Gratiano mocks –'love me and leave me not' (V.i.150) – were common, emphasising the value of tokens as keepsakes. See Kunz, *Rings*, 242; Bullen, *English Garner*, 305/67; Bury, *Introduction*, 25, 2.

[80] Antonio urges Bassanio to 'let him have the ring' – 'Let his deservings and my love withal/Be valued 'gainst your wife's commandment' (IV.i.449–51) – precisely the priority that Portia subtly points out as illegitimate in V.i. Note that 'forfeit' was defined as 'penalty for transgression': see Fischer, *Econolingua*, 77.

ring becomes a symbol for the transfer back of the claim and authority of love. Antonio, made to hand it back to Bassanio personally, is officially surrendering his claims, as one would by returning a love-token; with this, his 'bonds' in Bassanio 'are all determinate'.[81] So the ring re-enters the closed Portia–Bassanio nuptial circuit from the homosocial bond of 'friendship' between Antonio and Bassanio. In legal terms, it is a proof of Bassanio's error and, less overtly but more crucially, of Antonio's transgression. At the same time, it clinches a contractual deal rather different from the spousal that it is advertised to symbolise supremely and sacredly. Portia's ring also places marriage in a contractual economy, and thus recalls and contrasts with Leah's ring which Shylock 'would not have given . . . for a wilderness of monkeys' (III.i.122–3) – the only thing to which Shylock attaches a worth distinct from money value. Rings, being tokens as well as precious jewels, can connote several kinds of value, and in the context of spousals, can place 'romantic' love in the nexus of exchanges where it belonged in society. An understanding of the institution of marriage is itself a clue to the economic construction of social and private existence, as *The Merchant* brilliantly shows. The problem is precisely the risk of conflating the different values. Particulars of marriage procedures in the period indicate the inseparability of their transactional associations from their sentimental ones.[82]

A complex treatment of the circulation of tokens is to be found in *All's Well*; the circulating objects, conveniently, are rings. The first ring is given by the King to Helena as a 'token' (V.iii.85). Helena gives it to Diana as an instrument of the bed-trick to secure Bertram. Bertram hands it over to Lafew as an 'amorous token' for Maudlin (V.iii.68–76), but it becomes, to the King, a proof of Helena's death and, possibly, Bertram's foul play. The second ring, equally, participates in a whole range of economies, becoming a different token with each change of hand. A symbol of family honour, it was Bertram's heirloom. But Diana's demand of it as a confirmation of Bertram's oaths suggests the power of the ring to clinch a love contract; indeed it lends Bertram's 'wooing' of Diana the ceremony of a spousal (IV.ii.66), and his words echo Portia's marital offer of person and property:

---

[81] Shakespeare, Sonnet 87.
[82] See Sheehan, 'Formation and Stability', 228–63, and Gillis, *For Better, For Worse*, passim. See also Humphrey's wooing of Luce in Beaumont's *The Knight of the Burning Pestle*, I.i.140–9, with a glove which has a price-tag attached.

> Here, take my ring.
> My house, mine honour, yea, my life be thine,
> And I'll be bid by thee.   (51–3)

The 'band of truth' (56) by which Diana charges him to observe her directions could well be this ring – Swinburne's 'holy band of Wedlock' (*Spousals*, 209). In conjunction with Bertram's words, this 'subarration' would technically count as a promise of marriage. In terms of Bertram's intention, though, it turns out to be a token, rather, of 'such a Contract as *Judah* made with *Thamar* . . . that he should lye with her, which bargain he concluded by delivering her a Ring . . . afterwards . . . committing filthiness with her, and begetting her with Child' (209).

This ring acquires a further valency in its promised exchange with the first ring which, at this point, stands for Diana's chastity (IV.ii.45–9). In deed, though, it is Helena's chastity that is going to be its operative but invisible counterpart. It will, Diana says darkly, 'token to the future our past deeds' – 'token' here meaning 'to signify' as well as, literally, 'embody', if the 'another ring' of Diana's description is the yet uncracked ring of Helena's virginity (60–5),[83] the putting of which 'on [Bertram's] finger in the night' will lead to her pregnancy. The bawdy sense is reinforced by the verbal echo of Bertram's letter to Helena which posited, by linguistic juxtaposition, a cause-and-effect relationship between getting the 'ring upon [his] finger' and showing 'a child begotten of [her] body' (III.ii.57–9). It recalls 'Nerissa's ring' (*MV*, V.i.307) and the implications of Portia's reproach of Gratiano for parting with it:

> . . . your wive's first gift,
> A thing stuck on with oaths upon your finger
> And so riveted with faith unto your flesh.
>   (V.i.167–9)

It also reinforces the connection between the legal importance of rings in marital contracts and the legitimising power of consummation in a doubtful marriage.[84] The means of Helena's triumph reminds us of Anne Yates's success in establishing her marital claim on her elusive and reluctant handfasted husband George Johnson (who has, like Bertram, made a second marriage of sorts) by proving, through alibi, that 'they have

---

[83] Cf. *Hamlet*, II.ii.427–8; *R&J*, II.i.24; *AYLI*, III.ii.271–2; *AW*, III.v.92. On the sexual symbolism of the ring, see Partridge, *Shakespeare's Bawdy*, 25, 96, 179. See also Thompson, *Motif-Index*, H 433.1; de Vries, *Dictionary*, 386–7.

[84] *Spousals*, 73, 148–50, 219–21, 224; Houlbrooke, *Church Courts*, 60; Furnivall, *Child-Marriages*, 56–7.

laine together in bed'(1562–3);[85] it also recalls the case of Walkden v. Lowe (1561) where the birth of a child – a demonstrable proof of copulation – vindicates Jane Walkden's marital claim and invalidates Richard Lowe's later marriage.[86]

The sexual metaphor of the ring hinges on its shape which is also the main focus in its other symbolisms. Being a thing of nought that can be filled up or entered into, it stands for the vagina, and for the potential sexual errancy as well as vulnerability of women. In this function it acts as a metonymy, a detached attribute held up for the object it pertains to, thus also resembling the notion of the fetish.[87] It can, moreover, stand in, as a synecdoche (part for the whole), for the woman herself: Mariana, in *Measure*, is 'nothing' because of the indeterminacy of her sexual status – 'neither maid, widow, nor wife' (V.i.177). It is the finger entering it that determines the identity and value of the ring. As Martine Segalen writes, of nineteenth-century French marriage rituals, 'The wife is the ring, she is the circle which her husband will force.'[88]

Next to rings, gloves were among the commonest love-tokens in Renaissance England, and are structurally similar to the ring.[89] Fingers, the objects of insertion in both cases, had their own sexual associations.[90] The ring and the glove come together in sexual synecdoche in Middleton and Rowley's *The Changeling* (1622).[91] At I.i.225, Beatrice-Joanna drops a glove – her agency in it is left tantalisingly obscure – and Deflores picks it up. Beatrice, instead of coolly accepting it as a courtesy, flares up and flings down her other glove: 'There, for t'other's sake I part with this,/ Take 'em and draw thine own skin off with 'em' (229–30). The needless violence of her indignation results in a physicality in her imagery that induces Deflores' lewd response to this act of giving an intimate article of her clothing:

---

[85] Furnivall, *Child-Marriages*, 57–9; for similar instances, see NNRO DN/ACT/4, Bk 4A, 129; ibid., DN/ACT/5 Bk 7A, 68; ibid., DN/ACT/6, Bk 7B, 303. A handfast was the symbolic gesture of clasping hands through which many informal or unsolemnised marriages were contracted; see Barton, 'Wrying but a little'; Cook, *Making a Match*.

[86] Furnivall, *Child-Marriages*, 56.

[87] On fetishism, see Freud, *On Sexuality*, VII, 65–8, 347–57.

[88] Segalen, *Love and Power*, 57–8.

[89] Bullen, *English Garner*, 295–305; Evans, *English Posies*, passim; Houlbrooke, *Church Courts*, 60. See de Vries, *Dictionary*, 216–17, on its associations of physical intimacy and the notion of a perfect fit.

[90] Ibid., 185. Besides the obvious association with the penis, the middle finger or *digita impudica* was supposed to be used in coition. Cf. Barry, *Ram Alley* (1611), 288–9, on a widow 'as a pie . . . /That hath many fingers in't before'.

[91] Middleton and Rowley, *Changeling*.

> Here's a favour come; with a mischief: now I know
> She had rather wear my pelt tann'd in a pair
> Of dancing pumps, than I should thrust my fingers
> Into her sockets here . . .   (231–4)

In the context of Beatrice's compulsive visceral awareness of him, the glove thrown in hate becomes a perverse token of 'favour' and prefigures her acceptance of his 'service' (II.ii) in murdering Piracquo, by which she has also, unawares, made a contract to accept his sexual service. For, in sexual relationships, giving can bind as fast as receiving. Alice Berry not only discovered a ring sneaked into her glove by Marketman but he also 'snatched' a 'handkercher' from her, a structure of exchange and reciprocity being thus established by force.[92]

Meanwhile the 'thrusting' fingers are verbally linked, in Alibius and Lollio's exchange (I.ii.26–31), with the woman's 'ring', establishing the metaphoric contexts for the terrible confrontation of III.iv. Deflores' 'token' (26) to Beatrice – the dead man's finger with the ring sticking fast to it is a symbolic possession of her virginity as well as her person, for both were symbolically given over to Alonso by 'the first token' (33) of betrothal. Unmoved by the murder, Beatrice is appalled by the finger: Deflores remarks scathingly, 'Why, is that more/Than killing the whole man?' (29–30). This is a comment on both the power of the visible sign and the potential of synecdoche to sanction a perverse detachment of a part from the whole. Nor does he allow Beatrice to dissociate the 'whore-dome in [her] heart' (144) from the giving away of her virginity to Deflores (117–49) – demanded physically, since he has already laid claim to it metaphorically. They are as inseparable as ring and finger – 'we should stick together' (84): the 'deed' of murder, which is also the sexual 'deed' (both contract and act), has made them partners in mind and flesh. Beatrice's attempt to quit their liaison with payment is met with contempt, ''Twill hardly buy a capcase for one's conscience' (44), and an unsparing emphasis on the more-than-professional contract she has entered:

> I could ha' hired
> A journeyman in murder at this rate
> And mine own conscience might have slept at ease.
>   (68–70)

One thinks of Joan Swift of Faversham who, after declaring her love to Thomas Wood, lost interest and offered him a 'sow and piges

---

92 CCA, X.10.21, 81–v.

condicionally that he wold forsake her'.[93] But Marcia Mace pointed out
that this was 'to sell hym awaie' and it would not set her 'conscience' free
from the bond. But Beatrice's reaction also recalls the outraged bewilderment of Joan Stuppell who, eager to get rid of an obsessed George More,
found herself forcibly saddled with rings and things sent via third parties,
which were then used to make a case for her obligation.[94] That we are
made to think of both situations at once is a measure of the complexity
of the play's treatment of 'intention'.

'THE ARTIFICE OF SIGNS'

Synecdoche and metonymy are attributes of the evidential process itself.
The perversity of tokens in law is illuminated in drama by an exploration
of material items of proof in terms of tokens of recognition, from an
Aristotelian perspective.[95] The discussion of such tokens as proof, and
thus as elements of a well-made plot, was central to Aristotle's analysis of
dramatic structure in tragedy and the associated hierarchy of proofs.
This tradition was transmitted (with modifications) to English Renaissance writers through such commentators on Terence and New Comedy
as Donatus, Melancthon and Willichius, and Latin rhetoricians such as
Quintilian, revived by way of humanist education, and found its way into
dramatic writing as well as the toolkit of dramatic analysis in the period.[96]
The evaluative classification of recognitions in the *Poetics* is based on a
hierarchy of the means of recognition.[97] The best methods are 'probable
incidents' and the worst are 'inartistic', where the signs are material
objects – 'the artifice of signs and necklaces'. This corresponds to
the hierarchy of proofs in the *Rhetoric* (1.1.11, 1.37 and 2.25.8): here, the

---

[93] Ibid., X.10.16, 57–v.
[94] Ibid., X.10.18, 154v.
[95] I have been guided here, and inspired, by Cave, *Recognitions*, 10–78; 221–60; and Eden, *Poetic and Legal Fiction.*
[96] On the complex transmission history of Aristotle, see Herrick, 'Comic Theory', 61–88, 179–88; Altman, *Tudor Play of Mind*, esp. 130–47; Hutson, *Usurer's Daughter*, Chs. 5 and 6; and Cave, *Recognitions*, 273–5. In the sixteenth century, the Latin tradition was undoubtedly the most familiar vehicle. The Greek tradition joined it gradually, and piecemeal, depending on availability of translations into Latin (cf. the transmission of Pyrrhonism in the 1560s, after Sextus Empiricus was translated). Related narrative traditions, such as Boccaccio's *Decameron* and its legacy, also fed into Castelvetro's mediation of Aristotle's poetics. See Cave, *Recognitions*, 8, on Aristotelian theory as part of 'an active stock of critical knowledge', and 275, on how 'the dialogue between Aristotelian poetics and romance had reached England before Shakespeare imagined his experiments in the genre', even though the tradition was yet to be fully assimilated in England then.
[97] Aristotle, *Rhetoric and Poetics*, 16, 1455a 16–21.

best proofs are entechnic or artistic, constituted by probabilities; the worst are *ta semeia*, or atechnic, material signs, divorced from rhetorical demonstration. However, even in his discussion of the highest tragedy, *ta semeia* creep in through the back door. The poet's handling of the 'marvellous' (*Poetics* 24), for instance, makes the narrative handling of improbables rather like a recognition through *semeia*. Nor are material signs free of rhetoric: Aristotle's apparently confusing phrase for them, 'the artifice of signs', is ultimately revealing. The Aristotelian dilemma results in what Terence Cave calls 'paralogism', consisting of 'inferring an antecedent from an inadequate consequent . . . the name in logic for the procedure by which contingent clues are made to yield positive identities'.[98] This obscures the probabilistic causal inference claimed for 'recognitions' and defined in opposition to 'signs and tokens', which actually hinges on these very accidentals. As a result, 'recognitions' move into literary traditions which, from their theoretical inception, combine a use of tokens with an awareness of their ambivalence.

Quintilian, who was one of the main writers through whom Aristotle's *Poetics* became known in England in the sixteenth century, adapted it slightly. For instance, he translates *semeion* as *signum*, and might seem at first glance to be reversing the Aristotelian hierarchy by giving necessary signs the status of non-necessary signs that can be ground for inferences. But in fact, this is only a shift in terminology, and the artistic evaluation of proofs remains substantially unchanged.[99] Quintilian is really following Aristotle's division in the *Rhetoric* where, unlike the *Poetics* which defines 'signs' as inartificial objects, there are two kinds of signs – necessary ones, and 'simple signs' which are an intermediate category between infallible signs and probabilities, being refutable but on occasions eloquent in conjunction with argument. Even so, Quintilian is careful to stress the limits of such 'probable' use of signs and their distinction from argument (*Institutio*, 5.10.11–13), and re-harnesses them to that which is palpable to the senses – 'presents itself to our eyes' – (5.9.14–15, 5.10.13) – like Aristotle's infallible signs. The Aristotelian hierarchy, thus, remains a relevant model for analysing our primary material. What had been added to it by the time our plays were being written, however, is the notion derived from Terentian practice that what is probable, and therefore less certain than infallible, and in need of

---

[98] Cave, *Recognitions*, 249. Originally, of course, *paralogismos* is a term used by Aristotle.

[99] Quintilian, *Institutio*, 5.1.1, 5.8.1, 5.8–9. See also Herrick, *Comic Theory*, 29, 180.

argument, is paradoxically productive of belief in dramatic plots which are essentially controversial.[100] As Quintilian notes, 'Plots composed for the Stage are called Arguments' (5.10.11). But this does not prevent dramatists from using them to highlight the resistant element of dubiousness ensconced within probability, just as Terentian drama, while capitalising on deliberative process as well as inartificial proof, also showed up the fallibility of non-discursive evidence presented before the eye, as with the staging of the faked signs of Glycerium's pregnancy in *Andria* (III.i).

Underdowne's translation (1569) of Heliodorus' *Aethiopica*[101] – a major vehicle of romance plots, a mediator of Aristotelian ideas in fictional practice, and the great precursor of English tragicomedy – articulates the problem of tokens and their connections with probability and narrative art. When Theagenes urges Cariclea to disclose the tokens that will reveal their identities and save their lives, she argues,

Tokens . . . are tokens to them that know them, but to those that know them not, and can not understand the whole matter, they are but vaine treasure . . . And put the case that Hydaspes knowe some of them who shall perswade him that Persina gave me them as a mother to her daughter? The surest token . . . is a motherly nature . . . (Bk IX, 253)

The focus is the same as in church courts – the difficulty of discovering the intention and context behind the giving. Yet, in the recognition scene (Bk X), concrete tokens combine with narrative devices to create what Cave would call a 'saturation' of evidence, convincing Hydaspes that Cariclea is his daughter. His lingering doubts about the manipulability of proofs are given over to the reader who is left to puzzle out in her or his head the connection between the evidence and the conclusion, the extraneousness of what convinces and the intrinsic natural facts which do not.[102] Drama can tellingly juxtapose the ambivalence of the tools of knowledge in recognition with those of proof in situations of trial. The essential similarity in the two structures of experience is their attempt to proceed from ignorance to certainty, whether the object of knowledge is an intention or an identity. There are instances in art and in history, from the trial of Cariclea (*Aethiopica* X) to the 'story' of Martin Guerre, where

---

[100] Cf. Altman, *Tudor Play*, 136, quoting Melancthon on Terence: 'for where is the place for counselling, reasoning, and planning if not in doubtful affairs?.'

[101] Heliodorus, *Aethiopian History*.

[102] The *Aethiopica* was well known not only to Renaissance English dramatists including Shakespeare (See *Twelfth Night* V.i.107–8) but also, interestingly, to Swinburne (*Testaments*, 163).

the two coincide. My contention is that the 'scandal'[103] of anagnoristic signs helps us understand certain perversities of legal evidence. The problematic relation between the externality and accidentality of signs, and the truths of identity that they reveal, provides a suggestive framework within which to view the slipperiness of legal tokens, the implications of their function of endowing visibility and their detachedness from the entities they represent.

The ring-metaphors that led to this discussion are a trope for some of these problems. In the anagnoristic tradition, the ring belongs to the category of material, adventitious proofs, along with scars, handkerchiefs, hair and jewellery.[104] In law, it is a symbolic, external and fragmentary index to multifaceted situations and inward intentions.[105] The impropriety of judging whole by part, invisible by symbol, is underlined by an interplay of metonymy and synecdoche surrounding the ring.[106] It stands for a promise of marriage and also the female genitalia; its synecdoche includes its power to represent a woman and to signify an entire situation by its physical participation in it. Legally, as well as theatrically and mimetically, it bodies forth what cannot be decently shown. This is specially germane to contemporary marriage laws which granted the sexual act a vital status in confirming uncertain unions. Proof of copulation could turn a *de futuro* contract into matrimony and render a clandestine marriage inviolable. It could also grant marital rights to a party where gifts and gestures had created grounds for expectation.[107]

The circulation of the rings in *All's Well*, thus, combines the impropriety of prostituting sentimental value with the scandal of female honour circulating in a fetishised form.[108] Bertram's terms of exchange in describing how Diana 'got the ring' (V.iii.217–19) classes both the ornament and virginity in the 'vendible' category (I.i.155). Silence and invisibility are the conditions of the bed-trick. Nowhere is the ring a more sufficient and more schematic synecdoche, since there can be few other situations where so much will hang on it. Once individuals' roles are taken on by the ring's

---

[103] My use of the word alludes to Cave's, and its extended application to the means of legal knowledge indicates certain connections.

[104] For its popular provenance, see De Vries, *Dictionary*, 386.

[105] For the suggestion that love-tokens visibly embody, see the posy in Evans, *English Posies*, i: 'A VILA MON GARDI LI MO' [Behold my heart: keep it for me].

[106] One type of the legal tool of 'distinction' is defined as 'whole into parts': see Maclean, *Interpretation*, III.

[107] See n. 84 above; see also *Spousals*, 40–1, 121, 226. On the role of sex in both clinching and proving a spousal contract, and its use in *AW*, see Mukherji, 'Lawfull Deede'.

[108] See Thompson, *Motif-Index*, Z.321; D.800–899 – the ring, in folk tradition, fits only one person.

impersonal materiality, one woman is easily substituted for another. Equally, when one's relationship with a person is determined by one's relationship to a part of her body, little is lost in making rings cement it. An exchange of literal rings makes a love-knot, but a substitution of figurative rings in the dark is the stuff of scandal.

More widely, the rings figure the uneasy relation between intentionality and 'proven' legal truths. Helena's ring is the proof on which the entire action of V.iii hinges. Its truth value is preferred to spoken forms of evidence, recalling Swinburne's suggestion of a distinction between the word's subjectivity and the object's solidity. The turning point in the Countess's attitude is marked by Diana's presentation of the ring – 'That ring's a thousand proofs' (198). Bertram himself stakes all on the ring:

> If you shall prove
> This ring was ever hers, you shall as easy
> Prove that I husbanded her bed in Florence . . .
>
> (124–6)

It is, of course, proved to be Helena's, and the marriage to be valid. Yet the nature of the truth that the ring proves remains dubious. The Swinburnian discomfort around error and the law's inadequacy to accommodate its moral implications lies at the core of the bed-trick (as in *Measure*).[109] Bertram thinks he sleeps with Diana, and if that consummation is to seal any marriage, it is his with hers – as indeed it legally would, since the 'news' of Helena's death, arriving before the bed-trick, has fulfilled the stipulated condition of Bertram's *de futuro* 'spousal' to Diana (IV.ii.71–2). Diana's claim in V.iii. to be his 'wife', in that sense, is legally warranted.[110] The fact that Bertram is 'quit' (297) is due to an arbitrary separation of fact and meant truth in the deed of darkness in Florence – a comment on the criteria of evidence in marriage laws, and their manipulability at the level of action. The trick cannot be 'lawful meaning in a lawful act' (III.vii.47), since the act is joint, involving two 'meanings'. 'Law presumeth' that the parties acted 'out of an honest affection' – and so Helena and Bertram's union is legitimate – 'and yet in conscience and before God, the same were unlawful' (*Spousals*, 227–8).[111]

---

[109] *Spousals*, 168–73 – the 'History' of the King of Cyprus's marriage by proxy with the wrong lady; and *Matrimony*, 122, on the 'error' of identities.

[110] In fact, this is double confirmation, for copulation would turn the contract into matrimony even if the condition remained unfulfilled. See *Spousals*, 219. Note also the likeness of this unrealised but acknowledgedly 'unlawful' contract to the marriage of Angelo and Mariana in *MfM*.

[111] By the same token, Isabella in *MfM* is complicit with the Duke in engineering an act of union that is less lawful 'in conscience' (and indeed in canon law) than Claudio and Juliet's sexual

Bertram's final condition in his pledge of love – 'If she, my liege, can make me know this clearly' – touches precisely on the discomfort surrounding the knowledge law brings, but it is forestalled immediately by Helena's assertion – 'If it appear not plain and prove untrue . . .' (V.iii.315–17). We know, of course, that in the world of the play, as in law, it cannot prove untrue – for, in Swinburne's terms, 'it doth otherwise lawfully appear'. Pregnancy itself, in visually representing a sexual truth, feeds into the sense of indecorum around the token.[112]

The homology between law and tragicomedy thus becomes clear, and the ring visibly connects the two: it ensures the right pairing necessary for the comic resolution, and is the legal ratifier of marriages in the French court. The sense of yet-ness must remain, since the play ends with a hint of the resumption of the cycle just run, with the King offering Diana the choice of a husband from his remaining retinue of gallants. Law and genre must continue their collusive coercion, and individuals as well as texts inserted into these systems must continue to establish slippery relationships within these, and to these, and must ever gesture to other spaces, elsewheres, in which to work out the precarious provisionalities that inflect some of the last words of *All's Well*: 'All yet seems well, and if it end so meet. . .' (V.iii.322).[113]

In the recognition scene of *Twelfth Night* (V.i), the revelation of identities begins with such proofs as 'a mole upon [the] brow' (242) and promises to continue through circumstantial evidence (251–2).[114] The end leaves us, as it does Orsino, with a sense of seeing double since the physical appearance that caused the errors still remains the same but the signs that have come to light have promptly turned the world of relationships upsidedown; such strange states, no matter how jokingly stated, are visually true, as of Olivia being 'betrothed both to a maid and man' (263). The 'conceit deceitful'[115] of 'a natural perspective, that is and is not' (217) is the anagnoristic counterpart of the legal dualities of *All's Well*; it clarifies how Bertram's trial, manipulated by Helena and Diana's monitoring of circumstantial evidence, is also a recognition scene built on a dramatic arrangement of 'inartistic' proofs, apparently leading inductively towards knowledge.

---

  consummation which is only, technically, sealing their engagement. See Nuttall, '*Measure for Measure*: The Bed-trick', on the ethical ironies of the legality of that bed-trick.

[112] *AW*, V.iii.304 – 'behold the meaning'. Cf. Walkden v. Lowe, p. 43 above.

[113] For a theory of the relationship between law and genre, see Jacques Derrida, 'The Law of Genre'.

[114] Cf. the natural accidents and narrative explanations leading to the recognition of *The Comedy of Errors*.

[115] Shakespeare, *Rape of Lucrece*, 1423.

While dramatic self-consciousness foregrounds the fictionality of generic arbitration in *All's Well* through a sense of the unresolved and irrecoverable, in *Measure* it points more explicitly to the close affiliation between narrative deceit and legal fiction: the play's sole plot-maker is also its supreme legal authority. The Duke's construction of the recognition scene is founded on his earlier crafting of the grave mis-cognition of the bed-trick, and the righting of wrongs at the end is premised on that deep ethical error; but all this is 'comic' ingredient, ostensibly in the interest of common good, fitting exactly the technical meaning of 'legal fiction' – a lie perpetrated by law for the sake of the commonweal.[116] Law and narrative are similarly mendacious in their operations, even as the 'fantastical Duke of dark corners' (IV.iii.157) is linked by nomenclature to Lucio, the declared 'fantastic' of the play.[117] The darkness and disguise surrounding the Duke and his operations also imply the voyeurism of the evidentiary system in stressing the need to prove sexual events in a public space.[118]

Voyeurism resurfaces in *Cymbeline*'s exploration of tokens. Indeed, the dangers of the metaphoric in the overall perception of experience receive their most vertiginous expression here. By a single grammatical move, a whole can be reduced to a part, an intrinsic property to a thing to be handled – a metaphorising complicity that Posthumus and Iachimo, troublingly, share. Its foundations are laid in the wager scene (I.iv.) where the meaning of the 'ring' keeps shifting till the precious Imogen herself, the ring of her chastity, the spousal ring, and its money value become almost inseparable.[119] Why else is there a sense of Imogen being violated in the bedchamber scene (II.ii), though nothing is actually done to her? Why the darkening shadows of Tarquin and of Tereus? It is because her whole body has been published when the bracelet changes hands among men, her virginity bartered when the ring is wagered, and forced when

---

[116] See Heywood's *Curtaine Lecture*, 6, for formulations about a legendary bed-trick that resemble the definition of legal fiction, and 252–3, an example of comments on the fictional plotting involved in the stratagem resulting in the neglected Queen bearing the King's son.

[117] See *First Folio*, 102 – 'The names of all the actors'.

[118] In Whetstone's *Promos and Casandra* (1578), a major intertext of *MfM*, the Duke's evidentiary operations belong to informers who have 'eyes will look into a Mylstone': Bullough, II, 442–513, esp. 449, 453, 474, 495.

[119] Cf. Iachimo's pointing up of conflated relationships at I.iv.153–4 – 'she your jewel, this your jewel, and my gold are yours'. The linguistic defilement of Imogen is to be understood in the context of a series of transferences – crucially from maidenhead to actual head, trunk to headless body, Posthumus to Cloten – symptomised in the play by words vengefully literalising themselves, and parts constantly becoming wholes.

'the ring is won' by Iachimo (II.iv.45). This also turns the theatrical space into a 'naughty court'[120] when Posthumus wants evidence of Imogen's adultery and Iachimo produces it. The mole under the breast, literally a part of the body, is the ultimate privy token – 'corporal sign' (II.iv.119) – that confirms the implications of the bracelet in the action of the play and clinches its synecdochic validity. Both Imogen's maidenhead and Post-humus' right to its possession pass into Iachimo's hands in a second marriage between the diamond she gave him and his reciprocal 'manacle', but this time, not in chaste union.

What makes these objects convincing to Posthumus is their visual vividness. We begin to understand the connection between the 'few thousand meaner movables' 'screwed to (Iachimo's) memory' (II.ii.29, 44) and the rings and things vividly described by many a deponent in church courts, who invariably 'remembreth not' the particulars of dates and words.[121] On the other hand, we realise their effectiveness as proof.[122] In the case of the supposed sexual offence in *Cymbeline*, the synecdochic ring and bracelet connect Iachimo's effective re-presentation of ocular proof in II.iv with his 'watching' (II.iv.68) of Imogen to make his 'inventory' in II.ii, sharpening the feel of illegitimacy surrounding the law's scopic power in culling evidence. The prying that results when the eye of man presumes to be the eye of God in order to embody the Eye of Justice is most sharply focused in sexual litigation where evidence of sex could prove both marriage and adultery. One remembers such depositions as Maria Haselwell's (1562), who crept out of bed at night to follow Margaret Monelay, suspected of habitual fornication with John Barnes, and 'did plainly perceyve . . . that they were nought together'; or Henry Spoore's (1576?), attesting the marital bond between Margaret Milner and Robert Ogle by describing how he 'rose out of his bedd and loked in at a wyndoo at them, and . . . saw ther doings.'[123]

The specifically sexual scandal of tokens in *Cymbeline* feeds into and complicates their anagnoristic scandal. Its most absurd expression is Imogen's mis-cognition of Cloten for Posthumus from 'legs' and 'hand' and 'brawns' and garments (IV.ii.301–32). The very figure of the synec-doche is literalised here in all the accidentality, externality and error it can

---

[120] See Symons v. Bredford discussed on p. 36 above.
[121] See Furnivall, *Child-Marriages*, 187–93.
[122] *Enargeia* or vividness is linked on the one hand with Greek *enargos* (sure proof), on the other, with *evidentia*, its Latin cognate.
[123] Furnivall, *Child-Marriages*, 91–2; Raine, *Depositions*, 95–6.

involve, the trunk serving for a body and an identity. But Posthumus' true 'recognition' is brought about by a combined operation of tokens and narrative *enargeia*. Just as Imogen's mole had to be provocatively de-scribed and Iachimo's acquisition of the golden exhibit vividly told, so, in the final scene, the 'diamond' ring upon Iachimo's finger initiates a narrative of its history to effect the disclosure (V.v.135–8). Suggestively, Posthumus' recognition of the facts does not coincide with his recognition of Imogen – he strikes her when she approaches him (V.v.229). In the rhetoric of legal procedure, as of fiction, the simple or natural sign is no more independent of artifice than artifice is of signs.

A decade after *Cymbeline*, Boccaccio's wager story finds its way through Bandello, Painter and Whetstone into Massinger's *The Picture*.[124] Here, Mathias, leaving his wife Sophia to fight in wars, is troubled by imaginary speculations of her temptations in his absence. To make his 'doubts' 'certainties' (I.i.150) he makes his friend Baptista devise a means of proof by his 'Art': a picture of Sophia which, if it changes from white and red to yellow, should indicate 'Shees . . . courted but unconquered'; if it changes to black, ''tis an assurance/The fort . . . /Is forc'd or . . . surrendered' (I.i.176–85). Reading signs becomes a venture in interpretation, the inher-ent hazard of which is established in IV.i when Baptista and Mathias 'interpret' (38) the changing colours to conclude that 'She is turnd whore' (36); for we know that she was tricked by Honoria into momentarily believing that Mathias had been false, and fleetingly tempted by the desperation of this belief – hence the combination of yellow and black that the two men puzzle over and misread. In a sense, the picture at a particular moment does reflect a mental state; hence Mathias' speech on the importance of mental sin in reply to Baptista's consolation, 'She's false but not in fact yet' (39). But the play makes him – and us – learn that the flowing stream of intentionality cannot be captured in an isolated, momentary representation; it is a complex whole that defies analysis in parts through the univalent reduction of designated signs. Sophia's indignation is directed at the illegitimacy of the device – 'A diuelish art, a spie vpon/My actions' (V.ii.3–4), and the absurdity of the enterprise (V.iii.76–9). She herself emerges as the triumphant natural object which alone can bring certainty and cure Mathias' error (V.iii.163) – her name means 'wisdom' – in recognition of which he burns the 'cursed picture' (213–15) and Baptista renounces his art. As a mimetic, cognitive and

---

[124] Massinger, *Plays and Poems*; see also Bullough, *Sources*, III, 199–286, 182–4.

legal instrument, 'the artifice of signs' meets with its most systematic rejection in this play dedicated to, and possibly played before, the members of the Inner Temple, and written by a dramatist consistently interested in legal processes.

Law is not the only sphere, any more than art is, where just and adequate representation is difficult to achieve. This chapter is not innocent of the synecdoche of signs. But if, in its self-aware critical endeavour, it has been able to gesture at some of the ambiguities of evidence in fields other than its own, this token will have served its purpose in more senses than one.

'Unmanly indignities': adultery, evidence and judgement in Heywood's A Woman Killed With Kindness

In August 1596, the Vice-Chancellor's room at Queens' College, Cambridge, took on the unexpected character of a 'bawdy court'.[1] Bridget, wife of John Edmunds, a Cambridge university employee, was brought to the Vice-Chancellor's court on a charge of adultery with William Covile of Queens' College. Over the next month, neighbours, colleagues and household servants deposed; after a brief period of protesting innocence, Bridget confessed and turned witness for the prosecution along with her husband; John sued for a judicial separation.

This chapter[2] is a reading of Thomas Heywood's *A Woman Killed With Kindness*, in the light of contemporary perceptions of adultery and practices of investigating and proving it within the household and in court.[3] I use the Edmunds case as my point of entry into this study, because it provides remarkable analogies with, and suggestive insights into, the

---

[1] CUL, V.C. Court I.3, 109v. I am immensely grateful to Elisabeth Leedham-Green for alerting me to this case. Sexual litigation in post-Reformation England usually came under the jurisdiction of ecclesiastical courts, which, for this association, were also known as 'bawdy courts'. V.C. Court III.5, item 63 explains why the Edmunds case was tried there instead. Covile is variously spelt in the court papers, the most common variant being 'Covell'.

[2] A shorter version of this chapter is Mukherji, 'Unmanly Indignities'. Sheen and Hutson's comments as editors helped me refine my argument. On the Vice-Chancellor's court in Cambridge, see Shepard, 'Meanings of Manhood', 19–24 and 243–93. For earlier accounts of this historically neglected arena of litigation, see Tanner, ed., *Historical Register*, 63–9; Peek and Hall, *Archives*, Chs. 10–11. On the Vice-Chancellor's court of Oxford, see Underwood, 'Structure and Operation'. Chancellor's courts in university towns had criminal as well as civil jurisdiction over not only members of the universities, but also townspeople who had 'privileged status' deriving from fourteenth-century trading privileges granting university suppliers certain exemptions and rights. In their civil procedures, Vice-Chancellor's courts resembled church courts, except that their jurisdiction spread wider, and they rarely dealt with marriage litigation or tithe disputes. But like ecclesiastical courts, they had significant regulatory power over the moral lives of university members and the inhabitants of these towns.

[3] The first Quarto of the play was published in 1607, but it seems to have been performed at the Curtain and the Red Bull since 1603. See Gurr, *Shakespearean Stage*, 222.

process that Heywood dramatises. The dramatic exploration of the social process of collecting proof brings into focus certain distinctly early modern perceptions of privacy and publicity, shown to be at play in the dramatic as well as the legal material. But the drama's self-conscious treatment of evidence suggests an affinity between theatrical and evidentiary representation, and helps establish the necessary inwardness of proof. Meanwhile, the focus on sexual misdemeanour and its specifically nuanced punishment becomes, for Heywood's play, a way of defining its own generic affiliations and investments; civility becomes at once a function of class sensibility and of genre.

A CAMBRIDGE SCANDAL

At a fairly early stage in the Vice-Chancellor's Court proceedings, John Edmunds volunteered his services to prove the case against his wife. Most curious among the various evidence presented by him as exhibits in court are a set of love-letters between Covile and Bridget, 'openlie redd then and there', leading to Covile's admission that they were indeed written 'with his owne hande'.[4] Most interesting for us are the remarkable material traces they preserve of the process of construction of evidence. The marginal comments and annotations at the bottom of the letters, written in a distinct hand from the letters themselves, were inscribed by Edmunds himself. Two of these letters he intercepted, and the third he procured from his wife. And then he annotated them.

The nature of the marginal notes reveals the purpose behind their writing. They consist of a series of details and definitions made with evidentiary intent. John is anxious to have his dates and facts straight. Careful cross-checking is in evidence.[5] Equally carefully, he marks all the statements that might possibly be cited legally as admissions of adultery. 'Confession', he scribbles next to the second sentence of the third letter: 'You & I must be both wyse', and underlines 'both wyse'. Where Covile frets that 'the greatest proofe he hath is the things I gave you', and asks for them back, the evidentiary import of these gifts is attested by John Edmunds's triumphant note: 'confess that he gave her dyvers things'.

---

[4] Figures 2.1, 2.2 and 2.3: V.C. Court III.5, items 66, 67a and 68 respectively.

[5] For instance, he notes an inconsistency in item 66, and remarks '26 day was Saterday' against Covile's statement 'Now is Saterday'. He has obviously cared to find out, at least as late as 23 August 1596 (when he came to possess it), that the given date of the letter, 26 October 1594, did not tally with an earlier remark in it about the day, and comments on it again in his summary at the bottom: '. . . written upon a Sonday if the date be true'.

Where Covile writes that he dares not write since her husband says she tells him everything, John scribbles: 'He durst not write. Knavery. This care of concealing is half a confession.'

The annotations suggest that John Edmunds kept returning to the letters in order to prepare them for presentation in court.[6] The impression of deliberate memorial reconstruction is supported by the palæographical evidence, the indecision over his noting down of the time of conveyance of the third letter and, most interestingly, the fact that the second letter (Fig. 2.2) was clearly torn up into seven even strips, but subsequently glued back together and annotated. The material form of these documents, thus, is itself 'evidence' – a visible and eloquent sign – of the process of the construction of proof, by which an essentially private act, or its product, is made an object of public display. These 'exhibits' also tell the story of how an injured husband in an adultery case sets about to collect and prepare, indeed, almost produce evidence with vindictive meticulousness when he takes on legal agency.

Yet the calculated conversion of these private letters into legal documents is shot through with more spontaneous expressions of moral condemnation and outrage. Alongside quasi-legal notations on details that may aid his case, John pens declamations such as 'Lye' (Fig. 2.2) or 'Impossible' (Fig. 2.3). In the first letter, he sarcastically writes, 'wisely done William' where Covile protests he has 'honored all bridges for [her] sake'.

The contents of the letters, meanwhile, inscribe the process by which adultery is registered within a close community, and how that impinges on the consciousness of the parties. The relaxed, pleasantly detailed and loving tone of the first letter – 'whylst others are eating of oysters I am wrytinge . . . Kisse mye Cuff . . . I never breathe but I think of you' – is clouded over in the second by a consciousness of risk and persecution. The third letter is uneasy in tone, cautious, even impatient – 'You are not so careful as you might be, to expect me to show kyndnes in such a

---

[6] In figures 2.1 and 2.3, the ink of John's comments is of two different degrees of distinctness. The ink of 'Confess:' written in a large script at the left-hand bottom corner of both these letters, is darker than that of the main marginalia and underlining in figure 2.1; in figure 2.3, it matches the marginal comments that are explicitly concerned with statements that may count as confessions, and the notes at the bottom on the circumstances of the receipt of the letters. 'He durst not wryte', 'trust no letter' and 'confess that he gave her dyvers things' are written in a paler ink in figure 2.3. The last of these, too, has to do with confession, but seems to have been more randomly written in before John had a chance to come back to the letter and re-read it. The marginal comments on figure 2.1, significantly, are less pointedly legal: they are all in the pale ink. The bolder annotations were presumably inscribed at a second or later reading, when the documents were being prepared for use in court.

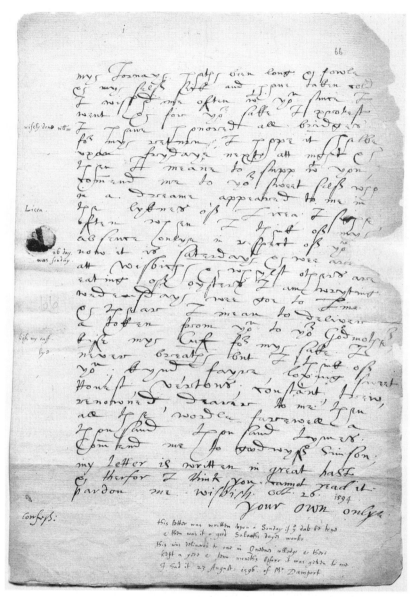

Figure 2.1. Love letter sent by John Covile, Fellow of Queens', to Bridget Edmunds, wife of John Edmunds, M.A., Peterhouse, and employee of the university. Cambridge University Library, Vice Chancellor's Court III.5, item 66.

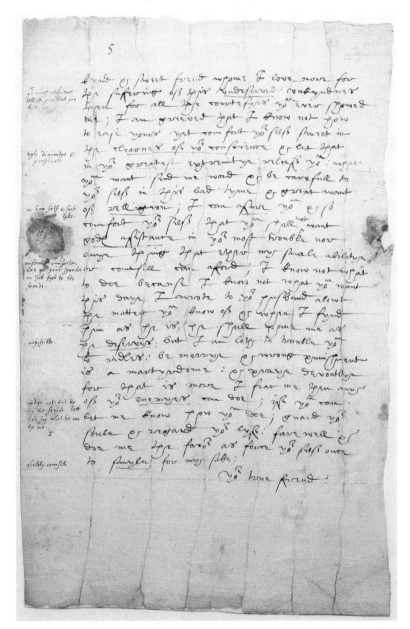

Figure 2.2. Letter from John Covile to Bridget Edmunds. Cambridge University Library, Vice Chancellor's Court III.5, item 67a.

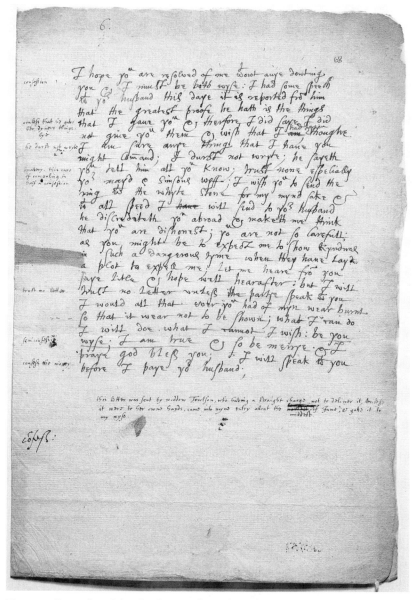

Figure 2.3. Letter from John Covile to Bridget Edmunds. Cambridge University Library, Vice Chancellor's Court III.5, item 68.

dangerous tyme when they have layd a plot to expell me.' He wishes his love-tokens to her 'wear burnt so that it wear not to be shown'. A wider community, watching, talking and judging, is glimpsed.

All this becomes more visible in the court records. 'Common rumour and popular gossip in the parish' are a legal factor from the outset.[7] One of John's witnesses is his maid Elizabeth Atkyn who had not only lain on occasions 'at the beddes foote' in Bridget's room, but 'carryed at diverse tymes diverse letters from her sayd mistris unto . . . Covyle, & from . . . Covile unto [her]'.[8] Other witnesses include Elizabeth Baker, an ex-servant, and the fourteen-year-old John Fletcher who ran errands for Covile and Bridget. Forty of their love-letters were 'sent secreatly . . . by myne owne servantes', Edmunds alleged. The servants almost come to embody the vigilant balance between trust and mistrust necessary in a small community functioning through aiding and abetting, informing and gossiping. They mediate between the male workplace on the one hand, and the parish and the home on the other.[9] Within the house, servants provide the link between the lady's chamber and the master's study.

This alerts us to the distinction between communal vigilance and the closer surveillance within the home, and gives us an impression of the domestic relations and spaces constituting the Edmunds household. The interior figures prominently in the testimonies. One day Atkins was in the kitchen when she heard 'Mr. Covill and her said Mistris . . . struglinge together [in the hall], whereupon she . . . came forth of the said Kitchen into the entrie that leadeth into the saide Hall'.[10] All this, while John Edmunds was 'in his studye'. Atkins, the mobile spirit of the household, conveyed the information to her master with alacrity, having first observed the aftermath of the 'acte' in the yard where Covile had gone out to 'coole him selfe'.

Both the centrality of the 'act' or 'fact' of adultery, and the importance of the act of seeing, come across in the courtroom drama. In affirmation of her 'private' report to John Edmunds, Atkins says that 'she had *seene* . . . Mr. Covyle & hir Mistris . . . at two severall tymes . . . committing adultery' (italics mine).[11] After hearing the suggestive scuffle,

---

[7] CUL, V.C. Court V.3, item 61.
[8] Ibid., item 72.
[9] This is the route travelled by the letter written in Wisbich in a moment of withdrawal from a festive household indulging in oysters, and deposited via several hands at Queens' with John rather than Bridget. The vital role of household servants as deponents in sexual litigation continued well into the 1630s: see Capp, 'Life, Love and Litigation'.
[10] CUL, V.C. Court I.3, 112v.
[11] CUL, V.C. Court I.3, 111.

She . . . did looke into the saide Hall . . . the dore . . . being open, and did then see the said Mr. Covyll and hir said Mistris . . . naughte togither . . . in a Chayre . . . by the fyre, her . . . Mistris . . . sittinge in the . . . Chayre, and Mr. Covyll haveinge his gown one, and she sawe hir Mistris hir heade then hange over the . . . Chayre, and her hands aboute Mr. Covills middle, and did then and there here [=hear] the said Mr. Covill blusteringe and blowinge verie muche, and afterwards did see him in the yarde . . . verie redd in his face.[12]

John Edmunds senior recollects his visits to his son's house while Edmunds junior had been away, in vivid terms:

[he] firste knockinge at the doore, hath opened [it] and gone in, and hath found . . . Covill and . . . Bridget Edmunds in the hall there togither alone, she then beinge barelegged, without anie hosen on, and . . . her peticote not laced; and . . . he did see . . . Mr. Covill . . . barelegged and hir peticoate unlased as aforesaid, reaching with her hand towards some place there . . . and he . . . askinge hir what she . . . would have . . . she said that she was then reaching of an apple out of her Cuborde for [him] . . .

The testimonies, as well as the assumed basis of the court's reading of them, are an interpretation of certain images. They also indicate that it did strike people to lock chamber doors on certain vital occasions.[13] Yet, a great deal of 'private' interaction went on in the 'hall', a space that was social in relation to the bedchamber and the study, but 'interior' in relation to the outside world, though separated by, and accessible through, an 'entry' and an unlocked door.

These testimonies further communicate a sense of a complex and comprehensive experience of interior space that is translated into theatre by many of the contemporary plays dealing with adultery, or murder associated with adultery. They allow a reconstruction of distinctly early modern notions of privacy within the home and in the parish, and their relationship with sexual litigation. Heywood's *A Woman Killed With Kindness* places adultery in a context of domestic economy and communal relations.

Drama, however, extends the problematic relation between 'private' and legal space by exploring the relation of these spaces to theatrical space. This is part of the plays' self-conscious treatment of the limits of theatrical representation, resembling and dramatising the problems of evidentiary

---

[12] Ibid., 112v.

[13] See the Edmunds' servant John Fletcher's deposition, CUL, V.C. Court I.3, 120–120v, and p. 77 below. See also V.C. Court I.3, 113, where John Edmunds senior deposes about how he knocked on his son's door before pushing the door open to go in and find his daughter-in-law Bridget 'barelegged, without anie hosen on', at play with Covile.

representation. The Edmunds case throws light on this connection by revealing some of the actual situations of witnessing and informing that bring about the legal exposure of adultery.

A WOMAN KILLED WITH KINDNESS

The study or the store-house

The initial confrontation between husband and wife following Master Frankford's discovery of Anne's adultery is halted by Frankford's self-announced withdrawal into his study for deliberation:

> I will do nothing rashly.
> I will retire awhile into my study,
> And thou shalt hear my sentence presently.
> (*WKK*, xii, 130–2)

The activities associated with the study defined its character as the gentleman's private chamber, a place of solitary retirement. Contemporary meanings of the word 'study' included 'reverie or abstraction', 'thought or meditation directed to the accomplishment of a purpose; studied or deliberate effort or contrivance', mental labour, reading, learning or reflection (*OED*). These, in turn, related to the use of the word to denote a room in the gentleman's house. The common associations surrounding this specifically male solitariness derived from the humanist notion of a man's need for spiritual withdrawal from the affairs of court, society and household. Montaigne's famous *arrière boutique* was, by extension, a mental space, 'a store-house'

[reserved] . . . for our selves . . . altogether ours, and wholly free, wherein we may hoard up and establish our true libertie, and principall retreat and solitarinesse, wherein we must go alone to our selves, take our ordinarie entertainment, and so privately, that no acquaintance or communication of any strange thinge may therein find place: there to discourse, to meditate and laugh as, without wife, without children, and goods, without traine, or servants. . .[14]

Having chosen 'treasures . . . that may be freed from injurie', a man should 'hide them in a place where no one can enter, and which cannot be betraied but by our selves'. Montaigne's 'treasures' are intangible possessions immune from loss or theft so long as the self is secure; his image of sequestration remains poised between the spatial and the mental.

[14] Montaigne, *Essays*, trans. Florio, I, 254–5.

When we first meet Frankford alone (iv), after his brief appearance as bridegroom in the crowded opening scene, the stage direction describes him as being 'in a study'. Both modern editors gloss 'study' as 'a reverie'.[15] But Van Fossen speculates that 'Frankford may well enter the stage from the "study", or central opening in the rear wall of the stage'.[16] Even if we accept that the primary purpose of the stage direction is to indicate Frankford's abstraction, the scene evokes elements of the iconography of the study, introduced as it is after four populated scenes, as a solitary space where the master of the house soliloquises reflectively. The other sense of studying, that of 'studied or deliberate effort', implicit in the later, more spatial, use of the word, reinforces the present scene's evocation of a private location. It also reveals how the play defines space not simply in terms of physical allocations, but through the organisation of conceptual relations between various household activities. The configuration of the space in which Frankford delivers his soliloquy changes immediately when Wendoll, Anne and Nick enter.

However, the treasures here inventoried by Frankford, albeit in the metaphorical form of ruminating upon them, are different from the 'riches' stored in Montaigne's *arrière boutique*:

> How happy am I amongst other men
> That in my mean estate embrace content.
> I am a gentleman, and by my birth
> Companion with a king; a king's no more.
> I am possessed of many fair revenues,
> Touching my mind, I am studied in all arts;
> The riches of my thoughts and of my time
> Have been a good proficient. But the chief
> Of all the sweet felicities on earth,
> I have a fair, a chaste, and loving wife,
> Perfection all, all truth, all ornament.
> If man on earth may truly happy be,
> Of these at once possessed, sure I am he.
>
> (IV, 1–13)

[15] See *WKK*, 19, and Van Fossen's Revels edition, 20.

[16] *WKK*, ed. Van Fossen, 20. Hosley, 'Discovery-Space', 35–46, notes that '*Enter* in Elizabethan stage-directions can mean "is discovered" . . . as in Marlowe's *Doctor Faustus*, "*Enter Faustus in his Study*"' (37). This 'discovery-space' was revealed by the drawing of the curtains of the two or three tiring-house doors at the rear of the stage of the Swan and, as he claims, of the First Globe (35). See also Gurr, *Shakespearean Stage*, 138 and 171, on the similar use of the study in Barnes's *The Devil's Charter* (1607). Beckerman, *Shakespeare*, cites seven Shakespearean instances of the use of the Globe discovery-space as a study (85–7). The Red Bull, one of the two theatres where *WKK* was staged most frequently (the other being the Curtain), also had a curtained discovery-space: see Reynolds, *Staging*, Chs. 6 and 7, and 158–60 and 134–5 for its frequent use as a study.

Frankford's solitary contentment becomes a bourgeois appropriation of the humanist notion of man's mental cabinet as a site of abstraction from his material and public life. His contemplation of his own status as a gentleman extends beyond his possessions to include less material riches – his learning and his companionate marriage – thereby redefining the very terms of his gentility. In the wedding scene, not only Anne's 'birth' but 'her education', and the 'equality' and 'sympathy' of this union of two 'scholars' is repeatedly noted.[17] The private space created by this soliloquy is where Frankford experiences and consolidates his sense of class.[18] This subjectivity, at once social and private, is what determines Frankford's judicial behaviour when it finds itself violated by adultery. The study becomes the site not only of his solitary stock-taking, but also of his later retreat to arrive at a 'sentence' on this violation.

The distinct associations of Frankford's study and of his 'studies' are akin to the secretarial pursuits invoked in Richard Braithwait's later prescription about the office in an earl's house, which 'is necessary for the Earl to know'. This is 'a chamber very strong and close', 'the keys [whereof] the Earl is to keep'. It contains account books, registers, letters

---

[17] *WKK*, i, 12–24, 55–72. Lena Orlin discusses this soliloquy to establish the 'Ciceronian context' for Frankford's generosity with Wendoll, and claims that 'the ethical energy in the main plot' is 'vested more in the relationship of Frankford and Wendoll than in that of Frankford and Anne' (*Private Matters*, 159–60). This is part of her larger argument that male friendship and kinship displace the woman or the marital relationship; that the notion of companionate marriage is 'functionally misleading' because displaced (178). I want to move away from such a polarity, suggesting instead that the very terms of 'companionate marriage' are defined in relation to a sense of equality which was indistinguishably made up of material and non-material affinities. The concept, understood thus, is not misleading but central to our understanding of the importance of Frankford's '[possession]' of 'a fair, chaste and loving wife' – not subordinated to, but equated with, even privileged over, his other possessions. Orlin's overall acute discussion leaves out the last part of Frankford's soliloquy, focusing on his marriage, when she establishes the supremacy of the context of friendship in relation to this meditation on p. 160. But this is a local discontent. Companionate marriage, I suggest, is essential to the gentleman's self-perception, most satisfying when it encompasses both material and mental properties, as with the rest of his existence. And this, I believe, does not inherently go against the grain of Orlin's more expansive and panoptic discussion of the play. But it is important to stress the humanistic underpinnings of the way in which Heywood makes 'companionate marriage' a defining attribute of gentlemanliness. This is analogous to how Thomas More's Xenophonic training of his wife is cited by Erasmus, among other signs of More's humanist education, to make a surrogate statement about its social utility, helping More on his way to court and to the King's 'household and his privy chamber': see Erasmus' letter to Ulrich von Hutten, 23 July 1519, in Erasmus, *Correspondence*, 15–25. Lorna Hutson alerted me to this analogy.

[18] On the need to extend gentlemanly civility, beyond wealth and heredity, to include certain cultural values and sensibilities, and thereby forge a self-image, see Bryson, 'Rhetoric of Status'. See also her *From Courtesy to Civility*, and Jones, 'The First West-End Comedy', 230–3, suggestive on the autonomy and mobility of the status of the early seventeenth-century 'gentleman', who could not be 'created' by the King any more than he could be alienated by attainder, as a nobleman with a hereditary title might.

patent, charters, deeds and similar papers, well-guarded from natural
hazards and human interlopers. These carefully protected items are
repeatedly referred to as 'evidences':

> . . . upon every drawing box is to be written the name of the manor . . . the
> evidence whereof that box doth contain . . . when the Earl . . . hath occasion to
> make search for any evidence . . . he may see by [the] roll whether the same be in
> that box or not . . . Also empty boxes and letters patents and other evidences . . .
> If there be occasion of search to be made for any evidence in this house (the Earl
> himself not being present), under two persons at the least should not enter
> therein . . . For the Earl ought to have more care of the safe keeping of his
> evidences, than either of his plate or jewels.[19]

The assumption behind this use of the word is the legal notion that
written and sealed documents were automatically valued as reliable evidence (as opposed to words and other less concrete proof).[20] Braithwait's
association of the methodical preservation of such documents with the
private preoccupations of the householder illuminates Frankford's use of
the associated space. It is here that he ruminated alone on the felicity of
his situation. It is here again that he settles his accounts in company with
none but God, arriving, as it were, at a spiritual decision as he re-emerges
to pronounce the 'judgement' on his wife before a waiting household:
'My words are registered in heaven already' (xiii, 153).[21]

---

[19] Braithwait, *Some Rules and Orders*, 17–18. See Orlin, *Private Matters*, 183–5, for the only other
critical discussion of this passage in relation to Frankford's study. In fact Orlin's 'Coda Three: The
Key and the Cogito' 182–9), the short chapter in which the Braithwait passage appears (more fully
cited), shares with my present chapter its concern with the householder's study as a private space.
She focuses on the study as a variation of the strong-box, locked away by the householder himself, a
symbol of the 'ambitions to protect and preserve records and objects of value' (185). She connects
'individual selfhood' with a patriarchal urge to possess and secure. While broadly in agreement
with her, I focus specifically on the evidentiary implications of such a space, both in Heywood's
play, and in Braithwait's passage. In her full-length chapter on *WKK*, Orlin places the action and
'the ugly ethic of the play' (156) in the context of the classical theories and moral philosophy of
friendship and benefice, Renaissance adoptions of these, as well as Renaissance warnings against
obligation and excessive generosity in friendship. Ultimately, her argument is about the subordin-
ation of the woman to the amicitious text's 'ethical intent' (161). In the process, however, she pauses
on the particularised depiction of the 'material surroundings of Frankford's "household"' (145), the
resultant 'proliferation of domestic details' which she says 'solidifies our perception of [his] status,
and, thus, of his investment in his household commonwealth' (146). Her discussion of the objects
of Frankford's house, and their relation to the notion of domestic possession and mastery, provides
a useful background to my more specific and selective consideration of household space. For a
more succinct comment on the link between amicitia and oeconomia in *WKK*, see Hutson,
Usurer's Daughter, 133–4.

[20] On the superior importance of deeds in contract law and the law of evidence, see Baker,
Introduction, 360–2 and 375.

[21] It is important to remember, however, that Braithwait was writing more than two hundred years
later, and this is an imaginative association rather than a historical point. Looked at more deeply,

The relation of John Edmunds's study and his workplace to his house-hold and to his preparation of evidence provides a suggestive real-life comparison. John is in his study when his wife and her lover have their 'sweetest sporte' in the hall.[22] The maid hears them from the kitchen and goes out into the 'entry' to spy on them.[23] The physical and hierarchical position of the study within the Edmunds household, then, is defined in two ways:[24] firstly, in terms of its spatial relations with hall, kitchen and entry, involving the factors of relative visibility and audibility; secondly, as a function of the householder's relations with the other inmates and their activities which, in turn, are associated with different parts of the house. The privateness of the study must be perceived as both a segregation from, and an implication in, the governance of the household. This generates the paradox whereby a gentleman's seclusion, while making space for his wife's adultery, also provides the space from which to exercise his judicial author-ity in punishing this domestic misdemeanour. The systematic preparation of the evidence of the letters is an activity associated with a man's studies in the wider senses of the word, though whether Edmunds actually filed and reworked the letters in his study can only be speculated on.

The sense of privacy in these texts is constituted by the notion of secrecy. The closeness of Braithwait's Earl's office, the confidentiality of John Edmunds's collection of evidence, and the moments of suspense generated in Frankford's house when he withdraws into his study, come together to throw light on the peculiarly early modern experience of privacy that forms an important context to the drama of discovery in *Woman Killed.* The connection of secrecy (itself a concept inextricable from a consciousness of the public) with private space is suggestively expressed in Angel Day's description of the gentleman's closet: 'Wee do call the most secret place in the house appropriate unto our owne private studies . . . a Closet'.[25] The husband's 'closet' in Middleton and Rowley's

---

Braithwait's larger narrative even suggests a difference of regimes: a distinction between the failure of knowledge that Frankford's evidentiary activities seem to signify, and the sense in which precisely this risk had been brought under control in Braithwait's oeconomy. Erica Sheen first alerted me to this difference in spite of my specific analogy – a difference that is somewhat elided in Orlin's more comprehensive analogy between that later imagined earl's household and that of the early modern gentleman.

22 CUL, V.C. Court I.3, 116.

23 See Capp, 'Life, Love, Litigation', 59–60, on servants' prerogative over household space, and therefore, over information.

24 On spatial hierarchy in the early modern English house, developing from the increasing differenti-ation of domestic spaces, see Orlin, 'Causes and Reasons', 19–75.

25 Day, *English Secretorie,* Part II, 109. For a related argument to mine, see Stewart, 'Early Modern Closet', though his primary focus is not on the surveillance of the feminine.

The Changeling (1621) contains the books and objects of his secret study. Alsemero himself explicitly states the covertness associated with this room, when he hands over its key to his friend:

> That key will lead thee to a pretty secret,
> By a Chaldean taught me, and I've made
> My study upon some . . .   (IV.ii.111–13)

The inwardness of Montaigne's storehouse becomes, in these texts, a prudent and worldly secretiveness that is essential to the management of domestic economy.[26]

The husband's proprietorial secrecy has its complement in the wife's or the adulterer's experience of privacy. Evidence operates at the interface between the two, and household servants mediating these two realms of secrecy have an important role in its production. This complex oeconomy is dramatised in *Woman Killed* where adultery is not only discovered through, but itself makes visible, the dynamic conjunction of spaces, people and relations constituting domesticity in the early modern household.[27]

Oeconomy and privacy

From the very beginning, the topography of the Frankford house is divided and distinguished. While the wedding party make merry in the parlour, the bride and groom withdraw into the bed-chamber (i, 75). The servants, meanwhile, 'have a crash in the yard' (ii, 4–5). As Jenkin supervises the clearing away (viii), specific associations of rooms are defined in terms of certain occupations and inmates: 'My master and guests have supped already . . . Here now spread for the servingmen in the hall . . . One spread the carpet in the parlour . . . More lights in the hall there!' (viii, 1–3, 13–16). Nick, in the meantime, waits in an undesignated space between hall and parlour; hence Frankford's surprise at finding him on inappropriate territory: 'what make you here? Why are not you/At

---

[26] Advice tracts for the landed classes throughout the first half of the seventeenth century abounded in instructions to maintain privacy as part of a proper maintenance of position, authority and domestic order. The advice of Richard, Earl of Charlbury, to his son to 'withdraw [himself] into [his] closett or some private part of [his] chamber' is given in this overall context (Huntington Library, EL 34/b/2, 16, 165). See Pollock's brief survey of the informal circulation of such literature in élite circles: 'Living on the Stage'.

[27] I use 'oeconomy' to denote the complex structure of household governance, including financial relations, marital interaction, spatial organisation and the supervision of servants. For the early modern deployment of this concept and its derivation from Aristotle and Xenophon, see Hutson, *Usurer's Daughter*, 30–41, and Orlin, 'Causes and Reasons', 11–12.

supper in the hall there with your fellows' (23–4). Nick explains he has been awaiting his master's 'rising from the board to speak to him'. Frankford: 'Be brief then, gentle Nicklas,/My wife and guests attend me in the parlour' (26–7). Whether the room in which the Frankfords and their guests dine is the parlour or a private room from which they retire after supper to a parlour for a game of cards,[28] the point is the care to maintain propriety and a *notion* of privacy through segregation.

The relation between the need to define private space in this representation of a genteel household, and the by now undisputed absence of privacy, as *we* understand it, in early modern England, needs to be comprehended in terms of contemporary architectural trends. Recent studies concur in detecting a distinct tendency towards a sharper definition and division of interior space for specific purposes through the Tudor and Stuart periods.[29] While much of this work concentrates on noble households and manor houses, Colin Platt has shown how pervasive these trends were across the social spectrum.[30] Household inventories confirm the impression of steady increase in the number of purpose-specific rooms at various social levels.[31] This is not to suggest that the common architectural patterns across a reasonable range of the social scale cancel out distinctions of lifestyle. But there *was* a shared dimension of domestic existence which can be understood partly in relation to the fluidity of class boundaries.[32]

---

[28] In manors of the gentry, the functions of the originally communal multi-purpose hall were being distributed, in this period, to several purpose-specific rooms such as dining chambers: see Orlin, 'Causes and Reasons', 41–8. But Catherine Richardson's assumption of an interrupted parlour dinner ('Properties', 136) is mistaken, as Jenkin says at the opening of the scene that his master and the guests 'have supped already' (viii, 1–2), and Frankford is said to be 'newly risen from supper' (s.d., 23), having finished it. This is why Nick was waiting. The further assumption that they have dined in the parlour could also be wrong in an interesting way, if we accept that the parlour is where they retire to, for cards and drinks, and the division of interior spaces could be even more nuanced and minute than the simple polarisation of hall and parlour would suggest. The prompt copy of the 1992 RSC production of the play by Katie Mitchell at the Pit (originally performed at The Other Place, Stratford, 1991) indicates the location of Nick's conversation with Frankford 'in corridor near dining room' (RSC archives, Stratford), suggesting that the dining room was taken to be distinct from the parlour.

[29] See Platt, *Great Rebuildings*; Friedman, *House and Household*; Orlin, 'Causes and Reasons'.

[30] Platt, *Great Rebuildings*, esp. Ch. 1.

[31] Skipp, *Crisis*, 62–3.

[32] See Harrison, *Description of England*, Bk I, Ch. 5, on the fluid boundaries between the first three of 'four degrees of people'. See also Wrightson, *English Society*, Ch. 1, which establishes that formal definitions of rank were in practice often overridden by a more comprehensive perception of gentility, determined by the related factors of landed wealth, lifestyle, exercise of authority and local recognition.

This context merits a little digression, as it helps us understand Frankford's social position. He is not a knight or esquire himself but mingles with them, and his marriage into the baronetry is generally acclaimed as equal. He boasts of his royal connection 'by birth'; so he is probably a gentleman by virtue of being the younger son or brother of an esquire. He talks of his 'mean estate' but mentions his 'revenues' and owns three or four manors (xvi, 8–9). His situation illustrates what Keith Wrightson sees as the 'permeable membrane' between gentlemen and titular lords, and explains the similarities between the internal workings of his household and the picture of life in noble houses emerging from recent research.[33] This context of social mobility also explains the fact that the Edmunds household seems to have functioned through spatial and human interactions that are, in a specialised sense, comparable to the dynamics of Frankford's country manor. John Edmunds senior was an alderman in Cambridge at the time of the case and died as a reeve – both highly respectable positions. He owned and occupied a house large enough to be rented. The son went to university, and was professionally a 'privileged' member of it; he was genteel enough to have been involved in the Latin college play of 'Fatum' with Covile,[34] a fellow in Divinity, and comfortable enough to have had men-servants as well as maids at all times, if not in the same abundance as Frankford.[35] His house was divided at least into hall, kitchen, entry, yard, bed-chamber and even a secluded study, and had more than one storey.[36]

However, this trend towards a multiplicity of purpose-specific rooms coincided with an increased number of corridors and stairways offering multiple access to the same space. Although some historians of private life have linked the emergence of stairways and corridors, along with more specialised rooms, with the 'new concept of privacy',[37] it is precisely these common spaces that could often compromise privacy. In the Edmunds house, entry and staircase provide convenient vantage points for servants and visitors to observe Bridget and Covile. In the Frankford household, it is in the undefined space – possibly the corridor between hall and parlour or hall and dining room – where the first act of quasi-legal 'informing'

---

[33] Wrightson, *English Society*, 23.

[34] See Nelson, *Records*, I, 367, and II, 973.

[35] See Wrightson, *English Society*, on the number of servants as a social index of gentility.

[36] On shared fashions and household possessions among knights, gentlemen and merchants, see Harrison, *Description of England*, 200. On the similarity of the spatial arrangement of farmhouses and cottages to that of 'those above', see Mercer, *English Vernacular Houses*, 74.

[37] See Pollock, 'Living on the Stage', 79.

takes place, as Nick reports his mistress's clandestine romance to his master, and the investigation is plotted (viii, 17–117). Catherine Richardson sees this corridor as one of the 'liminal', 'comfortless passageways' where Frankford is seen drifting away from his social status and domestic control, symbolised by status-denoting objects in designated spaces like the parlour.[38] Here, she argues, we see the disempowered private man instead, and pins it down to 'the absence of properties' in this scene.[39] My reading suggests that, rather than simply being 'a domestic space not designed to be a space', a neutral place of trapping-less privacy, such 'unlocated locations' are also sites of the householder's control through surveillance (just as the study is at once private and oeconomic).[40] After all, the perambulating master of the house was a figure of surveillance inherited from classical texts of household philosophy which informed humanist writing about good husbandry. Richard Whitford, in *A Werke for Householders* (1531), echoes the pseudo-Aristotelian *Oeconomicus* when he quotes the maxim, 'the steppe of the husbande maketh the fatte donghyll'.[41] Architecture itself reflected a situation where a growing sense of privacy was inextricable from a matrix of oeconomic interest and accountability.

This duality is also exemplified by the place of the private man's house in the community. This is the context in which domesticity – and its disruption – are placed in the anonymous *Arden of Faversham* (1592), another 'domestic tragedy' about adultery and murder. The implication of the personal and the domestic in a wider nexus of gazes and agencies that *Arden* dramatises is interiorised in Heywood's play. In part, this is a simple shift of focus from the place of the private in the community to the shared, threatened, but distinctly perceived privacy inside a household. But it has also to do with Heywood's focus on adultery as a situation that reveals aspects of marriage, private relationships and domesticity. Class itself becomes, here, a determinant of the internal dynamics of domesticity, relations and arbitration. The role of a larger community becomes an element in the consciousness of specific protagonists, especially Frankford and Nick. Its function in the story of the marriage, thus, is most apparent at the end, when its nature and presence become a factor in the way adultery is dealt with in the domestic courtroom.

[38] Richardson, 'Properties', 136–7.
[39] Ibid., 137.
[40] Ibid., 136.
[41] Whitford, *Werke*, F5v. On the provenance of *Oeconomicus*, see Hutson, *Usurer's Daughter*, 24, n. 21; 22. For its derivation from Xenophon, see Aristotle, *Economics*, x.

The fear of publicity is inherent to a situation of illicit love. But while Alice Arden is vexed by her neighbours' 'blabbing' (*Arden*, I, 135), Wendoll's imagery alludes to a more inward divulgence:

> Your husband is from home, your bed's no blab –
> Nay, look not down and blush.   (vi, 164–5)[42]

Wendoll's remark recalls Anne's awareness of her blush as a sign that betrays her shame, akin to her faults being written on her brow (vi, 154–6), even if the bed is a mute witness. The relationship between the privacy of the body and its responses, and their public, visible, expression, are based on premises of close observation and domestic surveillance – in this instance, in a sphere more intimate than the community.

The acts of watching and overhearing, likewise, are grounded in oeconomic relations within the Frankford household. The scene of temptation, which begins with Anne soliciting Wendoll, on behalf of her husband, to 'command/Even as himself . . . keep his table, use his servants . . .' (vi, 75–7), ends with Wendoll's implicit takeover of Frankford's wife and bed. The impropriety of this substitution is anticipated by Jenkin's jokes in the prefatory sequence. A servant is the first to register the dislocations resulting from an outsider's installation in a hermetic household. In the first of several scenes of overhearing, Jenkin's asides provide an ironic commentary on Wendoll's compunctious soliloquy (vi, 30–56). When Wendoll notices him and asks, 'What, Jenkin? Where's your mistress?' Jenkin answers, with no apparent connection, 'Is your worship married?' A puzzled Wendoll demands, 'Why dost thou ask?' Jenkin's answer is loaded: 'Because you are my master, and if I do have a mistress, I would be glad, like a good servant, to do my duty to her' (57–61). The definition of the master–servant relationship in a household is posited on a harmonious relationship between husband and wife; once that goes askew, the surrounding nexus of subsidiary relations is thrown into confusion. When Wendoll asks to be served dinner at Anne's 'private chamber' (xi, 90–2), the servants wonder if the 'new master' is '[playing] the knave with [the] old' (xii, 10–11).

The substitution that Jenkin registers in a casual, jokey way, and the others gossip about, is attacked by Nick, when Frankford invites Wendoll to command his men and his resources:

---

[42] 'Blab' is a word symptomatic of adultery; cf. Heywood's own *Edward IV* (I, 8): 'This tongue was never knowne to be a blab.'

> I do not like this fellow by no means:
> I never see him but my heart still earns.
> Zounds, I could fight with him, yet know not why.
> The Devil and he are all one in my eye.   (iv, 85–8)

When Sisly asks him to help Wendoll 'off his boots', Nick's resentment is expressed with passion:

> If I pluck off his boots, I'll eat the spurs,
> And they shall stick fast in my throat like burrs.
>
> (iv, 97–8)

One recalls John Fletcher's services for his mistress and the surrogate lord of the house, as Bridget and Covile play at cards and hold court in John's absence, at the same time as he keeps a faintly resentful eye on them, ready to furnish detailed evidence in court.[43] Servants are not neutral observers and reporters any more than evidence is an independent and depersonalised legal operation. When Nick reports Anne's infidelity to Frankford in *Woman Killed*, he implicates himself conspicuously in the domestic situation the impropriety of which he discloses:

> You knew me, sir, before you knew my mistress . . .
> 'Sblood sir, I love you better than you love your wife.
> I'll make it good . . .
> There's not room for Wendoll and me too
> Both in one house. O master, master,
> That Wendoll is a villain.   (viii, 34–5, 43–4, 51–3)[44]

Even as Wendoll assures Anne of his secrecy, Nick, unnoticed by them, swears to his own project of secret observation. The word 'close', used by both, captures the ironically complementary nature of a situation in which confidentiality is an attribute both of personal privacy and the gaze that threatens it. To persuade Anne, Wendoll stresses,

> I will be secret, lady, close as night,
> And not the light of one small glorious star
> Shall shine here in my forehead or bewray
> That act of night.   (vi, 146–9)

---

[43] CUL, V.C. Court I.3, 119v–120v.

[44] Nick's investment is also a function of an internal hierarchy among the servants. Sisly, Roger and Jack do not have the same access to the master as Nick. He is the one to interrupt Frankford's solitary study (iv) to announce Wendoll and to provide particulars to help his master decide if the visitor is 'worth receiving'. This anticipates his privileged role in the 'private' investigation of Anne's adultery while at the same time partaking of the activities of watching and talking that the servants engage in collectively (xi, 78–80).

Unheard, Nick immediately responds,

> I'll henceforth turn a spy,
> And watch them in their close conveyances.
>   . . .
>   I'll have an eye
> In all their gestures. . .   (vi, 174–80)

'Close' suggests both the sense of enclosure including the secondary association of concealment, and the alternative meaning, 'of proximity'. Its particular uses here underline the connection between the two senses, and define the atmosphere that engenders evidence.

The scenic structure of this episode sharpens the focus on viewing established by Nick's presence. The scene dramatises the act of seeing itself, and anticipates its more complex representation in the scene of Frankford's discovery. In the meantime, Nick's 'eye' becomes the principal evidentiary agent. His opportune discovery is recounted in entirely ocular terms: 'O I have seen such vile and notorious tricks,/Ready to make my eyes dart from my head' (viii, 19–20). Frankford persists that his 'eyes may be deceived' (86), but as a remedy, sets about to organise his own scene of viewing. This is conceptualised, however, as a drama of knowing: 'Till I know all, I'll nothing seem to know' (115). Nick's secrecy is harnessed, henceforth, to the secrecy of the suspicious husband seeking confirmation: 'be secret then/For I know nothing' (94–5). The covertness, deliberation and visual action that are employed to the cognitive end of evidentiary practice already coalesce in this exchange. It also registers the imminent takeover of the ocular agency by the husband's eye, in a reclaiming of lapsed husbandry: in Xenophon, 'the master's eye' was said to be 'the quickest way of fattening the horse' – a proverbial expression for a *domestos* in good order; as Ischomachus' paraphrase suggests, 'the master's eye in the main does the good and worthy work'.[45]

Staging evidence

The preparation for the grand disclosure is elaborately planned: duplicate keys must be moulded in wax and a letter must be brought in, as if to call Frankford away to business. Frankford's methodical construction of evidence 'by degrees' (viii, 218) is a variation on the husband's careful and

---

[45] Xenophon, *Memorabilia and Oeconomicus*, xii, 20, 471.

remarkably deliberate material construction of proof in the Edmunds case. Frankford stages a situation in which he can catch them in the act:

> And when they think they securely play,
> They are nearest to danger.   (223–4)

Incidents of organised spying are symptomatic of the deliberation behind such activity in early modern English communities, as attested by court records – the precise reason why they were perceived as 'spying'. As Martin Ingram puts it, 'spying cases did not represent normal, spontaneous, neighbourly behaviour but carefully planned, *legally purposeful* activity'.[46]

The project of discovery is set afoot in the dead of night, in silence and secrecy. The 'scene' that Frankford and Nick's journey through the house seeks to uncover has to be approached with Frankford's 'dark lantern' (20) – a lantern with an inbuilt arrangement to conceal its own light – an appropriate instrument for the covertness that is associated with the legal process through which illumination is reached.

At the threshold of his own house, Frankford imaginatively anticipates his movement through it as he goes over the keys one by one:

> This is the key that opes my outward gate;
> This is the hall door; this my withdrawing chamber.
> But this, that door that's bawd unto my shame,
> Fountain and spring of all my bleeding thoughts,
> Where the most hallowed order and true knot
> Of nuptial sanctity hath been profaned.
> It leads to my polluted bed-chamber,
> Once my terrestrial heaven, now my earth's hell,
> The place where sins in all their ripeness dwell.
> But I forgot myself; now to my gate.   (xiii, 8–17)

Frankford's rhetorical journey charts a movement towards discovery. The intricate network of gates and doors and chambers traversed in the discovery scene becomes a sinister realisation of the 'labyrinth of sin', the 'maze' that Anne felt herself engulfed in as Wendoll seduced her (vi, 159–60). Significantly, Anne's expression of bewilderment was met by Wendoll's triumphant metaphor of entry:

> The path to pleasure, and the gate to bliss,
> Which on your lips I knock at with a kiss.
> (vi, 161–2)

---

[46] Ingram, *Church Courts*, 245.

Frankford, standing with the keys of his own house in his hands, embodies the paradox of the cuckolded householder's situation. Adultery, in early modern England, was at once a personal and private misfortune, *and* a violation of ownership and usurpation of property. Frankford's handling of the keys suggests his control over the 'evidences' in his personal space, the whole house temporarily coming to stand for his 'chamber'. At the same time, his position is one of peculiar alienation, for the contents of his locked cabin are his wife and her lover, not what he has pleasurably hoarded but a store that has been emptied out. He has to enter from outside to penetrate an inner sanctum already occupied. His situation, thus, defines both his authority and his displacement from his bed and board. The key becomes at once a token of proprietorial access and of exclusion.

As he proceeds into the interior of his house, he takes not only Nick but also the theatre audience with him. The theatrical implication of this inward journey is underlined by Nick's comment as they negotiate the gate: 'It must ope with far less noise than Cripplegate, or your plot's dashed' (xiii, 18–19). Cripplegate was the very gate through which the audience passed to come to the Red Bull where, it seems, *Woman Killed* was most often performed.[47] The analogy with playgoing not only points up the fictional element in the construction of proof, but also the difference between the evidentiary 'plot' within the play, and the function of the dramatic plot in this scene. The former is aimed at anagnorisis, even if Frankford is almost convinced of the sight that awaits him, but the latter is concerned with *exposure*, for the audience already knows what Frankford is uncertain of. What lies beyond his 'last door' is framed as a 'spectacle' as Frankford pauses:

> O keep my eyes, you heavens, before I enter,
> From any sight that may transfix my soul.
> Or if there be so black a spectacle,
> O strike mine eyes stark blind;   (xiii, 27–30)

As he 'enters', however, he exits from the stage space. Immediately after his second 'entry' into the bedroom come dramatic exits from the inner chamber – 'Enter Wendoll, running . . . Frankford after him. . .'[48] The scene of adultery – the centre of the action – remains invisible to the audience. Even Nick has to stop short of the bedroom door. His role, like

---

[47] See *WKK*, 65, n. 18; *WKK*, ed. Van Fossen, 72, n. 18; Gurr, *Shakespearean Stage*, 222. Van Fossen assumes that Cripplegate had a reputation for creaking loudly when opened (72, n. 18).

[48] In modern editions, this ironic disparity between plot and stage action is further encoded by the insertion of additional stage directions (e.g. at ll. 34, 39–40) reinforcing the conflict between the two.

the playgoer's, is to watch Frankford enter and await his response to what he has seen. The scene stages evidentiary action rather than evidence, the act of viewing rather than the spectacle. 'The act of night' (vi, 149) is the 'act' of adultery, not, as in *Arden,* the murderous deed. It must, hence, remain enclosed by darkness in a playhouse. The door that blocks theatrical visibility is an appropriate symbol for the play's preoccupation, here, with both what cannot be shown, and the staged and constructed nature of seeing itself.[49]

Fletcher's deposition on behalf of his erstwhile master in the Edmunds case illustrates the relationship between the terms of theatrical and legal representation. Asked whether he saw his mistress and Covile 'lye together', Fletcher says he did not, but that one night, when his master was out and his mistress was 'almost in bedd', he saw Covile 'goe upp thither to hir'.[50] The candle in the room was put out by Covile, whereupon Fletcher was asked by his mistress to light it again. But he could not get into the room as Covile had shut the door 'against . . . him':

> and in the shuttinge of yt he did see . . . Covills white band and a peece of his . . . gowne did hange oute at the . . . chamber doare . . . All which he saith he might and did easilie see and decerne by suche lighte as came thorough two windows there, from the candle lighte either in the hall or kitchen of the same howse.[51]

The closed chamber door at which Fletcher's eyes had to stop is emblematic of the limits of evidentiary vision in sexual litigation. The conjunction of darkness and candle light filtering in through holes and corners, reminiscent of Frankford's 'dark lantern', captures the distinctive combination of invisibility and spectatorship that characterises the evidentiary experience.[52] But when Fletcher narrates this episode in court, the details of the closed door and the bits of garment caught in it become the metonymic tokens which imaginatively evoke in a legal space what the door's opacity conceals. Frankford, the informed husband, unlike Fletcher, the curious servant, can go into the room to witness the 'black . . . spectacle' (xiii, 29).

---

[49] For a comparable discussion of the unrepresentability of sexual evidence in *Othello*, see Maus, *Inwardness and Theater*, 104–27. But while she emphasises adultery as the crime that cannot be staged or seen, I show that the seeing itself is as highly constructed as the synecdochic strategies that Maus says substitute for full sight in drama (and which I myself demonstrate to function thus in the plays discussed in Chapter 1).

[50] CUL, V.C. Court I.3, 120.

[51] Ibid., 120v.

[52] In a suggestive theatrical invention, Mitchell's 1992 production (see n. 28 above) had two stage props in the discovery scene – Heywood's 'dark lantern', which they enter with, and a 'bright lantern' which Nick places on a raised surface once they are in.

But the use of stage space to mark the contrast between his vantage point and that of Nick and the audience dramatises the representational limits of the theatre, analogous to those of the courtroom.

However, the play is not merely staging the limits of its own medium. By focusing on the impossibility of showing certain sights on stage, it is making a more positive theatrical point about the motives of dramatic as well as legal representation, and about contemporary connotations of particular spaces and actions. The unseen bed-chamber is foregrounded as the end point of Frankford's inward journey. It contains the ultimate ocular proof that will enable him to '[place] his action' (xiii, 39), and the final 'scene' in the drama of disclosure that the audience cross Cripplegate to watch. Thus, the very denial of the bed-chamber's actual presentation on stage reinforces the sense of its climactic importance and the related notion of its sanctity and inaccessibility. Such facts as servants' pallets often being placed next to the beds, historians have suggested, prove the inappropriateness of applying notions of privacy to the bed and its associated activities in the early modern period.[53] But, given this sharing of private spaces, Heywood's theatrical segregation of the bed-chamber is all the more pointed. It brings alive an intangible, but nonetheless real feeling for privacy that could be experienced in spite of, and perhaps even because of the physical limits to it.[54] Significantly, beds were among the most commonly used large properties in the Red Bull, whose repertory contains at least seventeen scenes showing beds.[55]

While the bed-chamber itself remains invisible in the play, it is represented through a sudden appearance of people in garments associated with the intimacy of the bed. Wendoll is said to emerge from the bedroom 'running over the stage in a nightgown'. Anne comes out 'in her smock, nightgown and night attire' (xiii, 78). The breach of propriety involved in such exposure is registered by the servants: Jenkin exclaims, 'O Lord,

[53] See, for example, Orlin, 'Causes and Reasons', 185. For older, classic statements of this position, see Stone, *Family, Sex and Marriage*, and Ariès and Duby, eds., *History of Private Life*, III. Habermas, *Structural Transformation*, and Elias, *Civilizing Process*, share Stone's developmental chronology. For a critique, see Calhoun, ed., *Habermas and the Public Sphere*. On the historiography of gender roles and separate spheres, and the need for a more nuanced approach to what 'privacy' or 'publicity' meant to historical subjects, see Vickery, 'Golden Age', 384–414, and *Gentleman's Daughter*.

[54] See Pollock, 'Living on the Stage', for a similar argument for the existence of a concept of privacy, not to be confused with the material form that it took or lacked, though she focuses on the specific, politicised circumstances of the élite household.

[55] See Reynolds, *Staging*, 65–70, and Gurr, *Shakespearean Stage*, 171 and 175. On beds in Shakespeare, see Roberts, 'Let me the curtains draw', 153–74.

mistress, how came this to pass? My master is run away in his shirt, and never so much as called me to bring his clothes after him' (148–50). As Frankford goes for Wendoll 'with his sword drawn', 'the maid in her smock stays his hand' (68), and the servants enter the stage 'as newly come out of bed' (145). Bed-clothes, here, stand for an order of privacy that is defined through the possession and use of certain household objects, not merely through the increasing differentiation of space. Sisly's quip, earlier, as she carries the keys up to her mistress – 'I am neither pillow nor bolster, but I know more than both' (xii, 26–7) – touches on the association of some of these articles with the notion of sexual knowledge and secrecy. It is this privacy that is violated and made visible as the members of a household gather in a common space before one another and before an audience, in their bed-clothes.

One recalls Banquo's exhortation to the amazed crowd newly awakened and assembled outside the slain Duncan's bed-chamber:

> And when we have our naked frailties hid,
> That suffer in exposure, let us meet
> And question this most bloody piece of work.
> (*Macbeth*, II.iii.126–8)

Banquo's words reinforce the association of certain clothes with retirement into privacy, evoked earlier by Lady Macbeth's urging that she and Macbeth should 'retire . . . to [their] chamber':

> Get on your night gown, lest occasion call us
> And show us to be watchers.   (II.ii.63, 58–9)

Though the 'act of night' in *Macbeth*, as in *Arden*, is murder rather than adultery, it is verbally and imaginatively associated with a secret deed, implicated in the intimacies and tensions of the Macbeths' marriage. The murder itself is the joint act, closely committed.[56] The sleep-walking scene, lit by a taper – often a stage symbol for the approach to the bed-chamber – communicates a sense of vulnerability ('frailties') in offering a view of private guilt, associated with items of intimate use: '. . . infected minds/To their deaf pillows will discharge their secrets' (V. i.73–4).

It is significant that the disclosure in *Woman Killed* anticipates both the murder scene and the discovery in *Macbeth*.[57] Frankford's exclamation as

---

[56] So it does not matter that there were two grooms sleeping in Duncan's chamber. The secrecy and privacy inhere in the clandestine nature of the crime committed in that room.

[57] This is not to claim that the *Macbeth* scene is indebted to Heywood's. The analogy is a literary comparison of the ambience of the two scenes, and what that suggests of either treatment.

he halts outside the bed-chamber, 'O keep my eyes, you heavens, before I enter,/From any sight that may transfix my soul/. . ./O strike mine eyes stark blind' (xiii, 27–30), resembles Macduff's words as he stands outside Duncan's room and prepares Lennox for the spectacle within: 'Approach the chamber, and destroy your sight/With a new Gorgon' (II.ii.71–2).[58] At the same time, as Frankford '[treads] softly, softly' at 'dead midnight', from the eerie stillness outside the gate, through the 'general silence [that] hath surprised the house', towards the bedroom (1–26), he reminds one of Macbeth's 'stealthy pace,/With Tarquin's ravishing [strides] . . . /Moving like a ghost' through his palace towards the sanctum of 'curtained sleep' (*Macbeth*, II.i.49–60).[59] Though the moral structures of the two entries are different, for Macbeth goes to commit treason and Macduff to discover it, Frankford's journey combines the stealthy apprehension of Macbeth's progress and Macduff's investigative approach.[60] By collapsing the transgressive and the anagnoristic processes, it points up the ambiguity of evidentiary action. Frankford is, like Macduff, morally sanctioned to probe into the privacy of the bed-chamber, but there is something inherently sordid, almost illicit, about the process that is comparable to Macbeth's striding towards the sleeping Duncan.

The necessary murkiness of evidence collection in Heywood's play, however, is neatly absorbed into the ensuing drama of judgement and pardon which restores the gentility that has defined Frankford from his first soliloquy. The dirty business of ferreting out adultery is relegated to a single dark night of what Milton calls 'unmanly indignities', in which master and servant have to act in collusion.[61]

---

[58] Macduff's description of the 'sacrilegious murder' also configures it in architectural terms; it 'hath broke ope/The Lord's anointed temple, and stole thence/The life o' th' building!' (II.iii.67–70).

[59] The connection with Tarquin further links the clandestinity in *Macbeth* with an adultery plot, albeit fleetingly.

[60] For an analogous argument about the hero of revenge tragedy or the detective, whose hunt itself becomes ironically fearful and stealthy, and whose tracking takes on the clandestinity of the crime he seeks to detect or avenge, see Kerrigan, *Revenge Tragedy*, 59–87, esp. 65–73. The process of reconstructing evidence can itself acquire a kind of violence which makes the revenger figure or the Holmesian detective re-enact the crime being investigated.

[61] Milton, *Doctrine and Discipline of Divorce*, 337. It is in connection with the difficulties of proving adultery, much discussed in the wake of the severe penal statute of 1650, that Milton regrets the undignified means of investigation necessitated by the stringent evidentiary requirements of the Act. See ibid., 347, on the 'uncomely exigencies' that Henry VIII was reduced to, and the 'obscene evidence' required, to prove that Catherine of Aragon had been 'carnally known by Prince Arthur'. On the Act of 1650, and the proposals for amending it so as to admit 'reasonable presumption' rather than certain evidence as a ground for conviction, see Thomas, 'Puritans and Adultery', 278–80. Note that Milton argues for the jurisdiction of divorce as being rightfully a 'domestic prerogative', and most properly belonging to the husband (*Doctrine and Discipline of*

'Usage of more humility': judgement and mercy

When Frankford retires to his study to prepare the 'sentence', leaving Anne standing in her nightgown before the rest, she clinches the indignity of the exposure in conflating guilt and shame in such a situation:

> See what guilt is: here stand I in this place,
> Ashamed to look my servants in the face.
> (xiii, 151–2)

Immediately after, Frankford emerges and delivers the prelude to his verdict:

> My words are registered in heaven already;
>   . . . I'll not martyr thee,
> Nor mark thee for a strumpet, but with usage
> Of more humility torment thy soul,
> And kill thee, even with kindness. (xiii, 153–7)

The cruder evidentiary exercise, associated with the judicial process, is disclaimed, as the language invokes a higher order of justice. This recalls and smooths over the more frank coexistence of legal and divine notions of judgement at the moment of discovery, when Nick is impatient for his master to clinch the 'case' by entering the room, catching them in the act (xiii, 36–9), and Frankford desists from a violent action at the thought of damning 'two precious souls/Bought with my Saviour's blood' by sending them 'laden/With all their scarlet sins upon their backs' (xiii, 45–9). It also recalls the combination of a calculating evidentiary concern and a providential imagination simultaneously registered in John Edmunds's annotations of his wife's love-letters.

Frankford's 'sentence' defines its own refinement by contrast with more extreme and grosser forms of punishment – 'I'll not . . . mark thee for a strumpet'. The self-conscious decency of his 'usage/Of more humility' is recapitulated and underlined at the play's conclusion in Sir Francis's comment that Frankford's penalty would have been less effective, had he 'with threats and usage bad/Punished her sin' (xvii, 134–5). The repudiation of the implied vulgarity of 'usage bad' is configured in terms of a more Christian, more 'kind' judgement – 'a mild sentence' (xiii, 172).

Divorce, 343–4). This suggests the thin borderline between the Reformation notion of companionate marriage and the sort of dubious private justice that Heywood brings into scrutiny.

What Frankford decrees is, in effect, a separation from bed and board (159–81), the usual verdict of church courts in cases of proved adultery, when one of the parties sought 'divorce' on that ground. The commonest penalty for adultery was, in fact, public penance in a sheet.[62] But the generosity of Frankford's sentence is defined against Anne's imagination of severer punishments, expressed in her first, instinctive, fearful response to the exposure, and her plea for kindness:

> . . . mark not my face
> Nor hack me with your sword, but let me go
> Perfect and undeformed to my tomb. (xiii, 99–101)

Later, while she waits for her sentence, she expects, even craves, a greater, and cruder, penalty than what she would receive from ecclesiastical authorities:

> I would have this hand cut off, these my breasts seared,
> Be racked, strappadoed, put to any torment. (xiii, 136–7)

In part, this should be seen in the context of the debate over punitive attitudes to adultery that culminated with the Puritans' triumph in the Act of 1650, but which began as early as the mid-sixteenth century.[63] The Parliament's efforts to make adultery a criminal offence started with the penal bill of 1549. From 1584, the Puritans began to urge the Parliament to make adultery a felony, and by 1624 the death penalty had been proposed. Anne's visualisation of her defacement and death carries resonances of the Puritan attitude, and recalls Wendoll's half-humorous remark on her insistent talk of the soul's sin even as she succumbed to temptation: 'Fie, fie, you talk too like a puritan' (xi, 109). Nor was the fitness of the death penalty – or, more specifically, the rightful killing of the adulterous wife by the husband – an exclusively Puritan notion: its provenance in England was older and wider. Not only the Mosaic law but also humanists such as Erasmus and More had criticised the leniency of church courts, and endorsed the legitimacy of murdering a wife caught in the act.[64] This body of opinions provides the background to Nick's exasperation (xiii, 35–40, 50–1, 67–8), and Sir Francis's surprise at Frankford's 'too mild . . . spirit':

---

[62] See Emmison, *Elizabethan Life*, 281–91; Houlbrooke, *Church Courts*, 46, 70; Hall, 'Some Elizabethan Penances'.

[63] See Thomas, 'Puritans and Adultery', for a seminal discussion.

[64] Ibid., 269; Avis, 'Moses'. For Heywood's list of harsh penalties in ancient civilisations, see *Generall History*, 605–6.

> . . . Had it been my case
> Their souls at once had from their breasts been freed.
> Death to such deeds of shame is the due meed.
>
> (xvii, 20–2)

What may also lie behind Anne's lurid punitive images are the well-established municipal practices of whipping, striping, stocking and carting for sexual offences, at the initiative of local magistrates, justices of the peace and constables, on the ground that fornication was a breach of the peace.[65]

Interestingly, violent physical punishments such as 'breaking on the wheel' as well as husbands hacking unfaithful wives were part of a generic tradition as well. Italian tales of adultery, man's revenge and God's judgement, the sources for so many contemporary English plays about adultery, abound with such excesses. In Painter's novella, 'Of a Lady of Thurin', one of the source stories of *Woman Killed*, the lady 'taken in adulterie' is punished by her husband by being shut up and starved in a chamber with her hanged lover's corpse.[66] With a pointed difference, Heywood makes Frankford let Wendoll off with the thought that his own conscience pangs 'will be revenge enough', thanking the maid for staying his 'bloody sacrifice' 'like an angel's hand' (xiii, 69–76). The 'bloody revenge' formula is consciously evoked and then rejected: ' . . . Pray, pray, lest I live to see/Thee Judas-like hanged on an elder-tree' (77–8). Burton, in his *Anatomy of Melancholy*, writes about how 'adulterers . . . amongst . . . Italians at this present day . . . are to be severely punished, cut in pieces, burned, *vivi comburio*, buried alive, with several expurgations', and puts it down to 'incredible jealousy' – quite possibly extrapolating from literature into life.[67] In John Reynolds's *The Triumphs of God's Revenge*, which assembles a large number of 'histories' translated from popular Italian tales, combining the motifs of revenge and judgement in their treatment of murders and sexual crimes, the offenders are killed in appropriately hideous ways.[68] These stories of passion and violence fed

---

[65] Thomas, 'Puritans and Adultery', 265–6. See also Bond, 'Dark Deeds', 191–200, on the disparity between the lurid visualisations of punishment in homilies against adultery (e.g. Thomas Becon's, 1547), and the relatively moderate and non-violent penitentiary procedure (penance in a sheet) in early modern England. However, towards the end of the penance ritual in church, the homilies of repentance, and those against fornicators and adulterers, were read out to the offenders before the congregation. This effected an imaginative association between the milder ecclesiastical penalty and a residual homiletic severity harking back to the older Mosaic tradition.

[66] Painter, *Palace*, I, Novella 43.

[67] Burton, *Anatomy*, III, 285.

[68] Reynolds, *Triumphs* (1635). This is the 4th edition, and the first complete one (in six books), as it came out in instalments, and each edition was an addition on the previous one. On the history of its publication, see Mish, 'Best Sellers', 369.

into the stereotype of Italy already existent in England and expressed vociferously by Roger Ascham.[69] Fynes Moryson's comments are typical:

The Italyans . . . are most strict in the courses of Justice . . . Adulteries (as all furyes of Jelousy, or signes of making loue, to wiues, daughters and sisters) are commonly prosecuted by priuate reuenge and by murther, and the Princes and Judges, measuring their iust reuenge by their own passions proper to that nation, make no great inquiry after such murthers.[70]

Protestant judgement books such as Thomas Beard's *The Theatre for God's Judgements* (1597) constituted a related genre, as populist and vivid as the sensational tales of passion, and working similarly by illustrating their moral point through a series of 'histories'.[71]

Anne's apprehension and expectation of physical defacement and death, then, allude to a literary tradition at the same time as they suggest Puritan opinions and disciplinary practices. Significantly, Heywood's own compendium of examples, *The Generall History of Women*, written in the format of Reynolds's *Triumphs* and Beard's *Theatre*, sets itself apart from these in its express distaste of violent private revenge for adultery: 'much is that inhumane rashnesse to be avoided, by which men have undertook to

---

[69] See Ascham on 'the maners of Italie' and the 'bold bawdry' and 'subtlest shifts' of Italian literature, in Painter, *Palace*, xix. See also Nashe, *Unfortunate Traveller*, II, 301–2.

[70] Moryson, *Shakespeare's Europe*, 160. It is interesting that Italian tales seem to have determined perceptions of social and amorous behaviour in the Edmunds case. Bridget objects to George Mountain as a witness on the ground that '[he] read lectures to [her] of bawdry <viz: the pallace of pleasure as she termeth it' (CUL, V.C. Court III.5, item 69). Whether this was Pettie's *Petite Pallace of Pettie his Pleasure* (1576), or Painter's collection, these amorous stories are disputed in the trial. Mountain protests that he read out 'Bocchas in Frenche', where 'there was noe bawdry at all' – referring, presumably, to the *Decameron*, of which several pre-1596 French editions were available in the Cambridge libraries. Bridget, however, persists 'that she meanethe . . . an englishe booke . . . the Palace of pleasure' (ibid., I.3, 117). Italianate sonnet sequences are even seen to shape the narrative of adulterous love: one of Covile's love-letters alludes to the unattainable mistress in *Licia* (1593) by Giles Fletcher the elder, and echoes his prefatory sonnet in the address, 'kynd, fayre, loving, sweet, Honest, vertuous, constant, trew, renowned, dearer to me then all the worlde' (figure 2.1); see Fletcher, *English Works*, 81.

[71] On the populist affiliations and methods of Protestant judgement books, see Walsham, *Providence*. The frequent association of adultery and murder in ballads and pamphlets about contemporary crimes and their punishments is perhaps also due to the fact that the most notorious trials involved murder, and executions for murder were more spectacularly public events than adultery trials in church courts. Besides, husband-murder counted as petty treason, and so was punished appropriately. Thus, in moralistic pamphlets about adultery, the penalties for treason began to acquire an independent imaginative association with adultery. The title-page of Goodcole's *The Adulteresses Funerall Day: In flaming, scorching and consuming fire* is illustrated by the vivid image of a figure burning at the stake – legally associated with traitors and heretics rather than adulteresses. Indeed, Alice Clark, the unfortunate protagonist of the pamphlet, was tried as a traitor for having poisoned her husband. But Goodcole's tract, like popular literature and plays about such trials, is imaginatively preoccupied with the evils of adultery, and focuses on domestic morality in its homiletic exercise.

be their own justifiers, and have mingled the pollution of their beds, with the blood of the delinquents'.[72]

Frankford's stance, then, is not just the personal predilection of a character and a choice of 'mild' rather than Puritan measures, but also a means through which Heywood's essentially English play defines its generic distinction from the more extreme, crude and Italianate treatments of the subject. This, in turn, is an attribute of the 'domesticity' of his play, home-bred in both a national and a social sense. The enclosing of the process of justice within the household is an aspect of this comprehensive domestication. Both the interrogation (xiii, 108) and the adjudication (158) are conducted in Frankford's house. It is not as though actual law is never evoked so that the play itself becomes the legal arena. The judicial machinery is perceptibly present (iii, 92 ff.; iv, 6–7, v, 1–14), but placed separately in the sub-plot. This civilised containment of adultery and of the process of justice indicates the link of Frankford's 'kindness' with respectability and family prestige. Compare the testimony of Mr Swinnerton at the trial of Sir Edward Moseley for the alleged rape of his wife. When asked why he had delayed bringing the case to court and attempted private negotiation instead, he said, 'if he could satisfy me, that my Wife was consenting to it, I had rather wave the Prosecution, than bring my Wife and myself upon the stage; and this was my intent'.[73]

Staging kindness, forging kinship

The impression of a class salvaging its self-image through a refinement even in punishment and penitence is consolidated in the final scene where an entire fraternity of gentlemen surround Anne's death-bed. But the viewers of this spectacle are in a sense all insiders, bound together in a complicated network of obligations, tied by investments in the 'kindness' of kindred. The sub-plot, which I have chosen not to concentrate on, becomes most integrally linked with the main plot at this point. Sir Charles Mountford, impoverished, indebted and imprisoned for killing huntsmen of his enemy, Sir Francis Acton, is quit and freed by Acton's

[72] Heywood, *Generall History*, 248–9; but note the qualification: 'Neither is this discourse aimed to perswade men to too much remisnesse in wincking at . . . the adulterie of their wives . . . Disgracefull it was in Philip . . . of Macedon, who having conquered divers nations . . . could not govern one wife at home'. Frankford's response, ostensibly, is positioned between these two extremes, and hinges on the link between moderation and governance advocated in so many conduct books.

[73] *Harleian*, III, 476 ff.

magnanimity. To acquit this debt, Mountford offers him his own sister Susan, whom Acton has lusted after. The incipient ugliness of these interested acts of generosity is allowed a sudden transformation by Acton's last-minute change of heart and his offer to marry Susan (xiv, 133–45). Yet the play knows – and will not let us forget – the mercenary and obscene bases of these gifts. Susan perceives her brother's plan as a commodification of her self – to be presented 'as a token' (xiv, 59), and would prefer to save her honour and die (85). Sir Acton, as she points out, 'still exceeds [them]' – his debt remains too great to be repaid, and so the obligation remains eternal, albeit rhetorically converted into kindness. And yet, 'kindness' was the very word used by Acton earlier, to describe his cunning strategies of seducing and 'conquering' Susan (ix, 66). Susan herself sees clearly that 'this strange kindness' in Acton proceeds from ulterior motives (xi, 119–22). The freeing of Mountford, as Mountford himself realises, only made him 'lie bound/In more strict prison than thy stony gaol' (x, 94–5); 'his kindness like a burden hath surcharged me' (xiv, 63). But in that single act of magnanimity through which the 'pawn' becomes a 'wife' (xiv, 106, 146), the tone changes and a rhetoric of genteel alliances is forged:

> All's mine is yours; we are alike in state.
> Let's knit in love what was opposed in hate.
> Come, for our nuptials we will straight provide,
> Blest only in our brother and fair bride.
>
> (xiv, 153–6)

This moment of transition in the sub-plot from indignity to gentility is mirrored in the main plot in the final scene of Anne's death and the forging of a new amity between Frankford and his brother-in-law, defining the civility of a world where such alliances can not only survive, but are reinforced by the husband's 'kindness' in dealing with his wife's transgression. The unruly wife is replaced by a noble brother-in-law, even as good manners ensure more manors. This brother-in-law, of course, is the same Sir Francis (Anne's brother) who, in the sub-plot, wields his own brand of kindness. Thus the kinships forged in the sub-plot are themselves reasserted in the last hour of reunion, pardon and death. It is Francis who articulates this:

> O Master Frankford, all the near alliance
> I lose by her shall be supplied in thee.
> You are my brother by the nearest way;
> Her kindred hath fallen off, but yours doth stay.
>
> (xvii, 101–4)

The elegiac tone of the speeches over Anne's body is itself a genteel note, markedly different from the derangement and distraction at the end of so many Jacobean tragedies of adultery and revenge, and is almost self-congratulatory:

> . . . Brothers and gentlemen,
> All we that can plead interest in her grief,
> Bestow upon her body funeral tears.
> Brother, had you with threats and usage bad
> Punished her sin, the grief of her offence
> Had not with such true sorrow touched her heart.
>
> (130–5)

The 'grace and humanity' in Frankford to which Anne appeals is drawn into a highly wrought, hyperbolical scene of pardon that effectively completes the ascent of the action from the level of unmanly indignity. Frankford's restoration of the status of a wife and a mother to Anne (115–16), likewise, clinches his ultimate deviation from Anne's more Puritan expectations, as expressed at the moment of discovery:

> . . . To call you husband!
> O me most wretched, I have lost that name;
> I am no more your wife.   (xiii, 81–4)

The 'new [marriage]' reconciling the estranged pair at the end was a possibility allowed by the canonical divorce 'from bed and board', but not by extreme Protestant views of the finality of the breach caused by adultery.[74] Nor is Frankford the sole determinant of the play's closing ambience. The frail, self-starved, repentant adulteress languishing in her chamber is herself a figure of refinement, noticeably unlike the lady of Thurin in Painter's story, cruelly starved by her husband.

Perhaps the most remarkable, if elusive, detail comes earlier, with Anne's instruction to Nick after her lute has 'groaned' for her (xvi, 31–2):

> Go break this lute upon the coach's wheel,
> As the last music that I e'er shall make –
> Not as my husband's gift, but my farewell
> To all earth's joy. . .   (xvi, 72–5)

Being 'broken' alive on the wheel was a common penalty for offenders in the Italian tales of crime and punishment that lie behind so many

---

[74] See Dibdin and Healy, *English Church Law*; Houlbrooke, *Church Courts*, 67–75; Ingram, *Church Courts*, 171–8; and Baker, *Introduction*, 559–64.

Jacobean adultery plays.[75] The lute – in any case an instrument associated with women and their bodies in the literature of the period – becomes a symbol for Anne herself by the time its dying or breaking groan is imagined to be 'the last music that [she] e'er shall make'.[76] Thus, Anne's figuration of her own punishment effects a generic transformation, by which a horrible image of torture is evoked only to be turned into an exquisite and extended conceit. A delicate musical instrument comes to stand for the offender's body, as Anne takes upon herself a symbolic enactment of the mortification she feels is both her right and her due. The lute broken on the wheel is a perfect image for the refined yet physical penalty she inflicts on herself.

However, the less exalted basis of the impeccable resolution is not as perfectly blended into the 'grace' and 'kindness' of the scenes of judgement and pardon in Heywood's generic vision, as in the characters' perception. Even at the moment of genuine regret and self-awareness, Frankford reinstates his dignity through display as he bestows the most opulent monuments on Anne's grave

> . . . this funeral epitaph,
> Which on her marble tomb shall be engraved.
> In golden letters shall these words be filled:
> Here lies one whom her husband's kindness killed.
>
> (xvii, 137–40)

Funeral monuments and tombstones were among the most expressive symbols of family honour and class prestige in the period.[77] So they are peculiarly suited to communicating the compound of sentimentality and bourgeois respectability that characterises Frankford's milieu; the appropriate final expression of a sensibility that conflated 'fear of shame, regard of honour,/The blemish of [his] house' and '[his] dear love', during Anne's interrogation (xiii, 118–19).

---

[75] E.g. Reynolds, *Triumphs*, 14, 325, 512.

[76] For the association of women with the lute in drama, often in an erotic context, see *The Dutch Courtesan*, I.ii.136–61 in Marston, *Selected Plays*; Shakespeare's *1 Henry IV*, III.i.207–8; *Richard III*, I.i.12–13; *Henry VIII*, III.i.1; *Titus*, II.iv.44–5; *Pericles*, IV, Gower's speech, 25–6; and *Shrew*, II.i.38–159. Puns on musical instruments and women's bodies were well established. The first printed English book of music was called *Parthenia* (1612) – the maiden venture – and the second, inevitably, *Parthenia in-Violata* (1624)! Women with lutes were more common in the European Vanitas still-lives in the sixteenth and seventeenth centuries than in contemporary English art. But see the portrait of Mary Sidney, Lady Wroth, with an arch-lute (attributed to Marcus Gheeraerts, c.1620), reproduced in Strong, *English Icon*, 267.

[77] See Llewellyn, 'The Royal Body', and 'Honour in Life'. See also Belsey, *Shakespeare*, 90–101, and 108–20.

The proprietorial basis of Frankford's magnanimity and civility is emphasised earlier, in the judgement itself:

> Go, make thee ready in thy best attire,
> Take with thee all thy gowns, all thy apparel;
> . . .
> Choose thee a bed and hangings for a chamber;
> And get thee to my manor seven mile off,
> Where live. 'Tis thine; I freely give it thee.
> My tenants by shall furnish thee with wains
> . . .
> Choose which of my servants thou likest best,
> And they are thine to attend thee.   (xiii, 159–72)

This 'sentence' points up the fragility of the woman's experience of privacy in relation to her husband's property.[78] Clothing, bed and hangings – the very items associated in the play with intimate use, and with a private, even secret existence – are marked out, here, as Frankford's, though referred to as '[her] stuff'. For Anne, the privacy that certain possessions make possible is precarious, because her proprietorship is virtual. For Frankford, the act of judgement resolves the ambiguity of his evidence-collection, which involved a strange combination of ownership and alienation, the householder himself having to assume the role of a trespasser. That alienation is now foisted on to Anne, while Frankford's reassertion of his right over her property undermines the physical separation. Even the place of her banishment is one of *his* numerous manors (xvi, 8–10). The judgement, indeed, is no less an inventory than Frankford's soliloquy in the study – only, a more explicitly material one. It purports to 'freely give' to Anne the material elements of a privacy which it actually takes away from her. Paradoxically, her theatrical presence is henceforth consigned to her bed-chamber, associated now with self-mortification and death. Anne's response in self-starvation is an attempt to reclaim the dignity denied her by the inequality of the magnanimous verdict. Her body is the only private possession she is left with, and through its control, she can 'redeem her honour' (xiii, 135), and resist being assimilated into Frankford's objects of bounty, both material and intangible – manorhouses, beds and servants, as well as disproportionate and self-conscious lenience:

---

[78] Revealingly, Heywood's company paid out less for the play itself than for Anne's dress – 'vellvet & satten for the womon gowne of blacke vellvet': see *Henslowe's Diary*, I, 119v–120v.

> He cannot be so base as to forgive me,
> Nor I so base as to accept his pardon.
>
>   (xiii, 140–1)

Frankford's 'usage/Of more humility' carries resonances of a humiliation that can result from a calculated denial of the dignity of justice. It is precisely this humbling that Anne resists by her spirited self-abnegation.

But this scene, and Anne's gesture, remain precariously poised between Anne's self-presentation, and the risk of that being absorbed into the more elaborate theatre of her husband's kind judgement. After all, the humanist legacy of Frankford's oeconomic negotiations comes complete with the idea of theatrical correction of wives, foregrounding the avoidance of cruelty. Erasmus, in his *Colloquy on Marriage*, offers a sort of parable of 'kindness' in correction being a more effective way of disciplining a wayward wife than either the sanctions of ecclesiastical courts or the use of corporal punishment. This is the story of a More-like figure who decides to bring his wife into line by staging a threat of physical violence which is then not carried out. This he does with the help of his own father-in-law, '[preferring] to have her cured by [his] skill' rather than use 'blows', though he knows that violence is within his rights. The older man rises to the occasion with some relish, till his

speech grew so heated that he seemed barely to keep his hands off her. (For he's a man of marvelous cunning, capable of playing any comedy without a mask). Moved partly by fear, partly by truth, the girl promptly went down on her knees . . .

This is followed by extravagant pardon by both father and husband, and the ensuring of lifelong obedience. As a counter-example, the narrator, Eulalia, goes on to tell a story of a 'husband reformed by a wife's kindness'.[79]

The young wife's amazement into obedience is the function of a theatricality that also characterises the action of Heywood's play. In the sub-plot, the moment of staging a transaction becomes a way of reversing the transaction – Mountford offers his sister as a repayment of his debts, but the calculated theatricality of this extreme gesture of generosity is meant to 'amaze' the senses of his benefactor Acton. But Acton reverses this gift in offering to marry Susan and turning the dishonouring prostitution into an elevating alliance for Mountford. In the main plot, this self-reflexive theatrical transformation of indignity into civility is additionally harnessed to evidentiary concerns. The vivid, and vividly staged, rhetorical proof of

---

[79] Erasmus, *Colloquies*, 114–27 (120–2).

Frankford's kindness is designed to cancel out the meaner evidence culled in his shady, seamy nocturnal tracking, both the content and the process. The bed of erotic transgression, which we never have to see in the discovery scene, is replaced in our full sight by the bed of refined penitence and ostentatious lenity – now for the first time presented as a central property (xvii, 38). It is as if the unspeakable and unrepresentable are suddenly brought within the bounds of decency and representation, even as the tone of the play modulates. Yet this is achieved by an extreme application of the humanist and Erasmian notion of curing and cleansing through kindness. For here, too, is a bed where someone gets 'killed', like Desdemona, like Duncan, except that the kindred circle of witnesses can provide the perfect alibi. In a strange twist, the rhetorical proof of the less crude kind of evidence, often privileged by literary forms, becomes more dubious still than demonstrative proof. Its refinement becomes a function of insidiousness and persuasive fiction. Ethically suspect translation, even transference, masquerades as transcendence. In this general 'orgy of clemency',[80] impeccably staged, Anne's spectacular resistance seems as fragile as the lute she sends to be broken on the wheel, but all the more poignant because in danger of being upstaged through appropriation into a rather different drama where she is less an agent than a 'token'. Heywood's own representation, meanwhile, teeters between complicity and critique, as he forges a specifically civilised genre for his own play but also points up the dubiousness that such a knowing project might entail in human and moral terms. Its reflexivity about staging extends beyond the issue of physically representable evidence to the ethics of fashioning representability.

The full significance of 'kindness', thus, is part of the play's complex vision of the genteelness of its action. At once denoting an act of equity and a criterion of gentility, 'kindness' encapsulates the range of experience and attitudes that adjudication of adultery brings together in a bourgeois domestic set-up. The fact of adultery, after all, challenges both senses of the word. In *Woman Killed*, kindness, understood in this double sense, is what reunites the processes of evidence and of judgement in both moral and generic terms, albeit in an uneasy and self-aware union.

Though the real-life adultery case against Bridget Edmunds lacks such a neat and self-conscious ending, it helps us understand historically the domestication of justice in a play like *Woman Killed*, dealing with adultery as a private wrong, privately judged. It enacts the operations of justice

---

[80] A. D. Nuttall's phrase for the last scene of *MfM*, in '*Measure for Measure*: Quid Pro Quo', 239.

within a bourgeois middle-class home in the early stages of investigation, and reveals the containment of justice within the close-knit academic community at the end. While Covile is let off with a warning after compurgation by fellows of various Cambridge colleges,[81] the records do not offer space to Bridget for self-presentation, beyond telling us that she was subjected to public penance. Nor is she traceable among the surviving parish records, while Covile died a respected and well-placed man, as Sub-Dean of Lincoln Cathedral and Prebendary of Lincoln, and John Edmunds as a successful Cambridge businessman.

CODA

The current critical orthodoxy is that property – both in the theatrical and domestic senses – usually implies male proprietorial control in the early modern theatre. In the case of *Woman Killed*, especially, it has been widely argued that the abundance of objects on stage are a way of defining Frankford's material hold over his various spaces, and the vulnerability of his wife in relation to this.[82] Catherine Richardson, in particular, offers a detailed study of household inventories to argue how certain spaces filled with things, such as the parlour, theatrically signify the storage and display of wealth; and that the properties used in the play as a whole define ownership of spaces and enable the audience to read the 'past of the Frankford family, . . . its networks of kin and inheritance', as well as to mark 'competitive social distinctions'; she goes on to say that 'the banishment of Anne from the family home with a small number of possessions, can then be seen against this background, starker and more meaningful as a result'.[83] To a large extent, I have implicitly gone along with this view, and have certainly identified unacknowledged patriarchal perversities in the 'kind' treatment of the adulterous wife. However, there is one scene in the play which gives me pause. This is scene xv, where Cranwell enters to find Frankford searching each room of his house frantically, and asks him the meaning of this, since his wife has been 'dispatched . . . away' anyway. Frankford replies,

> O sir, to see that nothing may be left
> That ever was my wife's. I loved her dearly,
> And when I do but think of her unkindness,

---

[81] CUL, V.C. Court I.3, III, 114v.
[82] Notable recent instances are Richardson, 'Properties', and Orlin, *Private Matters*, 141–54.
[83] Richardson, 'Properties', 143, 148 and passim.

My thoughts are in hell, to avoid which torment,
I would not have a bodkin or a cuff,
A bracelet, necklace, or rebato wire,
Nor anything that ever was called hers
Left me, by which I might remember her.

(xv, 3–10)

Nick, at this point, discovers Anne's lute 'flung in a corner' (12). This single property, intimately associated with Anne, whether or not it was technically bought by Frankford, acts unmistakably as a memorial token with deeply personal associations and evokes a vignette of the moments of felicity that the couple did share. What it triggers off is this unwonted speech from Frankford, authentic in its tone of utter loss:

Her lute! O God, upon this instrument
Her fingers have run quick division,
Sweeter than that which now divides our hearts.
These frets have made me pleasant, that have now
Frets of my heartstrings made. O Master Cranwell,
Oft hath she made this melancholy wood,
Now mute and dumb for her disastrous chance,
Speak sweetly many a note, sound many a strain
To her own ravishing voice, which being well strung,
What pleasant strange airs they have jointly sung.
Post with it after her. Now nothing's left;
Of her and hers I am at once bereft.   (13–24)

Here, for once, the play is staging a rather different relationship to property than the obvious and much-expounded proprietorial one. 'Things' are shown to be capable of standing for feelings, values and relationships, not simply 'the trappings of an emergent bourgeois culture'.[84] The house suddenly becomes 'bereft', and the level at which this sentiment is registered is not the proprietorial one. The very movements of evidence-collection are reversed as Frankford is seen to 'search each room about [his] house', but this time in an act of coming to terms emotionally with these hollowed spaces and confronting the values they once stood for. In fact, this moment suddenly offers yet another way of reading the title, suggested by Wendoll's comment when, later, he visits Anne and finds her playing on this very token, the lute: 'I'll do my best good will,/To work a cure on her whom I did kill' (xvi, 99–100): the improper 'kindness' he showed to Anne (and 'her unkindness' too) must

---

[84] Ibid., 135.

share, with the kindness of gentlemanly judgement, the blame for the price that has been paid. It makes him realise, too, that he has 'divorced the truest turtles/That ever lived together' (48–9). It is only now, in loss, that the now-lost togetherness is glimpsed. If the 'companionate marriage' of the play had been *merely* a class arrangement, and the various objects merely possessions, they would not have borne such a sense of personal value, nor such a personal sense of loss.[85] The lute becomes a particularly eloquent symbol of the lost sharing – no wonder Anne chooses this, out of the numerous properties she is allowed to retain, to be broken on the wheel almost in figuration of her own self. This scene's simultaneous sense of emptiness, and the need to actively empty one's own space of memories of lost happiness, have less to do with specifically early modern notions of husbandry than with a cross-historically familiar emotionality. But it is precisely because this operates in a context of early modern oeconomic structures of feeling that it is poignant in a distinct way, and constitutes the irreducible surplus at the heart of the play which cannot be explained away by schematic readings of property and propriety. Other, more complex, sentiments are inextricably tangled with these percepts, not unlike the way in which emerging notions of privacy have been shown to be embedded in more orthodox circumscriptions. The pathos at the end of the play, when well-performed, extends beyond class-specific, self-conscious projection to an elusive sense of real pity and waste. This is what makes the play invite readers and directors again and again, and refuse to seal itself off entirely in some easy materialist parable.

---

[85] See ibid., 135, for an example of how the notion of gentlemanliness in *WKK* is often by implication reduced in criticism to 'the acquisitions made imperative by consumerism, . . . without which the definition of status has . . . become difficult to achieve'. No doubt, these acquisitions are important for the definition of class, and part of it, but they would not add up to Frankford's own sense of his status without the supplement of immaterial possessions which straddle the social and the deeply personal. See also nn. 17 and 18 above.

CHAPTER 3

Evidence and representation on 'the theatre of God's judgements': A Warning for Fair Women

Drama, amongst other staged spectacles, was the target of unceasing attack from moralists and reformers from the 1550s.[1] This virulent criticism, strongest in the 1580s and 1590s, was partly an expression of Protestant iconophobia, and partly a Puritan association of the theatre with moral and sexual laxity. Philip Stubbes's *An Anatomy of Abuses* (1584), one of the most outspoken works in this populous tradition, denounces plays for 'alluring . . . People . . . to Theatres and vnclean assemblies',[2] '*Venus* pallace, & sathans synagogue':

Do they not maintaine bawdrie . . . induce whordom . . .? . . . marke the flocking and running to Theatres & curtens . . . where such wanton gestures . . . such kissing and bussing, such clipping and culling, Suche winkinge and glancinge of wanton eyes . . . is vsed, as is wonderfull to behold. Then, these goodlye pageants beinge done . . . euery one brings another homeward . . . and in their secret conclaues (couertly) they play *the Sodomits*, or worse. (144–5)

His list also specifies the danger of examples 'painted before your eyes' by a 'Cosoners trick' (146). At the same time, such reformists recognised a need for visual representation and drama's efficacy as a vehicle. A particular kind of drama was allowed, as a concession to flawed, sense-bound human capacities which must be reached through concrete forms. Such images would be

---

[1] See Gosson, *Plays Confuted* and *School of Abuse*; Munday, *Second and Third Blast*; Crosse, *Vertues Commonwealth*; Ascham, *Scholemaster*; and, later, Prynne, *Histriomastix*.
[2] Stubbes, *Anatomy* (b), xi; 143. (This is a slightly different edition of Stubbes, *Anatomy* (a), which is an incomplete but fuller text. Page numbers refer to the former unless otherwise specified.) The first known anti-theatrical tract was Northbrooke, *Treatise*. The relevant secondary literature includes Barish, *Anti-Theatrical Prejudice*, Heinemann, *Puritanism* and Collinson, *From Iconoclasm to Iconophobia*, esp. 8 ff.

dyvysed to . . . *declare lyvely before the peoples eies* the . . . wickednes of the bisshop of Rome . . . and to . . . *open to them* thobedience that your subiects *by goddes and mans lawe* owe unto your magestie. Into the commen people thynges sooner enter by the eies, then by the eares . . . (italics mine)[3]

The anonymous 1590s play, *A Warning for Fair Women*, probably performed at the Curtain (among Stubbes's 'Venus pallaces'),[4] and centrally concerned with 'bawdie loue',[5] murder, and a defiance of God's law, distinguishes its own act of representation from the 'Cosoners trick'. It foregrounds its distance from its action by aligning itself with an existing body of opinions about the uses and abuses of drama; and by attempting to forge a generic identity legitimate by the moralists' own standards – 'honest & chast playes, tragedies & enterluds . . . for the good example of life, for the auoyding of . . . euill' (x). It is the '*abuses*' of dramatic exercises that Stubbes deplores (xii). The burden of the abuse seems to be borne by 'commedies', whose 'ground' is 'loue, bawdrie, cosenage, flattery, whordome, adulterie' (143). Tragedies are potentially but not inherently evil, and can be used to a proper end (x).

Significantly, it is Tragedy who, with whip and knife, sweeps the stage clear of Hystorie and Comedie in the Induction to *Warning*. She defines her genre against the 'abuses' of the other two. Comedie's description of her as 'mistris buskins with a whirligig' (*Warning*, 19), 'Murthers Beadle' (26) and 'pure purple Buskin, blood and murther right' (69) conjures up a lurid vision of Italianate revenge tragedies – or, at any rate, an unChristian, undignified and hamming tradition (50–64, 67–9) – recalling Stubbes's strictures on corrupt tragedies.[6] Tragedy's indignant reply not only distinguishes her role from comic levity (41), but also emphasises that she is no common cut-throat and blood-spiller in heated foreign lands (70–7), any more than her 'faire circuite' of 'Auditors' are injudicial (92, 83). Her

> . . . Sceane is London, native and your owne,
> I sighe to thinke, my subject too well knowne . . .
> (96–7)

In its conscious difference from a cruder form of tragedy and its assertion of native roots, *Warning* is comparable to Heywood's *Woman Killed*. Both

---

[3] *Discourse Touching the Reformation*, 179.
[4] See Gurr, *Shakespearean Stage*, 228. On the possibilities of Globe performances, see Hosley, 'Discovery-Space', 36.
[5] Stubbes, *Anatomy*, viii.
[6] Stubbes, *Anatomy*, 143. References to *Warning* cite running line numbers.

plays belong to the broader category of 'domestic tragedy', treating ordinary middle-class people rather than dignitaries or royalty; showing household catastrophes rather than state affairs; and focusing on the pivotal domestic relationship (marriage) and its desecration. They also share a preoccupation with the discovery of 'crime', as well as its theatrical representation. And yet, the two plays belong to distinct worlds: the common features only sharpen the difference. This chapter shows how generic investments determine the treatment of related issues, including privacy, discovery and 'domesticity'; and how the status of evidence radically differs according to these investments. In placing itself carefully within a genre which is not predominantly dramatic, *Warning* has to negotiate the problems of its use of the theatrical medium at the same time as it exploits its opportunities. What emerges is a theatre of judgement premised on a self-consciously transparent dramaturgy, but one that involves specific and complex viewing relations. The play seems steadfast in its providentialist project, though some tensions necessarily arise from the encounter between homily and drama, between God's theatre, man's, and the devil's, and therefore between different criteria of judgement.

THE DUMB SHOWS

The dumb shows are an early statement of the play's representational strategies, and of the nature of its engagement with signs – behavioural, legal, providential and theatrical. In *Woman Killed*, where Anne Frankford is won over by Wendoll's love, Nick, watching unseen, resolves to 'turn a spy' and 'have an eye/In all their gestures' (vi, 174, 180). In that scene, where Anne's agency is elusive, and where bodily expressions of inner states preoccupy her progressively, Nick's comment highlights the interface between evidence and 'gestures', an interface constituted by the act of interpretation, with all its ambiguities.[7] In *Warning*, by contrast, gestures constitute the well-established semiotic of the dumb shows: they are *performed* – a set of conventionally choreographed, collectively interpretable signs. The opacity of human gestures is replaced by the transparency of allegorical action. This aims to resolve the problem of representing ambiguous action in a play premised on an unmisgiving notion of correspondence between inner and outer; in a genre which

---

[7] Presumably, Nick sees the pair kiss as he enters; he has not heard the preceding dialogue, and they leave soon after he enters. Though he hears Wendoll's words at 161–2 and 164–5, the observed gesture is the prime impact on him here. Cf. Shakespeare, *WT*, I.ii, where Leontes watches and interprets the gestures of Hermione and Polixenes.

assumes God to be the ultimate overseer of human motives, as well as their sole discoverer to the world. Linked on the one hand with the inward, and on the other with the rhetorical and the constructed, the dumb show straddles divine and human vantage points, both what God sees and what He shows.

Symptomatically, these shows combine allegorical with real characters, a type identified by B. R. Pearn as the rare 'intermediate type' of dumb show typical of the 1590s when popular taste was turning away from purely symbolic spectacle to a more realistic mode integral to a play's action.[8] Tragedy summons the Furies, in the first show, to prepare a bloody banquet – all in good classical style. Then Lust and Chastity enter, morality fashion, but with the diners – George Sanders, a London merchant, his wife Anne, her wooer, and lover-to-be, George Browne, Mistress Drury the widow and go-between and her man Roger.[9] The ensuing action takes the place of the temptation scene, intervening between the scenes of Anne's resistance of Browne's courtship, and Browne's first attempt at murdering Sanders, clearly with Anne's consent. Mehl criticises the first dumb show as an evasive pantomime which avoids the dramatic challenge of showing Anne's conversion.[10] Mehl is right to spot that a crucial event in the plot is relegated to a dumb show, but misses the point of this relegation. The dumb show is a conscious choice of a mode of representation, articulating the play's particular notion of 'action'.

The last we hear from Anne Sanders before the first dumb show is her capitulation to Mistress Drury's persuasions to accept it as her fate – since the lines on her palms say so – that her husband is soon to die and she to be wedded to Browne, though her heart is not inclined to 'new affection' (759). Drury, the stereotypical bawd, seizes the moment:

> For this will hammer so within her head,
> As for the new, sheele wish the old were dead . . .
>
> (764–5)

Tragedy enters straight away, with a bowl of blood, and declares the function of the ensuing dumb show:

> Al we have done, hath only been in words,
> But now we come unto the dismall act . . .
>
> (776–7)

---

[8] Pearn, 'Dumb-Show', 385–405 (392); see Mehl, *Elizabethan Dumb Show*, 90–6; Foster, 'Dumb Show', 8–17.

[9] Compare the curious mixture of allegorical and real-life characters in the dramatis personae.

[10] Mehl, *Elizabethan Dumb Show*, 92.

'Dismall act' invokes a theatrical dimension, reinforced by a recital of stage props – 'curtains', 'hell' and 'tapers' (778–81). Tragedy makes a curious and specifically theatrical distinction between doing in words and doing in action: 'Al we have done, hath only been in words'; there has only been talk so far, no deed. But the notion of expressive action as a performative tool, fashioned according to rhetorical prescriptions, was current in psychological theories of inward passions and physical expression. Thomas Wright, in his important physiognomical treatise *The Passions of the Minde in Generall* (1604), writes

The internall conceits and affections of our minds, are not onely expressed with words, but also declared with actions: as it appeareth in Comedies, where dumbe shewes often *express* the whole matter, by gestures . . . The rhetoricians likewise . . . prescribe many rules of action . . . how much more liuely it *representeth* the conceits and affections of the minde, because that thorow the eares and the eyes of their auditors, they intend to imprint them in their soules the deeper . . . (italics mine)[11]

Paradoxically, 'words' are the more immediately expressive medium in our play, while the 'damned deed' (782) must be externalised through static symbols. But what *is* the deed?

The *word* 'deed' rings like a dismal toll through the play. Joane, finding her man John Beane nearly slain to death, exclaims, 'Wo worth him *John* that did this dismal deede' (1468), and anticipates Mistress Drury's hapless recognition of the *fait accompli*: 'thou wilt, alas/That ere this dismal deede was brought to passe,/But now 'tis done . . .' (1748). In the second dumb show, the murderous 'deed' is emblematically reconnected with the act of seduction:

enter Lust bringing forth Browne *and* Roger, *at one end mistres* Sanders *and mistres* Drurie *at the other, they offering cheerfully to meete and embrace, suddenly riseth up a great tree betweene them, whereat amazedly they step backe, whereupon* Lust *bringeth an axe to mistres* Sanders, *shewing signes, that she should cut it downe, which she refuseth, albeit mistres* Drurie *offers to help her. Then* Lust *brings the Axe to* Browne, *and shewes the like signes to him as before, whereupon he roughlie and suddenly hewes down the tree, and then they run togither and embrace.*

Tragedy explains that the tree 'represents' Anne's husband (1290). Anne could not be moved to murder him herself. So Browne 'gives the fatal stroke unto the tree' (1296). But Tragedy's qualification of Anne's innocence has been linguistically suggestive: '. . . though by them seduced to

---

[11] Wright, *Passions*, 124.

consent,/And had a finger in her husband's blood'. Ostensibly referring
to her 'consent' to the killing, the juxtaposition with 'seduced' simultaneously suggests a rather different order of consent. The description of the
murder is instantly followed by the sinful coupling in the explication of
the dumb show: 'Which being done, they then embrace togither/The act
performed, now *Chastitie* appeares', distraught (1299). The order of
events opens up the word 'act' to polyvalence, though it refers primarily
to the murder. As the common legal description of murder as 'fact' comes
up moments later with Anne 'repenting of the fact' (1302), one distinguishes the 'act performed', the act of adultery which can only be staged
through performative words and representative action, from the fact of
murder.[12]

Lest the action gets too expressive without descriptive checks to imaginative readings, Tragedy '[expresses]' the action after Anne's tearful
departure and Roger following Lust with his sword:

> What's here exprest, in act is to be done,
> The sworde is drawne, the murtherer forth doth run,
> *Lust* leads him on . . .
> The onely actor in this damned deed.   (1304–7)

The 'act' here is theatrical action, and the 'deed' in the final line now
means, exclusively, the murder. The following scene (viii) stages the
stabbing, but not lust in action. Yet, it opens with Browne's reference to
Anne's encouragement of the murder:

> Did I but waver, or were unresolv'd,
> These lines were able to encourage me,
> Sweet *Nan* I kiss thy name, and for thy sake,
> What coward would not venture more then this?
> Kil him? Yea, were his life ten thousand lives,
> Not any sparke or cynder of the same
> Should be unquencht in bloud at thy request.
>
>   (1309–15)

---

[12] See Glossary on 'fact'. The emphasis in law on the *fact* of crime is typically reiterated in providential
tales of crime, where crime *is* a self-evident fact. Cf. *Warning* 2246, 2421–2; Golding, *Briefe Discourse*,
219–20. Compare the descriptions of Stow and Holinshed, two other contemporary chroniclers of
the Sanders case, Apps E and F in *Warning*, 231–3 (232) and 234–6 (235). For an official reference to
'Saunders' [wyfe's] facte' (1573), see *Acts of the Privy Council*, VIII, 121, 105. See Martin, *Francis Bacon*,
77, on 'fact' as 'evil deed'. See Rollins, *Old English Ballads*, 347, for 'The wofull lamentacon of
Mrs. *Anne Saunders*' where Anne bewails her 'bloudy facte'. Compare Reynolds, *Triumphs*, Bk I, 63,
where wife-murderer Alibius '[hangs] for the fact'.

This letter will, later, constitute important evidence of Anne's complicity. Thus, while the real action of the play focuses on the killing, the symbolic action of the dumb shows connects the two deeds of blood – murder and adultery. But consciously or unconsciously, the word 'deed' both limits and multiplies signification. In the legal episodes (xiv–xvi), it is repeatedly used to denote the murder (2125, 2317, 2290–1). But the sense of sexual 'deed' is never quite effaced (2137–40), and is continued in the Officers' gossip about the fate of 'lustie *Browne*' (2163–9). The third dumb show gathers up the shifting and accreting connotations of the word 'deed(s)' (1780–4).

In retrospect, the first dumb show clearly encapsulates the key action at the outset, anticipating the association of murder with illicit desire. The central spectacle depicts the tussle between Lust and Chastity, as Anne '*thrusteth* Chastity *from her*', in a psychomachic tableau (812). By the time Tragedy rubs blood from her bowl on to the hands of the 'actors' in the 'impious deed' (856), the sexual and criminal strands of this sinful 'plot' (796) are indistinguishable. Browne's exhortation to 'sable night' to cover his 'deede of darknesse' in the next scene fuses the two associations:

> My guiltie soule, burnt with lusts hateful fire,
> Must wade through bloud, t'obtaine my vile desire . . .
>
> (910–11)

Thus, while the dumb shows claim representational autonomy, their purposeful indirection lends a density to the play's medium which would seem to run counter to its resolute moral simplicity. The mingling of murder and adultery through linguistic slippage undercuts the ostensible transparency of the shows. As allegorical action slides into real action – a triumphant '*Lust drinckes to Browne, he to Mistris* Sanders, *she pledgeth him*' – the real action itself becomes symbolic of another kind of pledging (just as the visible embrace of Browne and Anne in the second dumb show stands for the necessarily invisible act of sex), as psychological and behavioural allegories are combined.

'THIS TRUE AND HOME-BORNE TRAGEDIE'[13]

The conflation of lust and murder is more than just an ironic by-product of attempts to forge an emblematic mode of expression. It is a theme signalling *Warning*'s generic identity. The contemporary providentialist

---

[13] *Warning*, 2729.

corpus within which the play inserts itself frequently focused on actual events dealing with crime and punishment, presenting them as demonstrations of divine judgement, as miraculous as they were inevitable. Providentialism, broadly speaking, was the belief that all human action and natural phenomena are preordained and overseen by God, and a manifestation of the workings of His hand. Though it was particularly associated with Protestant thinking and polemic, several classical and medieval treatises on providence were also published in early modern England.[14] The distinct understandings of providentialist thought produced an appropriately mixed popular literary genre, combining stern Protestant narratives of judgement with lurid elements derived from various un-Protestant fields. The best-known anthology of providentialist 'histories' was Thomas Beard's *The Theatre of God's Judgements* (1597), followed by John Reynolds's *The Triumphs of God's Revenge* (1621–35), both introduced in Chapter 2. Alongside, there was a vast body of moralistic pamphlets drawing on native, topical events, usually of crime and punishment. Sometimes they told of incredible occurrences, marks of God's judgement for human wickedness.[15] The familiarity of the examples was meant to strike home the moral message; their emphasis was, like that of our play, on the 'true and home-borne' nature of the instances. Anthologies of tales or 'histories', on the other hand, combined home-bred examples with far-flung ones, from distant lands of profligate habits, but appropriately 'domesticated' and familiarised.

For such publications, both murder and sexual immorality were highly marketable subjects. When the two combined, there could be no better: witness the Italianate judgement tales that found their way into Beard and Reynolds. But the interesting feature is an imaginative association between the two, whether or not they coincided in the same story.[16] As Reynolds puts it, 'Lust is a sin which for the most part goes accompanied with other enormities, as having adultery and blood both attendant of her.'[17]

Penalties for sexual sins are often discussed in terms identical with the punishment for homicide, though their legal statuses were significantly

---

[14] The authoritative study of providentialism in sixteenth- and seventeenth-century England is Walsham, *Providence*: on different strands within providentialist discourse, see 8–20.

[15] See the typical and suggestive title of Munday's *A View of Sundry examples . . . straunge murthers, sundry persons perjured, signes and tokens of Gods anger towards us*. On the Calvinist contribution to the notion implicit here, see Kendall, *Calvin*. On its medieval legacy, see Vance, *Mervelous Signals*.

[16] See T.M., *Blood for Blood*, Bk II, 53 – a typical inheritor of Beard and Reynolds, often recycling their 'Histories'.

[17] Reynolds, *Triumphs*, 90–1.

different. This I believe derives from the Calvinist ancestry of much of this corpus, albeit filtered through a rag-bag of older popular beliefs, some even of Catholic origins.[18] The main strands feeding into this association in popular providentialism were a broadly Puritan connection, derived largely from Mosaic law; adultery tales, often with violent ends demonstrating divine retribution; and the decalogue tradition, associated during the Reformation with Calvin's sermons. Not only did the Calvinist context explicitly connect the natures of adultery and murder as offences, rather than simply linking them through a theory of appropriate penalties, but also underlies the source of *Warning*. Arthur Golding, author of *A Briefe Discourse of the Murther of G. Sanders* (1573), the direct source for *Warning*, translated several of Calvin's works, including the *Treatise concerning offences* (1567). This treatise repeatedly links diverse offences. Straight after the prohibition against murder, Calvin introduces 'The xxxviii. Sermon' including 'Thou shalt not be an Advouterer' (18)[19] through a comment on the juxtaposition – God's rather than his:

... But here God *interlaceth* a lawe that forbideth to commit adulterie ... For ... if wee bee unchast, wanton, or of beastly conversation: we must not think that God is contented with us. Uprightnes & Sobernes are things inseparable: for God Hath ioyned them togither in his lawe ... (224)

Golding's *Briefe Discourse* stresses that 'the steps of a harlot leade downe unto death' (228). Anne, proved guilty of complicity in her husband's murder, is sentenced to death. But her conversion to illicit love is seen as the *primum mobile*. After the legal proceedings, she is remembered as a 'harlot', her harlotry being associated with both deaths – crime as well as punishment.[20]

Part of the suggestiveness of the sex–murder association through designated gestures in the play has, of course, to do with the limits of contemporary theatrical representation. In *The Changeling*, a play belonging more to Reynolds's world of lust, vengeance and judgement than to the refined domesticities of *Woman Killed* or the scrupulous

---

[18] See, e.g., Goodcole's tracts *Heavens speedie hue and cry* and *The adulteresses funerall day* (1635). Cf. Walsham, *Providence*, 70–5 (75).

[19] Calvin, *Treatise*, 224. 'Advouterer' is often used for 'adulterer' in this translation (225).

[20] Cf. Webster, *WD*, III.ii.108–9: 'Next the devil, Adult'ry,/Enters the devil, Murder'. Saxey, *Straunge and Wonderfull Example*, suggests how, in printed tracts or ballads, the sexual aspect of a sensational murder could be abstracted from its criminal context. Saxey includes the Sanders trial without mentioning that it was a murder trial; the judgement is configured as a 'fayre warning' against adultery (A8).

pieties of *Warning*, the finger Deflores cuts off the slain Alonzo's body and presents to Beatrice-Joanna becomes a symbol of the overlap between death and sex. Both murder and adultery are unrepresentable, secret acts occurring in the closet in the last scene, and can only be heard in the form of a suggestive 'dying' moan, almost in instant answer to Tomazo's call for 'a recompence for murder and adultery', a 'cause' so 'urgent in blood' (V.iii.140–1, 136–7). The providential end is common to both plays, but *Warning*, like its source tract, pre-empts a response that may have more of relish than of piety in it, while the dramatic interest of *The Changeling* lies elsewhere. *Warning*'s own emblems owe more to the specific dangers of the exemplary genre, forestalling attacks such as Stubbes's, which do not even spare plays with an apparent moral purpose:

[Plays on religious subjects are sacrilegous because Christian themes] . . . are iested at . . . or . . . enterlaced with . . . wanton shewes, vncomely gestures . . .[21]

Even Beard makes a careful distinction between 'pure and holy . . . embracings' and the 'vnlawfull Gestures' and 'kisses of . . . lecherous wretches'.[22] Such distinctions are analogous to *Warning*'s use of dumb shows to represent 'lecherous' embraces through 'pure' gestures, given that sex and death come as a package in this genre.

Significantly, the play suppresses two episodes of obvious dramatic potential, both mentioned in the source. In *A Briefe Discourse*, Anne Sanders 'was delivered of childe & churched' after Sanders's death and before her arraignment, but while the case was already in progress (219). This is quickly passed over in the play, with a bare mention of Anne's confinement (2343–5). Since the date of the commencement of her relationship with Browne is left unspecified in all the sources (Golding, Stow and Holinshed), and the play chooses to relegate that whole chapter to dumb shows, it is impossible to calculate possibilities of an illegitimate pregnancy. But in a case centrally involving adultery, the pregnancy of a woman implicated in her husband's death would have aroused speculation. It would also be lucrative material for drama. Likewise, the fascinating episode of Mr Mell the prison minister who falls in love with Anne, tries to cover up her fault, and is publicly and spectacularly punished, is only fleetingly present in the play.[23] Such excisions seem to

---

[21] Stubbes, *Anatomy*, 140–1. See Calvin's distinction between 'gestures and words' in *Treatise*, 227.
[22] Beard, *Theatre*, 425–6.
[23] Golding, *Briefe Discourse*, 221–2. *Warning*, 2484–2522.

be strategic. The problem, precisely, is that these events are too dramatic, and could hamper the play's self-fashioning as a purely providential project. What even Golding could do, in words chaste and few, the playwright needed to be wary of, because his medium had a vexed status. Even among the Puritan exponents of the didactic potential of enargeic drama, there was a simultaneous awareness of the risks, owing to the risky mediation of style and tone. The depiction of evil was meant to be exclusively aimed at arousing horror, and must exclude involvement, or aesthetic delight:

> when the . . . sins of men are . . . shown in action, as though before our eyes, even the crimes of the most abandoned of men, yet some dread of divine judgement and of a horror of sin should appear in them: no exultant delight in crime or shameless insolence should be displayed.[24]

'THE SPECTACLES OF GOD'S LAW'[25]

As in most adultery plots, and notably in *Woman Killed*, secrecy is an initial imperative in *Warning*. Mistress Drury advises Browne that the 'oportunitie' for a first meeting 'must be watch'd, but verie secretly' (286–7), and Browne seals the pact with a promise of reward conditional upon reciprocal secrecy (319–20). Domestic topography also seems as central to the representation of adultery here as in Heywood. As Browne approaches, Anne is discovered sitting 'at her doore' (s.d., 322),[26] awaiting her husband's return from the Exchange – a moment marking the inception of their relationship. This liminal space is eloquent of how adultery was perceived and experienced: the rupture of a personal, intimate stability which involved, at the same time, a violation of ownership and usurpation of property. The need for privacy was proportional to the publicness of the legal 'fact' of adultery. Thus, the threshold of the bourgeois household suggests the curious location of the marital and the domestic on the thin line between interior and communal, private and public. Adultery defines, and is defined by, this territory.[27] In *Woman Killed*, we saw 'close conveyances' in love and 'close' surveillance coming together in the closeness of domestic space. The secrecy woven by Browne, Drury and Roger is comparable to Wendoll's in Heywood's

---

[24] Bucer, as quoted in Wickham, *Early English Stages*, II, Part II, i, 330.
[25] Golding, *Briefe Discourse*, 227.
[26] Described by Anne defensively as her 'his [her husband's] door' (364).
[27] On the domestic threshold as a representational emblem of the distinction 'between home and world' in early modern Dutch painting, see Schama, *Embarrassment*, 570–96.

play. But the analogy ends there. For the complementary closeness of the investigator transposes itself on to a very different evidentiary structure in *Warning*. When Drury calls Roger her 'heart's interpreter' and exhorts him to be 'secret' (442–3), an instructed audience would remember that the one and only 'heart's intrepreter' is God, in whose eyes all secrets are already always apparent. This scene places criminal psychology within a providentialist context. The negotiation of social and amorous privacies in *Warning* gives way to a need to secure a different order of privacy, as Browne resolves to go ahead with his 'black deed' (855, 915). Macbeth-like, he exhorts the night to hide his intentions (910–15, 1347–8). His acute awareness of the public gaze just before his execution becomes inseparable from a larger structure where he sees himself as a spectacle for diverse onlookers, human and divine, external and inward (2387).

A comparison with the language and imagery of another domestic play, Yarrington's *Two Lamentable Tragedies*, also partly based on a much-publicised contemporary murder, underlines the generic and moral underpinnings of the notions of secrecy and revelation in *Warning*.[28] Here, key and closet, secrecy and invasion, enclosure and entry are part of the preliminary drama of 'a hart wide open to receive/A plot of horrid desolation' (A2v):

> The plots are laide, the keyes of golden coine,
> Hath op'd the secret closets of their harts . . .
>
> (A2v)

When these terms are later applied to detection and disclosure, they are already theologically laden. In the second part of *2LT*, Falleria's scornful defiance of God's power to witness and his assurance in the inviolability of his sinful secret (the murder of his orphaned nephew) are touched with proleptic irony, like Mistress Drury's smugness:

> The God of heauen can truely testify,
> Which to speake plaine, is nere a whit at all. *To the people.*
> Which knowes the secret corners of my heart . . .   (B)

To the hired ruffians, he 'ope[s] the closet of [his] brest' and urges 'cunning secrecie' (Dv). The language of concealment only anticipates the inevitability of disclosure:[29] remember Swinburne's warning about

---

[28] Yarrington, *2LT*.

[29] Cf. the image of God as spy in the ballad, *The Complaint and lamentation of Mistress Arden* (1633?), in *Arden*, App. 4, 165–8. Compare Yarrington, *2LT*, B3.

'the tribunal of the Infallible Judge, to whom all things (how secret soever) be all naked and open' (*Spousals*, 198). But while in Swinburne's legal treatise, such 'asides' imply an awareness of the necessary limits to evidentiary processes, in *Warning* this consciousness exposes human presumption in attempting secrecy. 'Discovery' does not entail the suspense of the doubting husband's nocturnal investigation, nor the uncertainty surrounding the judicial resolution of anagnoristic plots. Instead, it is an uncovering, a revelation as inevitable as it is indubitable. The status of signs and tokens, correspondingly, is radically different. This involves a reversal of the spectatorial relations in secular adultery plays such as Heywood's. The drama, in exemplary 'domestic' plays about crime and punishment, is configured as the theatre of God's judgement.

The single most important collection drawing together all these elements of providentialism, and almost defining it as a genre, Beard's compendium *The Theatre of God's Judgements* straddles Protestant moralistic agenda and sensationalist presentation.[30] Complete with specific evidentiary strategies, it provides an elementary framework for the providentialist dramaturgy developed in such plays as *Warning* and *Two Lamentable Tragedies*. Its narratives of discovery '[lay] open' to the reader, as upon a stage, the spectacle of God's judgements, to chasten sin-beclouded humanity:

. . . murderers, whoremongers, adulterers rauishers and tyrans shall here see by the mischiefe that hath fallen vpon their likes, that which hangeth before their eyes . . .[31]

Individual 'histories' are foregrounded as theatrical 'spectacles'. Steven Gardiner, upon celebrating the burning of Ridley and Cranmer, promptly came to a 'wretched end, with his tongue all blacke and swolne, hanging out of his mouth horribly: a spectacle worthie to be beholden of all such bloodie burning prosecutors' (62). 'It was a lamentable spectacle . . . the gouernor of Mascon, a Magitian, whom the diuell snatched vp in dinnerwhile, and hoisted aloft' (119). These pictorial presentations are illustrated with the same vivid woodcuts that accompanied contemporary ballads, broadsheets, chapbooks and popular pamphlets, many of which claimed a Protestant moral agenda.[32] Such strategic uses derived sanction from a

---

[30] On the providentialism of Beard's encyclopaedia, see Walsham, *Providence*, 65–115.
[31] 'The Preface', A4; Avi (v).
[32] Cf. Watt, *Cheap Print*, and Walsham, *Providence*, on the strategic use of images by the supposedly iconophobic Puritan propagandists.

perceptual psychology which privileged ocular impressions over mere spoken words.[33] This was a practical theological appropriation of the notion of the affective image in classical rhetoric, harking back to Aristotle's notion of the psychagogic, enargaeic image, and its further development as *imago* in Quintilian.[34] It is a justification commonly reiterated by writers of graphic cheap print, resulting in a mixture of styles consistent with the way they assimilated older, fabular, material into reports of current events and the Protestant exemplary context.

This justification is extended to a defence of the theatre against Puritan criticism. Heywood, himself an actor, gives three examples to illustrate the moral power of theatrical representation in his *Apology for Actors* (1612), including 'the domesticke, and home-borne truth' of the performance 'of the old History of Fryer Francis' in Lynne:

> . . . presenting a woman who insatiately doting on a yong gentleman, had . . . secretly murdered her husband . . . As this was acted, a townes-woman . . . finding her conscience . . . extremely troubled, suddenly skritched and cryd out Oh my husband, my husband! I see the ghost of my husband . . . threatning and menacing me.[35]

The play proved to be a 'Mousetrap' for the woman who had committed a similar crime long ago. Eventually, judicial inquiry established her confession as fact. This story, evidently current at the time, is cited by Master James in *Warning* (2037–47) – a narrative inscription which projects the play as morally purposive, working on individual conscience through visual reconstruction.

A more general notion of history as theatre, and recorded examples as ocular evocation, was part of the Calvinist background. Beard was one of the many inheritors of the German Lutheran pastor Andreas Hondorff, whose *Prompuarium exemplorum* (1575)[36] was translated into Latin by Philip Loncier as *Theatrum Historicum* (1575) which ran into thirty editions by the 1680s.[37] This enormously popular translation heavily influenced a

---

[33] Cf. Wright, *Passions*, Bk 5, esp. 150.

[34] On the psychological image in Aristotle, see *De Anima* III and IV. Its connection with the legally convincing image emerges from a collateral reading of *De Anima*, *Ethics* and *Poetics*: see Eden, *Poetic and Legal Fiction*, 62–111. Quintilian draws out the implicit Aristotelian connection between the psychological and the rhetorical or artistic image; his *imago* is a combination of the two – the rhetorical-poetic image which relies on the vividness of the psychological image to come into existence: see *Institutio*, 10.7.15.

[35] Heywood, *Apology*, 57–8.

[36] On Hondorff's legacy, see Walsham, *Providence*.

[37] Hondorff, *Theatrum*.

compendium of judgement tales spectacularly told by the Calvinist minister Jean Chassanion, *Histoires mémorables* (1586), the immediate source of
Theatre, though Beard was familiar with the genre's ancestry.[38]

This illuminates the second configuration of spectatorial relations implicit in Beard's narrative and title. God is not merely the omniscient
spectator, but also a maker of theatrical shows. He not only sees into
human intention and hidden things but also theatrically uncovers these –
and in the process, His own intention – through 'manifest tokens' that
we, as spectators, can read (Preface). This effects a curious reversal of roles:
the judge himself becomes the object of vindication. The proofs that
lead to a crime's discovery also prove the logic of divine retribution, 'as
by this meane sinne is discouered and made knowne unto vs, so is the
punishment also of sin set before our eyes' (Preface). Hence Golding's
antithesis between 'secret faults' of men and the 'open judgements' of
God.[39]

This complex spectatorial structure is linked to a duality inherent in
the Calvinist notion of divine signification, captured in Calvin's phrase
'a manifest evidence of that his *secret operation*'.[40] Calvin's God is a
vigilant overseer: 'our eyes must rest on the *watchfulness* of God'.[41] But
His own ways are essentially inscrutable: Calvin stresses his '*secret* bridle',
and the impudence of '[attempting] to fathom his secret counsels'.[42] Yet
there is a simultaneous need for the obscure design to be made legible
to man. So the hidden God is said to '[give] daily and marvellous proof
of his Providence'.[43] Underlying much of Renaissance providentialism
in general, and Calvinist epistemology in particular, is the tradition
of Augustinian sign-theory.[44] The face of the world, to Augustine, was a
set of visible symbols configured as 'proofs' that 'that was the Creator
whom they his creatures ought to serve in that law'.[45] But what is evidence is also theatre. As in medieval and Augustinian thought,[46] Calvin's
God

---

[38] Chassanion, *Grand Jugemens*; Beard, *Theatre*, 66: marginal note on Loncier.
[39] Golding, *Briefe Discourse*, 216.
[40] Calvin, *Defence*, 24.
[41] Ibid., 7. Cf. Beard, *Theatre*, 66, on 'God's watchfull eye'.
[42] Calvin, *Defence*, 16, 18 and 8.
[43] Ibid., 17. See also Beza, *Job*, for a classic example.
[44] See Colish, *Mirror*, Ch. 1. On the Augustinian inheritance of Calvinism, see Todd, *Opacity*,
  Chs. 2–4, and Shuger, *Sacred Rhetoric*, Ch. 1. For focused formulations in Augustine, see *De
  Trinitate* xv.xi.20 and *De Magistro* xiii.43.
[45] Augustine, *City of God*, Bk IX, Ch. 12, 133–4; Ch. 13, 135.
[46] See Colish, *Mirror*, 1–7.

manifests his presence by clearer and brighter proofs . . . the Church [being] . . . the most immediate theatre of his glorious Providence.[47]

Commentators such as Calvin and Beza, like Augustine before them, took it upon themselves to teach men how to read divine stagecraft. The popular Calvinism of cheap Protestant print implicitly adopted a similar stance in 'reporting' spectacles of divine intelligence on the 'theatre of his . . . Providence'. As *Briefe Discourse* claims to extend God's work by plainly publishing the process of discovery, so *Warning* seeks to make legible the drama of divine justice which finds a mere instrument in the legal system.

Golding's phrase, 'the spectacles of Gods lawe', then, captures the duality of God's revelations which are premised at once on His insight into all things invisible and His selective unveiling of his own secret purpose. His apology for writing about the event shades off, appropriately, into a defence of God's dramaturgy:

When God bringeth such matters upon the stage . . . His purpose is that . . . his judgements, should by the terrour of the outward sight . . . drive us to the inward consideration of ourselves.[48]

The point of making a public *spectacle* of Browne, Drury, Roger and Anne was that

their faults came out in the open Theatre, & therefore seemed the greater to our eyes, and surely they were great in deede: neyther are ours the lesse, biecause they lie hidden in the covert of our hearte. God the searcher of all secrets seeth them, and if he list he can also discover them . . . Lette every of us looke into himselfe (but first lette him put on the *spectacles* of Gods lawe . . .) (italics mine)[49]

Golding's description posits a relationship between the two senses of 'spectacles' – stage shows displayed before our eyes, and glasses lent us to see through and see better, as God does.[50] The action both consists of,

---

[47] Calvin, *Defence*, 6–7. On continuities between English Reformation theology and medieval scholasticism, see Grimm, *Reformation Era*, and Todd, *Opacity*, Ch. 3. On Augustinian ideas and Protestant poetics, see Shuger, *Sacred Rhetoric*, Ch. 3.

[48] Golding, *Briefe Discourse*, 226.

[49] Ibid., 227. Cf. *2LT*, D2v.

[50] This latter sense of 'spectacles' – a device for supplementing defective eyesight – was already current in Elizabethan English, its earliest recorded use being in 1386 (*OED*). One of the Elizabethan uses cited, interestingly, is from Thomas Norton's 1561 translation of Calvin's *Institutes* I.ii.b: 'Being holpen with spectacles . . . they begin to read distinctlie' – evoking exactly the same context of hermeneutic aid as Golding. The word was also used more generally as 'a means of seeing, something made of glass' (*OED*, IIa). See OUA, Hyp/B/4, 315r, for an early modern use of 'spectacles' in this sense in legal documents. See Wright on the distortive function of the 'green

and is viewed through, the 'spectacles of Gods lawe'. These two kinds of watching set the parameters for *Warning*'s drama of discovery. The play, of course, stages again what is already a divine drama of retribution. So its demonstrative exercise, while anxious not to compete with God's drama, inevitably acquires an aesthetic dimension, and a poetic of divine judgement evolves on the Elizabethan stage.[51]

'SURE THE REVEALING OF THIS MURTHER'S STRANGE'[52]

The world of the play is full of various portents and signs. The created world is but an instrument of God, and even registers and manifests intentions and consequences yet to become facts. John Beane's sweetheart Joan, maid to 'Old John', expresses her misgivings in a scene that is, strangely, like a pastoral interlude, or a play from another world, and sounds a little like the muddled reminiscing of Juliet's nurse:

A thousand good morrowes gentle *John Beane*, I am glad I met ye . . . I have been so troubled with ye all night, that I could not rest for sleeping and dreaming: me thought you were grown taller and fairer, and that ye were in your shirt, and me thought it should not be you, and yet it was you; and that ye were al in white, and went into a garden, and there was the umbrest sorte of flowers that ever I see: and me thought you lay down upon a green banke, and I pinned gilliflowers in your ruffe, and then me thought your nose bled, and as I ran to my chest to fetch you a handkercher, me thought I stumbled and so waked: what do's it betoken? (1023–34)

In a similar vein, catching something of the cadence of Falstaff '[babbling] of green fields'[53] and something of the eldritch, Beane replies,

Nay, I cannot tell, but I like neither thy dreame nor my owne, for I was troubled with green Meadowes, and buls fighting and goring one another, and one of them me thought ran at me, and I ran away, that I swet in my sleepe for feare. (1035–9)

These forebodings would seem to be merely the muddleheaded fantasies of the unlearned, when Old John breaks into the conversation

---

spectacles' of passions (*Passions*, 49–51). The other, more common connotation of 'spectacle' as a public display had various extensions in usage. One of these even contained the notion of something exemplary (*OED*, IIb).

[51] For the place of supernatural signs and proofs in Aristotelian poetics and rhetoric, see Eden, *Poetic and Legal Fiction*, 16–17; see also Quintilian, *Institutio*, 5.7.35 – more familiar to the writers of the English Renaissance.

[52] *Warning*, 2019.

[53] Shakespeare, *Henry V*, II.iii.17 – the Hostess's description of Falstaff's death.

commonsensically: 'Tut, feare nothing . . . dreames are but fancies' (1040–1).[54] But in fact the informed reader would register these as meaningful. Old John himself is later struck by his horses '[breaking] out' unwontedly and decides they are 'bewitched' (1431–3). This is minutes before he and Joan stumble upon the slain John Beane in the woods. Joan concurs that it must be a *dies mali* – 'dismall daie':

> . . . did ye look in the Amminicke? if it be not, then tis either long of the brended cow, that was nere wel in her wits since the butcher bought her calf, or long my dreame, or of my nose bleeding this morning, for as I was washing my hands my nose bled three drops, then I thought of *John Beane*, God be with him, for I dreamd he was married, and that our white calfe was kild for his wedding dinner, God blesses them both, for I love them both well. (1436–44)

Joan's dream is curious in its psychologically realistic mixture of sensible signification and dream-like nonsense, like Old John's dream about marrying Mistress Sanders (1041–5).

Such signs are systematically mobilised to construct a semiotic that at once indicates providential operation and serves a legal agenda. Tokens in the drama of divine judgement become aids to judicial discovery – establishing, in the process, the projected status of the legal system itself. Joan's double nose-bleed, for instance, while partly dream-speak, also evokes familiar socio-legal practices that find their clearest expression later, with Beane's unexpected revival. Though mortally wounded by Browne, Beane miraculously survives. The general refrains are from the world of *The Winter's Tale*: 'Why it is past beliefe' (1912–18), 'Tis verie strange' (1942). The suspense is built up until Beane is suddenly wheeled into the Mayor's office as a witness, on the back of Browne's desperate claim, 'He doth not live dare charge me with [murder]' (1981). The impact on Browne is devastating:

> Swounds, lives the villain yet?
> . . .
> I gave him fifteen wounds,
> Which now be fifteen mouthes that doe accuse me,
> In ev'ry wound there is a bloudy tongue,
> Which will all speake, although he hold his peace,
> By a whole Jury I shalbe accusde.   (1987–99)

The sight of the wounds stimulates Browne's imagination to immediately visualise a judicial situation. But what is imagined is next made real. In

---

[54] Cf. Arden's ominous dream, and Franklin's dismissal of it as 'fantasy' in *Arden*, vi.

the midst of general amazement, John Beane 'openeth his eyes', 'lookes upon [Browne]', provides the all-important confirmation and 'sinckes' dead (1992–2004). All exclaim on this 'wondrous worke of God' (2011–14). The purpose of this sustaining turns out to be evidential (2072). As Golding states:

> . . . M. Barneses man [Beane] having ten or eleven deadly wounds, and being left for dead, did by God's wonderfull providence revyve againe . . . was founde by an old man and his mayden . . . and conveyed to Wolwich, wher he gave evident tokens and markes of the murtherer, and so continewing still alive till he had bin apprehended and brought unto him, dyed the next Monday after.[55]

The implication is reinforced in the play by a dramatic compression of time: Beane drops dead the moment he has breathed out his testimony: 'in the case of blood,/God's justice hath bin stil myraculous' (2020–1). But wonder, here, is specifically connected to the secular legal operation.

The agent in this particular revelation is not only Beane's presence but his wounds. They are like those eloquent signs, 'sweet Caesar's wounds, poor poor dumb mouths' inscribed into the 'piteous spectacle' of Caesar's body, that Antony '[shows]' the Romans and bids 'speak for' him.[56] But in *Warning*, it is God who plants 'a tongue in every wound' and plays 'Antony' to 'ruffle up' Browne's spirit. Beane's wounds are both a witness to, and a sign of, the murder, at once accusing Browne and striking his conscience with all the power of a mnemonic token. He is moved emotionally and morally to instinctive repentance and immediate confession, like the woman 'moved' to confession 'by the sight' of her crime onstage (2046–7). This allows orders for court proceedings to be issued, while the Mayor and Barnes compete at telling 'stories' of providential discoveries leading to confession and justice. For the wounds are legal tokens too: divine rhetoric is appropriated by the legal system, even as the anagnoristic plot is played out inextricably at three levels – socio-legal, providential and moral.

The specific detail which places the scene firmly in the context of popular providentialism is the curious event Barnes remarks on:

> See how his wounds break out afresh in bleeding. (1991)

This is not quite, but very much like, bier-rite or 'cruentation'[57] – the judicial custom whereby the murder suspect would be brought into the

---

[55] Golding, *Briefe Discourse*, 218.
[56] Shakespeare, *Julius Caesar*, III.ii.224–6, and 198; 227–9.
[57] From Latin 'cruentare', 'to bleed'.

presence of the corpse, and sometimes made to touch it. If the corpse bled, he would be proved guilty, and innocent if it did not.[58] Deriving from the same imaginative principle as the older ritual of trial by ordeal or combat, this is one of the superstitions which survived the rationalisation and relative secularisation of criminal justice, well into the sixteenth century; there are even a few recorded instances of the practice from the seventeenth.[59] Its use in coroner's inquests was the most institutionalised form it took;[60] even in post-Reformation England, it counted as potentially admissible legal evidence. The underlying sanction was purely providentialist. Beard refers to several instances, and in a tone which suggests standard practice:

. . . finding vnknown murders, which by the admirable power of God are for the most part reuealed, either by the bleeding of corpses, or the opening of the eye, or some other extraordinarie signe, as daily experience doth teach.[61]

A 1574 gaol record from Brecon cites a coroner's inquest where the jurors ordered the nephew of an old woman found dead in a field to touch the body

for . . . if the person hadde byn thoccason of her deathe, the same person handling the bodye, it would appere by bledinge or some outward aperaunce.[62]

In *Warning*, John Beane is not quite dead when his wounds bleed. But the phenomenon would still be recognised as a variant on bier-rite. Several variations are indeed noted in contemporary murder reports. In Henry Goodcole's *Heaven's Speedie Hue and Cry* (1635), the murderer himself bleeds from the nose, confronted with the body of his victim.[63] *Sundrye Strange and Inhumaine Murthers* (1591) tells of a killer who

---

[58] See Gittings, *Death*; Gaskill, *Attitudes*, 220 and 230. See also Robbins, *Encyclopaedia*: 'Bier Right'. For examples of the practice in early modern England, see the entry in CRO, DDX 196, 10 (1572); Gittings, *Death*, 109.

[59] On the medieval ordeal, see Bartlett, *Trial by Fire*, esp. 73–87. See also Lea, *Superstition*, 217–370; on bier-rite as a form of ordeal, see 315–23 (spelt 'bier-right'); on the history of wager of battle as a judicial institution, see 93–216. Compare the ritual trial-by-drowning of suspected witches, persistent in early modern England.

[60] On forensic evidence and symbolic testimony, see Gaskill, *Attitudes*, 266–70. On coroners' inquests, see 250–3.

[61] Beard, *Theatre*, 303–4. Compare 46–7. Cf. also *True Report*, C2v; *Sundrye strange and inhumaine murthers*; *The most horrible and tragicall murther*.

[62] PRO Gaol Files. Brecon, 968/13; Owen, *Elizabethan Wales*, 181. In this case, unlike the 'histories' commonly reported in judgement stories, the corpse did not bleed, suggesting that the boy was innocent. Though the jury were satisfied, the English law ordered further enquiries.

[63] Goodcole, *Heavens speedie hue and cry*.

assumes he is discovered when his children's corpses start bleeding in his presence, and confesses in panic.[64] Clearly, bier-rite was thought effective as evidence in bringing the guilty party to confession, affliction of the conscience being often inseparable from a psychologically strategic use of the discourse of providential discovery. Rationalists like Thomas Ady tried to explain the ritual in psychological terms.[65] Certainly, there are recorded instances of judicial authorities using it to elicit confirmation from suspects.[66] Beard cites a Danish example where all the suspects had to lay their hands on the dead man's breast; as soon as the guilty man did so, 'the bloud gushed forth . . . so that vrged by this evident accusation, he confessed the murder'.[67] The scene of Beane's testimony thus suggests the superstitious, rhetorical and pragmatic aspects that combined to form providentialist evidentiary practice. Even the emphasis on the victim's dying words reflects a reality of legal attitude: in an age where evidence-collection was relatively informal but all-important, forensic skills being limited, obtaining this almost symbolic testimony before the victim died became desperately urgent.[68] When this is combined with cruentation and confession, as in *Warning*, the impression of providential incontrovertibility is overwhelming. Other tell-tale 'marks' are assimilated into this structure: Browne's bloody hose (1510), like the 'bloud on [Mosby's] hose and pursse' that incriminated Thomas Arden's killer in 1551 and is described by Holinshed as 'tokens';[69] Beane's description of Browne's garment and his distraction (1680–1, 1714–16); and the letter exhibited during Anne's trial, written by Drury and 'read . . . twise' by Anne before being sealed (2301–6), a sign of her implication in the murder.

In *Arden*, too, that other 1590s 'domestic tragedy' on a contemporary case of adultery and murder, Alice is brought to confession by the judicially arranged presentation of Arden's corpse (xvi, 1–2):

> Arden, sweet husband, what shall I say?
> The more I sound his name, the more he bleeds.
> This blood condemns me, and in gushing forth
> Speaks as it falls and asks me why I did it. (3–6)[70]

---

64 *Sundrye Strange and Inhumaine Murthers*, A4r–v.
65 Ady, *Candle*, 131.
66 CUL, EDR, E9/6/5v.
67 Beard, *Theatre*, 303. Cf. 304.
68 See Gaskill, *Attitudes*, 237–40 and PRO, STAC 8/152/12.
69 Holinshed, *Chronicles*, II, 1062–6: *Arden*, App. 2, 158. For Beard's use of 'tokens', see *Theatre*, Ch. XI.
70 Compare Holinshed, *Chronicles*, 157.

Most dramatic treatments of the ordeal of the bier foreground its visual impact and its rhetorical potential. Lady Anne's exclamation, in Shakespeare's *Richard III* when Henry's corpse gushes blood at the appearance of Richard, is verbally reminiscent of Antony's purely rhetorical display of Caesar's body, except that Henry's bleeding is an evidence of crime rather than a moral spur:

> O gentlemen, see, see dead Henry's wounds
> Open their congeal'd mouths and bleed afresh!
> Blush, blush, thou foul lump of deformity;
> . . .
> Thy deeds inhuman and unnatural
> Provokes this deluge most unnatural. (I.ii.55–61)

The phenomenon is configured here as a visible expression of a secret and unnatural act of blood, and Nature's exact and opposite reaction to it. This reveals the assumptions behind the semiotic of supernatural signs which informed judicial process, and found its way into crime literature.

THE ORDER OF SIGNS

One way of understanding how plot-making works in this 'theatre' is to examine the various tokens that circulate in the play, and how their meaning and function shift. Precise distinctions are made between categories of signs, as between superstition and a correct reading of providential tokens. The first 'signs' we register are the yellow spots on her fingers that Anne notices one morning, which convince her that something is amiss (670–2). This is an opportune moment for cunning widow Drury – surgeon, palmist and bawd. A little vignette of domestic strife over authority and 'credite' in the household (iv, 559–659) soon turns into a more sinister scene of '[persuasion]' (502). As Anne tries to rationalise what she has been resenting as her husband's imperiousness in denying her money to pay for her knick-knacks for one night, until he has repaid an 'obligation', Drury seizes her chance: 'Good fortune, thus incenst with her husband,/I shal the better breake with her for Browne' (607–8). We cannot simply read this scene as a feminist manifesto. We are alerted from the outset as to where the real danger lies. As Sanders's man warns,

> Feed not my mistris anger, mistris *Drewry*,
> You do not well: to morrow if she list
> It is not twice so much that she may have it.
>
> (626–8)

The dramatist does seem to be sympathetic to Anne and alive to the issues at stake. But Drury's patently corrupt instigation and Anne's own more affectionate reassessment of Sanders's instructions train us to read the episode within the context of an overall happy and loving marriage. So, when Drury grabs her hand as Anne muses on her yellow spots, what follows is meant to come across unambiguously as a piece of machination:

> . . . I see disciphered,
> Within this palme of yours, to quite that evil,
> Faire signes of better fortune to ensue,
> . . . See you this character
> Directly fixed to the line of life?
> It signifies a dissolution,
> You must be (mistris Anne) a widow shortly.
> *Anne.* No, God forbid, I hope you do but jest.
> . . .
> Have you such knowledge then in palmestrie?
> *Drury.*
> . . .
> What makes my house so haunted as it is,
> With merchants wives, bachlors and yong maides.
> But for my matchless skill in palmestrie? (674–92)

She proceeds to 'read' what is 'playnely figurd' by the 'Ladder of Promotion' in Anne's hand – her destiny to marry 'a gallant fellow' richer than her husband (697), one whom she has recently 'had some speech with' 'neere about [her] doore' (731). Anne remonstrates that she does not 'wish to be promoted so', for 'My *George* is gentle, and belov'd beside,/And I have as good a husband of him,/As anie wench in London' (700–3). But she is weak-willed, and eventually accepts that what is set down by 'destenie' must be, and that, as Drury says, ''tis lawful, one deceast to take an other' (750). We are never shown the transition between this resignation and the active desire to see the 'one deceast', for what immediately follows is the first dumb show. We are left, instead, with Drury's shrewd observation:

> For this will hammer so within her head,
> As for the new, sheele wish the old were dead . . .
> (767–8)

This scene explores the psychology of superstition, its relation to a popular and uninformed version of Calvinistic predestinarianism, and how these can be manipulated to affect the human mind. The signs played on here are no tokens of Providence, but 'proofs' in the employment of a cunning rhetoric of persuasion. Prefaced by Drury's consent to be Browne's 'Orator' (541), and later referred to as her triumphant 'perswasion' (1096), this section illustrates the ungodliness of palmistry as it was popularly practised. Mistress Drury's real-life counterparts were women such as Judith Philips, 'a professed cunning woman, or Fortune-teller', whose activities are described in a 1595 tract:

> but now when this dissembling minion [Philips] espied her time, she requested to see the widowes [tripe wife's!] hand . . . [and said] I see by the Art of Palmistrie in your hand, and by mine owne skill, that you are borne to good fortune, likewise I know you haue had many rich proffers in the way of marriage: I haue had said the widow indeed . . . Then said this deceitfull woman againe, a Citizen dwelling vpon London Bridge, hath bin an earnest suter vnto you, and hath receiued a ring with fiue Diamonds in pledge of loue, but the Ring you haue againe. And so there was another Gentleman loued you well, which once would haue kissed you, and vsed you harshly, by that token instriuing with him, your hat fell into the Sowse Tub. At which words, said the Trype wife, I thinke you know all things.[71]

Needless to say she has been told these details by her confederates. Earlier in the scene she pretends to tell fortunes by reading the face (A3b–4a).

It may seem odd that Joan, who has accurate premonitions and tokens, should be the character to talk about 'amminicks', in a play where the embodiment of palmistry is the stereotypical con-woman Drury. Indeed, what is the place of rationalist scepticism in a play so preoccupied with portents of supernatural intelligence? Such confusion, however, may be due to the anachronism of applying our own notions of binaries to early modern ways of thinking. In a period where natural philosophy was itself changing, contemporaries had trouble deciding on the status of phenomena, because boundaries between categories were necessarily contingent.[72] The early modern distinction between the preternatural and the supernatural turned on the idea that the former could only work *within* nature, not against it; the devil *could* be its agent. The latter, by contrast, was above nature, and so could go against it; this power belonged only to God. Miracles and unnatural events like corpses bleeding were the province of the supernatural in this specific and exalted sense. As dreams and forebodings fall on the border between natural and supernatural, the diffusion of

---

[71] *Brideling*, B2b–4a.
[72] See Clark, *Thinking with Demons*, Part II, on early modern distinctions between 'natural' and 'demonic' magic (213–50), and their relation to the divine.

imaginative literature such as our play is best understood as the reflection of a culture where such boundaries were fluid, and 'grey-area' phenomena could be aligned with one or the other category, often according to strategy. As for the relation of palmistry to providential tokens, there was a well-established antinomy between astrology and Protestant Christianity, especially Calvinism. Calvinists objected that astrology posited planetary determinism as a profane substitute for providential determinism.[73] This distinction is generally endorsed by the play. But palmistry was not usually considered part of the 'science' of astrology even by those who claimed that astrology was part of mainstream natural philosophy. Nor was this camp a minority.[74] Interestingly, a large section of this group was involved in the industry that produced almanacs, widely considered to be a form of popularisation of the new science.[75] Even Calvin, in his *Admonition against Astrology Iudiciall*, seems to distinguish between 'the trewe Astrologians' and 'these speculative fools which walke aboue the cloudes'.[76]

The network of true and false signs in *Warning* reflects the Calvinist notion of providence, which requires an act of mental balance between the notion of mystery in obscurity, and its affirmation through external symbols of the absolute, selectively visible but ultimately incomprehensible power of providence.[77] Besides, like other shades of Puritanism, Calvinism had its pastoral and propagandist needs, and *Warning* shows how it was intertwined with popular Lutheran tenets. Consequently, the providential poetics of the genre dealing with miraculous discoveries and judgements has its own 'scandal': the palpable, almost titillating 'wonders' function like

---

[73] See Calvin, *Admonition*, Bvii–v; Howard, *Defensative*, Fulke, *Anti prognosticon*, Chamber, *Treatise* and Hypericus, *Two common places*. On the controversy over astrology, see Capp, *English Almanacs*, Ch. 5.

[74] See ibid., 180. See Kassell, 'Simon Forman's Philosophy', on astrology in Elizabethan London; Kusukawa, 'Aspectio' and 'Providence' on its relation to astronomy. A clue to the play's differentiation between palmistry as quackery and the art of reading providential signs is the distinction, in contemporary natural philosophy, between signifiers that were single and those capable of multiple signification. 'True' astrology, perceived within the Copernican tradition as an offspring of astronomy, and based on mathematical units for calculation, was meant to consist of single signifiers, whereas 'arts' such as physiognomy and palmistry were seen as being premised on signs which could mean various things, and needed to be interpreted, thus giving way to hermeneutic uncertainty; see Johannes, *Brief Introductions*. Historical work has so far been confined to astrology, mostly as a scientific or 'hermetic' study; surprisingly little has been done on palmistry as such. But see Porter, 'English Treatises', on chiromancy.

[75] Capp, *English Almanacs*, Ch. 6, section i.

[76] Calvin, *Admonition*, Bvii and Ci.

[77] See Muir, *Ritual*, Chs. 5 and 6, on the impact of the Reformation on ritual theory, and the implication of Zwingli and Calvin's assertion that the Mass was a metonymic representation. See Kibbey, *Interpretation*, 54, for Calvin's comments on transubstantiation – suggestive of the 'earthly sign' as a figure of God.

the 'inartificial' signs that occupy the lowest place in the Aristotelian hierarchy of tokens and yet are often the most effective ones in dramatic plots. Protestant writers, like their God, needed examples that would make a quick impact on the popular imagination. It was perceived as vital, however, to control the hermeneutic of divine displays by instilling a common structure of semiotic equivalence. The dangers of free interpretation are hilariously illustrated by the story Thomas More recounts in his *Dialogue concerning heresies* (1529) of a simple fellow who, hearing of the sudden collapse of a church during evening prayer, exclaimed, 'now you see what yt is to be at evensong whan ye shold be at bere baytynge'!⁷⁸

WHEN WE WERE CHILDREN WORDS WERE COLOURED (HARLOT AND MURDER WERE DARK PURPLE)⁷⁹

What makes tokens legitimate in *Warning* is a moral congruence between intention and symbol, inward truth and external form. One of the earliest to be set in circulation is that designated token, a ring, offered by Browne in words resonant of a spousal contract:

> Wear't for my sake, and if ye do me good,
> Command this chaine, this hand, and this heart bloud . . .
> (267–8)

But it is not to his beloved that he offers it in holy contract, but to Mistress Drury the bawd, to seal a mercenary pact whereby she procures Mistress Sanders's love for him. To an informed audience, the giving and receiving of this ring is an inauspicious travesty of a spousal gift, an outrage of the decorum of signification, and so a sign of profanity.

When Browne does send a 'token to [his] love' through Roger, it is a handkerchief dipped in Sanders's blood (1386):

> Give this to mistris Sanders, bid her reade
> Upon this bloody handkercher the thing,
> As I did promise and have now performed . . .
> (1411–13)

In its statement of promise and performance, this gesture enacts a perverse marriage sequence, like the contract of blood between Deflores and Beatrice-Joanna, sealed by Deflores' self-assertive gift – her lawful fiancé's

---

⁷⁸ More, *Dialogue*, 258. Compare Vaughan, *Spirit of Detraction*, Aiⁱ, warning against an all-too-easy reading or fashioning of signs, contrary to 'the secrets of his government'.
⁷⁹ MacNeice, *Collected Poems*, 214.

finger with her ring upon it. Inevitably, the correspondence between intention and reception breaks down; what Anne reads in the handkerchief is quite different from what Browne would have her read:

> Oh shew me not that ensigne of despaire . . .
> It is a kalendar of bloody letters . . .   (1935–7)

It resurfaces later as a determinate legal token in court. Drury's testimony reveals that it was a love-'token' from Anne to Browne, 'which after was sent backe,/Imbrude in *Sanders* bloud' (2336–8). But complete with as many holes as the 'wounds [Browne's] hand hath given him' (1388–9), it combines the personal and the memorial as well as partaking of the theatrical decorum of providential tokens.

What it visually contrasts with in the trial scene is the climactic token of the play – the white rose that Anne Sanders wears in her bosom,

> In token of my spotlesse innocence,
> As free from guilt as is this flower from staine.
>
> (2313–14)

As we have seen, colour symbolism was established with the very first dumb show, with Anne veiled in black, Chastity in white. At the bloody banquet, Anne was still 'attended by unspotted Innocence' (821), till Tragedy entered with her bowl and rubbed their hands with blood. On stage, the visual impact would be vivid: crimson would become an emblem for lust and murder (855). Remember, too, the discriminative smearing of individual diners: Anne, at that stage, had only a finger dipped in scarlet.

By the time Anne enters the courtroom spectacularly with the white rose, then, colour is a readily perceived index of moral condition. Anne's first words in court are 'Not guiltie' (2296–7). She then goes on to deny charges which the audience already knows to be true. The Second Lord remonstrates that '[she does] not wel/to use such speeches' when 'the case is too too manifest' (2309–10), before going on to ask her what the rose is all about. His words place the episode within a given epistemological frame, with its own criterion of evidence. Within a few lines of Anne's declaration of her self-fashioned token, the court's attention, and the audience's, turns to the gory handkerchief: a context is prepared for the debased use of recognised and hallowed tokens. Suddenly, now, the Second Lord remarks, in response to Anne's righteous indignation at the court's casting away of an innocent,

> It should not seem so by the rose you weare,
> His colour is now of another hue.   (2374–5)

It is not explicitly specified what colour Anne Sanders's rose turns to. But the iconography suggests purple or crimson. A colour association for states of the soul seems to have been a feature of plays broadly in this genre: witness Merry's scaffold speech in *2LT*:

> But that the blood of Iesus Christ hath power
> To make my purple sinne as white as Snowe.
> 　　　　　　　　　　　　　　　(K1v–K2)

In any case, the audience know exactly how to read the *theatrical* sign of Anne's rose changing colour. The only rightful dispenser of signs in the play's world is God. It is for him to make things manifest; any attempt at a counter-semiotic is an act of presumption which is bound to be exposed as spurious.[80] The Second Lord's words 'too too manifest' echo providentialist writing in both literary and theological traditions. Witness Calvin:

And although there be no deede done, no nor any thing fully agreed upon: yet will not God leave such doings unpunished: for it is too too manifest that they were attempted.[81]

Interestingly, Calvin is here discussing the inevitable visibility, to God, of not only lewd action but also unchaste intentions. But the ambiguous phrasing further suggests the clarity of what God makes visible to the world, so that the earthly agents of his law can implement justice. The evidence is for the judiciary to note, as the Mayor does in *Arden*: 'See, see! His blood! It is too manifest' (xiv, 401). The distinction between the *phenomenon* of divine signification and the *metaphor* of the eye of law is collapsed: one is but an instrument of the other. The status of tokens as signifiers is altogether untroubled in this scheme of things.[82]

Also implicit in the trial scene is the impossibility of competing with the rhetoric of the providential theatre. Many of Beard's stories vividly suggest a hierarchy between God's spectacles and man's:

a certaine Coniurer that promised a too curious . . . Prince, to present vnto him vpon a stage the siege of Troy . . . but he could not performe his promise, for another sport and spectacle more hideous and ougly to his person; for he was taken away aliue by a diuell . . . (*Theatre*, 120)

In Beard's story about Simon Pembroke, a scene of judgement in court is hijacked by the act of divine adjudication, and the metaphor of the 'theatre of God's [judgement]' is strangely reified:

---

[80] Cf. Drury's false claim of being able to read Anne's future, 'manifest as day' in her palm (674).
[81] Calvin, *Treatise*, 227.
[82] See Golding, *Briefe Discourse*, 223.

In . . . 1578 . . . Pembrooke . . . being a figure setter, and vehemently suspected to be a coniurer, by the commaundement of the Iudge appeared in the parish church of S. Sauiour at a Court holden there: where, whilest hee was busie in entertaining a Proctor, and leaned his head vpon a pew . . . the Proctor began to lift vp his head to see what hee ayled, and found him departing out of this life, and straightway he fell downe ratling in the throat, without speaking any one word. This strange judgement happened before many witnesses, who searching him, found about him fiue deuillish bookes of coniuration . . . so that euerie one confessed it to be a just judgement against Sorcerie . . . (126–7)[83]

Warning is careful to align its own judicial drama with those of God, and to distinguish both from the doomed inset drama Anne seeks to stage. Her non-verbal gesture, in shadowing the dumb shows, only draws attention to its lack of the moral transparency of the play's own visual tokens. The white flower which she falsely tries to use almost as a legal emblem, in the faith that signs are easy to manipulate in a world where they can straddle various significations, is itself transformed irrevocably into a divine token. *Warning*'s theatrical rhetoric, by contrast, is quickened by cognitive content, seeking to mirror rather than rival the divine semiotic. Its providential plot is distinct from Drury and Roger's 'plot' (857), the 'complot' of Anne and her lover (1554), and Anne's rhetorical plot. Anne answers the Second Lord's comment on the rose's altered colour with a rhetorical assertion of innocence:

> So you wil have it: but my soule is stil,
> As free from murder as it was at first.
>
> (2376–7)

She intends her defiance to have a similar effect as Vittoria Corombona's false but convincingly triumphant assertion of honesty in Webster's *The White Devil*. But, in the moral universe of *Warning*, Anne's attempt is merely desperate. Significantly, no rose is mentioned in Golding, Holinshed or Stow; it seems to be dramatically invented to give imaginative expression to ideas suggested by, and at play, in the trial.

That inward guilt should be made visible in an exemplary way is part of early modern punitive theories, evident in the practice of making sexual offenders do penance in public places wrapped in blue or white sheets, often with a notice of their offence stuck on to their clothes. Mr Mell, in Golding, has to watch Anne's execution from the pillory, 'with apparent notes and significations of his foolish demeanour', 'with a paper pinned

---

[83] Cf. Yarrington, *2LT*, H2v–H3v on the linguistic association between judicial and theatrical spectacle.

upon hys breast, wherein were written certain wordes in great Letters conteyning the effecte of his fact, to his open shame' (222).[84] The popular notion of branding of criminals is a version of this.[85] Such publications in popular judgement narratives are an attempt to extend or simulate externally what God manifests in a way more integral to the body. Corpses of unrepentant miscreants turn black and stink.[86] The body of a lascivious Antwerp lady 'was Metamorphosed into blacke and blewe . . . and her face (which before was so amorous) became most deformed and fearfull to looke vpon'.[87] At the more doctrinaire end, we have Calvin's biblically sanctioned assertion:

> St. Paule . . . telleth them that there remaineth some scarre there still printed in the bodie of the whoremonger, so that his body is put to reproach by it.
> (Efe. 1.15 and 59.3)[88]

Contemporary physiognomy offered a model of behavioural expressivity that could be easily adapted to ideas of providential signification; this, in turn, could link judicially punitive marking and involuntary but providentially determined physical expressions of sin. Thomas Wright exclaims, 'How hard is it, a fault with face not to bewray?'[89] Such assumptions provide a context for understanding the full implication of Wendoll's assurance that not even starlight 'Shall . . . bewray/That act of night';[90] or Frankford's offer to 'blush for [Anne]' (xiii, 86); or Alice Arden's despair that the blood on the floor 'will not out' 'Because I blush not at my husband's death'.[91] So Anne Sanders exclaims, at the horror that the bloody handkerchief represents, 'are not my deeds ugly?/ Then let my faults be written in my face' (1563–4).

There is in all this a sense of decorum which the guilty mind itself often feels, and even embraces, once repentance has struck. Paradoxically, it is this very awareness of visibility that prompts Anne to fashion her own symbol, once the instinctive initial remorse is overcome, as if the judicial procedure is a field of representation that she must play on its own terms.

---

[84] Compare Beard, *Theatre*, 122.

[85] *WKK*, vi, 154–7, xiii, 136–7. Cf. Frankford's visualisation of Anne's 'spotted body', the 'stripe of bastardy' on their children, and her shame being 'charactered' on their brow (xiii, 121–6). This complements heraldic signs representing honour, explored in Shakespeare's *Lucrece*.

[86] Beard, *Theatre*, 64; cf. *Devil's Conquest*.

[87] Stubbes *Anatomy*, 72.

[88] Calvin, *Treatise*, 226. Cf. Beard, *Theatre*, 369, on the pox as a sign that 'an Adulterer sinneth against his owne bodie', combining the notion of appropriate penalty with visible sign of sin.

[89] Wright, *Passions*, 26. See 30 on blushing.

[90] *WKK*, vi, 147–9.

[91] *Arden*, xiv, 255, 259.

When finally resolved to confess, she wishes 'no longer [to] cloake [her] guiltiness before the world' (2607). It is the desire of self-exposure that now moves her, in contrast with the earlier desire for concealment:

> . . . were my breast transparent,
> That what is figurde there, might be perceiv'd,
> Now should you see the very image of poore
> And tottred ruines, and a slaine conscience . . .
>
> (2654–7)

The tragedy of the actively repentant conscience, ironically, is a lack of devices to make the inward condition evident. Anne's image of her 'slaine conscience' becomes a stilled, internalised dumb show in the theatre of the heart.

THE THEATRE OF CONSCIENCE

Given how 'manifest' 'the case' already is legally, when Anne Sanders and Anne Drury are brought to trial, it is remarkable how doggedly the court officials persevere with bringing them to confess and repent, and to make Browne confess Anne's part in the murder. The Lord Justice, instead of rounding off the trial with the necessary sentences, delivers a long speech stressing that Divine justice 'yet reserves a place,/Of gracious mercie, if [she] can repent' (2349–53): 'And therefore bring your wickedness to light' (2354). The aim is an ostensibly spiritual rather than legal recognition – an uncovering of the self. Just after Browne *has* brought his own wickedness to light, through confession, the Lord Justice extends the work of the judiciary into an inward realm:

> And [God] can save whom al the world condemnes,
> If true repentance turn thee to his grace.   (2247–9)

The Sheriff, likewise, persists with Browne, after all the convicts have been sentenced, and Browne is about to hang:

> Now at the houre of death, as thou doest hope
> To have thy sinnes forgiven at Gods hands,
> Freely confesse what yet unto this houre,
> Against thy conscience (*Browne*) thou hast concealde,
> *Anne Sanders* knowledge of her husbands death.
>
> (2433–7)

As Browne reasserts her innocence, the Sheriff presses on again (2450–3); the tediousness, even obsessiveness, of his efforts is registered in Browne's resistance – perhaps the dramatist's concession to ungodly humour and human reaction. 'Let her confess what she thinkes good:/Trouble me no more master Shiriff', he says, hoping he has heard the last of this (2454–5). But the indefatigable Sheriff will not give up: '*Browne*, thy soule knows' (2456). This time Browne replies, with barely concealed exasperation, 'Yea, yea, it does: pray you be quiet sir' (2457). In the next scene (xix), Master James struggles with the conscience of the Minister who tries to protect Anne – the Mr Mell of Golding's tract. Finally, the prison divine comes into Anne's cell and urges her to 'acknowledge and confess' her fault; again, this is legally irrelevant, because Anne is about to be led off to execution. The emphasis on the soul's health stems from the need to impress that the judicial process is doing God's work; and that trials have demonstrative value rather than rhetorical interest. The evidence of the conscience will 'satisfie the world' (2430), as if the world's satisfaction also rests on achieving the moral end, not just the right punishment.[92] The drama of disclosure, being God's, should encompass body and soul, and promise a happy end hereafter.

Yet, precisely those aspects of divine judgement that distinguish it as providential and perfect in this genre also make it liable to seem unChristian. Typically, the discovery or punishment occurs in the same place as the crime; criminals are affected in the very faculties they used in their offence, for 'it pleaseth God . . . to pay men in their owne coyne, and measureth the same measure to euery man which they have measured unto others'.[93] So, in a tract by William Saxey, Brustar and his concubine are found dead 'by the beddes side, his right thigh and right arme, which often-times hadde imbraced this harlot . . . burned with fire', and her 'heathen partes', equally aptly, 'burnt to the breaste'.[94] Arden, himself a victim whose murder is avenged, is, however, repaid in his 'own coyne' by God in being killed 'in that plot of ground/Which he by force and violence held from Reede'.[95] Similarly, George Browne must 'suffer' 'where [he] did the fact', and his brother 'where [he] laid his act' (2420–3).

This perfect fit is part of the decorum integral to the fantasy of justice.[96] One component of decorum in judgement tales is the instantaneousness

---

[92] On 'satisfaction' or 'restitution' in the early modern theory and practice of confession, see Bossy, 'Social History of Confession', 25–7. See also Tentler, *Sin and Confession*.

[93] Beard, *Theatre*, 389.

[94] Saxey, *Straunge and Wonderfull Example*, Biiv–r.

[95] *Arden*, Epilogue, 10–11. Compare T. M., *Blood for Blood*, 317.

[96] Nor was 'punitive symmetry' peculiar to early modern England: see Schama, *Embarrassment*, Ch. 8 (583).

of the penalty with the offence. The liberties taken by the author of *Warning* with the temporal sequence of events in the Sanders case, are of a piece with the providentialist collapsing of the gap between the moments of crime and retribution.[97] But the principle of exact repayment makes providential narratives remarkably similar to revenge plots. The God of judgement tales can appear surprisingly close to a wrathful, avenging power effecting nemesis, unlike the Protestant God of mercy. His plots, like many of Reynolds's or Beard's, are less akin in spirit to Christian piety than to those revenge tragedies that *Warning* distances itself from in the Induction. The generic vision of such a God is summed up by the conclusion to the 'history' of 'Overbury and Turner', one of the four topical instances added by 'T. M.' to his rehash of Reynolds:

For our good God hath a revenging hand, and scourging whip to punish sin, adultery and blood being alwayes rewarded with shame, infamy, misery and death.[98]

A different note must be reaffirmed at our play's conclusion, pointing a different moral. So Browne must die with the conventional scaffold speech on his lips, with the usual recitation of his sins – including the abuse of 'Sabboth dayes' and the neglect of sermon-attendance (2465–7), both favourite Puritan targets. Roger and Drury open up their souls in confession to God's grace. Anne's repentance-speech is followed by her piteous farewell to her children, accompanied by the gift of a copy of 'Bradford's workes' (2703). These are the *Godly Meditations* of John Bradford, Protestant martyr (d. 1555), who also wrote, among other things, *A Sermon of Repentance* and a *Treatise on Predestination*. This appropriate gift signals the generic affiliation of the play, and forestalls any possibility of it being read otherwise.[99] In these final scenes, the drama of judgement is taken over by a sort of divine tragicomedy; at the same time, the judicial procedure is narratorially plotted into a trajectory of discovery–punishment–repentance–salvation. In her confession, as quoted in Golding, Anne '[thanks] God' for not letting her sin at her will,

---

[97] Kerrigan, *Revenge Tragedy*, Ch. 7, is superbly suggestive on the 'problem of punishment in time', and its relation to the need for recapitulation in revenge narratives.

[98] T. M., *Blood for Blood*, Bk VII, 'History 5', 353.

[99] Bradford, *Godly Meditations* and *Two notable Sermons*. The contents of the former indicate a specifically Calvinist preoccupation with the subjects of hot debate between Calvinists and its detractors – predestination, free will and election – emphasising the need for, and assurance of, God's mercy upon repentance and confession.

to the daunger of my eternall damnation, but that he hath founde out my sin, and brought me to punishment in this world, by his fatherly correction, to amend, to spare, and save me in the world to come . . .[100]

Indeed, Golding's own text is a telling clue to the play's anxieties and investments. In *Warning*, the detailed realism of the depiction of legal procedure leads to the even more public and spectacular event of the execution. Once Browne is led away, 'the people's eies [having] fed them with [his] sight' (2386), we see two carpenters under Newgate salaciously talking of going to see the scandalous executions, and of Smithfield being 'full of people' (2535–50). The historical reality of the scenario is attested by Golding's description of 'so great number of people, as the like hath not bene seene there togither in any mans remembraunce', and of crowds hanging from 'chambers whose windows and walls were beaten down to looke out at' (220). Golding painstakingly foregrounds the distinction of his moral narrative from such tittle-tattle as the gossip about the crowd-pulling 'arraignment of this lustie *Browne*' in *Warning* (2163). But in the process he allows a vivid glimpse of how such an event 'ministreth great occasion of talk' and 'breede much diversitie of report' (216). Golding's acute awareness of the risk of being read as prurient is not unlike Freud's anxiety with his case histories. He pre-empts notions of voyeurism around God's spectacular stagings, stressing that they are 'not to the intent that men should gaze and wonder at the persons, as byrdes do at an Owle, not that they should delight themselves & others with the fond and peradventure sinister reporting of them . . . no surely, God meanest no such thing' (226). God's ends are different, and these are implemented by the judiciary, since, in Richard Hooker's words, '*All powers are of God*'.[101] Indeed, Hooker's emphasis on the need for 'contrition' as the end of 'confession' illuminates Golding's rhetoric:

When the offense doth stand only betweene God and mans conscience, the counsell is good which St. Chrysostome giveth, *I wish thee not to bewray thyself publicly . . . I carrie you not into a theatre or open court of many of your fellow servants . . . Disclose your conscience before God, unfold yourselfe to him.*[102]

So the fact that Golding's God brings misdeeds 'out in the open theatre' (*Briefe Discourse*, 227) is projected as a necessary stage of disciplinary example in a more comprehensive drama that is ultimately between

---

[100] Golding, *Briefe Discourse*, 229. Compare Allenso's dying speech in *2LT* (K).
[101] Ibid., 398. See Lindley, 'Stubbornness', 343–4, on Hooker's focus on the centrality of penitence in confession.
[102] Hooker, *Laws*, III, 51–2.

man and God, and which ideologically separates discipline from what has become, over time, its Foucauldian coordinate of punishment. While the language of conscience is shown to be appropriated by the public, institutional voice – that of judge or Sheriff – Drury and Anne's final conference opens up a recess within the secular institution of the gaol, where confessional is privately experienced. The prison attendant is requested to leave the two women alone to 'conferre/Of things that nearly do concern [their] soules' (2566–8).

Within the intimacy of this psychomachic dialogue, we witness Anne feeling herself 'strangely changed' (2606). This process of conversion is necessary before the women can confront the prison chaplain and declare they are 'resolv'd' (2637), in the relatively less private scene following. Golding's protestations are especially understandable in the light of such accounts as Saxey's, which dwell on the lurid details of secret whoredom indulged with much the same fervour as Puritan descriptions of the lewd playhouse practices or gruesome punishments. Interestingly, Saxey, who includes the 'example' of 'God's heauy wrath' on 'Mystres Saunders', also cites that of Ovid's banishment 'for writing the books, of the Arte of Loue', and enticing 'the youths of London to practise continuall experiments & interluds of the Arte of bauderie'.[103] Golding's position must have been particularly awkward as a translator of Ovid as well as of Calvin, which perhaps underlies his obsessive caution.

Golding's emphasis also lends a generic specificity to providential dramaturgy. God's plot is tragicomic, letting men and women

runne so long upon the bridle, till it seeme to themselves, that they may safely do what they liste, and to the worlde, that they be past recoverie unto goodness: and yet in the end catching up with them in their chiefe pride, he raysed them by their overthrow, amendeth them by their wickedness, and reviveth them by their death, in such wise blotting out the stain of their former filthe, that their darknesse is turned to light, and their terrour to comfort. (*Briefe Discourse*, 226)

The temporal calculation and control underlying this plan qualifies Anne's thanks to God for not letting her have the 'reigne and bridle of sinning' (229) – for she has been allowed to run just long enough 'upon it' for God's plot to come off roundly. Admittedly, this is a different operation of *felix culpa* from that wielded by terrestrial tragicomic authorities. But it is similar in the seeming latitude allowed, the knowing wait for the most effective moment, and the definitions of 'comfort', 'light'

---

[103] Saxey, *Straunge and Wonderfull Example*, C–Cv.

and happy endings from the point of view of the arbiter. Further, the climax is made the more striking and effective to the gazing world by reserving the 'overthrow' – which is also the 'revival' – for the last moment, after the sinning mortals have waded too far in, having had no obstacle either from the world or from their conscience, both of which are monitored by God.[104] Such an agenda also provides a narrative justification of the sometimes unavoidable time-lag between sin and punishment. The narrative sequence itself is meticulously organised: the acknowledgement and the repentance are deferred 'to the last part of this matter, to which place those things do more peculiarly pertain' (219). After the executions, the final section of the *Discourse* is introduced: 'Now remayneth to shewe what is to be gathered of this terrible example' (225). The generic sense of decorum is intertwined with the telos of the providential plot: 'Now let us proceede to the incidents that happened from the times of their apprehensions to the time of their deathes, and so to the admonition, which is the conclusion and fruite of this whole matter' (220). The final agenda is to bring the convicted parties to 'willing confessing . . . which as yet they obstinatly concealed' (221). This is the pattern underlying *Warning*'s drama of conscience, its progress from darkness to illumination. The potential scandals of a spectacular providential play have to be bleached out for this theatre of recognition to fulfil its aim – not mere retribution, but a true knowledge of the soul and its relation to God.

The question remains as to whether the dramatic presentation of such events has inherent pitfalls which run counter to the theological agenda. The play, after all, is not a tract. For one thing, an inevitable theatrical dimension would be evoked by some of the stock dramatic ingredients used by the play. The 'handkercher' dipped in Sanders's blood, to a 1590s London audience, would undoubtedly recall that originary retributive token on the Elizabethan stage, Horatio's napkin, 'besmear'd with blood', which Hieronymo preserves to propel his revenge plot in *The Spanish Tragedy* (c.1587).[105] The most sensational providential

---

[104] Cf. Calvin, *Defence*, 17: '. . . He gives full rein to the foolish counsels of men; and seeming not to notice their great preparations, frustrates, by the issue, all their hopes.' Cf. Beard's fishing metaphor in *Theatre*, 'Preface': 'For albeit for a time they sleepe in their sinne and blindness, delighting in their pleasures . . . yet they draw after them the line, wherewith (being more ensnared than they are aware) they are taken and drawne to their destruction.' The idea of a conscious dramaturgy often comes complete with the notion of last-minute tragicomic reprieve even in the less consciously Protestant volumes. See T. M., *Blood for Blood*, on the spectacular last-minute abortion of the execution of Felicia, condemned by planted evidence (63).

[105] Kyd, *Spanish Tragedy*, II.v.51. Kyd's play was being performed in London all the way through from 1592 to 1602 (Gurr, *Shakespearean Stage*, 223).

token of the play – the rose changing colour – would presumably be the
product of a sleight of hand (Anne turning round and swapping flowers),
or vinegar, or a concealed bladder made to burst as Anne turns back for a
moment: some ploy that would be immediately recognised as a standard
device of the theatre.[106] Divine mystery thus stands in danger of appearing
to be theatrical manipulation, aligned in providentialist discourse with the
devil's frauds, or the 'Cosoners trick'. But perhaps the most significant
inconsistency in the play, threatening to undercut its pious self-projection,
is the fate of George Browne. Browne's trial is straightforward, as he
pleads guilty immediately. But he repeatedly makes two points. One is a
protestation of Anne's innocence. The other is a plea not to be hanged in
chains, but to be granted a decent burial:

> I know the Law
> Condemnes a murtherer to be hangd in chaines,
> O good my Lords, as you are Noble men
> Let me be buried as soone as I am dead. (2232–5)

He is immediately reassured: 'Thou shalt, thou shalt, let not that trouble
thee' (2236–7). His earnest prayer not to be made a prey to birds and the
watching millions after death is one that the audience have been led to
expect the judiciary to fulfil, being an instrument of a merciful God. As
Browne is taken out of the courtroom, he piteously reminds the officials
of his requests: 'Save poore *Anne Sanders* for shees innocent:/And good
my Lords let me not hang in Chaines' (2263–4). The awareness that he is
lying about Anne is unlikely to provide the audience a moral justification
for his subsequent treatment. As we have seen, the dramatic tenor of the
scene where the Sheriff labours to bring him to total confession acts in
Browne's favour; the audience, let into a secret from which Browne's aside
excludes the Sheriff, are drawn into complicity with Browne and surely
find his defiant and desperate loyalty to Anne not entirely untouched
by heroism of an order that is fundamentally alien to providentialist
discourse:

> Have I not made a covenant with her,
> That for the love that I ever bare to her,
> I will not sell her life by confession,
> And shall I now confesse it? I am a villaine.
> I will never do it . . .
> I will confesses my sinnes, but this conceale.
>
> (2438–45)

---

[106] Unfortunately, there are no extant details about the staging of the play.

While the play manipulates theatrical space to stage the various spaces encompassed by the process of divine judgement, the axis of audience participation makes a straightforward moral impact problematic. The audience's spectatorship, in a sense, is like God's, straddling open and secret utterance. The play, as the intermediary between the displayed and the enclosed, grants the audience that privileged double perspective corresponding to the double mechanism through which the Protestant legal system seeks to accommodate a jurisdiction over public and private, execution and repentance, body and soul. Yet, if the theatre allows us to hear the intimate dialogue with Drury in the recesses of the disciplinary prison which converts Anne to repentance, it also allows us to hear Browne's aside when he holds out against the Sheriff's inquisition and lies for love (2438–45, 2447–9). Unlike Anne's final confession to the prison Doctor in the same isolated room, Browne's is made only to the audience, not to God's representative – a theatrical token that is not, after all, in God's control; a secret shared only with the spectators in the playhouse. The excess of the Sheriff's zeal works in a similar way, anticipating the overbearing attempt of Duke Vincentio-as-Friar in Shakespeare's *Measure* to 'arraign' the pregnant Juliet's 'conscience/And try [her] patience' (II.iii.21–2) in the seclusion of a prison cell, and creating complicities and sympathies quite at variance with the agenda of staging juristic authority as the temporal inscription of a law that originates from a divine source beyond challenge. Juliet's reply not only intercepts the Duke's self-important sermon but declares the 'joy' of the 'sin' and 'shame' she repents, both her union with Claudio and its fruits (II. iii.35–6).[107] Similarly, Browne's success in resisting the State's attempt to ferret out the last secret '[locked] in the wards of [his] covert bosom'[108] fleetingly bestows value upon a love that the play has portrayed as purely criminal. *Warning* has indeed been presented as an agent of judicial investment in the individual's soul: a galvanising fiction that separates the urge to control the private site of truth that is the individual conscience from the more benign, non-inquisitorial investment of a Christian State in ensuring its subjects' salvation. But it also comes close to becoming an agent of its exposure.

---

[107] See Greenblatt, *Shakespearean Negotiations*, 140, and Hanson, *Discovering the Subject*, 68–9, for related readings of Juliet's response. But the premise of Juliet's 'tranquil acceptance of her "shame"' that Hanson accepts from Greenblatt's reading (which she usefully qualifies) does not do justice to the effect of her voice in the theatre – far from being passive, as Hanson suggests by contrast with Isabel – Juliet – like Isabel, is at once a 'powerful voice' *and* 'corporeal signifier'.

[108] Phrase used by the Duke in *MfM*, V.i.11.

Troublingly, this is a Reformist play, and Browne's resistance at a moment when he enlists theatrical sympathy evokes the equivocation associated at the time with Recusant defensive strategy against the Crown's investigations. But it would also smack of the common law disapproval of inquisitorial procedures and compulsions to testify against oneself. Browne of course is protecting not himself but his beloved, but his equivocation in referring the Sheriff to Anne herself for any confessions about her sin (2454–5) would amount to acting on 'mental reservation' – a device for countering precisely the trap of self-incrimination which common lawyers condemned and associated with canonical procedure dating back to the twelfth century.[109] Elizabeth Hanson explores this discursive knot as a context to the definition of subjecthoood in relation to torture and inquisition, and illuminates the potential conflict between its use by the State and its rejection by common law which aligned it with Continental methods deriving from Roman law.[110] Torture was used to elicit confession in English courts outside the common law jurisdiction (such as the Star Chamber or Privy Council), and was perceived as a tool of persecution by Catholic martyrs and common lawyers alike. Yet, as Hanson reminds us, common lawyers and jurists such as Thomas Smith, Edward Coke and Francis Bacon were all involved in inquisitory torture at some point or the other in their executive functions, trying Recusants for treason and applying methods that were theoretically anathema to the law of the land but legitimised by the Crown. *Warning* focuses some of these contradictions by bringing the legal and theological investments of the State into a dubious compound, in the very act of trying to project their integrity. Trapped in the interstices between the Protestant and, to a degree, common-law notion of the authority of conscience, and the proto-canonical investment of the State in controlling the conscience and demonstrating that control, it produces the paradox of a criminal sharing his guilty secret with the audience rather than with the Sheriff. Teetering between embodying the judiciary's job and revealing it, between accessing privacy and staging the strenuous process of such accession, the resolutely pious *Warning* risks slipping out of its self-defined homiletic parameters into poetic representation, if only at moments. Thus, even this middling sort of play becomes something more than a document in early modern providentialism to its literary readers, and acquires possibilities of poetic unruliness

---

[109] See Wigmore, *Evidence*, 266–92.
[110] Hanson, *Discovering the Subject*, esp. Introduction.

against 'God's law'. It does not, of course, show us Anne's execution. That exemplary public display is allocated to the execution of Browne, the chief criminal, presumably in a dramaturgical attempt to imitate the balance between inward and outward spectacles that God's law negotiates. No doubt, Browne's contrite scaffold-speech intervenes between his confiding in the audience and his execution, thus providing generic 'satisfaction'. But the moment he 'leapes off' (2479), the Messenger announces the Council's decision to hang his body 'in Chains' at Shooter's Hill and the Sheriff affirms '[it] shall be done certainly' (2480–4).[111] Even Roger Browne becomes a 'subject': by staging the potential of subjective resistance, the play inscribes the limits of an investigative method and discourse that use discovery as a device for regulating the soul.[112] The fate of John Beane, who is granted a less defined subjectivity, nevertheless inscribes another inconsistency that complicates our response. We see John die immediately after identifying Browne, and later absorbed into the narrative of forgiveness and spiritual concern: 'with a constant voice, [he] praid God forgive Browne, and receive his soule, and so departed' (2061–3). But this is said soon enough after Beane's on-stage death for the audience to register that they have seen no such thing. The dramatic medium, for all its sanitisation, resists perfect assimilation into the ideology of genre or the playwright's deliberate programme, by intimating yet another kind of evidence; one that casts doubt on the project of theatrical providentialism itself.

---

[111] The mind leaps forward to Wordsworth, so haunted by an accidental boyhood visit to the spot near Penrith where 'A murderer had been hung in iron chains' (1805) and the gibbet remained to evoke the scene, that the moment not only formed a 'spot of time' in *The Prelude* (302–11 in Bk I, 1799, 231–45 in Bk XI, 1805 and 1850), but also found its way into *Salisbury Plain* (1795 and 1841). Significantly, *Salisbury Plain* was conceived 'to expose the vices of the penal law', as Wordsworth wrote to Francis Wrangham (Wordsworth, *Letters*, 159).

[112] I use 'subject' here in the sense defined by Hanson in her excellent study of subjecthood in the context of the inquisitorial projects of the Elizabethan State in *Discovering the Subject*: 'the site of thought and origin of action', not just 'authority's subordinate' (2–3).

CHAPTER 4

'Painted devils': image-making and evidence in The White Devil

Webster's *The White Devil* explores its relation to legal representation and adjudicatory principles. In doing so, it shows unflinchingly that both legal and theatrical evidence are artful. But it is to the superior artifice of rhetorical and performative evidence that persuasion belongs; and it is with these that the play aligns its own art. It uses law as a tool not only to explore its own medium but actively to vindicate and privilege it, and to offer a radical hierarchy of proofs that defies institutional morality. The specific notion of artificial reasoning, familiar in rhetoric and jurisprudence, is deployed in this theatrical self-assertion.

This chapter approaches the issues of evidence and judgement through an examination of 'colour' in its legal, rhetorical, theatrical, theological and physiognomical senses, all of which are brought into play against one another in *The White Devil*, and define its engagement with, and position on, 'evidence' – image-making, legal proof and rhetorical tool. 'Colour', thus, provides a hermeneutic tool for the critic to explore the relation between legal and theatrical persuasion in the play, with rhetoric linking the two. After all, rhetoric was the discipline which engaged most systematically and centrally with the notion of evidence outside the law in the early modern period. But while the argument largely rests on the intricate links between the legal and rhetorical meanings of colour, and their ramifications in related discourses, it does not suggest that this nexus is already present in the audience's consciousness, though much of it would have been more familiar to Webster's audience than to us. Rather, 'colour' is a principle that the dramatist consciously deploys; through which several fields of cognition are aligned, and which, in its various interconnected senses, becomes a central constituent of the play's affect. The theatrical audience's judgement, like that of the audience in a courtroom, is challenged and influenced by the colour Vittoria gives to her plea; this consummate act, in its conflation of theatrical and judicial performance, inscribes the 'colour' used by Webster himself in presenting the case of his 'white devil' to the judgement of his audience.

As 'evidence' is integrally connected with image-making in this play, it is necessary to identify the structures and contexts of spectatorship the play sets up, and how that process instils a consciousness of colour.

'SPECTACLES FASHIONED WITH SUCH PERSPECTIVE ART'

The White Devil is centrally engaged with ways of seeing: with fashioning, presenting and viewing spectacles, with reading and misreading visible signs, and with optical, hermeneutic and ethical double-vision. This is signalled early on in the play. Flamineo, courtly hanger-on and cynical commentator, is also a bawd between his sister, the 'fair' Vittoria Corombona (I.ii.6), and her lover, the Duke of Bracciano. Having set the two up for an illicit rendezvous, Flamineo packs Bracciano away in a closet as his brother-in-law Camillo enters, and proceeds to taunt Camillo in an exchange that delineates the anatomy of jealousy:

FLAMINEO: It seems you are jealous. I'll show you the error of it . . . I have seen a pair of spectacles fashioned with such perspective art that . . . 'twill appear . . . there were twenty. Now, should you wear . . . these . . . and see your wife tying her shoe, you should imagine twenty hands were taking up of your wife's clothes . . .
CAMILLO: The fault there, sir, is not in the eye-sight –
FLAMINEO: True, but they that have the yellow jaundice think all objects they look on be yellow . . .   (99–110)

The audience, alerted to the notion of perspectives of viewing,[1] are now suddenly called upon, along with Camillo, to look: 'See, she comes' – '*Enter* \ Vittoria] Corombona'. From the moment of her first appearance, Vittoria is presented as a spectacle for us to absorb and assess as Flamineo provides a running commentary in a strange counter-blason-in-prose:

What . . . \a] flattering knave might . . . write sonnets to her eyes, or call her brow the snow of Ida, or ivory of Corinth, or compare her hair to the blackbird's bill, when 'tis liker the blackbird's feather? . . . (I.ii.114–19)

---

[1] What Flamineo describes is 'anamorphic' painting, which was a variation on perspective art, and worked by providing a radically different and more meaningful perspective when viewed not from the front but at wide angles. Webster seems to use 'perspective' here in a generalised and slightly indiscriminate way to describe art that creates alternative or multiple viewpoints. On the relation of Renaissance perspective art to the literary imagination, see Gilman, *Curious Perspective*. On 'perspective' in visual art, see Gombrich, *Image and the Eye*, esp. 189–201, 208–13, 224 and 256–70. On anamorphism in relation to 'perspective', see Turner, *Dictionary*, 484–91.

Vittoria is a 'dark lady' – too dark not only to merit sonnets praising her fairness, but also too foul, as Flamineo knows, to merit her husband's vexation. Implicit here is a correspondence between inner and outer; but what we see on stage is, presumably, a charismatic and glamorous woman (or a pretty boy in a dress). Flamineo himself has conceded her physical beauty (6–7). An early pointer, this, to ironies that open up around the notions of outward appearance and internal state, and are deployed through a play on the concepts of colour as well as the physical realities of colour itself.[2]

An accepted colour symbolism suggesting opposite colours standing for opposed moral states pervades conversations. When Francisco (Duke of Florence), brother to Bracciano's Duchess, Isabella, accuses Bracciano of having Vittoria as his 'strumpet', Bracciano defies his 'black slander' (II. i.58–60). Swift comes the rebuttal:

> Thou hast a wife, our sister; would I have given
> Both her *white hands* to death, bound and locked fast
> In her last winding sheet, when I gave thee
> But one.   (64–7)   (italics mine)

Cardinal Monticelso welcomes the 'proofs/Of her black lust' that will compromise Vittoria's credit at her trial (II.ii.7), and calls Lodovico a 'foul black cloud' 'raising' the 'devil' (V.iii.99; 88–9). Even the parodic Lawyer inveighs against Vittoria's 'black concatenation/Of mischief' (III.ii.28–9). The devil, for sure, is black in this play: Flamineo's partner Zanche the Moor is the 'devil' that is said to 'haunt' him (V.i.86). His own greeting of 'precious gipsy' (158–61) – followed by 'infernal' (218) and 'foul nest' (234) – is resonant in a play where 'white' connotes both complexion and sexual purity, and also, more generally, an innocence of crimes of blood. At her trial, Francisco cannot imagine Vittoria 'hath a soul so black/To act a deed so bloody', the 'act of blood' being, ostensibly, the murder of her husband Camillo (III.ii.183–90).[3] But the colour of blood, if less polyvalent than black, has already acquired an association with both red hot passion and black murder. The two senses of 'blood' are collapsed when Vittoria, dying, cries out, 'O my greatest sin lay in my blood./Now my blood pays for 't' (IV.vi.240–1). Set up as an external sign of inner state, colour almost comes to embody the emblematic principle of viewing. So Flamineo can

---

[2] Most recent criticism addressing 'colour' in Renaissance drama focuses on race and identity: see Loomba, *Gender, Race*; and Hall, *Things of Darkness*.

[3] The same act is later described as 'the black deed' (V.iii.251). So, black and red seem equivalent when pitted against white. This is complicated by the abundance of papal red, of which more later.

damn Mulinassar – Francisco disguised as a Moor – by denigrating 'the morality of your sunburnt gentleman' (V.i.185). So Zanche can live out her stereotype, albeit with a twinkle of the eye, when, thinking she has entrapped Mulinassar in a profitable match, she brags, 'It is a dowry,/ Methinks, should . . . wash the Ethiop white' (V.iii.261–3). But this is a more manipulable notion of colour than Flamineo's.

Spectatorship and audition, meanwhile, are dramatically inscribed in I.ii, as Camillo exits and Bracciano enters to join Vittoria, while Vittoria and Flamineo's mother Cornelia eavesdrop (s.d., 205). Flamineo and Zanche provide the commentary on the lovers' dalliance centre-stage (214–15), while Cornelia despairs. Their asides effect an acoustical differentiation of space, at once reinforcing metadramatic awareness and extending the action beyond the stage. The theatre audience share the positions of the three onlookers on stage, while the lovers, unmindful of what is going on around them, become almost a tableau.

As their erotic badinage progresses, they exchange rings, and Bracciano launches into bawdy word-play: 'My jewel for your jewel', 'Nay, lower, you shall wear my jewel lower' (225–8). But Flamineo mediates this figurative speech to the audience, ensuring their complicity in the visualisation it suggests: 'That's better – she must wear his jewel lower' (225–9). At this point Vittoria offers a different order of figuration – 'A foolish idle dream' (232–56). She tells the Duke she thought she was sitting under a yew tree in a churchyard at midnight, when 'there came stealing in/Your duchess and my husband'. One of them bore a pick-axe, the other a rusty spade, 'And in rough terms they gan to challenge me/About this yew.' Bracciano interjects briefly – 'That tree'. Vittoria's rejoinder, 'This harmless yew', pointedly puns on 'you'. For it is this yew that Camillo and Isabella accused her of intending to uproot. For this, they vowed to bury her alive; Camillo began to dig with his axe, and Bracciano's 'fell Duchess', 'like a Fury', 'voided out/The earth and scattered bones', while Vittoria sat helpless and trembled, but 'could not pray'. But then there arose a storm, which 'let fall a massy arm/From that strong plant,/And both were struck dead by that sacred yew/In the base shallow grave that was their due'. 'Excellent devil!', exclaims Flamineo, registering her ingenuity, 'She hath taught him in a dream/To make away his duchess and her husband'. Bracciano, no fool, takes the cue and offers an exposition of this vivid image:

> Sweetly shall I interpret this your dream.
> You are lodged within his arms who shall protect you,

From all the fevers of a jealous husband,
From the poor envy of our phlegmatic duchess.
I'll seat you above law and above scandal,
Give to your thoughts the invention of delight
And its fruition . . . (260–6)

What Vittoria has just etched out for the mind's eye is no real dream, but a piece of metaphoric representation. 'Invention of delight' indicates that Bracciano has rightly understood it as a rhetorical artefact, at the same time as 'seat you above law and scandal' posits a different order of values from those of law and society.[4] It is not the dream but its narration that is the object offered by Vittoria and dramatised by Webster, aimed at a specific end – powerful suggestion leading to persuasion. So the deadly pact is sealed in the promised 'fruition'. Another way to describe this dream would be to call it a consummate act of insinuation. Another name for which, in rhetoric, would be 'colour'.

'COULORS OF ELOQUTION'[5]

It is time to consider the rhetorical status of images such as these, in relation to the concept of colour as it unfolds its crevices, accretes meaning and brings together several discursive fields. The aim is to come to an understanding of the categories of images that the play itself deals with, and how it positions its own act of representation. Bacon's fragment *The Colours of Good and Evil* (1597) is an ideal starting point for examining the precise nature of insinuative colour as perceived in the period.[6] But the Baconian notion of colour itself has to be studied in relation to the neo-Ciceronian school of rhetoric that was familiar to most schoolboys, let alone students of law, or young men like Webster who went to the prestigious Merchant Taylors' School.[7]

In the classical rhetorical tradition, colour came closest to meaning ornament – an appealing and persuasive appearance.[8] Thomas Wilson, in his *Arte of Rhetorique* (1553), recommends '[beautifying] oure talke wyth diuers goodlye coloures . . . that our speache maye seme as bryghte and

---

[4] On 'invention', see Glossary. On amorous interaction as a cryptic code, symptomatic of the law of love, and pitted against conventional laws of court and society, see Goodrich, 'Gay Science', 113.

[5] Peacham, *Garden*, Prefatory letter.

[6] Bacon, *Works*, VII, 77–92.

[7] On the provenance of Cicero and his followers in sixteenth-century England, and in school curricula, see Skinner, *Reason and Rhetoric*, 19–65, esp. 22–3. On Webster's early life and education, see Bradbrook, *John Webster*, 1–27.

[8] On *ornatus* in rhetoric, see Skinner, *Reason and Rhetoric*, esp. 138–9.

precious, as a riche stone is fayre and orient'.[9] By extension, the figures or tropes of rhetoric which performed this function themselves came to be known as the 'colours of rhetoric'.[10] So Puttenham, in his *Arte of English Poesie* (1589), explicates the rhetorical notion of 'ornament' in terms of 'figures and figurative speaches, which be the . . . colours that a Poett setteth upon his language'.[11] As Peacham writes in his *Garden of Eloquence* (1577), 'Fygures of Rhetoricke . . . fashion a pleasant, sharpe, euident and gallant kinde of speaking', so that 'reason seemeth to be clad in purple', rather than 'walkyng . . . naked'.[12] Erasmus' dictum that style 'sets [a thing] forth to be viewed as though portrayed in colour . . . so that it may seem to be painted, not narrated',[13] draws upon Quintilian's prescription of representing the facts as though to paint them to 'the mind's eye' – suggesting the link between colour and evidence in the rhetorical sense – *evidentia*, or *enargeia*.[14] So Wilson writes that 'translation' through colours is 'referred to . . . the sense of seing'.[15]

The more specialised sense of 'colour' in Bacon, then, is not unrelated to the relatively common visual meaning of the word. He offers 'a table of colours or appearances of good and evil . . . as places of persuasion or dissuasion', an essential feature of deliberative rhetoric. But the Baconian notion emphasises the implication of 'places of persuasion and dissuasion'. 'Colours' are discursive fields, not unlike the original rhetorical sense of 'common places', a recognisable and recognised resource which provides devices for making a piece of oratory convincing. These precepts can be drawn on and used either in support of, or against, any particular set of arguments; the art of colouring lies in the skilful, opportunistic and effective application of such available devices to aid the cause at hand:

the persuader's labour is to make things appear good or evil . . . so it may be represented also by colours, popularities and circumstances, which are of such force, as they sway the ordinary judgement . . .'[16]

---

[9] Wilson, *Rhetoricke* (1553), 90. On colours in classical rhetoric, see Skinner, *Reason and Rhetoric*, 138–9, 195–8, 273–4 and 368–9.
[10] See, e.g., Wilson, *Rhetoricke*, 90v–94v. But see Skinner, *Reason and Rhetoric*, 19–65 and 138–9 on the technical distinction between *ornatus* and colours or tropes.
[11] Puttenham, *Arte*, 138.
[12] Peacham, *Garden*, Hiiii v; cf. Wilson, *Rhetoricke*, 85v.
[13] Erasmus, *On Copia*, 47. On the humanist/rhetorical education in English schools, and the popularity of *De Copia*, see Clarke, *Classical Education*. See also Sonnino, *Handbook*, 1–14.
[14] *Institutio*, 8.3.62. See also Eden, *Poetic and Legal Fiction*, 88.
[15] Wilson, *Rhetoricke*, 91. Cf. Fraunce, *Arcadian Rhetorike*, 15.
[16] Bacon, *Works*, VII, 77.

Precisely how is this swaying of judgement to be achieved? Invoking Aristotle on 'signs or colours of apparent good and evil' in *De Augmentis*, Bacon nevertheless goes on to define the ways in which his notion of colour differs from, adds to, and improves upon Aristotle's, 'for their use is not more for probation than for affecting and moving'.[17] The Baconian notion of the affect of colours has to be understood in the context of his larger theory of rhetoric,[18] where the appeal of rhetorical devices is to the 'Imaginative or Insinuative Reason' which stimulates through vivid embodiments and suggestions, evocative images and illustrations.[19] With the hasty, barely acknowledged proviso, in obvious danger of being unfulfilled or subverted, that a responsible user of rhetoric will refrain from 'colouring that which is evil',[20] Bacon goes on to expound on the specific kind of figuring forth involved in the exercise. What rhetoric does to invisible 'inventions' is to 'make pictures of them so that they may be seen':

> For since they cannot be showed to the sense in corporeal shape, the next degree is to show them to the imagination in as lively representation as possible, by ornament of words . . . Again, if the affections themselves were . . . pliant and obedient to reason . . . there would be no great use of *persuasions and insinuations to give access to the mind*, but naked and simple propositions and proofs would be enough. But the affections do on the contrary . . . raise such mutinies . . . that reason would become captive and servile, if eloquence of persuasions did not win the imagination from the affections' part . . . (italics mine)[21]

This is the precise operation that Bacon identifies as colouring in *Colours*:

> . . . reasons . . . if they . . . have more life and vigour put into them by these forms and insinuations . . . cause a stronger apprehension, and many times suddenly win the mind to a resolution.[22]

Webster's Vittoria Corombona knows this, and is a master at it. The vivid representation that will work on the 'Insinuative Reason' finds its perfect embodiment in Vittoria's narration of her dream. Suggestion is of its essence. It is interesting that Bacon also stresses the importance of strategic address in the exercise of deliberative rhetoric, in contrast with logical proof, for 'the proofs and persuausions of rhetoric ought to differ

---

[17] Ibid., IV, 458.   [18] Ibid., 454–93.   [19] Ibid., III, 383.
[20] Ibid., IV, 456. He eventually offers the inevitable defence that 'rhetoric can be no more blamed for knowing how to colour the worse side, than logic for teaching how to make fine sophisms. For who does not know that the principle of contraries is the same, though the use be opposite?' (457). Well, quite!
[21] Ibid., 456–7. In *WD*, of course, the traditional components of reason and affection are reversed.
[22] Ibid., VII, 77.

according to the auditors'.[23] The success of Vittoria's device would depend entirely on the suggestibility of a specific intended audience. Sure enough, it hits the mark. The value of this artistry does not lie in whether its matter is 'true' or 'false' but in its persuasive force in a particular circumstance. This is the inherent implication in Bacon's *Colours*, but becomes more explicit in his collection of pithy sayings for, and then against, a given set of topics: *The Antitheses of Things*; they are, in fact, very similar to the arguments and counter-arguments, colours and counter-colours in *Colours*, as Lisa Jardine demonstrates in her discussion of Bacon's rhetoric.[24] The 'antitheses' are artful contrivances, tools of a systematic and strategic exercise in image-building: 'as skeins or bottoms of thread which may be unwinded at large when they are wanted'.[25] They are good because they work, not because they communicate virtuous or truthful ideas. An audience that is tuned in will take the cue, as Bracciano does. Vittoria's dream is both a 'coloured device' in the Baconian sense and a piece of oratory built on the figures or colours of rhetoric in a more general sense, the text of the dream itself turning on an elaborate conceit.

A comparison of the contents of this supposed dream with the dreams and second dumb show in *Warning* clarifies *The White Devil*'s distinct understanding of rhetorical colour. Joan's portentous dream, or John Bean's, though mediated by narration like Vittoria's, are actual signs, devoid of 'colour'.[26] Old John dismisses dreams as 'fancies' (1040–1), but they turn out to be accurate intimations of impending disaster. The point about Vittoria's dream is that it *is* but 'fancy': it has no truth value, any more than Zanche's strategic narration of a dream of art in a minor and comic key (V.iii.226–48). It is not surprising, then, that in *Warning*, Mistress Drury takes a bribe from Browne and agrees to 'be [his] Orator' (539–41). It is she who uses rhetorical tricks to work on the imagination of the gullible Anne. Drury's machinations are as unambiguously fake as her 'palmistry' is a ploy. Persuasion is clearly the devil's domain, and criminal insinuation is pitted against a self-consciously emblematic theatrical rhetoric, announcing itself through the moral symbolism of the dumb shows.

---

[23] Ibid., IV, 457.
[24] Jardine, *Francis Bacon*, 224–6 and 219–24. On the notion of paradox in Bacon's theory of rhetoric, and the relation of the *Antitheses* to the *Colours*, see Wallace, *Francis Bacon*, 51–85, esp. 65–70. For a (possible) instance of Bacon's preoccupation with 'paradox', see the apocryphally Baconian 'Christian Paradoxes' in Bacon, *Works*, VII, 289–97.
[25] Bacon, *Works*, IV, 472.
[26] *Warning*, 1023–4.

The White Devil has its own dumb shows – by this time, a dated and crude device.[27] In fact it has two, both in II.ii, enacting the deaths of Isabella and Camillo respectively, at one level similar to that in Greene's *Friar Bacon and Friar Bungay,* showing us gesturally what is actually happening right then.[28] By the end of the scene, both Bracciano and the Conjuror-cum-presenter exit hastily:

> . . . we are now
> Beneath [Vittoria's] roof. 'Twere fit we instantly
> Make out by some back postern.   (50–2)

The assumption would be that Camillo is being killed in another room in the same house (his house) – shown by the second dumb show – where Bracciano has the nerve to lodge with the Conjuror.[29] But the spectacle of Isabella's killing shows her in Bracciano's house. This foregrounds the aesthetic nature of the shows, suggesting their close kinship with theatrical reality, even as the second show shades off intriguingly into the actual. These are visions conjured up by 'strong-commanding art' (22), and watched by Bracciano through 'spectacles of glass' (s.d., 23). The Conjuror is careful to distinguish it from the 'sophistic tricks' of necromancers (6–8), the cheating of jugglers (10), and 'a whole ream of almanac-makers, figure-flingers' 'that only live by stealth,/Since they do merely lie . . .' (16–18). What *he* is about to show, however, is 'art' (22, 32), complete with musical accompaniment, like Paulina's artifice at the end of *Winter's Tale* (35–6), and Bracciano has to put on a 'charmed' night-cap to be able to view it. The Duke seems to understand the nature of the promised shows:

> . . . to show me by your art
> How the *intended* murder of Camillo
> And our loathed duchess grows to action.
>   (1–3) (italics mine)

These are spectacles that conflate times and spaces – showing both murders in the same space, and ending with the apprehending of Vittoria, Flamineo and Marcello, and Francisco's discovery of Camillo's murder (6–52) which seems to take us into real time, leading straight on to Vittoria's trial. The actual disclosure of Isabella's murder within the play

---

[27] Bradbrook, *Themes and Conventions,* 14, 18, 27–8, 44.
[28] Greene, *Friar Bacon,* xiii.
[29] This seems almost universally assumed by critics and editors alike. See the Revels edition by Brian Gibbons (1984) and New Mermaids by Elizabeth Brennan (1966): II.ii.o.i., n; and II.ii., n, respectively.

happens later, at the end of III.ii, when young Giovanni appears in black and breaks the news to his uncle, Francisco. Throughout the second dumb show the operative words are 'as 'twere': Flamineo lays Camillo 'folded double as 'twere under the horse'; Monticelso, Francisco and their army 'go as 'twere to apprehend Vittoria' (s.d., II.ii.37). And yet, the switch to the urgent present after the shows (l. 48–), does suggest an immediacy of event. So, are we to think that the dumb shows are tricks that prospectively show Bracciano, and us, what is to happen? Or are they meant to be presenting in formulaic form what is actually happening at that moment? Do they figure forth the substance of events, or the shadow? The answer, probably, is 'both'. What they certainly do is dislocate our perspective, and make us think about the *rhetoric* of the image, and its implications for dramatic representation, rather than of straightforward correlation between representation and reality. These relations become shifting, slippery. Crucially, unlike *Warning*'s dumb shows, *The White Devil*'s inscribe spectatorship in the figure of Bracciano. His may be a privileged perspective, but we share it. Might that suggest that the playwright finds his surrogate in the Conjuror, and that the dumb shows inscribe the symbolic character of representation itself, rather than simply being a stock representational device? Bracciano also happens to remain a sharp and receptive viewer of images – dreamt, fabricated, or conjured. For the conjurations too are 'inventions', like Vittoria's dream; their elusive 'colour' needs to be correctly interpreted. Bracciano's response to them is comparable to his earlier response to the dream-narration, if less comprehending: ''Twas quaintly done, but yet each circumstance/I taste not fully' (39–40). 'O, 'twas most apparent', replies the Conjuror, and explicates it (48 ff.). The double sense of 'apparent' is fully exploited – both what is evident, and what is but external, or simular.

In this play, in some senses, 'nothing is/but what is not'. Indeed, the moment in IV.i. when Isabella's ghost appears recalls the 'unreal mock'ry' of Banquo's ghost.[30] Yet we are left in little doubt as to the reality-status of the apparition. Francisco, meditating on revenge for his sister's death, first thinks of calling for her picture, to 'fashion [his] revenge more seriously' (97–9).[31] But then he changes his mind and opts for something altogether more mind-forged: 'no, I'll close mine eyes,/And in a melancholic thought I'll frame/Her figure 'fore me' (100–2). '*Enter* Isabella's Ghost'. Francisco sits up:

---

[30] Shakespeare, *Macbeth*, I.iii.131; III.iv.106.
[31] Cf. Vindice's 'study's ornament', his beloved's skull: Middleton, *Revenger's Tragedy*, I.i.14–16.

> . . . Now I ha't – how strong
> Imagination works! How she can frame
> Things which are not! Methinks she stands afore me;
> And by the quick idea of my mind,
> Were my skills pregnant, I could draw her picture.
>
> (102–6)

Eventually, Francisco banishes the image – 'Remove this object;/Out of my brain with't!' And the Ghost exits. It is, however, the playwright's choice to have bodied forth a visible ghost on stage – for his trade, too, is in 'shaping fantasies'.[32] Like Banquo's ghost, or Old Hamlet's in the closet scene, Isabella's too is a theatrical presence.

Francisco's rejection of the ghost as an aid to meditation suggests a link between the function of the imagination with the Catholic practice of meditating upon an object, or a semblance, to incite religious affection:

> . . . What have I to do
> With tombs, or death-beds, funerals, or tears,
> That have to meditate upon revenge?
>
> (IV.i.115)[33]

It also recalls that piece of picture-making inscribed within the already inset spectatorial scene of the dumb shows. While Bracciano sits watching the Conjuror's images, and we watch him, Isabella is shown poisoning herself in kissing her husband's picture revealed by drawing the curtains. This event, itself presented through a vivid image, enacts almost symbolically the danger of idolatry that was associated, in Reformation England, with Catholic habits of making, focusing on and worshipping pictures.[34] Indeed, this is a play which, unlike many others set in Italy, makes much of the Catholic context of the setting, including even a papal election that can be traced back, albeit approximately, to history.[35] But the Catholic

---

[32] Shakespeare, *MSND*, V.i.5. This famous speech by Theseus, on the embodying power of imagination, uses exactly the phrase Francisco uses about the ghost – 'strong imagination' (V.i.18).

[33] On Catholic meditative practices and their use of images and objects, see Duffy, *Stripping of the Altars*, esp. 301–37; and 313–27 on the *ars moriendi*, or rituals connected with 'death-beds, funerals, or tears'. Martz's *Poetry of Meditation* is an early critical landmark in this field, but its evaluation of the importance of spiritual exercises such as those instituted by Ignatius Loyola for the Jesuit Counter-Reformation in England has been criticised as disproportionate. Sullivan, *Dismembered Rhetoric*, offers a balanced overview, especially of the role of rhetorical invention and amplification in meditation. See also Watt, *Cheap Print*, 131–256, for iconophobia and iconography in popular Protestant culture; and Aston, *England's Iconoclasts*.

[34] The curtain further suggests theatre as image-making.

[35] For Webster's sources, and the historical context, see Florio, *Letter*, and 'Fugger newsletter'; Boklund, *Sources*. See Dent, *John Webster's Borrowing*, on verbal and literary debts.

associations do not function as a simple criticism of the pictorial imagination. The play is preoccupied with various orders of images, with inventions and creatures of the imagination; with the drawing of pictures –
insinuative, suggestive, iconic, legal and memorial. Its audacity lies in
foregrounding the dubiousness of some of these sorts of image-making,
and then quite consciously situating itself in this nexus, and challenging
our responses in spite of the awareness it instils; in giving us, first, the
colours of things, and then pleading with 'colour' for forms of being we
have learnt to recognise as less than 'fair'. The scene that brings together
these various modes of imagining is the trial, which also brings into focus
Webster's engagement with the relation of the visual imagination to the
law and the theatre.

'THERE IN THE RING WHERE NAME AND IMAGE MEET'?[36]

The Catholicism of the setting is explicit in III.ii, the 'Arraignment of
Vittoria'. The scene appears to be set in an ecclesiastical court of some
description – presumably a consistory court in Rome.[37] In attendance are
Duke Francisco, six ambassadors, a lawyer, Vittoria as defendant, with a
guard, Flamineo and Zanche. The presiding judge, Cardinal Monticelso,
is dressed in 'scarlet' (70–1): this, clearly, is cardinalate red, meant to
signify holiness and *gravitas*. The colour red, here, is aligned with moral
and judicial authority in accordance with the ostensible iconographical
structure of the play, and the society in which it is set. The lawyer's robe,
presumably, is black.[38] Their meanings are supposed to be self-evident:
red and black are perfectly appropriate colours for representatives of
justice in a 'spiritual' court.

Also present to watch, uninvited and unwelcome, is Bracciano, who
ostentatiously spreads his 'rich gown' (s.d., 3) on the floor to act as a stool,
since there is no place assigned to him. His presence immediately layers
up the scenic structure: the audience share his vantage point, anticipating
the way they are going to be made part of the court audience. Vittoria is

---

[36] Auden, *Selected Poems*, 25, 'O Love, the interest itself'.

[37] However, this trial has components of several jurisdictions and procedures, and cannot be read as a
literal representation of any one kind. For instance, Vittoria's social status combined with the
presence of the ambassadors evokes a 'trial by Peers' rather than a church court trial. But the
context would be recognised by Webster's audience primarily as a canon law procedure. The
Roman setting would effect an imaginative superimposition on a more familiar scenario closer to
home. A Jacobean audience were routinely used to performing such 'double-think'.

[38] On the colour of legal robes, see Baker, 'History of English Judges' Robes'.

commanded by Monticelso to 'stand to the table', and the lawyer to 'fall to the plea' – suggesting standard legal procedure, and the associated furniture (8–9). The spatial organisation is confrontational. The lawyer opens his interrogation with an extravagant gesture towards Vittoria – '*Domine judex converte oculos in hanc pestem mulierum corruptissimam*' ('My lord judge, turn your eyes upon this plague, the most corrupted of women') (10–11). Recalling Flamineo's announcement of Vittoria's first appearance, the lawyer's presentation frames her straight away as a spectacle. The lawyer being positioned, like Vittoria, between the judge and other dignitaries on the one hand, and between Bracciano and the theatre audience on the other, his presentation of her works on both the theatrical and the legal planes. But the pompous Latin immediately drives a rift between the audience at the Roman law court, and the one in Jacobean London. 'What's he?' Vittoria asks out of turn, inserting herself into the legal procedure, and then goes on to ask the judge to order the lawyer to 'speak his usual tongue', or she 'will make no answer' (11–14). Francisco remonstrates with her – 'Why, you understand Latin' (14). Vittoria's reply extends the forum of her trial, as well the range of her addressees:

> I do, Sir, but amongst this auditory
> Which come to hear my cause, the half or more
> May be ignorant in't . . .
> . . .
> . . . all this assembly
> Shall hear what you charge me with.   (15–20)

Notwithstanding Webster's much-quoted expression of disdain for the audience, after the failure of the play's opening performance at the Red Bull,[39] he is here writing the audience into the judicial space, through Vittoria's gesture. Vittoria aims her persuasion not just at her judges in court but also to the jury of the audience who are both present and not present. In this instance, their ignorance of Latin becomes not a cause for contempt, but a call for accessibility as a mark of fairness. Implicit in this scene is a contrast between two notions of the trial jury's assumed function. The jury Vittoria appeals to corresponds to the new common-law model of impartial, independent evaluators of testimony presented in court and assessors of 'facts' (i.e. alleged criminal acts supported by various evidence), as opposed to the earlier model outmoded from around

---

[39] 'To the Reader', *WD* (6–7), where Webster complains about the lack of 'a full and understanding auditory' on the first night.

the middle of the sixteenth century – that of a jury of neighbours or peers, men who already had information about the defendant and shared aspects of the role of witnesses.[40] In the pre-trial scene, Francisco comments on the shrewdness of Monticelso in having '[obtained]/The presence of all the grave lieger ambassadors/To hear Vittoria's trial' (III.i.1–3): their assuredly adversarial opinion will lend weight to the case of the prosecution which is self-confessedly based on merely circumstantial rather than substantive evidence (4–8). The presence of the dignitaries and the notion of credit associated with them carry overtones of the procedures of trial by peers in early modern England. Where noblemen indicted for capital offence were tried in court when Parliament was not sitting, the Lord High Steward acted as judge and the peers (in the specific sense of 'lords' rather than the more general common-law sense of 'equals') as the jury in the name of 'Lord triers', and the decision was by majority.[41] When Parliament was sitting, the tribunal was the House of Lords, and the Lord High Steward presided while the peers were the judges. In either case, the presence of worthy nobles evokes, in the cross-jurisdictional way typical of Webster's trial scenes, a point of judicial reference that is challenged and undercut by Vittoria's articulate preference for the 'ignorant' jury of people who would assess the conjunction of her performance and 'facts' rather than speak from prior opinion or knowledge. Significantly, there was much discontent in the period over the failure of the system to appoint learned and well-respected men to juries and recruiting, instead, from the 'simple and the ignorant'.[42]

The 'credit' Vittoria seeks (22), however, is at once legal and histrionic. Since she must be made into an image, she fashions herself actively as a rhetorical sign in the most inclusive sense, and beats the prosecutors at their own game. The rhetorical underpinning of the legal situation is foregrounded: the Lawyer, exasperated by her interruptions, exclaims that 'the woman/Knows not her tropes nor figures', nor 'grammatical elocution' (39–42). The differences among various levels of rhetoric begin to appear. Vittoria's defence is to adopt a superior art, and marshal the colours of rhetoric to fashion a factually untrue plea which is more convincing and effective as 'evidence' in her 'wider' court than the cruder

---

[40] See Introduction, n. 11, above; esp. Shapiro, *Culture of Fact*, 13, and Hutson, 'Rethinking "the Spectacle of the Scaffold"', 37–8.

[41] On trial by peers, see Baker, *Oxford History*, 520–1; Stephen, *History*, 161–5; Drinker Bowen, *Lion*, Ch. 12, provides an evocative account of the trials of Henry, Earl of Southampton, and Robert, Earl of Essex, by peers.

[42] Larkin and Hughes, eds., *Stuart Royal Proclamations*, no. 77.

proofs flaunted by the prosecution; to attempt, in other words, to give 'colour' to her plea.

COLOURING A PLEA

The slippage from rhetorical to legal, or vice-versa, is natural and easy, not only because of the familiar overlap between the disciplines, but also, more specifically, because 'colour' had a technical legal meaning in the period, which any law student would have been aware of. To 'give colour' to an opponent in pleading was a notion conceived in the fourteenth century, and had become common procedural practice in English law by the fifteenth. Originally it was used in assizes of novel disseisin, but was also used derivatively in trespass and some other forms of action.[43] It was a device, a fictional means of putting the case, used by defendants if they wanted a discussion of the points of law in court, and a consideration of the parties' rights, before the case went to the technically unlearned jury. It took the form, most typically, of the defendant offering his own description of the plaintiff's case, to suggest that though there was indeed a conflict, the basis of the plaintiff's complaint was legally unsound; the premise that the plaintiff was wronged was misconceived, because he had no rights in the first place. For instance, my cousin takes me to court for having evicted him from his property. I, as defendant, admit that I have indeed thrown him out of the said premises, but that the property never belonged to him in the first place, because though my father, the original owner, gifted my cousin, his nephew, a deed, it was never validated because he never parted with his property which eventually passed into my hands by inheritance. This would force the plaintiff to redescribe the issue, and, more importantly, the justices to engage with the facts of the case in detail. This variation on what is known as 'confession and avoidance' in common law would prompt an unplanned and genuine discussion.

The interest of the device lies in its patent fictionality. It was an instrument of art, discarded once persuasion had been achieved. As Donald Sutherland puts it in his seminal article on the legal history of 'Colour', 'what the defendant said about the plaintiff's claim was not true, and not expected to be true, but pure sham, pure fiction'.[44] So much so

---

[43] On disseisin, see Glossary; and Baker, *Introduction*, 262–71.

[44] Sutherland, 'Legal Reasoning', 182–94 (184). For other legal writing on 'colour', and its continuing use in the early modern period, see Stephen, *Treatise*, 1–3, 183–7, 498–503, 500–3, 600–1, 662–3; and

that standardised forms of 'colour' became available in the fifteenth century, so that the same claim was used by hundreds of defendants in a variety of cases.[45] Once the plaintiff replied to the defendant's 'colour', no one bothered about the precise claims of the colour: the purpose of giving colour had been achieved, a discussion of the specific basis of the plaintiff's case had been initiated. Aimed at persuasion, its overlap with rhetorical colours is obvious. It was an attribute of style, wit and performative skill, rather than an instrument of factual truth. The device almost amounted to an unexpected interjection which arrested, and called for a restructuring of, the procedure in order to accommodate the demand of the colour-giver. A plea could be regarded legally as a 'bad plea' if it did not use colour where it could have, or should have done.[46] Colouring was an important attribute of what was known among the Inns as 'the science of well pleading' which was premised on the straightforward construction of an artefact in law. Implicitly, the need for colour was based on the court's need for concreteness of facts.[47] But vividness was severed from accuracy of fact and set adrift, exactly like rhetorical colour being cut loose from its assumed mooring in ethics. 'Colour' thus embodied a paradox at the heart of legal procedure.

In the sixteenth century, when the common-law practice of giving colour had become so much of a received convention as to have been taken on trust, rather like a 'precedent', we still find Christopher St. German vexed over the moral and epistemological implications of this piece of falsehood in his *Doctor and Student* (1523–32).[48] St. German was well-versed in canon, civil and common law. Significantly, his interest, as a legal theorist, lay primarily in the relationship of the law of England with the law of conscience.[49] In this, his position is not unlike Henry

on 'implied colour', 499 and 501. See also Chitty, *Practical Treatise*, 1, 2, 182–8, 496–521 and 600–1. The difference between 'confession and avoidance' and 'colour' is that the former was meant to be based on factual truth; not so the latter.

[45] As late as 1803, 'colour' in pleading was perceived essentially in the same terms as in the medieval and early modern periods, e.g. Potts, *Law Dictionary*: 'Colour . . . a probable plea, but false in fact, and hath this end to draw the trial of the cause from the jury to the judges' (111–12).

[46] Sutherland, 'Legal Reasoning', 186–7.

[47] Ibid, 189–90.

[48] St. German, *Doctor and Student* (hereafter, 'St. German').

[49] St. German's position here is at first confusing, but ultimately revealing. He is reviewing the indigenous common law, rooted in the constitution of England, from the point of view of the law of Rome which still constituted the main body of theoretical legal literature in the 1520s, and a literature in which he, like Swinburne, was well-versed. On his ambiguous position in relation to the Reformation, see St. German, xi–xx. Many of the concepts he wrestles with hark back to the *Corpus Juris Civilis*. Whether it was the influence of humanism, a shared intellectual heritage,

Swinburne's, later, in the smaller and more specific field of canon law. Also, like Swinburne, St. German had practical experience of law, having been a Middle Templar and Master of Requests;[50] and like him, mainly concerned with mediating legal principles to the lay reader. One of St. German's main concerns, as of Swinburne, is to reconcile conscience to the law of the realm as administered in courts, whether they be secular or ecclesiastical. What troubles them both is that the connection might not be obvious enough for the multitudes to grasp, so they find rhetorical means and compositional formats enabling them to raise, and thus pre-empt, doubts regarding the truth value of law. We have seen how Swinburne casts his treatise on spousals in the form of 'ampliations' or objections to the existent law, and his answers, leading to discussions and justifications of points of law. St. German, almost half a century earlier, chooses a more explicitly dialogic mode, working through questions, objections, answers and explanations that pass between a Doctor of Divinity and a student of law, ultimately seeking to establish in digestible form the correlation between God's law and that of His deputies on earth.

This concern inevitably leads to a discussion of 'colour'. The Student explains the rationale behind using colour to the Doctor with reference to a tenancy dispute:

And therfore to the intente that matter may be shewyd and pledyd before the iudges rather then before the Jurye/the tenauntes vse to give the pleyntyffe a colour/that is to say a colour of accyon wherby it shall appere that it were hurtfull to the tenaunte to put the matter he pledyth to the iudgement of xii men/& the moost comon coloure that is vsyd in suche a case is thys/when he had pledyd that such a man enfyffed him as before apperyth: it ys vsyd that he shal plede ferther and say that the pleyntyffe claymyng in by a colour of a dede or feffement made by the sayd feffour before the feffement made to hym/where nought passyd by

or the more practical need of common law (in the main lacking a definitive body of written statutes at this stage) to absorb, adapt and appropriate some of the intellectual and hermeneutic concerns of Roman law, or whether it was because the same conceptual problems had to be encountered, English legal thinking in the sixteenth century is far more intertwined with the intellectual structure of the civil law than has been commonly granted. Maclean raises this possibility as a starting point for his study: see Maclean, *Interpretation*, esp. 1–66 and 179–202. St. German's treatise, curiously, goes unnoticed by him, possibly because St. German writes about the law of the land! But see Macnair, *Law of Proof*, 45, for Egerton's admission of the concurrence of the two legal traditions. The assimilation and appropriation of Civil law tenets by the common law of England was, in imaginative terms, similar to the appropriation of Catholic modes of presentation by Protestant propagandists in the English Reformation. After all, St. German was an anti-clerical pro-Reformist himself, but not an extreme or radical, or an entirely theoretical one.

50 See Leadam, ed., *Select Cases*, civ, cv, cvi, cix and cxv; and St. German, xi.

the dede entred/vpon whom he entryd and askyth Jugement yf the assyse lye against hym.[51] . . . And in such case the iuges may not put the tenaunt from the plee/for they know not as Juges but that it is trew/and so if any defaut be it is in the tenaunt & not in the courte. And though the trouthe be that there were no suche dede of feeoffment made to the playntyf as the tenaunt pleadeth/yet methinketh it ys no defaut in the tenant for he dothe it to a good intent as before appereth.

This piece of casuistry does not go unnoticed. The Doctor remonstrates:

If the tenaunt know that the feoffour made no such dede of feoffement to the playntyf/than there is a defaute in the tenaunt to plead it/for he wyttyngly sayth against the trouthe/& is holden by al doctours that euery lye is an offence more or lesse . . . & therfore he sayth that the playntyff claymyng in by the colour of a dede of feffement where nought passyd . . . knowyng that there was noo suche feffement it was a lye in hym and a venyall synne as me thynkyth.[52]

The Student justifies this lie on the grounds that it is used in self-defence and 'to auoyde fro his neyghboure the daunger of periurye'; that just as rulers and governors are justified in extracting confessions from miscreants by suggesting their crimes are well known even when that is not the case, 'yet it is noo offence to saye they were so informyd bycause they doo it for the comon welthe' (297). This, of course, is the classic argument behind legal fictions.[53] St. German's treatise, along with Littleton's *Tenures* (c.1455, pub. 1481), Fitzherbert's *Abridgement* (1514–16), Perkins's *Profitable Booke* (1530), Finch's *Nomotechnia* (1613), Coke's *Commentary on Littleton* (1628), and suchlike institutional books, written from the early sixteenth century onwards, formed an important part of the recommended legal education at the Inns in the late sixteenth and early seventeenth centuries.[54] From the 1550s onwards, the sole supremacy of oral methods of legal learning, and of manuscript material, came to be balanced by a stress on the private reading of printed legal literature: treatises like those mentioned above, which would provide 'great booke skil, or muche beating of their braine by anie close studie, or secret musyng in their chamber'.[55] Such pioneering figures as Edward Coke

---

[51] On feoffment, see Glossary. On real property, feudalism and feoffment, see Baker, *Introduction*, 282–94.

[52] St. German, 293–7 (294–6).

[53] See p. 51 above, and Maclean, *Interpretation*, 138–42.

[54] See Prest, *Inns of Court*, Ch. 7, but esp. 126, 132 and 143–4; Baker, *Introduction*, 214–21.

[55] Wilson, *Rhetoricke*, 21. This transition, related to the increasing availability of print, has implications for the history of reading in the sixteenth century, especially in London, and the contribution of law to the wider patterns and practices of readership.

and Simonds D'Ewes actively advocated this programme until as late as the 1620s. Webster was a bencher at the Middle Temple from 1597, and is almost certain to have read *Doctor and Student.*[56]

The Doctor's classification of lies involves a distinction among types that roughly correspond to the categories of poetical falsehoods outlined by Augustine, and inherited by the Christian rhetorical tradition that combined with, and adapted, the classical (Aristotelian) heritage to form the complex literary theory of the English Renaissance. St. German's Doctor talks of three kinds of lies:

> yf it be of malyce & to the hurte of his neighbour/than it is called (mendacium perniciosum) and that ys dedely synne. And yf yt be in sporte and to the hurte of no man/nor of custome vsyd/ne of pleasure that he hathe in lyenge/than that is venyall synne/and ys callyd mendacium iocosum. And yf yt be to the profyte of his neighbour and to the hurt of no man then it is also venyall synne/and is callyd . . . mendacium officiosum. And thoughe it be the leest of the thre yet it is a venyall synne & wold be eschewyd.[57]

This is very similar to the originally Augustinian classification of *falsa* (false things) into *fallax* and *mendax.*[58] *Fallax* was a lie intended by the speaker/rhetorician to deceive, while *mendax* was a fabulous kind of falsehood, to please rather than deceive, and so, ethically acceptable. Poetic fiction, or, by extension, imaginative fiction, is discussed as being analogous to that of law not only by Aristotle and Augustine but also, following them, by Sidney, who justifies the poet's lies, albeit through a simplification of the Aristotelian analogy, as 'profitable invention' for the good end of demonstration or instruction.[59] This could as well be described as 'mendacium officiosum': the differentia here, as in Aristotle, Augustine and St. German, is 'intention'. Significantly, Bacon uses the word 'fallax' repeatedly when he follows the statement of each 'colour'

---

[56] On the influence of St. German, see Kahn and Hutson, *Rhetoric and Law*, 8; Harris Sacks, 'The Promise and the Contract'.

[57] St. German, 295. The Doctor's doubts here are, of course, set to rest by the Student's explanation.

[58] Augustine's *falsa* consist of imitations, artificial or natural: see St. Augustine, *Soliloquies*, 72–86; *St. Augustine Against the Academics*, 81–5 and 146–7. See Eden, *Poetic and Legal Tradition*, 112–75 on these categories in the Aristotelian and Augustinian traditions; and Introduction, Ch. 1 and Ch. 4, Section 4.4, on the provenance of these rhetorical traditions in the intellectual inheritance and climate of the English Renaissance. The debate on things false or true ultimately applies to categories of images: imitation itself is a mimetic image, whether false or true. Truth in imitation is linked by Augustine to the notion of *Imitatio Christi*. On *fallax* and *mendax* in theology, see Sommerville, 'New Art of Lying'. On the dependence of scholastics and humanists alike on the *mendax/fallax* distinction, see Maclean, *Interpretation*, 140–2.

[59] Sidney, *Apology*, 124. The *Apology* was published around 1580. Sidney's works were published and republished throughout Webster's youth.

with a set of counter-illustrations; 'the fallax of this colour' is the usual phrase introducing these counter-arguments.[60] Indeed, his list of colours and counter-colours is entitled 'A Table of Colours or Appearances of Good and Evil, and their degrees, as Places of Persuasion and Dissuasion, and their several Fallaxes, and the Elenches of them'.[61] The category of 'fallax' implicitly invokes the contrasting category of mendax, which is clearly the exercise a successful user of colour engages in. The interrelatedness or sharedness of these various fields – common 'places', if we like – of the uses and notions of colour is implicit in the manipulation of colours in Webster's play.[62] In the case of drama, the idea – and the phenomenon – of the image or the imitation or, if we prefer, the *evidentia*, acquires a specially concise focus because of the given medium. *hite Devil* expertly and knowingly exploits this focus and makes it resonate against the ostensible moral structure of its action.

'SUCH OPEN AND APPARENT GUILT'[63]

Various senses of colour are set off against one another in the arraignment of Vittoria – colours of rhetoric, physiognomical notions of expressive colours, face-painting and cosmetics, Catholic pictorialism, and 'colour' in pleading. The exchange in which all these different senses come into play is that between Vittoria and Monticelso, once Monticelso takes on the role of prosecuting lawyer and confronts Vittoria with the charges against her:

MONTICELSO. I shall be plainer with you, and paint out
      Your follies in more natural red and white
      Than that upon your cheek.
VITTORIA.   O, you mistake.
      You raise a blood as noble in this cheek
      As ever was your mother's.
MONTICELSO. I must spare you till proof cry whore to that.
      Observe this creature here, my honoured lords,
      A woman of most prodigious spirit
      In her effected. (III.ii.50–9)

The different levels of 'colour' implicit here constantly overlap with, or slide into one another, and ultimately relate, and contribute, to the idea of

---

[60] Bacon, *Works*, VII, 77–92.
[61] Ibid., 78. On *elenchus*, see Glossary.
[62] Bacon talks of these 'places' as self-evident loci available to pleaders, 'ready prepared, and handled and illustrated on both sides': *Works*, IV, 422.
[63] *WD*, III.iii.56.

legal colour that informs the trial scene and its dramatic impact. Monticelso says that he, unlike the lawyer, will be blunt and use a truth-telling rhetoric. One cannot but use 'paint' in any representation, but truthfulness is most itself when most like the red and white of the natural body; his painted depiction of her follies will not only be more direct than the lawyer's legal bombast, but also more natural in its red- and whiteness than her harlot's painted cheek. No, she replies, for her cheeks look red at the moment only because he has called up a blush from the blood that he shares with her and his mother.

The overall thrust of this scene, as engineered by Monticelso, is to present Vittoria to the court as an evident spectacle of corruption: 'Observe this creature here, my honoured lords' (57). All of her, he suggests, is eloquent of her sinfulness. Her impudence is writ large on her bearing: 'She comes not like a widow; she comes armed/With scorn and impudence. Is this a mourning habit?' (121–2). So invested is he in visually impressing Vittoria's moral bankruptcy that even the fact of using false colour on her face becomes a visible index of it. The fairness of her form is meant to stand for the hypocrisy of her soul: 'If the devil/Did ever take good shape, behold his picture' (216–17). The 'pictures' Monticelso draws, of whore and murderess, are part of his attempt to control the image of the defendant. These are pitted against Vittoria's own self-projection. An underlying assumption behind his exercise is the physiognomic notion we have already encountered, that the inner condition expresses itself in physical signs. Thomas Wright, in *Passions of the Mind*, asserts that

wise men often, thorow the windowes of the face, behold the secrets of the heart . . . so the hearts of men are manifest vnto the wise . . . (27)

He proceeds to tell the story of Alexander the Great who, being warned that Philip, his trusted physician, intended to poison his medicine, made a gamble. He drank the medicine offered to him by Philip, at the same time as he handed over to him the letter warning him of this supposed conspiracy, intently observing Philip as he read the letter:

. . . he beheld him continually in the face, supposing that if he had been faulty, some token would haue appeared in his countenance: When Philip had read the letter, he shewed more tokens of displeasantness, than of feare: which, with the louing words of the Physitian, assured *Alexander* of his seruants fidelitie . . . By this example, superiours may learn to coniecture the affections of their subiects mindes, by a silent speech pronounced in their very countenances. (28–9)

Macbeth expresses exactly this notion of the expressiveness of the outward when he marvels at his wife's unchanged countenance despite the visible presence, as he imagines, of the conscience-tormenting ghost of Banquo: 'When now I think you can behold such sights,/And keep the natural ruby of your cheeks'.[64]

This belief was not purely a denizen of imaginative literature, any more than it was confined to a specific discipline. Law itself was informed with this idea, and counted on it in certain areas, though there is no documentary evidence to suggest that its legal application was gendered. One of the reasons why defendants in criminal trials were allowed no counsel but could – and indeed had to – speak for themselves as best they could, was the idea that this might provide supplementary evidence by way of expressive gestures which would help the court in coming to a verdict. Raleigh, famously, was not allowed benefit of counsel in his treason trial.[65] Ferdinand Pulton of Lincoln's Inn writes in his treatise *De Pace Regni* that upon a plea of not guilty to an indictment of treason or felony, the defendant

must answer it in proper person, and not by Atturney, or councell learned: for this plea of not guiltie doth tend to the fact, the which the party himselfe doth best know, and therefore he can best make answer vnto it. And if his councell learned should pleade . . . for him, and defend him, it may be that they would be so couert in their speeches, and so shadow the matter with words, and so attenuate the proofes and euidence, that it would be hard or long to haue the truth appeare. Also if the partie himselfe defend it, peradventure his conscience will pricke him to vtter the truth, *or his countenance, or gesture will shew some tokens therof,* or by his simple speeches somewhat may be drawne from him to bolt out the veritie of the cause, which would not be won of men learned in the Law, who endeauour to speake prouidently, and artificially . . . (italics mine)[66]

This not only states the connection between legal psychology and contemporary physiognomy, but also the assumption that the best proofs are self-evident and natural, even if legal procedure be an artifice. It is as though what law discovers belongs to nature and has objective status.

---

[64] Shakespeare, *Macbeth*, III.v.113–14. Cf. *Leir*, xv, 1172–7, in Bullough, *Sources*, VII, on the idea of a 'dumb shew' of facial expressions: the dumb show as a theatrical device works on the same premise as physiognomical notions of legible correspondence between gestures and being.

[65] See Stephen, 'Trial', 184, on denial of the benefit of counsel to those accused of treason.

[66] Pulton, *De Pace Regis*, 184v–185. For other legal references, see Baker, *Legal Profession*, 286–7. This, incidentally, illuminates Lucrece's psychology, in Shakespeare's *Lucrece*, when she desists from making her case in a letter to her husband and waits for an occasion when her gestures and expressions 'may grace the fashion/Of her disgrace, the better so to clear her' (1317–21); she has constructed the scene of disclosure as a trial where she needs not only to tell the truth but to prove her own chastity.

Such positivism is precisely what Vittoria's trial scene destabilises, along with any physiognomical or legal notions of a straightforward correspondence between inner and outer, hidden and visible. Inherent in Vittoria's defence in her verbal match with Monticelso is the hint that Monticelso is not merely commenting on artificial colouring of the face but questioning the functions of Vittoria's natural body which, instead of expressing her 'intention' as bodies are meant to, gives out false signals. This is why his claims and accusations teeter on the brink of suggestive contraries: his attempt to demonstrate and throw into relief Vittoria's ostensibly unmistakable viciousness is overpowered by his anxiety about the opacity of her exterior which, in turn, is constructed as a type of deceptiveness in itself. The blushing that is normally a manifestation of inner beauty and modesty are, in Vittoria's body – no whit less 'prodigious' than her 'spirit' – expressive of false modesty, just as her physical fairness gives a lie to a soul ridden with 'black sin'. Her very physical being, Monticelso implies, creates a false semiotic. There is an almost imperceptible transference, in the exchange quoted, from a contrast between the lawyer's parodically 'deep eloquence' and Monticelso's plain speaking, to an ethical distinction between Monticelso's transparent language and Vittoria's impenetrable appearance which is a false semblance of her true nature.[67] In Augustinian rhetorical terms, the latter belongs to the category of *falsa*.

The unyielding selfhood that gains a specifically legal focus in the trial scene is, however, part of the play's more general, and uniformly gendered, sense of a threateningly unknowable core – centred on Vittoria at all times. The desire to pierce the façade and discover the inner truth is figured through an almost cannibalistic image, produced by the sick imagination of Bracciano who is insensibly provoked by the contrived love-letter sent to Vittoria by Francisco, which he (Bracciano) is meant to, and does, intercept. Flamineo stokes the fire, not without a hint of mockery:

> Ud's foot, you speak as if a man
> Should know what fowl is coffin'd in a baked meat
> Afore you cut it up.   (IV.ii.19–21)

Bracciano rasps back:

> I'll open't, were't her heart. What's here subscribed –
> '*Florence*'? This juggling is gross and palpable. (22–3)[68]

---

[67] Cf. Claudio on Hero's 'false' blush, and the treacherous 'evidence' of her body': *Much Ado*, IV.i.33–8.
[68] Cf. Ford, *'Tis Pity*, IV.iii.53–4.

And then he proceeds to misread the letter grossly and palpably to the audience, who know it is forged, and is not, as he thinks, evidence of Vittoria's infidelity. His urge to discover escalates rapidly till he begins to sound like the ranting stock jealous-husband figure (like Bassanes, a butt of jokes in Ford's *Broken Heart*) as he charges at Vittoria:

> Come, come, let's see your cabinet, discover
> Your treasury of love-letters. Death and furies,
> I'll see them all.   (76–8)

His frustration at the ultimate inaccessibility of the inward is made fun of by the dramatic medium through the excess and luridness of his imagery: the naïveté of signification implicit in his desire has no place in Webster's dramaturgy, any more than in Vittoria's performance – or indeed her being.[69] Lodovico's label for Vittoria's condition – 'such open and apparent guilt' (III.iii.56) – sounds hollow as we experience the play, and is reduced to a fantasy of the law, and of the stereotypical male imagination.

Interestingly enough, the physiognomic discourse of the time itself turns out, on closer inspection, to be self-divided. No sooner does Wright assert that 'the hearts of men are manifest to the wise', than he qualifies it with a theologically informed proviso:

. . . not that they can exactly, vnderstand the hearts which be inscrutable, and onely open vnto GOD, the coniectures thay may aime well at them: for as he which beholdeth his face in the water, doth not discerne it exactly, but rather a shadowe, then a face; euen so he that by externall phisiognomy and operations, will diuine what lyeth hidden in the heart, may rather conceiue an Image of that affection . . . then a perfite and resolute knowledge . . . (*Passions*, 27)

Other writers concede even more: in a little-known quasi-medical and quasi-physiognomical tract called *The Optick Glass of Humors* (1607), the

---

[69] Significantly, Bracciano's violent urge to uncover is aimed at riddling in the letter – 'A haltar on his strange equivocation!' (34). His impatience with it aligns him temporarily with the investigating and prosecuting bodies. When he exclaims, 'How long have I beheld the devil in crystal?' (IV. ii.88), he echoes Monticelso in the trial scene (III.ii.216–17). Ultimately, this indignation stands for law's inability to deal with paradox and opacity.

The dramaturgical statement here seems similar in its impulse to that final lurid gesture in Ford's *'Tis Pity*, where Giovanni scoops out Annabella's heart and enters with it – presumably a sheep's heart – at his dagger's end. That is as much a comment on the impossibility of possessing the inalienable core of another's being, as the present moment is on the impossibility of complete knowledge or hermeneutic control over an invisible intention. But while in *'Tis Pity* the theatrical gesture becomes in the end a statement about the condition of human love, here it is more engaged with the relation between inner and outer in law, drama and life. Ford's *coup de théâtre* is also, of course, time's revenge, and the theatre's, on a trope bled dry over generations of conventional love poetry and certain varieties of effete drama.

author, 'T.W.', drifts suggestively from an assertion of the inner–outer correspondence into a rumination on how easy it is to get it wrong.[70] In Chapter 3, 'Whether internall faculty may be knowne by the externall phisiognomy and visage', guidelines for reading the former through the latter give way to a set of qualifications which, like Swinburne's 'Ampliations' and St. German's Doctor's objections, make more impact than the affirmations of the technique; just as doubt is often a more emotive force than certainty. The tenor takes over from the vehicle, to say that Ulysses's appearance was misleading. But T.W. persists with reassurances: for instance, Ulysses's speech would reveal the inner man (D2). But what about Aesop, who wanted no deformity externally, yet 'what beautie had he not mentally?'; there is always the possibility of 'a leaden rapier in a golden sheath', 'wrinkled faces . . . vnder smooth paint', 'a gaudy outside and a baudy . . . inside', 'a faire . . . corps, but a fowle . . . mind' (D2v–D3). The world-view of popular providentialist texts which provided the background for plays like *White Devil* is transformed, as Webster throws a challenge at the semiotics of conventional judgement, even in the very person of the paradoxically named 'white devil' of the play. The dubiousness of the evidentiary valency of physiognomy is harnessed to a wider scepticism about the notion of evidence.

The blood on Vittoria's fair cheeks, however, also professes to be no less chaste than Monticelso's mother's. The idea of sexual depravity dances around the other, more obvious meanings. It is already implicit in Monticelso's accusation of her tainted colour. Vittoria picks up on this, and slams back a commensurate, if equally implicit insult: allusions to parentage in the period were, more often than not, infused with suggestions of cuckoldry, and of one's mother's lack of chastity. So, Vittoria's blood being as noble as his mother's suggests, subtextually, that her incontinence was only as bad as the one that produced him. Nor is this suggestion missed: 'I must spare you till proof cry whore to that' (III.ii.56); this rejoinder takes us straight into the domain of misogyny and sexual slander.

'COLOURED ABUSES'[71]

All this spills over quite naturally into a yet further level of signification, with theological overtones. Monticelso implies Vittoria is false: so her

---

[70] T.W., *Optick Glass.*
[71] Phrase used of the Church of Rome, in contrast with the clear crystal of the Protestant faith, in Batman, *Christall Glasse,* t.p.

appearance, instead of being a true manifestation of her inner state, is rosy and fair. But the falsity here is almost signified by the use of artificial colours. Cosmetics for women were used in the period, and often condemned in Puritan moralistic literature such as Stubbes's *Anatomy*.[72] Allusions also appear in a variety of plays. Romelio, in Webster's *Devil's Law-Case*, says that Jolenta's 'pale face/Will make men think [she] used some art before,/Some odious painting'.[73] In Barry's romp of a play, *Ram Alley*, Will Small's whore, Francis, protests how she, a country lass, was taught the corrupting arts of the court, including face-painting: 'sleeking, glazing', 'mercury water, fucus' (I.i.67–71). Cosmetics were also associated with Catholicism in Protestant eyes. The Church of Rome, the Pope, indeed the Catholic creed itself, were frequently attacked for hypocrisy in sermons and other anti-Catholic propaganda. The habit of worshipping painted images combined with the precise accusation of deceit to form the notion of a gaudy exterior giving a lie to the inner decadence of the 'Romish faith'. It is this ugliness that Thomas Adams seeks to expose by enabling his audience to see through the false appearance in his sermon, *The White Deuill* (1612):

. . . I will spend a little time, to vncase this *white Deuill*, and strip him of all his borrowed colours . . . a guilded hypocrite, a *white-skind* Deuill.[74]

It is easy to see how this complex of associations lent itself to a gendered application. The Church of Rome became the scarlet whore of Babylon, a seductress luring souls into corruption rather than righteousness, leading astray with false show of fairness rather than signalling the path to moral rectitude:

It is a complexion for lust, who, were she not painted ouer with religious shew, would appeare as loathsome to the worlde, as she is indeede . . . Thus hypocrisie can put bloud in your cheeckes, . . . and better your colours; but you may be sicke in your consciences, and almost dead at the heart . . . *God shall smite thee, thou painted wall;* and off with your vermillion dye with the riuers of brimston.[75]

The very terms of Adams's condemnation recall the colour terminology of Webster's play, first performed in the same year.[76]

But inherent in the idea of Catholicism as a richly painted hollowness is an implicit dualism between a use of colour as a stable sign of hypocrisy in

---

[72] See Plat, *Delightes for Ladies*, for literature on cosmetics.   [73] Webster, *DLC*, III.iii.3–4.
[74] Adams, *The Works*, 43.   [75] Ibid., 45–6.
[76] On the possibly intertextual relation between Adams and Webster, see Dent, *Webster's Borrowing*; Aitken, 'John Webster and Thomas Adams'; Waage, *White Devil Discover'd*, Ch. 9.

as much as external allure is necessarily incongruent with inner corruption, and an understanding of colour as a straightforward moral index in as much as true nature needs must show its true colours externally. So Thomas Adams, in his sermon *The Black Devill* (1615) quotes from Jeremiah (13, 23) on the title-page: 'Can the Black-Moore change his skin? Or the Leopard his spots? Then may ye also do good, that are accustomed to do euill';[77] and then also writes the complementary sermon, *The White Deuill,* representing hypocrisy itself.[78] He claims to present 'Impiety in the true colours . . . look here, and detest it'.[79] Adams is conscious of his use of two notions of colour, and colour words, and presents them almost as two contrasting principles of composition, two aesthetics dictated by the different characters of the two quarries:

The *White Deuill,* the *hypocrite* hath beene formerly discouer'd, and the sky-coloured vaile of his dissimulation pulled off. I am to present to your view and detestation a sinner of contrary colour, swarthy rebellion . . . an *Apostate* falling into the clutches of eight *vncleane spirits.* Needs must he be fowle, that hath so many fowle deuils in him . . . If *Hypocrisie* there, were iustly called the *White Deuill; Apostasie* here may as iustlie be called the *Blacke Deuill.* In the former was a *white* skinne of profession drawne ouer an vlcerous corps: here hyde and carcasse . . . seeming and being, outward profession and inward intention, are *blacke,* foule, detestable. Therefore we call him the *Apostate,* or *blacke Deuill.*[80]

Colour as an expressive metaphor seems as manipulable as colour itself.

We can now locate Webster's deployment of colour in a whole discursive network current at the time. But the burden of sermon literature is the moral dubiousness of the artificial: this is the point on which Webster's own position is distinct from the moralising Roman Cardinal who spouts Protestant invective. It is also a point on which such simple polarities as corrupt-Catholic and righteous-Protestant do not hold in this play, though it does come complete with skulls and ghosts (IV.i.102 ff.; IV.iv.124 ff.), beads and prayer-books (V.i.69), cardinals and popes. In a typically anti-papist vein, the Jacobean clergyman and religious controversialist Oliver Ormerod comments on Catholic image-making:

The Heathen . . . were the first inuenters of images: . . . [which] . . . were but inuentions of their . . . braines, very vnlike their originals . . . The like may be said

---

[77] Adams, *Black Devill,* t.p.   [78] Adams, *White Devill,* 32–60.
[79] Adams, *Black Devill,* A4.   [80] Ibid., B4, 6.

of your supposed imaginary gods, for they are but *Pigmalion's* pictures, workes of your deuising, as vnlike the originals, as *Catrina* and *Phrine* were to *Venus*.[81]

Such images fall under the category of 'Semblances', defined here as false likeness, or untruth (47). To understand the play's position in relation to Pygmalion's art, we need to go back to Renaissance rhetoric where the same terms as those of Protestant propaganda, and the same figures of disapprobation, were applied to literary language and rhetoric.

'THOSE BRITTLE EVIDENCES OF LAW':[82] THE ORDER OF IMAGES

In trying to fashion a Protestant poetic, Sidney warns against using 'Eloquence' so as to let it be 'disguised, in a Courtisanlike painted affectation'.[83] The wariness of a deceptively coloured language is perceived in terms identical to anti-Catholic polemic both in their content and in their predominant metaphor. An artificially made-up woman becomes a figure for moral falsity in expressive modes no less than in religious discourse. But this is only one of two perceived possibilities of 'the goodly and bewtifull colours of Eloqution'.[84] For as in physiognomy, so in rhetorical theory, the notion of deceptive or manipulable surface coexisted with another, more extractive model, one that saw 'colour' as an implement for making visible rather than obscuring 'true' or inner nature. Only, here, the latter is a function of art rather than physical nature. Let us revisit, one last time, that initiatory work of artifice in the play, Vittoria's dream, and the response it elicits as Bracciano 'sweetly . . . [interprets]' it:

> I'll seat you above law and above scandal,
> Give to your thoughts the invention of delight
> And the fruition.   (I.ii.264–5)

The product of her imagination meeting his will be an 'invention of delight', and its fruition will lie in Bracciano's giving form to her insinuative idea or image.

'Inventio', in rhetoric, referred to the finding of *inherently* persuasive matter, with the purpose of applying them in individual cases. Some arguments, however, were not dependent in the same way on the art of rhetoric: their credibility derived from external, objective sources. Aristotle calls these *atechnoi pisteis* (inartificial proofs) in *Rhetoric* I,

[81] Ormerod, *Pictvre of a papist*, 28.   [82] *WD*, III.ii.89.
[83] Sidney, *Apology*, 138.   [84] Peacham, *Garden*, Prefatory letter.

corresponding to *atechnic* signs of recognition in *Poetics*, already discussed in Chapter 1.[85] These were empirical phenomena rather than integrally rhetorical artefacts; merely needed to be reported or presented, rather than re-presented, re-created and mediated by any art. In law, they could be documentary evidence, objective facts, testimonies, oaths, depositions, confessions under torture or rumour. Both Aristotle and Quintilian grant their particular utility in forensic oratory. But at the same time, the Aristotelian distinctions between kinds of proofs and persuasions, signs and recognitions, preserved with modifications in Quintilian, are not neutral but hierarchised.[86] The legal counterpart of the internally probable application of *entechnic* signs which brought about the best kinds of recognitions in *Poetics*, are the *entechnoi pisteis* (artificial proof) of *Rhetoric*. Inartificial proofs, like inartificial signs, were inferior tools of persuasion, albeit more effective in a court of law.[87] *The White Devil* pits Vittoria's *entechnic* means of persuasion against the cruder judicial operations of institutional law, and of her prosecutors. A hierarchy is already subtly inscribed when Bracciano says he will 'seat [her] above law and scandal', the latter almost standing for such evidence as rumour, testimony and precedents.[88] Meanwhile, that aspect of proof which is wholly the work of rhetorical art,[89] the superior order of suasion, becomes associated with Vittoria's 'invention of delight'. Wit and skill and art are posited as alternative and rival to law in its social operation.[90] For the delight, here, belongs to the interface between an artificial image and its

---

[85] For an overview of the relation between legal and rhetorical 'proof', see Skinner, *Reason and Rhetoric*, Ch. 3. See also Quintilian, *Institutio*, 5.10.11 ff.

[86] See Chapter 1 above, pp. 45–7.

[87] On inartificial proofs in Renaissance literary theory and rhetoric, see Joseph, *Shakespeare's Use*, 309–12. Serjeantson, 'Testimony and Proof', 195–236, demonstrates the erosion of this hierarchy in philosophical and scientific theory later in the century, largely through the new centrality of 'experiment' in the Royal Society's work. But he also stresses the continuing influence of the older tension between law's (even common law's, by the beginning of the seventeenth century) admission of, say, 'testimony' (an inartificial instrument) to the category of 'evidence', and the denial of this stature by rhetoric and natural philosophy (see esp. 212–13). According to the latter disciplines, external arguments could only confirm, not inform; they could not illuminate the nature of things, and so could not be considered 'evident'. This is precisely the distinction of perspectives that Webster plays on in Vittoria's trial. As late as 1646, Thomas Browne denigrates inartificial argument as 'a weaker kind of proofe', lacking the 'probable inducements of truth': Browne, *Pseudodoxia Epidemica*, I, 40.

[88] On gossip, information, opinion and scandal as motivating factors behind legal procedure, see *CSPD*, Elizabeth I, 12.239.114; Martin, *Francis Bacon*, 1–3; Quintilian makes specific reference to previous judgements, rumour, confessions and so on in his discussion of inartificial proofs: see *Institutio*, 5.1–7. For Cicero's version, see Cicero, *De Oratore*, I, 280–2. For a dialectical list of inartificial proofs, see Du Moulin, *Elementa*, 154–5.

[89] Quintilian, *Institutio*, 5.8.1: 'quae est tota in arte constatque rebus'.

[90] Note the contradiction between jurisprudential thinking and common-law practice implicit in the acknowledged importance of objective proofs in the courtroom, and the acknowledgement in legal

reception; it spills over from the invention to its recognition by 'an understanding auditory'.[91] The narration is the site of *jouissance*, at once theatrical, rhetorical and linguistic.[92] The very category of 'delight' drives a wedge between aesthetic and moral criteria straight away. Nor is it an anachronism to cite Barthes here. Renaissance rhetoric is inscribed with an awareness of what we would now call *frisson* in the best oratorical performance; witness Wilson:

there is no substance of it self, that will take fire, excepte ye put fire to it. Likewise, no mannes nature is so apt, streight to be heated, except the Orator him self, be on fire, and bring his heate with him . . .[93]

This is why the Iachimos of this world are the most captivating narrators – his audience '[stands] on fire', as engaged and receptive, at one level, as Bracciano to Vittoria's account.[94]

But aesthetic delight is by no means the only attribute granted to the argument of art by rhetoricians. Roman rhetoricians like Quintilian and Cicero, widely studied in Webster's England, almost equate the capacity to 'invent' artificial proofs with the ability to use common 'places' of rhetorical arguments, and by extension, a mastery over the application

---

philosophy that the construction of proofs from probability is the superior legal dialectic. The principle of *ratio artificialis* was granted pride of place in English legal thinking throughout the early modern period: see Giulani, 'The Influence of Rhetoric'. Coke himself once granted that causes 'are not to be decided by natural reason but by the artificial reason and judgement of law': *Twelfth Part*, 65. Abraham Fraunce's comments, too, indicate that this was an accepted field of debate, and there were several attempts to assert and commend the artistic component in legal logic: 'Ramus diuideth an argument into artificiall and inartificiall, wherevpon Piscator tooke occasion of reprehension. For I see no reason, sayeth hee, why testimonies should be called inartificiall argumentes, seeing that there is as good Arte shewed in applying them, as in finding other argumentes: and if in Art there ought to bee nothing without Art, either Inuention wanteth Art, or testimonies are not inartificiall, they answer him thus, They bee not called Inartificiall, for that they want Art, but because they argue not of themselues . . .' But this answer does not satisfy Fraunce, 'for the testimonie of God argueth most absolutely of itselfe, neither can wee well say, that his testimonies were not to be beleeued, vnlesse hee were verus, bonus, iustus &c. sith wee cannot distinguishe these so from his diuine essence, but that whatsoeuer is in God, is God: and therefore it is an infallible argument, God spake it, therefore it is so . . . neyther neede wee seeke for any artificiall argument to confirme it, as wee doe in the testimonies of men': *Lawiers Logike*, Dii. Interestingly, Fraunce's argument is premised on a distinction between the truth value of divine evidence and that of the human court. This relates to the difference between the self-evident providential proofs discussed in Chapter 3, and the kind of proof privileged and used by Webster's *WD* where evidence ultimately becomes a question of aesthetic representation; the rhetorical distinction between artful and artless proof is not only enacted in drama but also mapped on to a generic polarity.

[91] See n. 39 above.
[92] Barthes, *Pleasure of the Text*, passim.
[93] Wilson, *Rhetoricke*, 73v and 90 for an explicit connection between 'colour' and the 'iuce' of narration.
[94] Shakespeare, *Cymbeline*, V.v.168.

of colour. And this is where the 'extractive' model comes into play. For finding a given device and using it with ingenuity and effect is also a way of bringing certain arguments to light from their hidden places, a concept related to the Baconian notion of the 'discovery' of the 'hidden law'.[95] This is of course an attempt to redefine rhetoric's relation to truth. The responsibility of the discerning reader should be to look for more than simple mimesis in art. The Crassus persona in Cicero's *De Oratore* claims that colouring an argument is not simply to dress it up in attractive but borrowed robes. It is to draw forth the nature of things and paint them 'in their full light' by realising their inherent form,[96] just as Bracciano's delighted comprehension of the true intent of Vittoria's recreation of a mental picture is also a figuring forth of it: he literally paraphrases her narration in terms of the material shape it is intended to take.[97] The delight itself is in the recognition and realisation.

The image as an instrument of proof is almost a platitude in rhetoric, and its psychology has already been addressed. What is significant in this specific context is that the image, too, is distinguished into kinds. The simple psychological image or *phantasm* and the rhetorical-poetic image or *eikon* (*imago* in the Latin Aristotelian tradition) are overlapping but distinct forms of images in Aristotle. The distinction, stated more explicitly by inheritors like Quintilian, is that the latter is the refined, more artful and more effective version of the former.[98] And it is the *eikon* which comes closest to the *imagines agentes* of the later rhetorical tradition (see especially the *Rhetorica ad Herennium*) in that they are both premised on vividness and particularity; these are the images through which artificial memory operates, because the properties that aid memory are also those that are most effective in a court, and offer the maximum incentive to motion or judgement. Simple metaphors and similes, too, can be part of this larger category of images designed for maximum impact.

It is possible now to detect a hierarchy, even a competition, among the various types of image-making in *The White Devil*. We have already considered the dumb shows in II.i, and Francisco's memorial image of Isabella in IV.i, resorted to after a consideration and rejection of finding a real picture. Then there is Bracciano's ghost appearing to Flamineo in V.iv, the status of which remains indeterminate. But it is Vittoria who

---

[95] See Martin, *Francis Bacon*, 72–104.   [96] Cicero, *De Oratore*, I, 47.

[97] See Briggs, *Francis Bacon*, 79–80 on Jonson's dedication to Wright's *Passions*: how Jonson 'takes for granted a relation between ornament, persuasion, and the nature of things', and how the colours of Wright's art body forth the passions they paint.

[98] See Eden, *Poetic and Legal Tradition*, 85–96.

is both the central image and the central artificer. Once the general context of framing her as a spectacle has registered, the more specific but repeated attempts to script her into images are thrown into relief as varieties of the same exercise. While the lawyer's ocular presentation of her is recognisably parodic, the ostensibly more sophisticated and professional legal presentment of her by Monticelso is essentially enacting the same process through the trial where Vittoria already is, theatrically, the central spectacle.

The specific literary or rhetorical form this is taken up into is the Theophrastian 'character': 'This whore, forsooth, was holy' (III.ii.77). Vittoria challenges his picture of her promiscuous life, and questions his label for it: 'Ha? Whore – what's that?' (76). Monticelso, in reply, puts a name to the exercise, a name that would immediately suggest to its Jacobean audience the popular contemporary genre of character-writing, based on a word picture of character-types:

> Shall I expound whore to you? sure I shall;
> I'll give their perfect character . . .   (78–9)

With this, he launches into a twenty-three-line rhetorical exercise in precisely such a genre, through a series of metaphors and analogies answering, in highly formulaic form, the repeated rhetorical question, 'What's a whore?' (78–101). Nor is this Monticelso's only attempt at representation. He appeals to another normative stereotype: the virtuous widow. Vittoria is a widow, but far from an ideal one:

> And look upon this creature was his wife.
> She comes not like a widow; she comes armed
> With scorn and impudence. Is this a mourning habit?
> (119–21)

Quick to recognise his strategy, Vittoria retaliates: 'This character 'scapes me' (101). Monticelso presses on with his emblematic picture-making, fixing Vittoria more and more in stock, bloodless iconography. A shrewd addressee, she fashions her counter-images to meet her accuser on his own ground, using rhetorical re-description to project a 'self' with such colour of authenticity that it wins conviction despite our knowledge of her criminal responsibility. The admiration aroused in some members of the court audience attests to her success.[99] Our own response surely has

---

[99] For example, the English Ambassador's response at 107, 140, and 181–4 (as opposed to the French). On the possibility that his moderate response to her case inscribes the value given to equity in the English system, see Haberman, 'She has that in her belly', 110.

more affinity with Bracciano's quickening to her 'invention of delight' than with the Cardinal's bitter venom which is denied the poetic stature that she is granted.[100] When she flings an insult at Monticelso's inferior image-making, she wrests a stature that has little to do with legal fact or moral valency, and everything to do with performance and artifice. And who is to tell that it does not indeed reveal an inner quality in its 'full light'? Or to decide what is the semblance and what the true image?

> These are but feigned shadows of my evils.
> Terrify babes, my lord, with painted devils.
> I am past such needless palsy. For your names
> Of whore and murd'ress, they proceed from you,
> As if a man should spit against the wind,
> The filth returns in's face.   (146–51)

She is inviting a comparison between the two-dimensional sketches with which Monticelso tries to script her, and her own superbly protean expressive presence. It is, after all, 'the eye of childhood/That fears a painted devil', as some of the audience might even have retained from *Macbeth* (II.ii.50–2). If Monticelso's paintings just about qualify as simple psychological images, the self Vittoria portrays and presents is a splendidly crafted *eikon*. Monticelso proceeds now with exactly the sort of proof that is inartificial and inferior in rhetorical terms – petty details about 'who lodged beneath [her] roof that fatal night/[Her] husband brake his neck' (153–4), and '[marking] every circumstance' (118). He produces concrete objects as evidence, such as letters (192 ff.). He is correct. But he does not persuade. Vittoria lies. She arrests us, and our imagination. Turning colour on its head in more senses than one, she asks,

> Condemn you me for that the Duke did love me?
> So may you condemn some fair and crystal river
> For that some melancholic distracted man
> Hath drowned himself in't.   (203–6)

Monticelso persists with the match: 'If the devil/Did ever take good shape, behold his picture' (216–17). But by the time he flouts his art, the play has trained the audience to discern the poverty of his relentlessly schematic characterisation:

---

[100] At Bracciano's least-dignified dramatic moment, ranting like a jealous cuckold over a piece of deception by Francisco, he echoes the Cardinal's language, and uses the same reductive method vis-à-vis Vittoria: 'Where's this whore?' (IV.ii.44).

> I yet but draw the curtain; now to your picture.
> You come from thence a notorious strumpet . . .
>
> (243–4)

What we have before our eyes to compare with this is Vittoria herself, who rounds off her defence with a masterly *conclusio.*[101] Condemned to a house of convertites, she lashes out her defiant reply, as disdain and scorn ride sparkling in her eyes:

> It shall not be a house of convertites;
> My mind shall make it honester to me
> Than the Pope's palace, and more peacable
> Than thy soul, though thou art a cardinal.
> Know this, and let it somewhat raise your spite:
> Through darkness diamonds spread their richest light.
>
> *Exit* Vittoria . . . (289–94)

The jewel imagery challenges the very basis of Monticelso's condemnation of her false radiance, instead of getting round it. This is not a dramatic creation that can be summed up in unidimensional 'characters'. Interestingly, Webster himself was a past-master at the genre, having written, with Overbury, a book of characters.[102] Among his characters is 'An ordinarie Widdow', constructed around stereotypical features of cunning, avarice and incontinence. In fact, the terms of description are verbally similar to Monticelso's comparison of Vittoria with the rotten apples of Sodom and Gomorrah, ready to disintegrate (III.ii.63–5): 'Thus like a too ripe Apple, she [the ordinary widow] falles of herself' (*Characters*, 39). But in the play, the comment is placed by being put in the mouth of a specific fellow character. Webster also has a 'character' for 'A vertuous Widdow', who becomes a 'monument' herself, a 'Relique', a figure of devotion consecrated to the memory of her dead husband (38). But when he creates the Duchess of Malfi who is, even less equivocally than Vittoria, the heroine of her play, she is no 'wrinkled' relic, no pious retiring votary, but a woman of youth, beauty, and sensuality, as she woos her steward Antonio:

> This is flesh and blood, sir,
> 'Tis not the figure cut in alabaster
> Kneels at my husband's tomb. Awake, awake, man,
> I do here put off all vain ceremony,
> And only appear to you, a young widow . . .
>
> (*DM*, I.i.443–7)

[101] On the rhetorical 'part' of *conclusio*, see Sonnino, *Handbook*, 243.
[102] Webster and Overbury *Characters*, 15–61.

The status of emblematic figuration in *White Devil*, likewise, is a world apart from that in his *Characters*, as is the play's own position in relation to it. The representational principle underlying the Theophrastian exercise is – and is perceived by Webster to be – premised on a notion of signification similar to the one informing the ostensible rhetoric of physiognomical theory. That is why it is placed with less sophisticated forms of image-making in the play's hierarchy of mimetic modes rather than with the superior art of dramatic characterisation. Webster's Vittoria stands in the same relation to the Theophrastian 'whore' ('this character escapes me'), or to the 'Ordinary Widdow', as the theatrical medium does in relation to character-writing.

'WHERE MEANING SHALL REMARRY COLOUR'[103]

It would, therefore, be a profound mistake to conclude from its uses of anti-Catholic ideas that this is a Protestant play.[104] Protestant or Puritan semiotics assumed, disingenuously or otherwise, a correspondence of inner and outer, a decorously straightforward mode of signification which runs counter to the very basis of dramatic representation. After all, the term for psychological strategies of acting in classical dramatic theory is *hypokrisis*, a word originally so applied by Aristotle. Nor is it an accident, as Kathy Eden points out, that 'the Renaissance *hypocrite* originates in the Greek theatre, the Renaissance *actor* in the Roman law court'.[105] In his forensic demonstration of her hypocrisy, Monticelso declares in court, with prophetic certainty, that Vittoria is a counterfeit, a promising exterior that will prove bitter inside, and brittle, like Sodom's apples:

> I will but touch her and you straight shall see
> She'll fall to soot and ashes.   (III.ii.66–7)

But she does not. If this were the theatre of God's judgement as in *Warning*, Vittoria would surely crumble before our eyes. Anne Sanders's rose does change colour, visibly, in that court. Monticelso's image inhabits the wrong genre for it to work, either visibly or figuratively, just as his epideictic demonstrations inhabit the wrong judicial forum. Both sides

---

[103] MacNeice, *Collected Poems*, 214: 'When we were children'.
[104] This is the impression given, for instance, by Alison Shell's otherwise splendid discussion of anti-Catholic imagery in *WD* in *Catholicism*, 43–8 (an assumption also accepted as a given in Haberman, 'She has that in her belly'). Middleton's *A Game at Chess* is an interesting contrast.
[105] Eden, *Poetic and Legal Tradition*, 5.

deal in figuration and representation, but the impact belongs to Vittoria's performance, not the Cardinal's. Colour itself stands for two entirely different entities in the two plays, and their disparate generic worlds. What is a mere physical property in *Warning,* becomes an attribute of art, oratory and pleading in *White Devil.*[106] Opacity becomes the ultimate act of self-definition and integrity rather than an index of untruth or deception.[107] Vittoria makes sure that her slaughterer knows that her pallor in death is 'for want of blood, not fear' (V.vi.226). Zanche, attaining – Charmian-like – dignity in death, is 'proud' like Aaron the Moor, that her hue will protect her from the indignity of self-exposure: 'Death cannot alter my complexion,/For I shall ne'er look pale' (V.vi.229–31).

From that early moment of recognition, when Flamineo identifies the moral status of Vittoria's artistic image, Webster marks the fact that Vittoria is the 'devil' of the play (I.ii.251, 257–9), but then surprises us into finding ourselves of the devil's party. The iconic colours of the play are countered and ultimately dislocated by the persuasive colour of Vittoria's legal defence, which in turn is premised on her mastery over the colours of judicial rhetoric. The play's own plea lies in the change of colour it grants Vittoria, from her emblematic presentation by others, to her self-fashioned images eschewing any naïve correlation between truth and representation. Its case, no less than Vittoria's, is coloured: it wins over an audience in spite of their original conviction. So much so that it grants a 'woman dipt in blood'[108] the strange power of this condemnation of institutionalised spiritual authority: 'O poor charity!/Thou art seldom found in scarlet' (III.ii.70–1). This is the utterance that rings true, not

---

[106] See Daston, 'Marvelous Facts', on the debate over evidence centring on divine miracles. In the contentious field of debate over testimony as a form of evidence, a significant strand of thought distinguished between 'necessary' and 'probable': human testimony was at best probable, while divine testimony was 'necessary', and thus amounted to sufficient proof in this tradition. See Serjeantson, 'Testimony and Proof', 206–7. But as Serjeantson argues, probability, in the rhetorical and dialectical traditions of the early seventeenth century, was the privileged kind of proof, as it induced belief through internal reasoning rather than, like testimony, merely confirming through authority the inferences drawn from external arguments. The point of his essay, however, is to chart the shift from this idea to an alignment of testimony with 'fact' in later scientific thinking, as the notion of 'fact' itself drifted from law into natural philosophy, most notably with Locke.

[107] Note that even in Heywood's *WKK,* subtler and more complex than *Warning* in its treatment of adultery, a mark of conscience upheld in the behaviour of the adulterous Anne is that she constantly feels shame, and blushes, both at the thought of inevitable public discovery, and in actually public situations after her sin is detected (e.g., vi, 154–6, xiii, 151–2); note esp. vii, 155–6: 'Women that fall not quite bereft of grace/Have their offences noted in their face' – a premise that the play observes in its sympathetic treatment of Anne. That too is a different world from the 'whore's triumph' that *WD* provides (II.i.239) in spite of the virtuous Isabella.

[108] Middleton and Rowley, *Changeling,* III.iv.127–8.

Monticelso's oracular warning, preceding this, of her imminent destruction. Here is a reversal of traditional colour symbolism through a consummate application of colour in pleading and discourse. In her next spectacular appearance, Vittoria wears bridal white (V.i) – the originally presented 'devil' progressing, through the play, to reclaim whiteness as an achieved value. The Cardinal, in *his* next ceremonial entry (IV.iii), changes clerical crimson for papal white – the holy man showing up in his true colours as the hypocrite, the white devil. By now, we have learnt to read visible signs as complex, and potentially manipulable, capable both of consciously inward signification, and false and superficial correlation. The instrument that focuses as well as clinches this procedure is the dramatic employment of the legal device of giving 'colour', and the implied analogy between legal and theatrical persuasion. Thus, paradox itself becomes a heuristic tool; the attribute of an art that turns the legal notion of credit on its head, bound up as the *fides* of testimony was with moral precepts and the ethical standing of a witness or a defendant.[109] Authenticity is so redefined that the most poignant that any utterance in the play comes close to being, in the midst of pervasive courtly hypocrisy, is probably this, from the dying Bracciano, murderer, adulterer, and fool: 'Where's this good woman? Had I infinite worlds,/They were too little for thee. Must I leave thee?' (V.iii.17–18). Here is indeed almost a touch of the *Antony and Cleopatra* music.[110] Likewise, when Flamineo admires his nobly dying sister for that 'She hath no faults, who hath the art to hide them' (V.vi.247), we know better than to regard this 'art' as simple deceit; it is a function, rather, of an order of existential sophistication and complexity that is more truth-confronting than a simple correspondence of colour and content.

---

[109] See Serjeantson 'Testimony and Proof', esp. 216–17.

[110] Bracciano, like Antony, I think is meant to be not-very-young; a 'fond duke' (IV.iii.54) who, 'in [his] prime age', 'neglect[s] [his] awful throne for the soft down/Of an insatiate bed' (II.i.30–2). His passion for Vittoria, like Antony's for Cleopatra, is a seasoned statesman's obsession. And Cleopatra, too, is another dark lady triumphant through her own dignity, her deeply self-constitutive rhetoric, and her supremely theatrical act of defiance cum self-slaughter. These are creatures, all, of dazzling plurality: 'one way like a Gorgon', 'the other . . . a Mars' (*Antony and Cleopatra*, II.v.116–17). And yet, how different is the music of these lines that follow, from Bracciano, within minutes of those quoted above: 'How miserable a thing it is to die/'Mongst women howling!' (V.iii. 35–6). This is where the ultimate character of these plays inhere, encompassing in the same span the extremes of lyricism and horror, spiritual vindication and unflinching nihilism. Think of yet another strain that surprises us, the celebrated Ophelia music of Cornelia's half-crazed offering of flowers and herbs to standers-by, as she bends over her son Marcello's corpse (V.iv.66–80), followed rapidly by the Lady Macbeth strain of 'Can blood so soon be washed out?' (82–95). By this time, though, Webster is also having a field day, 'doing' various Shakespearean modes with ease, and sometimes with the uncaring élan and excess of a pastiche!

The place of the stage, then, is ultimately not with monolithic Protestant truth, but with the swiftly changing optical sites of anamorphic paintings, with the myriad colours of self-fulfilling rhetoric, and with the artifice of *entechnic* signs. Theatrical reality is ultimately the evidence of images; images that are, in this play, foregrounded, deployed and manipulated, as triumphantly as Vittoria's rhetoric, to leave the audience seeing double, 'with parted eye'.[111] Through the play of images, 'characters', 'colours' and emblems, we learn to perceive the poverty of what in art history would be called 'the single stationary eye'.[112] This is where art wins over theology, persuasive proof over demonstration, and multilayered representation over reductive and single truth. This, again, is the awareness the theatre brings to its own representational medium, while legal writers on the whole do not, because they are differently invested in the register of single meaning; inscribing such an awareness of the fluidity of signs would run counter to the positivism of the institutional discourse of law. Vittoria, like Shakespeare's Cressida, both 'is, and is not', what she is ostensibly given to be. No more is theatrical personation. No more indeed was the Renaissance art of pleading – learnt, among other means, through those learning exercises in the Inns which Webster must have been familiar with at the Middle Temple: 'moots', or sessions of arguing both for and against a proposition or a hypothetical 'case', described by Sir Thomas Elyot as a 'shadowe or figure of the auncient rhetoricke'.[113] The lawyer and Justice Sir Paul Eitherside in Jonson's *The Devil is an Ass*, or Mosca's jibe that lawyers 'could speake/To every cause, and things mere contraries', and 'with most quick agility' 'turn/And re-turn' (*Volpone*, I.i.271–5), are comic-satiric comments on the potential for the purely rhetorical, and an exoneration from moral conviction, in legal training itself. The irony of dramatic trials is often the way they relativise 'truth', complicate arbitration or even make it impossible, while the business of law was to arrive at judgement.[114] *The White Devil* deploys the twin space law itself inhabited but could not articulate, due to its disciplinary investments. The 'mock trials' were supposed to provide the basis for a practical 'science' which its theoretical

---

[111] Shakespeare, *MSND*, IV.i.189–90.
[112] Gombrich, *Image and the Eye*, 196.
[113] Elyot, *Governour*, i, 148–9. In ancient rhetoric, one was supposed to be able to argue every case *in utramque partem*.
[114] I disagree with Haberman's claim ('She has that in her belly', 109) that plays, which 'necessitate closure', are to be contrasted with legal practitioners who seek to perpetuate conflict. I argue that law, like drama, is a 'social event', and is invested in resolutions, though abuses of legal practice might prolong conflict.

proponents claimed, right through the Elizabethan and Jacobean periods, to be an instrument in establishing indisputable and positive truth![115] The most frequently cited authority on the principles of law in the period was, after all, Justinian, who stated that 'we honour truth and we wish our laws to tell only of things that really are'.[116]

This chapter, then, indicates the scope of drama's engagement with law. This relation does not have to be merely critical of legal process, or self-reflexively critical of the limits of theatrical representation, though my earlier chapters show how such critiques are common and can be extremely subtle. A self-aware analogy with law allows Webster's play to assert its similarities with law's fictions, but its superiority over law's semiotics. R. S. White, in his influential work, *Natural Law in Renaissance Literature*, argues that 'poetic justice is the literary equivalent of natural law'.[117] *The White Devil*, I suggest, provides a challenging counter-example to this claim. As such, it makes its dialectical point more forcefully than plays like *Dr Faustus* or *Macbeth* (which, too, complicate the relation between dramatic and ordinary notions of judgement), because it actively locates the drama in a legal framework. It confounds our assumptions by flouting what White calls a 'model' 'at the heart of literary theory of the times'; one which he says 'closely mirrors the basis of Natural law . . . that people are in some fundamental ways attracted to good and repelled by evil, and that they know the moral status of what they are doing or what they have done' (7). Webster observes the second part of this premise, but flings an aesthetic challenge in the face of the first, thereby complicating the model endlessly, and with endless sophistication.[118] Part of my attempt, here, has been to understand the nature of a particular aesthetic, and its forging of a judicial structure that is radically incompatible not only with courtroom logic but also with anything resembling natural law.

---

[115] On Webster's legal education and background, see Bradbrook, *John Webster*, 1–46. On 'moots', see Prest, *Inns of Court*, Chs. 6 and 7, esp. 117–19. On the importance of 'invention', 'wit' and 'memory' in these exercises, see ibid., 117, and Plucknett, *Early English Legal Literature*, 80–90. For surviving notes from these readings, see Baker, *English Legal Manuscripts*. See Dugdale, *Origines Juridicales*, for a discussion of the rhetorical purpose of this practice.

[116] *CJC*, Codex, 7.5.

[117] White, *Natural Law*, 7.

[118] This is also the main difference between my reading of the play and Haberman's. While Haberman sees Vittoria's challenge and triumph as a 'moral victory' ('She has that in her belly', 110), I argue that it is aesthetic and performative, and consciously pitted against morality, whether natural or corrupt. This is why it cannot be read straightforwardly as 'equitable drama' (115). *WD*, contrary to how it has been sometimes read, challenges the notion of drama's ethical supremacy over law by dissociating aesthetic complexity and representational sophistication from ethical superiority.

CHAPTER 5

Locations of law: spaces, people, play

Edward Heath, a young student at the Inner Temple between 1626 and 1631, listed his expenses in a little notebook.[2] He spent most of his money on playgoing, and certainly more time at the theatre than at Westminster sessions. He mentions 'goeing to a play' forty-nine times in his eleven-page diary; each visit cost between 1s. and 2s. He even appends a separate list, 'A note of All the Playes which I have seene', quarter by quarter. 'For goeing over to the beare garden' on one occasion, he spent 1s. 6d. The combined pleasures of the other bank made the boat-ride worth the price. 'Goeing by water' nine times cost him £2. 3s. In his more virtuous hours, Edward also paid 'for goeing by water and seate at the Starchamber', and spent between 1s. and 1s. 6d. on a seat each of the six times mentioned. But neither these sessions, nor paying 6d. 'for a seate at the Crosse' several times, excluded less pious entertainment. He bought '10 playbooks' on a saunter around 'Pauls Crosse', but no law books! Edward's other expenses certainly give us a sense of his priorities, often endearingly appropriate for a boy of sixteen. Out of his total allowance of £180 for nine terms, received from his father, the distinguished lawyer Sir Robert Heath,[3] Edward spent significantly not only on the above pursuits, but also for 'a paire of gloves', 'a beverhatt', on paying 'the boy at the danceing schoole', for cherries, 'apricockes' and strawberries, 'for a picture to give my mother', 'for changeing a paire of red silke stockins for a french greene', 'for hireing a coach to Hyde Park', 'at Greenewich when we went

---

[1] Barry, *Ram Alley*, Prologue, 1. No records of pre-eighteenth-century performances survive. References are to running line numbers.

[2] BL MS Egerton 2983, 13–24. John Baker kindly alerted me to this document.

[3] On Robert Heath and Edward's careers, see Kopperman, *Sir Robert Heath*.

to kill a bucke', 'for a black satten cap', 'for a seagreene hatbond', and 'for seedes for my bird'. He also kept losing money 'at tenis'! He spent remarkably little on legal activities, as Baker points out in his article on Edward Heath.[4] Perhaps John Davies's epigram about Publius was not so far from reality after all:

> Publius student of common law,
> Oft leaves his bookes, and for his recreacion:
> To Paris Garden doth himselfe Withdrawe[5]

The affinity between the theatre and the law court observed so far inheres in their shared evidentiary and representational concerns. But, as young Edward's daily journal suggests, the traffic between the theatre and the courts was more than a matter of dramatic metaphor, or discursive exchange or appropriation. The worlds of Westminster and Southwark, of the Inns and the private theatres, jostled against each other more substantially than prescriptive, Puritan writing about London would suggest. 'Paul's Churchyard' stood in the middle – a space shared by sermonists and their audiences; printers and sellers of popular cheap print; crowds flocking to the 'bawdy courts' in St Paul's Cathedral;[6] scriveners' stalls from which newsbooks speedily circulated far and wide; students from the Inns; and sellers and buyers of law books and legal texts.[7] The anonymous author of *Zepheria* (1594) condemns his lady to the following fate, as the subject of his poem:

> Thy face being veiled, this penance I award
> Clad in white sheet, thou stand in Paul's Churchyard.[8]

The metaphor unites the multiple associations of the site: penance rituals of Paul's church court for sexual misdemeanour, the selling of books in the churchyard, and a general sense of publicness. Paul's was also the hub of news: it was customary

for the principall *Gentry, Lords, Courtiers,* and *men of all professions not meerely Mechanick,* to *meet* in *Pauls Church* by eleven, and *walk* in the *middle Ile* till

[4] Baker, 'Edward Heath', 75–6.
[5] Davies, *Elegies*, 148, no. 43. Cf. ibid., 150, no. 47, where gallants visit 'Paris garden cocke-pit or the play'; and Isabella Whitney on law-students' frequenting of plays 'every Sunday at the least' (1573): *Sweet Nosegay*, E7v.
[6] On London church courts, and the supremacy of St Paul's within Middlesex, see Gowing, *Domestic Dangers*, 30–58.
[7] Map 1 , 21 (numbers refer to grid-squares).
[8] *Zepheria*, Canzon 36, F2v. On bookselling in Paul's Churchyard, see Blayney, *Bookshops*.

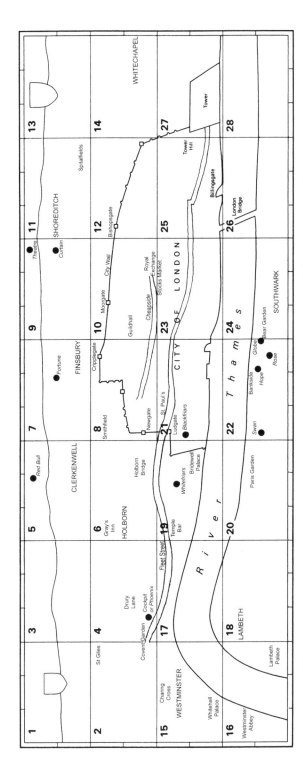

Map 1. A map of theatrical and legal London, showing the geographical overlap between the Inns and the theatres, especially their proximity to the private theatres.

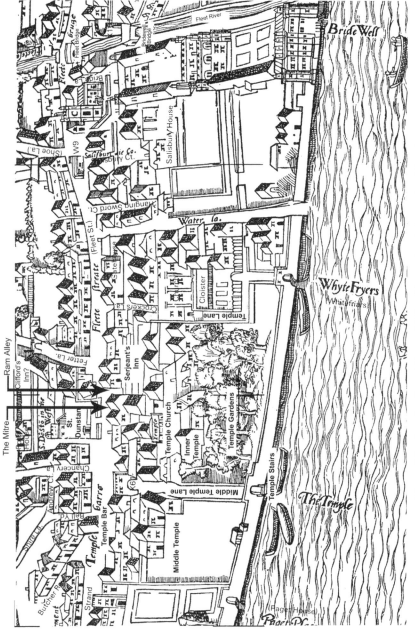

Map 2. Map locating Ram Alley and Mitre Tavern in relation to legal London.

twelve, and after dinner from *three*, to *six*; during which time some discoursed of *Businesse*, others of *Newes*.[9]

The nave was haunted by fortune-hunters, hoping for contacts and contracts. So Sir Oliver Smallshanks in Lording Barry's *Ram Alley* condemns his son Will, a would-be 'complete gallant' (1539), to 'get [him] a grey cloak and hat/And walk in Paul's amongst [his] cashier'd mates' (1578–9). Nor was Paul's detached from the bear houses, inns and playhouses across the Thames in Southwark – a mere boat-ride away.

Ram Alley (1608) and its comic engagement with law must be understood in this context of bustle and busy exchange. Despite the Prologue's disclaimer, its world is that of satirical city-comedy.[10] A comic counterpart of the 'domestic tragedies', it is also, in its specifically metropolitan character, akin to *Warning* (a notable exception to the general rule that Elizabethan domestic tragedies based on contemporary events are inspired by 'news flashes from rural parishes and county towns', while comedy inhabits the metropolis).[11] Relying on the actors' and audience's shared experience of its 'home-bred' context, *Warning* declares, 'My Sceane is London, native and and your owne,/I sighe to think, my subject too well knowne' (95–6). The urban locations it deploys are precisely those that Anne Barton identifies as the habitual domains of comedy:[12] the 'Exchange' (292), 'Lumberd streete' (933), 'the Spittle' (982–3) with its customary Easter sermons, Cornhill, and of course Fleet Street. Characters even correct each other's sense of direction within a specific neighbourhood by referring to familiar landmarks (302–5). This detailed 'domesticity' is one that *Ram Alley* shares with *Warning*.[13] Its action is set in and around the seedy Whitefriars district, a site at once of law and of roguery, and stretches across Gray's Inn, Temple Bar, St Paul's Cathedral, the Royal Exchange, and the courts of Westminster on the western side.[14] The publication of Stow's *Survey of London* in 1598, and the formation of a distinct popular urban identity, underlie both plays.

---

[9] Osborne, *Traditionall Memoryes*, 65 (Kr).

[10] On legal satire, see Tucker, *Intruder*, Ch. 1.

[11] See, e.g., Barton, 'Comedy and the Ethos of the City', in *Essays*, 302–28 (304).

[12] Barton, 'Comic London' in *Essays*, 329–51 (341–2).

[13] Map 2 gives us a sense of the terrain covered by the action of *Warning*, as also, roughly, *RA*. Theatres, and buildings used as theatres, are interwoven with these landmarks, suggesting how legal London overlapped with theatrical London. See Whitefriars in 19, adjacent to Temple Bar; Blackfriars in 21, south of Paul's and Fleet Street; Cockpit just above Fleet Street in 4. The public theatres are around Paris Garden (Publius' haunt) and the Bear Garden on the south bank, and north of the City wall.

[14] See Lady Politic Would-be's sneer at the 'Whitefriars nation' (*Volpone*, IV.i.198).

In *Warning*, this urban familiarity is harnessed to '[letting] wonder be familiar'.[15] But it provides *Ram Alley* the context for its legal themes. Here, 'home-[bredness]' is inseparable from an unerring feel for the pulse of city life, where law's centrality was often social rather than technically pertaining to law courts. Its distinct interest in law entails a knowing vision of legal life in relation to performance, as also to the localised spirit of comedy. The minute legal realism, combined with satirical typification, is reminiscent of 'character-writing', something of an Inns of Court genre in the 1590s.[16] Like many other plays put on at private theatres by children's companies, *Ram Alley*, performed by the King's Revels Children at Whitefriars, seems to speak to a London audience with its share of Inns-men.[17] Whitefriars was located in the heart of legal London: on the south side of Fleet Street and adjacent to Serjeants Inn, Inner Temple and Temple garden, across which stood the Middle Temple and Temple Bar.[18] As Thomas Nashe, like Edward Heath, testifies, there was no shortage of law-students at the public playhouses on the south bank: already in 1592, 'gentlemen of . . . the Innes of Courte' are listed by Nashe among those who spent money at these theatres.[19] John Earle, as late as 1628, comments on how 'Innes of Court men' would be 'undone' without the theatre, and certain favourite actors.[20] But the so-called private theatres were specially known for their repertory of satirical comedies, often about law and lawyers, as well as for their legal audience.[21] In fact, one of the earliest records of a Blackfriars audience comes from an Inns of Court student: Henry Fitzgeoffrey's *Satyres and Satirical Epigrams: with Certaine Observations at Black-Fryers* (1617). The trope of judicial spectatorship, then, was underpinned by a social and geographical connection. Nor was Beaumont the only dramatist to invoke the judicial metaphor for audience response at Blackfriars; the editors of Shakespeare's first Folio (1623) defiantly wrote, in their Preface 'To the great Variety of Readers':

---

[15] Shakespeare, *Much Ado*, V.iv.70.
[16] See Manningham, *Diary*, 1–26.
[17] Barry was the impresario of the company in 1607–8, after which he fled to sea as a pirate to escape legal action for debt, until he became a seaman and trader. See Corbin and Sedge's introduction to Barry, *RA*. Significantly, the Children of the King's Revels evolved from Paul's Children who had played, among many other satirical comedies, Middleton's *Michaelmas Term*, known for its legal satire.
[18] The private theatres were all close to the Inns – see Map 1.
[19] As quoted in Gurr, *Shakespearean Stage*, 200.
[20] Earle, *Microcosmographie*, H3r.
[21] On legal satire in plays by children's companies at private playhouses, see Shapiro, *Children of the Revels*, 51–8; Gurr, *Shakespearean Stage*, 18.

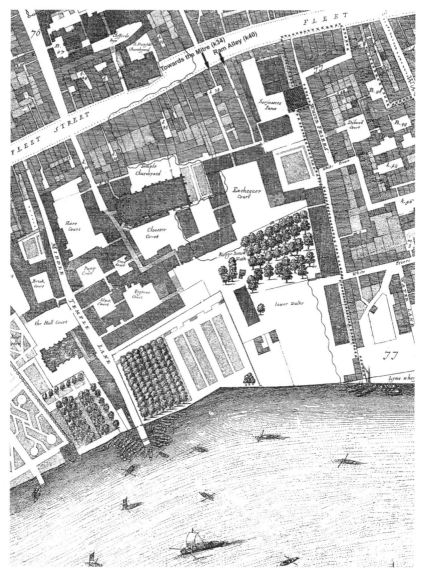

Map 3. Close-up of the neighbourhood south of Fleet Street which housed the Mitre Tavern (k34), the lane leading out of its back-door and to Ram Alley (k40).

And though you be a Magistrate of Wit, and sit on the Stage at Black-friers, or the Cock-pit, to arraigne Playes dailie, knowe, these Playes have had their trial already, and stood out all Appeales . . .[22]

Quomodo in Middleton's satirical city-comedy, *Michaelmas Term* (1605), played by Paul's Children a couple of years before Barry's play, testily addresses the spectators as 'all you students at Inns of Cozenage'.[23] *Ram Alley*, similarly, has abundant satire on law, and it is perhaps in an attempt to make up for it to an original Inns of Court audience that it offers in-jokes about the credentials of its so-called lawyer, Throat:

> He never was of any Inn-of-Court,
> But Inn-of-Chancery. . . (733–4)[24]

Widow Taffata, likewise, mocks Will Smallshank's shirt as 'more foul than an Inn-of-Chancery tablecloth' (1545–6).

But such finer distinctions do not preclude a larger sense of the legal culture as something spread over the major and the lesser inns; across taverns, alleyways and courtyards around official legal institutions; and involving men of law of various descriptions. Full of 'gear' and 'quillets' (423, 438), Throat is 'parcel lawyer, parcel devil, all knave' (95), 'one that professeth law, but indeed/Has neither law nor conscience' (108–10). He himself admits being but 'the dregs and offscum of the law' (417), having never been called to the Bar. But it is precisely such men '[sitting] on the skirts of law'[25] who made up the crowded margins of the profession, laying claim to a semi-legal status by virtue of their association with the Inns of Chancery and any other 'legal' connection. Throat's abode in Ram Alley is the physical centre of the comedy, a stone's throw from the Inner Temple, the Middle Temple and the Serjeants' Inn, and on the south side of Fleet Street, diagonally opposite Fetter Lane which connected Fleet Street with Holborn.[26] It was populated principally by lawyers and Inns-men – 'many a worthy lawyer's chamber/Buts upon Ram Alley'

---

[22] First Folio, 7 (A3). The Cockpit, another 'private' theatre, opened in 1617 in Drury Lane, near the Inns (Map 1, 4).

[23] Middleton, *Michaelmas Term*, II.iii.141–2.

[24] This distinction is a measure of the play's inwardness with the legal culture. On Inns of Chancery, see Glossary. On their history, see Megarry, *Inns*.

[25] Day, *Law Tricks*, 579. Cf. Lurdo, the pettifogger of that play, and Tangle in Middleton's *The Phoenix* (1603). On the 'lower branch' of the legal profession, see Brooks, *Pettifoggers*.

[26] Close-up in Map 2; 19 in Map 1. Ram Alley itself is in sharper focus in Map 3 – a close-up of the neighbourhood south of Fleet Street which housed the Mitre Tavern (k34), the lane leading out of its back door and to Ram Alley (k40), diagonally opposite St Dunstan's Churchyard.

(488–90) – and it ran down to a narrow lane which led straight to the Temple. The Mitre, where Will and his entourage sup after '[mumbling] up a marriage' (882), was on Fleet Street and backed onto Ram Alley, through which rogues could escape from the law, because it was both discreet and claimed the right of sanctuary.[27] Throat tries to fend off the pursuers of Francis (Will's whore), a veritable Doll Common, in Act III:

> . . . Are you mad?
> Come you to seek a virgin in Ram Alley
> So near an Inn-of-Court, and amongst cooks,
> Ale-men, and laundresses? . . .   (1283–6)[28]

The reputation of London's legal quarters inspired nostalgia: Throat bemoans that the over-studious Inns-men of his time are not a patch on 'those gallant spirits' who ensured that no 'wench' 'could pass an Inn-of-Court' without being laid (1029–41).[29] But bawdry and law are not only associated through the sexual customs of the legal community. They also compete in unscrupulous money-making (32–2). Constantia marvels at Adriana's lawyer-rivalling skills in securing lovers for her mistress, Taffata (278–80); Will identifies 'a lawyer and a whore' as his two 'suckers' (56). Law-tricks are consistently associated with sexual tricks, both being integral to London life.

Indeed, like Middleton's Tangle, Throat is fertile with 'tricks in law' (I.i.123). His central trick (II.ii.667) is to outwit Will Smallshanks, who, with his friend Boutcher's cooperation, has persuaded Throat to marry him to Constantia Somerfield, the heiress he claims to have stolen. The plan is that when Will brings his bride, Throat will steal her and inherit the money – with his legal know-how, he will make sure that before Will can do anything about it, he has made the marriage 'sure'. And so he does, only to discover at the end, to his utter horror, that he has been tricked into marrying Will's whore Francis passed off as Constantia. Will, a 'cashier'd younger brother' (2067), sets out at the beginning of the play

---

[27] Sugden, *Topographical Dictionary*, 426. Cf. Brome, *Damoiselle*, IV.i (E4).

[28] See Jonson, *Staple of News*, II.iv.35; or Chettle and Day, *Blind Beggar*, IV, 1633–4 on Ram Alley's reputation for cooks, ale and sex. When Will says he will sup at the Mitre, proceed to the Savoy, and then 'Go to't pell-mell for a maidenhead' (892–6), he is playing on the name of the most disreputable tavern on the alley, the Maidenhead, near the Temple end: see Sugden, *Topographical Dictionary*, 426. Shoe Lane, where Throat's coach is to pick up his bride, is seen in Map 2, off Fleet Street, West of Fleet Bridge.

[29] For an available contemporary 'character' of an Inns-man, see Overbury, 'Fantastique Innes of Court Man', 45–6. Cf. Justice Shallow's past 'bona robas' and 'swingbucklers' in Shakespeare, *2 Henry IV*, III.ii.21–4.

with three objectives: to marry off his Francis, to secure an advantageous match for himself, and snap up any unexpected profits on the way. So, besides seeing her well settled, he uses Francis-as-Constantia to procure a gift from his father Sir Oliver Smallshanks, and then beats his father to the rich widow Taffata's bed and board. All the gulling of the play eventually leaves Boutcher to regret his neglect of his true love Constantia, and his vain pursuit of the widow Taffata; Constantia, who has followed him around as a page, discloses her identity, and all ends happily – except for an outraged Throat clamouring for legal redress.

It is easy to assume that *Ram Alley* pits comedy against law, since both law and its practitioners are objects of satire. But numerous non-legal protagonists aim to outwit Throat at his own game, while Will, the master-plotter, turns out to be as legally informed as the 'open-throated lawyer' (132) is fallible in law's application. As Boutcher comments, he '[undoes] the lawyer's hands' and '[overthrows] him at his own weapons' (2499). Though he asks Throat to 'leave this firk of law' (1287), in his feigned indignation at the lawyer running off with his bride, the real law-trick turns out to be his – and it is one which the play trusts the spectators to admire. Fully aware of the combination of quasi-legal formalities that Throat would think of, to clinch his marriage, he contrives to make all of them possible, and waits until Throat has verbally and publicly ratified each one of these, including consummation. Its legitimacy so insistently asserted by the lawyer himself, even the discovery of Francis's identity cannot unmake the match. Comic destiny is aligned with cunning intelligence which functions through law-tricks: thus, several spheres of plotting are united. Law emerges as a body of measures which can be bent through ingenious opportunism, not just a specialised, sealed-off skill.

The larger sense of the tricksiness of law in the hands of clever users does not preclude specific legal information. The ploys centre around marriage law – so notoriously fluid that any impressive combination of the associated formalities could ensure a perception of incontrovertibility. Will advises his father Sir Oliver to make his clandestine match legitimate with the judicious use of a dubious priest, and of sex to clinch the contract (615–19). But this is not the only way he exploits the thriving market for unlicensed priests and brief-hunting lawyers spawned by the contested field of making and unmaking marriages. So Throat and Francis are 'tied fast by heart and hand', and 'deliver'd by an honest priest/At St. Giles in the field' (1255–8). Will's quasi-legal ploy, proceeding from a canny instinct for the manipulability of the law, locates comic dramaturgy in a terrain familiar to the play's audience: 'Come now to Ram Alley. There shalt thou lie, till I provide a priest' (648–9). Comedy here joins hands with law in self-delighting complicity, using their shared space to deploy its own stratagems. Boutcher, though astounded, resolves to support the knave – paralleling audience response (649–52).

The sub-plot, too, revolves around marriage practice. Taffata offers Sir Oliver a conditional handfast, but he will take no risks:

> We'll lie together without marrying,
> Save the curate's fees, and the parish a labour . . . (1441–3)

But Will arrives at Taffata's place the night before his father is to seal his match, woos and wins her at sword-point, insisting on the standard means used to legalise many an 'unsanctified [match]' (I.i.190): 'Clap hands, contract, and straight to bed' (2131). Sir Oliver arrives too late, to find his son and his betrothed '[scambling] out the shaking of the sheets' (2168). Among other dejected suitors, Boutcher, smitten by the widow, and tricked by her into thinking she is interested, indignantly asks her:

> Have not thy vows made thee my lawful wife
> Before the face of heaven? . . .   (2296–7)

Will now steps forward, revealing the better route to a lawful marriage in the face of this informal court. The plot's various threads converge. Throat threatens to 'star-chamber [them] all for cozenage' and sue for divorce, but Will jeers, 'She's your leeful, lawful, and true wedded wife' (2460–2). Throat's discontent is mildly rebuked by Francis:

> Good sir, be content.
> A lawyer should make all things right and straight;
> All lies but in the handling. I may prove
> A wife that shall deserve your best of love. (2485–8)

Quite apart from the third, bawdy sense, this is also a comedic reprimand. Comedy has ever been intolerant of whingers: in *Ram Alley*'s world, the law which colludes with comedy is the only law that has a place. Michael Shapiro observes that the combination of subtle flattery and open parody that many of the Children's company plays directed at the legal members of their audience worked partly by a demarcation between generations.[30]

---

[30] See Shapiro, *Children of the Revels*, 41, on the 'dual protection of saturnalian misrule and juvenile impunity' enjoyed by these companies, and 54, on the 'taste for saturnalian mockery' in the revels of the Inns.

Quomodo in *Michaelmas Term*, who rails against his law-student son, is a typical example of an unappealing older character whose anti-legal satire was acceptable to young gallants from the Inns who could identify with the canny younger generation in the play. In *Ram Alley*, the satire on law shades off into a robust sense of how law's flexibility lends itself to comic and prudent use by down-on-luck but clever tricksters fending for themselves in the city. The direction of sympathy recalls the lawyer William Fleetwoode's account of an intercepted clandestine marriage in a secret corner of the Temple church in his letter to Burghley (1575).[31] The protagonist – penniless 'Tasse' – was trying to marry Sir Robert Drury's daughter, a forty-year-old heiress. But Drury would give her nothing as she was marrying against his will. Fleetwoode's 'pity' went to 'the poore yonge man', and not only did he configure the episode as comic drama but, amusingly, had only one grudge: 'Nothing in this little comedie did more offend me, than that . . . they chose the rather to marrye in the Temple, because it was supposed to be a lawless churche' – a hilarious comment on the uses of London's legal quarters.

Unsurprisingly, the word 'trick', primarily used for legal and sexual ploys, is increasingly associated in *Ram Alley* with plot-words or the notion of play. Will himself provides the usual generic winks in the final comic arbitration, welcoming 'remedy' through forgiving and forgetting (2308–9). Only Puritan values remain a negative criterion, subjected to taunts amidst the parodic reversals and recognitions (2245–9). The unwieldy, irrepressible metropolis is opposed not to the world of Fleet Street, Mitre Tavern or Ram Alley, but to the civic authorities who strove to ban playing and restrict this mingled pulse of city life. Even the ineffectual Captain Face has a place here: ''tis not for fear/But for a love I bear unto these tricks,/That I perform it' (1746–8). In its opportunistic, malleable social practice, law in Ram Alley belongs as much to the men and women who frequent its courtyard and precincts, as to legal practitioners. Indeed, the play's full title equates the sites of law, the pranks of lust, and the ploys of comedy: *Ram Alley or Merry Tricks*. A Jacobean audience could hardly miss the pun on 'meretrix' ('prostitute').

This collusion is physically represented in the crowded tavern scene (IV.ii), with the Sergeant, the whore Francis who is now the lawyer's wife, and Throat's assistant, 'nimble Dash', who is plotting to get a bail for Francis as well as a 'writ of false imprisonment' and damages for 'suits in

---

[31] Wright, ed., *Queen Elizabeth*, 20.

law' (1625–8). The Sergeant, however, presses a further charge on Francis, that of owing money on a gown for a bawd. She protests that she paid for that gown with the four pounds and sixteen pence given to her by a Clerk of Chancery. As the Sergeant strikes a sexual deal with her, Captain Face enters and asks the Drawer whom he has been serving so long:

> DRAWER: I attend a coventicle of players.
> FACE: How, players?
>   Is there ever a cuckold among them?
> DRAWER: Jove defend else; it stands with policy
>   That one should be a notorious cuckold,
>   If it be but for the better keeping
>   The rest of his company together.
> FACE: When did you see Sir Theophrastus Slop,
>   The city dog-master?
>
>   (1674–82)

The possible allusion to a specific rival company underlines the overlap between theatrical culture, city entertainments, legal activities and the tavern crowd. It illustrates the generation of 'news which now supplies/ The city with discourse' (198–9), and the role of certain social spaces in that process. This is the world of the satirical Epigrams of Sir John Davies, himself a Middle Templar, whose 'Philo'

> Doth practise Phisicke, and his credit growes,
> As doth the ballade-singers auditorie,
> Which hath at Temple Bar his standing close,
> And to the vulgar sings an ale-house storie.[32]

'KEEP THE WIDOW WAKING': AN EXAMPLE FOR 'YONG MEN THAT ARE POOR'

An alehouse story such as that of Davies's ballad-singer at Temple Bar furnishes the matter of a 1623 Star Chamber case, fit to be a Jonsonian play.[33] Here are the dramatis personae:

[32] Davies, *Elegies*, 146, no. 38. See Map 2 for Temple Bar.
[33] PRO, STAC 8/31/16, A. G. Coventry (Attorney General) v. Tobias Audley etc. for forcible marriage to widow Anne Elsden. The records are fairly comprehensive, including several lists of interrogatories, depositions, and the full text of the ballad which incited a libel action. My recounting of the case draws from the whole set of records collectively; specific references are indicated where necessary. The legal proceedings are summarised in Sisson, *Lost Plays*, 80–124.

Motley crowd of Londoners:

Tobias Audley, *tobacconist*
Nicholas Cartmell, *minister and quack physician*
Mary Spencer, *prostitute*
Marjorie Terry, *bawd*
Francis Holliday, *conjurer and fortune-teller*
Robert Taylor, Thomas Hopkins and Francis Wise, *taverners*
Edmund Ward, *lawyer*
Benjamin Garfield, *gentleman, Beadle and Master of Bridewell, son-in-law to Anne*
Anne Elsden, *a widow richly left*

Theatre folk:

Thomas Dekker, John Webster, William Rowley and John Ford, *playwrights*
Ellis Worth, *principal actor of Queen Anne's Company from 1612*
Aron Holland, *owner of the Red Bull theatre*
John Snow, *parishioner of St. Giles and theatre-goer*

The primary scene is set in two taverns. One is the Greyhound on Fleet Street in Blackfriars, not far from Whitefriars theatre where *Ram Alley* played, and the very place where the abducted 'heiress' of the play (Francis in the guise of Constantia) is taken by Throat, before taking a boat at Bridewell.[34] The other is the Nag's Head in Cheapside. Toby Audley was a smart young man about town, but 'lived by selling of tobacco and hott waters, and . . . was very poore and needie'. Anne Elsden was 'worth 3000 li'.[35] She also possessed 'a great personall estate', in addition to her inheritance on widowhood.[36] Taffata-like, she was pursued by several fortune-hunters, Toby being the most resourceful. He first tried to trick Anne into a marriage at the Greyhound where he assembled a group of cronies, promising them 'gould enough': Rector Nicholas Cartmell, in debt and looking for profit, Edmund Ward the supposed Inner Temple 'lawyer', and Francis Holliday, akin to Jonson's Subtle. Meanwhile, Margery Terry lured Snow et al. to visit the tavern that night.[37] When Audley appeared with Anne, his associates pressed 'drugges' and wine upon

---

[34] See Gurr, *Shakespearean Stage*, 216; *RA*, 1085–6. See Map 1, 19 & 21. From Fleet Street – a legal street if ever there was one – to Bridewell, the prison, is a route through the two most prominent private theatres, Blackfriars and Whitefriars. The Nag's Head in Cheapside is just north-west of the Greyhound (probably within grid-square 8). Map 2 shows the boat-stairs at Bridewell.
[35] PRO, STAC 8/31/1.   [36] Ibid., 8/31/64.   [37] Ibid., 8/31/1.

Anne, to 'intoxicate and distort her senses, that hee [Toby] might draw her to what hee would'.[38] The morning after, the jolly crew 'inticed' a 'verie much distempered' Anne to Lambeth, where they applied yet more wine. Then they took her to St George's Fields where Simon Holliday '[con-iured]' her, till 'she became sencles'. They now 'came with her to Nag's Head in Cheapside to effect a match'.[39] None of this is far from *Ram Alley*'s world of rogues and tricksters, and the London marriage market.

Then comes 'Act II'. Though 'weakened' in her 'sences', Anne still had enough 'memory' to refuse 'to marrie the said Tobias'. So Cartmell 'infused and mingled' some special drugs 'into wine' which was forced down Anne's throat, 'so that her senses were taken from her'. At this point, a tavern boy '[carried] upp a Booke in the said room' – the Book of Common Prayer.[40] As Terry and Spencer put it,

> Anne Ellesden sat in a Chaire . . . unable to stand, and . . . Cartmell read some parts of the words of matrimonie, what pleased him; but when . . . Anne should have said after the said Cartmell, shee . . . could not speake a word . . . Marie Spencer tokke her by her chinne and shaked her, and made her crie oih, oih, and thise were all the wordes they said they could gett from her.[41]

Cartmell also effected a kind of handfast between them. This account, corroborated by several depositions, recalls the many disputed contracts discussed in Chapter 1, where the factual evidence of formalities were *presumed* to express mutual consent – but in fact often did not.

After 'marriage' and supper, Audley and his company had 'a bedd . . . sett upp in a roome in the said naggs Head Taverne'[42] 'and did after consummate the same marriage, and lay there together . . . not only that night but allso on the next night' (and a third elsewhere), ensuring that 'the churchwardens came & found them in bed together'.[43] Anne awoke from the nightmare to declare 'that shee was married to none but to her grave'. Wise, the vintner, and Ward, the 'lawyer', then presented 'the license' and said, 'looke yow heere yow old hagge, yow have cosened others, but now yow are cosened yourself'. The reports make a harrowing read:

> . . . on the Sunday morning next . . . Anne . . . then lieing in bedd . . . and exclaiming that some rogues had robd her and gotten away her keys . . . Marie Spencer and Margery Terrie councelled [Audley] to go to bedd *with* her and make much of her, and so stopp her exclama*c*ions, unto w*h*ich . . . Audley replied, that hee had as leive goe to bedd to an old Sowe.[44]

---

[38] Ibid., 8/31/2.   [39] Ibid., 8/31/2–3.   [40] Ibid., 8/31/3.
[41] Ibid., 8/31/5.   [42] Ibid., 8/31/3.   [43] Ibid., 8/31/64.   [44] Ibid., 8/31/4.

Audley took a stupefied Anne's house-key from her pocket, and went with Wise to get various valuables from her house and '20 li. . . . to buy them all drink.' A second raid yielded goods worth 1,500 li. The profits were shared in a general ambience of self-congratulatory jubilation – vividly evocative of gulling episodes in city-comedies, but with a particularly heartless edge. Anne was dowsed in yet more wine and forced to stay. Finally home a few days later, she 'remained senseless for 9 or 10 days'.[45]

The recurring details in the depositions are those on which the court demands information. The most curious recurrence is the legal enquiry about particular scenes in the tavern. The 'personal responses' of the defendants repeat the descriptions in affirmation or denial:

. . . hee did not *perceive* . . . anie vintners boy . . . bringing in anie Apricockes unto . . . Anne . . . But . . . one of the boyes of the . . . Taverne did . . . *pretend* . . . hee came from one of her Tenaunts, w*h*ich was done in a deriding manner, while . . . Anne remained in her distemperature . . . another boy, in another roome . . . did knocke w*i*th a pott, as if they wanted wine, and then the boy that counterfeited the said message answered, anon anon Sir acted at the Red bull in the play here called Keepe the widow waking.[46]

Enter the theatre. This deponent, John Snow, had seen the play that was the subject of the next 'act', bringing dramatists and impresarios to court. Audley's machinations had not only resembled a dramatic scenario but *provided* one. The interrogatories, remarkably, are based on reports of scenes acted in a play at the Red Bull at the time, itself based on the story of Anne Elsden, recreating the events in the two taverns. The interrogators ask the defendants and witnesses whether the staged incidents had indeed happened 'as is acted at the bull'. The legal process constantly refers to the drama for its own investigative purpose. The dialogue between law and drama could hardly be more immediate. A list of questions put to Audley's entourage asks:

. . . did you or any other . . . put a vyntners boy into wenches apparell and caused [him] w*i*th an emptie baskett to tell . . . Anne that hee had brought a baskett of Apricockes . . . did you or any other of yo*ur* Company . . . there knocke w*i*th a pott and vpon the same knocking did a boy of the said howse answere anon anon S*i*r, and is not or hath not the said manner of knocking . . . bene since acted vpon the Stage at the Red Bull when the plaie called *keepe the widowe waking* is acted or played there.

---

[45] Ibid., 8/31/5.   [46] Ibid., 8/31/5.

... were you privie consenting or acquaynted with the contryving acting or playing of the plaie or Interlude called *Keepe the widowe waking* by whom was the said contrived and whoe gave Instruccions for [its] contryving ... how often hath [it] bene acted or plaied at the Red Bull ... did you goe thither of purpose to see the same played ... .[47]

The tavern crowd seem to be revisiting the Boar's Head Tavern in East-cheap: 'anon, anon, sir' is a refrain familiar from the tavern scene in *Henry IV* where Hal, playing a silly game at the drawer Francis's cost, keeps calling out his name 'so that his tale to me may be nothing but "Anon"'.[48]

Webster, Ford, Dekker, Rowley and company were sued for libel by the Puritan Benjamin Garfield, Anne Elsden's son-in-law. They were accused of having made a play out of his family's misfortunes, spawning a salacious ballad. It is implied that they shared in the booty too, contriving with Audley's mates in protracting this exploitative event. The ballad, apparently based on the play and deriving its refrain from the play's title, was exhibited in court. Its humour works at the expense of widow Elsden, making Tobias into a comic hero (like Fleetwood's 'Tasse'), with the wit to achieve what others could not:

> He wisely tooke with him along,
> lest he should fail through speakeing,
> A Lawyer with a nimble tongue,
> who kept the widow wakeing.

And here is the moral:

> Therefore lett yong men that are poore,
> come take example here,
> And you who faine would heare the full
> discourse of this match makeing,
> The play will teach you at the Bull,
> to keepe the widdow wakeing.[49]

The ballad is a virtual advertisement for the play, sung strategically outside Anne's chamber-window in her son-in-law Garfield's house in Clerkenwell, almost adjacent to the Red Bull where the play was showing.[50] Here Garfield intervened, making it a Star Chamber matter. A set

---

[47] Ibid., 8/31/62.
[48] Shakespeare, *1King Henry IV*, II.iv.31–3.
[49] 'Bill of Informacion', 26 November 1624, in PRO, STAC 8/31/16.
[50] See Map 1, 5, for the Red Bull in Clerkenwell.

of interrogatories are directed at whether the rogues' collusion with the theatre extended to the ballad-writers:

. . . have you or any other in yo*ur* hearing . . . published sung read or told the Contents of the said Ballett was made of . . . Anne Elsden or the plaie acted in shew or token of her goeing from Taverne to Taverne and there kept watching by Tobyas Audley and others or caused or *pro*cured the said . . . Ballett to bee sung . . . neere the Chamber wyndowe of the said Anne . . . whether was the said plaie or the . . . Ballett made in disgrace of . . . Anne.[51]

A tailor testifies that he heard a stranger, Richard, claim that 'he made the said . . . ballad being at a play and did after he had seene the . . . play' and that he lived 'neere St. Pulichers church and was a book seller'.[52]

The transmission trajectory is from tavern to stage, and stage to street, via ballad-mongers. The missing link is between the first two stages. How did the dramatists acquire such a specific, salacious plot? This takes us back to what is known about the lost play. It was conceived as a double-bill: 'a play called the Late Murder in Whitechapell, or Keepe the Widow waking', as stated in Thomas Dekker's deposition which claims that

hee wrote two sheetes of paper conteyning the first Act of [this] play . . . and a speech in the last scene of the last Act of the boy who had killed his mother, w*hi*ch play . . . was licensed . . . And this def*endan*t is not guiltie of any complot, combination or conspiracy w*i*th one Toby Audeley or any other nominated . . .[53]

If Dekker is to be believed – and no one mentions the playwrights' presence in the taverns – there must have been some other route through which the story found its way into the drama. But all that the two parts of the play shared was their foundation upon contemporary scandals leading to trials. Significantly, the two protagonists (one comic and the other tragic in characterisation) were both tried at the same Old Bailey sessions on 3 September 1624, at the gaol delivery from Newgate.[54] The 'murder at Whitechapel' also resulted in two ballads. One was entered in the Stationers' Registers in the name of Richard Hodgkins: *The Repentance of Nathaniel Tindall that killed his mother* (1624); the other in the names of John Trundle and Hodgkins: *A most bloudy vnnaturall and vnmatchable murther Comitted in Whitchappell by Nathaniel Tindall vpon his owne*

[51] STAC 8/31/16, 62.
[52] Ibid., 'Deposition of John Griffin'.
[53] This autographed deposition is interesting on collaborative play writing, on which the legal records as a whole also throw light.
[54] MG, *Gaol Delivery Register*, III, 128–37, esp. 128b; and *Gaol Delivery Roll*, 636/92. For the Grand Jury's Bill against Nathaniel Tindall, see MG, *Sessions Roll*, 636/88.

mother . . . (1624).[55] Richard Hodgkins, incidentally, is probably the same as the 'Richard Hodskyns' mentioned in the Star Chamber bill:

> Audley and the other Confederates . . . [agreed] to drawe into their practise one William Rowley . . . deckers, Richard Hodskyns, Aron Holland Thomas Fuller clerk Raph Savadge and others being Com*m*on enterlude players, and contrivors of libellous plays and balletts . . .[56]

Dekker's deposition mentions 'instructions for the contriving' of the play 'by one Raph Savage', and Ellis Worth's corroborates this information. The overlapping names reinforce a sense of a theatrical cum cheap-print collaboration, and evoke a news-hungry market, waiting to snap up any lucrative trifles emerging from scandalous legal events. The reports also suggest the possibility of playwrights jostling with ballad-makers at sensational trials. This brings us to the elusive issues of court audience, the transmission of information from law court to yellow press, and the role of drama in all this.

'IN OPEN COURT'

Dramatic representations of court-space, proceedings and audience do not usually correspond to specific procedures exactly. They tend, rather, to be composite and fictional, conflating spaces and jurisdictions. Sometimes they are even apparently contradictory. Consequently, the vision they offer has been largely ignored or dismissed as fictitious. I propose, instead, that the fictionality itself demands address. Alongside a carefully contextualised reading of drama in relation to concurrent cultural practices, it is sometimes necessary to work back from dramatic portrayals to social realities and cultural perceptions.

Webster's *The Devil's Law Case* (1623), a play much concerned with representing legal procedures, provides a perfect case study. Here, the principal legal conflict is between Romelio and his mother, the widow Leonora, who falsely accuses him of bastardy in open court to avenge his supposed murder of Contarino, who is her daughter Jolenta's betrothed, but also the object of her own desire. When Romelio tells his mother, with the studied nonchalance of a master-plotter, that he has released Contarino from his agony by killing him, Leonora is first heartbroken, then vengeful. She tells her maid, Winifred, of

---

[55] Arber, *Transcript*, IV, 120, 123.
[56] See n. 49 above.

> ... such a plot
> That never mother dreamt of ...
> The law shall undo him.
>   (III.iii.349–54)

He 'has six lordships left him', 'but he cannot live four days to enjoy them' (380–1). 'Have you poisoned him?' Winifred asks (382). 'The poison,' she declares,

> ... shall be given him
> In open court; I'll make him swallow it
> Before the judge's face ...   (384–6)

Yet, when Leonora's case assumes scandalous dimensions, Contilupo exclaims that it

> ... deserves
> Rather a spacious public theatre,
> Than a pent court for audience ...
>   (IV.i.98–100)[57]

'Pent' suggests both secrecy and confined space. How does this square with Leonora's insistence on public shaming in 'open court'? Does this contradiction invalidate the historical value of drama, or does it address a reality that escapes the formal discourses of legal documentation? We are invited to reassess the nature of legal realism in the drama, and the reconstructive status of dramatic fiction.

How open, then, was the 'open court'? In play after play, we encounter people declaiming about, appearing in, revealing to, having to confront, and being judged in, an open court.[58] Isabella, in *The White Devil*, re-enacts Bracciano's private, symbolic ritual of divorce (refusing to sleep with her), declaring that this is as official as a public, witnessed, legal event:

> As if in throngèd court a thousand ears
> Had heard it and a thousand lawyer's hands
> Sealed to the separation.   (257–9)

---

[57] Whether there is the specific idea of a 'public' as opposed to 'private' playhouse is open to speculation; the main point seems to be a wider contrast between the relative publicness of theatrical and legal spaces.

[58] For an example of the currency of the phrase in legal history writing, see Baker, *Legal Profession*, 269 and 289. On the fluidity of the contemporary definition of a court, see 'The Changing Concept of a Court', in ibid., 153–69; and 270 and 289 on the fictive equation in law between 'in open court' and 'out of court'.

In Ford's *The Lady's Trial*, Spinella, challenged by her husband, despairingly but proudly refuses counsel:

> . . . let me appear,
> Or mine own lawyer, or, in open court,
> (Like some forsaken client) in my suit
> Be cast for want of honest plea . . .
>
> (II.iv)[59]

Leontes, in *The Winter's Tale*, configures Hermione's trial as a public event:

> . . . for, as she hath
> Been publicly accus'd, so she shall have
> A just and open trial.   (II.iii.203–5)

Hermione remonstrates that she has been 'hurried/Here, to this place, i' th' open air' before she has regained strength (III.ii.104–5).[60] Openness is at once a spatial perception and a function of the 'public', thus almost safeguarding fairness.[61] Conversely, a prose work such as Heywood's *A Curtaine Lecture* (1637), which cites Juvenal against '[litigious]' women who 'blusht not in open court to be her own Advocate and plead her own causes in publicke assemblies', also attests to the perception of the court as a public space.[62] A similar sense of undesirable publicity is registered in private letters such as the Countess of Southampton's to her father, begging that her marital trouble should be privately 'ended by some counsellors', 'for very loth I wolde be to have my name come in tryall in open courte'.[63] We also remember Swinnerton's decision to waive the prosecution for his wife's alleged rape, rather than 'bring my Wife and myself upon the stage'.[64] The notion of the 'open court' is equally ubiquitous in depositions, indicating an accepted connection between

---

[59] In Ford, *Dramatic Works*, II.

[60] Presumably the 'place' is a courtyard in the palace where people can watch the trial – a space defined by the royal presence and the structure of the event.

[61] See Thomas Churchyard's poem, *Honour of the Lawe*, A3v.

[62] Heywood, *Curtaine Lecture*, 11–12. Compare 41, on Seneca's account of a vestal virgin who, for the minor sin of writing a witty verse about the sweetness of marriage, was 'summoned into open Court'; and 70–1, on how 'in the open face of the Court and at the barre at which her cause was then pleaded, [Virginius] slew [Virginia]'. Clearly, the court was 'open' in a time-honoured proverbial sense. It is the continuity and reinforcement of this rhetoric in early modern England, and the specific historical underpinnings of the phrase, that interest us. The present report of these classical examples is, after all, Heywood's, especially the story of Virginius where he does not follow an earlier chronicler but narrates the spectacular court-event himself.

[63] As quoted in Merton, 'The Women who served Queen Mary and Queen Elizabeth', 182.

[64] *Harleian*, III, 476.

arraignment and publicness. In a 1590s Requests case, Collard's plea against the Countess of Rutland was successful 'vppon the open hearing and debating of the same matter' in court;[65] Janet Device is said to be 'sworn and examined in open Court' at her brother's trial for witchcraft in 1613.[66] Star Chamber notices also use the phrase, referring to the judges' opinion being 'published in open court'.[67]

But there must have been severe physical restrictions as to how public these events could be. Historiographical orthodoxy assumes that actual trials were in fact dry written business, conducted in the presence of a few officials, allowing for little chance of dialogue – suggesting that dramatic, confrontational trial scenes are largely fictional.[68] Historians of law have on the whole concentrated on procedural details, or the communal relations leading to prosecution, avoiding questions of audience size and composition. This is understandable, as very little survives by way of factual information about what exactly went on in court sessions.[69] What interests us as historians of culture now was not important, or even relevant, to clerks of courts and notaries public then, who kept records of court proceedings. Certainly, the courtroom was often too small to host an 'open' event: the ecclesiastical courtroom in Chester (the only surviving sixteenth-century church court) would scarcely accommodate fifteen people. Even Westminster Hall, where onlookers had free access, would have had very poor audibility, and limited space for each court in simultaneous sessions.[70]

Figure 5.1 – to my knowledge the only extant contemporary picture of a courtroom scene in early modern England – shows two courts in sessions in Westminster, the King's Bench on the left and the Chancery on the right. The courts are contained within cubicle-like enclosures, and the King's Bench is overlooked by a two-tiered gallery. Individual courts have very little seating space, and the foreground shows a general mingling of litigants, lawyers and members of the public. This gives an odd impression of smallness and closeness combined with the sense of a crowded public space. The coexistence of Leonora's perception of court-space with

---

[65] PRO, Req 1/19, 126–8.
[66] Potts, *Wonderfvll Discoverie*, D2v, F; compare D2 and Iv: Anne Whittle and Janet Device's examinations 'in open court'.
[67] Burn, ed., *Star Chamber*, 9.
[68] A recent formulation of this view, albeit in a balanced approach to 'reading' the norm of common-law practices, is Macnair, 'Reading the Evidence'.
[69] For a recent admission of the inadequacy of documents, and therefore of historical writing, on what exactly happened in courts, see Sharpe, *Instruments of Darkness*, 215.
[70] See Baker, *Introduction*, 44.

Figure 5.1. 'The Courts of King's Bench and Chancery in Westminster Hall', mid-seventeenth century; by anonymous draughtsman, possibly Dutch; British Museum, reproduced in *Legal London: an Exhibition in the great Hall of the royal Courts of Justice* (London, 1971), no. 9.

Contilupo's becomes suddenly comprehensible. Webster, we must remember, had an intimate knowledge of legal practices in London as both a law-student and a defendant. Perhaps the apparent conflict between Leonora's and Contilupo's remarks is the internal difference where the meaning lies.

The audience's nature and size are frustratingly elusive entities. Yet inevitably, the people present, and the structures within which they interacted, defined the space, and how public or private the trial event was felt to be. Such notions as privacy are often seen as anachronistic in the early modern period.[71] But imaginative literature reveals a distinct sense of privacy and publicness – only, their material and perceptual components were different from those in our times. Chapter 2 has already demonstrated the nature of these perceptions, in connection with adultery. Romantic love is another construct often seen as inapplicable to earlier periods.[72] Yet literary texts are eloquent with accents of love as we understand it.[73] Literary and non-legal representations of legal experience provide a specific field for examining such notions. A genre that is particularly revealing of a trial's human and social components is pamphlets generated by well-known trials.

But first, a sketch of the legal context for trials of various sorts, without attempting to go into individual jurisdictional details. Ecclesiastical or consistory courts were held in local cathedrals, with the Archbishop's court at York or the Court of Arches in Canterbury being the next step up; the Court of Delegates in Lambeth Palace acted as the appellate court, while the Court of High Commission was the Star Chamber's ecclesiastical counterpart. These administered canon law and dealt not only with sexual litigation, but also clerical matters and defamation cases. Church court trials were conducted *in camera*, on the basis of prior deposition, but were placed within a structure of public authority. In line with trial procedure, they began with 'information' by churchwardens and ended, often, with communal shaming or penance rituals. But, as Martin

---

[71] Ariès and Duby, *Private Lives*, III; Stone, *Family, Sex and Marriage*; Amussen, *Ordered Society*, esp. 2. See p. 78 above.

[72] See Stone, *Family, Sex and Marriage* and *The Past and the Present*; Slater, 'Weightiest Business'; Shorter, *Making of the Modern Family*. For an early but influential statement, see Zeldin, *France*; Irving Singer accepts this premise in *The Nature of Love*.

[73] Bertram's remonstrance to the King's infliction of a bride on him is an instinctive expression precisely of this: 'I cannot love her' (*All's Well*, II.iii.145). Cf. CCA, X.10.12, 151–52r, on how Anne Austen, pressured by her guardians to marry Robert Launsfield, said she 'could not fynd in her hart to love hym in such sort' – an essentially personal and instinctive articulation of 'love' in the face of social expectation and form.

Ingram points out, 'the courts sometimes left such hallowed precincts [as the church itself] to go on circuit, and sessions were held in such improvised surroundings in parish churches or in inn parlours'.[74] The participation of the community in the overall procedure was significant, and not limited to the trial stage alone. The initial stages of Information, Inquisition and Presentment, leading up to official prosecution, were heavily dependent on informants from local communities and parish ministers working hand-in-hand with churchwardens who were responsible for supervising moral behaviour in a parish and bringing 'presentments' to court. In addition, there were annual visitation courts, convened in suitable locations on the itinerary, when bishops and archdeacons would visit particular parishes mainly to hear reports from churchwardens, but also to try and settle some of the business reported in those very sessions.[75]

Common law courts sat at various places across the country – above all, Westminster. These included the Courts of King's Bench, Common Pleas, Wards, and the Exchequer. Chancery, which sat across the hall from King's Bench, was the court of Equity, Requests being a branch of it. State trials *were* populated events, taking over the whole of Westminster Hall, as were trials by Peers of the House of Lords: at Throckmorton's 1550 state trial, the crowd overflowed outside the Hall. The Star Chamber had the least clearly defined jurisdiction, by virtue of its appellate nature – cases got referred to it from various inferior courts. The number of people present, and the scope for direct interaction between defendant and court, were restricted by the spatial and procedural structures of that court.[76]

But the central common law authorities also functioned through assizes, with a group of itinerant judges travelling through counties on circuits, holding trials in venues from town halls to marketplaces.[77] Many witchcraft trials (the greatest generator of trial literature) were held at assizes, the single most widespread shared legal phenomenon. Going to court, in the popular imagination, consisted of an amalgam of impressions derived from a whole range of litigation that the populace was exposed to. Though the outlines of such a percept are necessarily elusive, imaginative literature and popular pamphlets testify to its existence.

---

[74] Ingram, *Church Courts*, 2.
[75] Ibid., 43–6.
[76] For contemporary lists of courts and jurisdictions, see Coke, *Fourth Part*, and Crompton, *L'authoritie*.
[77] On criminal jurisdiction and assize trials, see Langbein, *Prosecuting Crime*, 104–25.

Heywood writes, in discussing law suits resulting from enforced marriages (strictly speaking a denizen of church courts), that 'who shall but Follow the Circuit in the Countrey, besides these trialls in the City, shall seldome find a generall Assises without some evidence or other given upon the like tragicall accidents'.[78] The sense of space communicated by non-legal literature is similarly conflative, and suggests an event rather different from what official history would have us believe. At her trial for witchcraft in 1634, Mary Spencer apparently found 'the wind . . . so loud and the throng so great, that she could not hear the evidence against her'.[79] A tract about a 1660 witch trial in Bury St Edmunds indicates dialogue and cross-examination in open court rather than a purely written submission of testimonies.[80] This is technically possible in criminal trials where no counsel was allowed to either prosecution or defence.[81] But it is not just a feature of treason trials but also evident, in a less technical sense, in smaller local courts such as these. Dorothy Durent is said to have repeatedly 'answered' questions 'asked by the court'. An elderly woman supposedly bewitched by the accused, she showed signs of miraculous recovery when judgement was delivered. The trial comes across vividly as a spectacular event, far from mere paperwork. Such expectation clearly conditioned both the behaviour of the parties involved, and the written and spoken reports. Although slightly later in time, this instance indicates the customary continuities of legal procedures through the seventeenth century. Earlier examples corroborate this impression. Although depositions were mostly written before the defendant's appearance in trial, the parties could speak in court, and perform. The examinations themselves were sometimes 'openly read'.[82] In many witchcraft cases, while the accused deposed earlier, third-party witnesses were involved during the trial, and spoke in court. While it is impossible to assess the exact dimensions of any attending crowd, even the local dignitaries attending assizes, such as sheriffs and JPs, would constitute a sense of communal

---

[78] Heywood, *Curtaine Lecture*, 101. See Ch. 1 (pp. 27–8) on how Calverley ended up being tried for murder at common law after a miserable enforced marriage; but the suit brought up the question of validity by canonical tenets in the first place.

[79] *CSPD, 1634–35*, 79.

[80] *Trial of Witches*, 2–3, 8. I have been led to several of the witchcraft cases by scattered references in the work of various historians, notably Jim Sharpe's. While their interest may lie elsewhere, their collective research has facilitated my search for trial accounts with information on court happenings.

[81] Significantly, civil cases, where no counsel was allowed, have generated the least amount of non-legal literature; the more obvious reason, however, was the less sensational nature of civil causes.

[82] Potts, *Wonderfull Discoverie*, P2.

presence in small towns and villages. The jury would often consist of members of the defendants' immediate community, forming a direct link to the known world outside the court.

Thus, the foregoing stages of law, from 'Information' through arrest and prosecution to final trial, involved, in both common law and ecclesiastical procedure, much local and neighbourly participation, inevitably creating the sense of a public event.[83] The audience depended on the publicity already given to a case; the Lancaster witch trial is a case in point:

> so infinite a multitude came to the Arraignement and tryall of these Witches . . . the number of them being knowen to exceed all others at any time heretofore, at one time to be indicted, arraigned, and receiue their tryall . . .[84]

That there was much drama at these sessions is clear from such tracts. Janet Device was brought to court, to testify against her mother, who

> cryed out against the child in such fearefull manner, as all the Court did not a little wonder at her, and so amazed the child, as with weeping teares shee cryed out vnto my Lord the Iudge, and told him, shee was not able to speake in the presence of her Mother.[85]

On being asked to identify any of the suspects at a later stage, Janet, 'in the presence of this great Audience, in open Court . . . went and tooke *Alice Nutter* by the hand, and accused her to be one'.[86]

Like many pamphlets, both the Lancaster and the Bury trial tracts were written by men who witnessed the proceedings. *Wonderfull Discoverie* is prefaced by a note by James Altham and Edward Bromley, explaining that they have imposed 'the labour of this Worke vpon this Gentleman, by reason of his place, being a Clerke at that time in Court, imploied in the Arraignment and triall of them'.[87] The dedicatory letter ends with Potts signing off 'from my Lodging in Chancerie Lane, the sixteenth of November 1612' – suggestive of the fluidity of legal information between London and the counties. Dugdale's account of Elizabeth Caldwell's trial for attempted husband-murder confirms this; both the incident and the prosecution happened in Cheshire, but 'diuers reports passed vp

---

[83] On the participatory nature of judicial functioning, see Herrup, *Common Peace*, passim. For an example of the role of 'general report' in judicial proceedings, see *The araignment & burning of Margaret Ferne-seede*, esp. A3–v.
[84] Potts, *Wonderfull Discoverie*, B. Cf. the trial of Elizabeth Caldwell, convicted, with her lover, for attempting to murder her husband: Dugdale, *True discourse*, B2v–B3.
[85] Potts, *Wonderfull Discoverie*, G.   [86] Ibid., P2.   [87] Ibid., A2v.

and downe the streets of London'.[88] Dugdale too was 'one then present as witnes, theire owne Countryman'.[89] This generic self-fashioning resembles the anxious self-definition of providentialist tracts about contemporary scandals. As Robert Armin says in *his* dedication,

> We haue many giddie pated Poets, that could haue published Report with more eloquence, but truth in plaine attire is the easier knowne.[90]

Not only do Bromley and Altham vouch for Potts's legal role in court, but add Bromley's testimony that he has corrected the text, ensuring that 'nothing might pass but matter of Fact'.[91] The claim, everywhere, is one of responsible and factual narration, with eye-witnessing as a ground for authority and assent – a classic instance of what Jan Schramm calls 'the way in which fiction seeks to . . . bolster its claims to authenticity by its appropriation of evidentiary paradigms' – except that these pamphlet-writers were using these paradigms to make the point that they were not writing fiction.[92] Nor is this confined to trials known to have been public events. In the pamphlet engendered by the courtroom drama in a 1591 Star Chamber case, John Pitcher's attempt to stab himself to death as he was being carried out of the Chamber to the Westminster pillory is described as an eye-witness account of a spectacle watched by many, though public access to the Star Chamber would have been significantly more restricted than at an assize court.[93] In 1605, Alexander Chocke, JP, and member of the jury, wrote a vivid 'report' (filed with Star Chamber papers) of an alleged witch, the 'bewitched' girl and her father standing within a few feet of one another in court and having a charged and spectacular exchange.[94] Such ostensibly 'factual' eye-witness reporting is carefully distinguished by the writers from the less responsible publishing through cheap print. Dugdale claims an objectivity that he alleges the various verbal reports lack.[95] Henry Goodcole, writer of *The Adulteresses Funerall Day*, also wrote *The Wonderfull discouerie of Elizabeth Sawyer a Witch* (1621), the chief source behind Dekker, Ford and Rowley's play, *The Witch of Edmonton*, first performed that year. In his note 'To the Readers', Goodcole explains that his chief motive for publication is an

---

[88] Dugdale, *True discourse*, A3v.   [89] Ibid., Title.   [90] Ibid., D4v.

[91] Potts, *Wonderfull Discouerie*, A3v. The printer's apology for work 'done in . . . great haste, at the end of a Terme' (A4), reinforces the impression of factual scrupulousness.

[92] Schramm, *Testimony and Advocacy*, xii; see also Ch. 1 on the status of eye-witnessing in early modern writing.

[93] *Fearefull Example.*

[94] PRO, STAC 8/4/10.   [95] Dugdale, *True discourse*, A3–v.

'Authenticall . . . Narration' to assert 'the truth of the cause' against the 'wound' it has been given 'by most base and false ballets, which were sung at the time of our returning from the Witches execution'.[96]

Ironically, precisely this second stage of further publication beyond the courtroom but emerging from it was perceived by the legal authorities as insidious and vulgar. The presence of people at trials who might report on the courtroom events constituted a part of the particular sense of publicity that protagonists in dramatic trials articulate. Goodcole and Potts laboured to distinguish their own enterprise from the 'ridiculous fictions' of 'lewde Balletmongers', fit for 'an ale-bench'.[97] But those 'fictions' could also have arisen out of access to the court's proceedings by the ballad writer whose version Goodcole and company heard on their way back. In reality, distinctions between vulgar scandal-mongering print and quasi-legal reporting was often rhetorical. Sensational providentialist tracts were printed and sold at the very shops offering more self-consciously 'judicial' reports: *Strange Newes of a prodigious monster* (1613), a blatant example of the former, jostled with *A detection of . . . three witches arraigned at Chelmsforde* (1579) 'at the little Northe-dore of Paules'. The direction of transmission outwards from the court in the Sawyer trial mirrors the Elsden case. Nor is this instance unique. George Chapman, defendant in a 1603 Star Chamber case, protests that he is not guilty of '[making] any such stage playe to be played vpon the *open stages* in divers Play Howses within the Cite of London to resemble and *publishe* the dealing of . . . John Howe etc.' (italics mine). The libellous work attributed to Chapman was *The Old Joiner of Aldgate* – 'played by the children of powles in a pryvate house'.[98] Here, it is private playhouses that are perceived to be 'open', not the 'open court' of law.

The spreading of the word from Contilupo's 'pent court' into the 'spacious public theatre', then, reflects a transmission from stage one to stage two of 'publishing'. It is also reminiscent of Monticelso's claim, in *White Devil*'s trial scene, that he is merely repeating in court 'what is ordinary Rialto talk,/And ballated, and would be played a'th'stage' (III. ii.245). The point, there, is the greater publicness of the theatre and the street than the court. Webster's distinction between two degrees of

---

[96] Goodcole, *Wonderfull discouerie*, A3–v. Compare Potts, *Wonderfull Discouerie*, A2v.

[97] Ibid., A3v. See Beard, *Theatre*, 438, on the providentialist antithesis between 'ribald' 'Ballads' and legal literature.

[98] PRO, STAC 8/8/2 (Coke v. Joanes, Howe et al.), 3, 8. Chapman apparently sold the 'playbook' for 20 marks to a merchant of the Staple (2).

publicity (Leonora's 'open court' and Contilupo's 'public theatre') fits the gradations of 'publishing' that the writers of trial reports make – but on that axis, the pamphleteers belong with the vulgar scribes. Writing *Devil's Law Case* the year before he appeared at Star Chamber with Dekker, Ford and Rowley on the charge of '[contriving] . . . libellous playes and balletts',[99] Webster must have known the various interfaces well – between ale-bench and court, court and stage, stage and street. The play carefully stages spectatorship and audition within the court, as a 'private' closet is prepared for Ercole and the officers who want to 'hear all unseen'; court space itself is further distinguished between secret/private and open/public (IV.ii.1–5). This would seem less curious then than now. Social hierarchy was often spatially reflected in such select courts as Star Chamber: witness Lord Keeper Egerton's 1595 order 'that the empty room at the East side of the [Star Chamber], of late inclosed with a doore' should be reserved for men of good account in the country and for gentlemen 'towardes the lawe'.[100] In getting the court ready for the trial, Webster's Sanitonella warns the court officers to 'let in/No brachygraphy men, to take notes' (IV.ii.26–7). 'First Officer' replies, as though such were routinely present, 'No sir?' (27). Sanitonella answers,

> By no means,
> We cannot have scurvy pamphlets, and lewd ballads
> Engendered of it presently . . .   (27–9)

He articulates precisely the anxiety that Goodcole, Potts and Dugdale pre-empt. But who *were* these brachygraphy men? Hovering on margins of legal space, they are clearly distinct from sanctioned reporters in West-minster Hall.[101] Could Webster and Dekker have been among them at the Old Bailey sessions on 3 September, taking notes on both the murder trial and the one for unlawful marriage, before going on to write *Keep the Widow Waking*, which spawned a salacious ballad and eventually landed them in Star Chamber? Indeed, what is the status of the play-text itself as 'brachygraphy'? What Webster dramatises is that elusive process whereby a legal event was transformed into a cultural artefact. He does so with a sharp feel for the possibility of transmissions that the trial event contained.

---

[99] *PRO*, STAC 8/31/16, 'Bill of Informacion, 26 Nov., 1624'.
[100] Hawarde, *Les Reportes*, 39.
[101] Cf. IV.ii.80–9, 30–4. On legal note-takers, see Baker, *Legal Profession*, 325, and Abbott, *Law Reporting*.

What also emerges from all this is an unquantifiable sense of audience presence – drawn from the experience of a range of litigation, irrespective of the highly variable size of audiences, often scant, yet significant in their conditioning of legal performance on various planes. Small wonder that legal history has found it difficult to arrive at inferences about the feel of a trial or events in court; nor is it surprising that plays might provide an anchor within the disjointed picture accumulated from chapbooks (possibly the earliest journalism in England).[102] The drama's understanding of 'court', and relative notions of private and public, are part of a larger aesthetic of representation (as distinct from reproduction). Rather than remaining merely fictive, it acquires a distinctive realism, because of its actual affinity with the contemporary socio-legal concept of a court. Walter Map, a twelfth-century courtier, wrote,

> The court is indeed temporal, changeable and various, stationary and wandering, never continuing in one stay. When I leave it I know it perfectly, but when I come back to it I find nothing or but little of what I left . . . yet the court . . . remains always the same.[103]

Insofar as it can be considered as a stable entity, the court was indeed symbolic. John Baker discusses how this fluidity was tied down to hierarchical structures in the sixteenth and seventeenth centuries; but it is clear even from his study that the fluidity died hard in public perception.[104] The functions of delegation and perambulation in this period, with the 'court' sitting at various places and at various times, meant that the understanding of the court was necessarily figurative. The original meaning of the word 'court' – a lord's house – also persisted in Westminster's being the royal court in both senses. The factors defining a space or an event were ownership and authority, specific structures and presences: *curia regis* was an amorphous concept, applying to what was generally perceived as a legal event in a legal space. No matter where a particular 'court' sat, 'the king [was] always present in Court in the Judgement of Law'.[105] Certain associated legal offices were also symbolically defined: that of Lord High Steward, for instance, came into being for one day only on which there would be a trial by peers; the Lord would come in with a white wand, emblematic of authority, which he would break at the end

---

[102] On newsletters describing state trials, and the growth of the more canonical 'pure newsletters', see Cust, 'News and Politics', 112, 60–90; Raymond, *Invention*, 1–19.
[103] Map, *De Nugis Curialium*, 1.
[104] Baker, *Legal Profession*, 153–69.
[105] Coke, *Twelfth Part*, 65.

to signify the dissolution of his power – curiously similar to Prospero's symbolic abjuration in *The Tempest*. The court was often as transient as the theatre. Yet what it stood for – judicial power – was constant. It could 'sit' in as un-public a space as the single chamber of a judge in an Inn of Court or Chancery, but the presence of the judge and officials and certain members of the community would rule out its perception as a private event. These events, by a legal fiction, would be considered to have happened 'in court', as Baker explains.[106]

This shifting, composite, largely symbolic notion of the court is exactly the sense in which it figures most often in drama. Ford's Spinella is never taken to an actual court of law; but her tribulation is nevertheless perceived by herself, and others, as a 'trial', just as Heywood's Anne Frankford, standing in her night-gown in front of her servants in her own house, still feels she is being put on trial publicly, and Frankford emerges from his private chamber to deliver 'judgement'. The very privateness of these legal operations underlines the inherent publicness of their conception. Alternatively, when Throat in *Ram Alley* asks for his 'chair' and 'gown' so that he can 'seem a lawyer' to the client at his door (I.iv.415–16), not only is he asking for the stage props that define legal office in the theatre, but also the symbols that make it recognisable in society. The fictionality of dramatic trials can address a real presence of metaphor within the social practice and understanding of law.

---

[106] Baker, *Legal Profession*, 162–3.

CHAPTER 6

'When women go to Law, the Devil is full of Business': *women, law and dramatic realism*

As its alternative title suggests, Webster's *The Devil's Law Case or When Women go to Law, the Devil is full of Business* is a play about women initiating as well as disrupting court procedures. When Vittoria Corombona, the brilliant, adulterous protagonist of Webster's better-known play, outperforms her accusers during her trial in the papal court, judge Monticelso remonstrates, 'she scandals our proceedings'.[1] The sense of 'scandal' attaching to women litigants – or simply women appearing in court – in much of early modern drama may appear to be a fictional stereotype. Women in plays often bring dubious suits, get up to strange tricks that throw legal procedure into chaos, and engage in shady sexual dealings. Is this purely a literary phenomenon? Women, after all, are generally thought to have had minimal legal agency and visibility in the period. A second set of associations further reinforces the sense of their 'unrealistic' representation in these contexts – that of an obscuring mystery which often conflates tricksiness with ritual.

This chapter shows how the two associative strands are linked in such dramatic treatments, and attempts to explain the particular brand of fictionality this combination produces. In exaggerating the hybrid nature of theatrical courtrooms, female litigant characters bring issues of representation into focus. But addressing the fictive representation of women at court within early modern plays can tell us a great deal not only about the drama's distinctive vision of law but also about women's actual legal experience. It is precisely the apparent lack of realism that constitutes the most effective medium – if we know how to interpret it – for understanding amorphous but historically specific facts about socio-legal perceptions and phenomena. I will return, in this chapter, to *Devil's Law Case* as my main example. We have seen in its treatment of court-space and audience how traces in imaginative literature can point us to historical realities

---

[1] *WD*, III.ii.130.

otherwise inaccessible. It is no accident that the play's other major pre-occupation is with that especially elusive field – the experience of women at law. Though the play's mimetic self-consciousness in representing such legal realities is rare, its treatment of such situations is far from an isolated instance.

At the open trial-cum-recognition scene at the end of Shakespeare's *Measure for Measure*, Mariana's testimony creates puzzlement and annoyance in court.[2] In response to the interrogatories of the 'judge', the Duke, she claims to be neither married, nor a maid, nor a widow. The Duke answers, 'Why, you are nothing then' (V.i.177). Lucio quips, 'My lord, she may be a punk' (178)! Mariana explains that Angelo 'thinks he knows that he ne'er knew my body,/But knows, he thinks, that he knows Isabel's' (202–3). Angelo exclaims at this 'strange abuse' (205). The paradoxes underlying Mariana's claims are, however, created by the ambiguities of marriage law in the period. Validity and illicitness could coexist in the same union, as sexual union could turn an uncertain or informal contract, or a *de futuro* spousal (which was really like an engagement), into 'full and perfect matrimony', though consent, not coitus, was meant to be the essence of marriage in canon law, and in spite of official pressures to solemnise marriages.[3] This is what underlies the breach between knowledge and intention in Angelo's position that Mariana's apparently contradictory description touches on. This, again, is the loophole that the women in the play exploit to engineer the bed-trick through which Mariana takes Isabel's designated place in Angelo's bed and thus turns her five-year-old future contract with him into present and irrevocable matrimony. The bed-trick is also the central device through which Helena, in *All's Well*, fulfils her absconding husband Bertram's conditions and makes his private resistance to his formal marriage invalid, without Bertram even being aware that he has slept with her, and not Diana.[4] The

---

[2] The gate of 'Vienna', constructed as a place for adjudication, combines both the sense of law court and royal (or ducal) court, and recalls the often figurative understanding of the 'court' in the period. The factors defining a space or an event were ownership and authority, specific structures and presences. Vincentio, 'Duke' of Vienna, here embodies the authority of the governor.

[3] See Ch. 1 above, passim; and p. 48 and n. 107. The most direct dramatic example of a union at once valid and less than fully legitimate is Claudio and Juliet's consummated handfast marriage in *Measure*. Witness Claudio protesting to Lucio, with a curious combination of innocence and guilt, that she is 'fast [his] wife' and that 'the stealth of [their] most mutual entertainment/With character too gross is writ on Juliet' (I.ii.126); the confused mixture of indignation and disgust in this assertion of a 'true contract' that is yet furtive and reprehensible is an emotional analogue to the lawful deceits that Helena and Mariana engage in.

[4] Sex was assumed to be the surest proof of consent: this is why it was seized upon by law as a validating or finalising factor in uncertain matches or engagements. Hence the quasi-legal logic of

last scene of that play, too, is a trial, where Diana's testimony elicits precisely the same impatience as Mariana's statements. Diana's claims are also apparently paradoxical – her spousal ring, she says, was not given to her, nor did she buy it, nor was it lent her; just as she claims that Bertram 'is guilty, and not guilty', 'knows I am no maid, and he'll swear to't;/I'll swear I am a maid, and he knows not' (V.iii.290–1). The response is that she 'does abuse' the court (293); Lafew, in a tone similar to Lucio's, says: 'This woman's an easy glove, my lord, she goes off and on at pleasure' (277–8). The jibe, significantly, is sexual.

Both these scenes demonstrate how law itself makes space for contradictions which can then be exploited by women and perceived by onlookers as deliberate, teasing mystification. At the same time, the mystification takes the form of a transition from recognisable legal ploys to a seemingly fictive performance in a romance mode. The bed-trick itself, as a typically female device, is poised between real law and fairy-tale law – being at once a function of historically specific legal provisions and a popular motif common, among other texts, to Italian novellae and tales of sex and bawdry and wish-fulfilment, which so many Renaissance English plays drew on.[5] Women in legal situations are repeatedly associated in the drama with doublespeak, contradictions, law-tricks, stratagems and sexual intrigue. But inseparable from these associations is a sense of mystery, operating through disguise, ritual and riddle. Mariana enters the court veiled and speaks inscrutably, while Helena is presented as a spectacle of romance transformation as she is ushered in like a miraculous emblem: 'And now behold the meaning' (V.II.305–6). The legal realism of both these scenes is disrupted, even transformed, by an entirely different order of legality as the women take over. It is almost as if realism yields to fantasy when it comes to dramatic representations of women at law. Yet both the sense of anagnoristic mystery and of tricks and ploys point to legal realities behind the discomfort with female litigants in early modern culture. In fact, the reason why women characters are the commonest repository of the fictive in dramatic trials is specifically connected with their actual legal status and roles. What, then, were these roles?

Bertram's holding out against that only validating criterion left him to resist, in an otherwise formalised and enforced marriage – as if by refusing to sleep with Helena, he can still somehow prevent his marriage from materialising. Helena, by abiding by his conditions, tacitly accepts that logic but uses hard-headed law to beat it, and fairy-tale ambience to present it. On the relation between pure fiction and legal thinking in Bertram's conditions and Helena's meeting of them, see Mukherji, 'Lawfull deede'.

5   On the provenance of the bed-trick in literature and in myth, see Doniger, *Bedtrick*. See also Desens, *Bed-Trick*.

WOMEN AND LAW IN EARLY MODERN ENGLAND

Common law allowed women very limited legal capacities. They suffered from their differential treatment by the law of inheritance, since primogeniture ensured male children's primacy. Above all, married women had no independent legal entity. They were *femmes covert* – covered, that is, by their husbands, unable to contract, sue or be sued in their own person. Criminal law was partial too: husband-murder was petty treason, but wife-murder was felony; adulterous wives lost their dower rights, guilty husbands were protected. However, certain jurisdictions, notably canon law and equity, were much more favourable to women. Married women were granted *femme sole* rights here, as in manorial courts and borough custom. But across several jurisdictions, more and more women took part in litigation directly or indirectly: their increasing legal visibility was not limited to their role as plaintiffs but also their frequent appearance as witnesses. There is controversy about women's permissibility in this capacity too. But as Swinburne writes in *Testaments*, though

divers do write, that a woman is not without all exception, because of the inconstancy and frailty of the feminine Sex, whereby they may the sooner be corrupted; yet I take it that their Testimony is so good, that a testament may be proved by two women alone.[6]

Archival evidence corroborates the impression that when women appeared alongside their husbands, in spite of little institutional right, in reality they often played a considerable role. They could not make their own wills, but often executed their husbands' wills. Unmarried women could also act as administratrices or executrices of their parents' estates.[7] However, unusual as it is, Elizabeth Buller, 'spinster', sues Thomas Clarke for debt in 1622 in her own person, through an attorney she employs to act on her behalf in the Chancellor's Court in Oxford.[8] Mary Astell suing

---

[6] *Testaments*, 187v–188. On debates over exceptions to witnesses, and how women were affected by status rule, see Macnair, *Law of Proof*, 185–230, esp. 201–2.

[7] On women's position in common law, see Erickson, *Women and Property*. Tim Stretton's *Women Waging Law* is invaluable, and has led me to several of the Requests case documents I study, though it deals specifically with that court. But see the subsection on 'Satire and Drama' in Ch. 2 where Stretton touches on Leonora in Webster's *DLC* as an importunate female litigant; however, he is interested in how drama reflects legal realities rather than drama's fictions and their relation to those of law. See also Kermode and Walker (eds.), *Women, Crime and the Courts*. I am much indebted to the directions suggested by these scholars.

[8] Bodleian, OUA, Chancellor's Court Papers, 1623/32:1, Hyp/A/34 (1623), 10v, 30r. I am grateful to Simon Bailey – Archivist, Oxford Chancellor's Court archives – for his help with these documents.

Henry Thornton in the same court in 1632 is another possible example, but not enough survives from this case for absolutely certain inference. What evidence exists does, however, suggest that she too was a single woman and not a widow, and suing *in propria persona*.[9] Though these are the only cases I have come across that involve an unmarried woman suing in her own right, this may be suggestive of a trend, and of grey areas in the less rigorously defined jurisdictions. It is striking at any rate, given that the historical orthodoxy has ruled out any such possibility outside of canon law.

General patriarchal ideology provided support to conservative legislation and legal opinion. Women were debarred from official business 'as those whom nature hath made to keep home and to nourish their family and children, and not to meddle with matters abroad, nor to beare office in a cittie or Common-wealth, no more than children or infants'.[10] Lord Keeper Egerton's order of 1595 called for keeping the court from being infested with 'base fellowes and women or other suitors, as it hath been'.[11] Chancery counsel Anthony Benn advised that women should be 'shutt out of all courts for their witt is so lyttell and theyr will so great'.[12] But on the other hand, there were measures being developed at law to help women circumvent their legal disadvantages, as, notably, in the Court of Requests. 'T. E.'s *Lawes Resolutions of Women's Rights* (published in 1632, but written at the end of the sixteenth century) – the first legal handbook for women - also indicates a need for a women's guide to maximising the available legal provisions, and getting round obstructive ones.[13] An interesting result of the coexistence of these two approaches is that the law itself created models of an acceptable kind of female participation. Women ought to be given protection by the law, many opined – implying that they should play supplicant, not combative, roles.[14] They would be treated sympathetically if they were plaintiffs, both technically and in spirit. An exhibit in a 1597 case, the Earl of Huntingdon's letter to the Masters of Requests, shrewdly distinguishes between 'the clamorous complaints and suite of . . . Watterson's wiefe' and 'the poore wyddowes [the plaintiff's] cause'.[15] The tenor of the objection to women litigants,

---

[9] Ibid., Hyp/A/34 (1623), 6–14.
[10] Smith, *Common-Wealth*, 28.
[11] Hawarde, *Reportes*, 39.
[12] BRO, L28/46, 51–v. Also cited in Prest, 'Law and Women's Rights', 187.
[13] On the purpose and possible readership of this treatise, see Prest, 'Law and Women's Rights'.
[14] See Stretton, *Women Waging Law*, 54, for a related argument about 'a right and a wrong way to go to law' specifically in relation to Requests.
[15] PRO, Court of Requests (hereafter, 'Req'), 2/157/478 (Watterson v. Byrkbeck).

more often than not, focused on their unacceptable insolence and clamorousness. Lord Keeper Egerton exploded one day in court in 1563, at an 'impudent woman' speaking out of her turn, insisting that 'no woman should be a suitor in any Court in her own person'.[16] Dame Eleonora Howche [?], widow, is said to have 'obstinatelie disobeyed as well a certen decree and order by her highnes said counsaill made'; this was to do with an 'obligacion'; so an order is issued to 'apprehend her person' and bring her to this court (Requests), for 'the said contempt, which seemeth to tend to the euill example of other her Maiesties duetifull and obedient subiectes'.[17] Mary Froome, widow litigant, was condemned to 'remayne prisoned in the Fleete . . . vntil she put in borde to vndergoe the punishment inflicted vpon her' for her 'clamorous sutes and continuall vexacions against William Froome *et al*'.[18] Persistence and clamorousness come up again in Magdalen Holland's 1599 Requests suit for debt; the case was dismissed, and

it [was] further ordered in regarde of the compl*ainan*ts many and ecseeding clamo*urs*, w*i*thout anie iust causes heretofore stirred and pursued, that if she . . . rest not satisfied . . . w*i*thout further trouble or clamo*ur* . . . order shalbe pr*es*entlie taken for such corporall punishment to be furthw*i*th vppon the said compl*ainan*t inflicted as by the statute is in this case provyded.[19]

The suggestion is that of abuse of court and troublemaking. Lady Russell was considered a particular nuisance because she annoyingly persisted with her property suit at the Star Chamber (1606) in defiance of the King himself, and even ignored the court lunch-break, 'vyolently and with great audacitie [beginning] a large discourse . . . for the space of half an howre or more'.[20] A tract on the Court of Chancery notes that

If a widdow for the advancement of her child or kinsman . . . make a Bond or gives goods & after takes a husband whoe knows not of this gift, my Lord will uphold the guift for the consideracions sake being naturall affeccion. But if a widdow doe contract marriage . . . & before consumacion thereof doe secretly . . . make Bonds or deeds of guift to the end to cosen her new husband, this my Lord by no meanes likes.[21]

The marginal note sums up the point of this passage: 'widowes guifts vpon naturall consideracons allowed & for Others disallowed'. This document is, for the most part, a list of precepts about legal procedure

---

[16] Ibid., 161.   [17] PRO, Req 1/18, 900.   [18] Ibid., 1/19, 618–19.
[19] Ibid., 827 (Holland v. Wilford).   [20] Hawarde, *Reportes*, 275.
[21] CUL, Gg.2.31, 471v (874v, original foliation).

in Chancery. In this prescriptive context, the same note-taker comments, earlier, that 'My Lord Keep*er* said that he now regarded yt Cawse where a woman have the *followinge* of it especially if she have a husband' (italics mine).[22] He goes on to add that Egerton (the 'Lord Keeper' in question) 'will in noe waies allow that a woman shalbe exa*mi*ned as a witness ag*ain*st her owne husband'.[23] These precepts recall Juan Luis Vives's advice to widows to find 'feble atturneys, or none at all': 'for naturally we hate them that have gret power and riches, and helpe them that have lytel'.[24] It also reminds one of the famous adultery trial in Webster's *White Devil*, where judge Monticelso's instinctive objection to the defendant Vittoria's court presence is based on her indecorous demeanour: 'She comes not like a widow; she comes armed/With scorn and impudence. Is this a mourning habit?' (III.ii.120–1).

We can now begin to see how the notion of acceptable models of female behaviour at court itself made space for strategy. Nor was this potential ignored. Elizabeth Symonds's bill of complaint in the Star Chamber case of Symonds v. Parry exemplifies the combination of a genuine plea for equity and a strategic epistolary rhetoric foregrounding the humility, poverty and helplessness of the plaintiff, a 'poore' widow.[25] As a natural corollary, women's legal influence was viewed with mistrust, even fear. Tim Stretton discusses various instances of women at the Court of Requests conducting legal affairs with, or through, their sons or husbands, or by delegation, even where they were not named as parties.[26] Similar modes of operating are evident in other courts too, or at any rate the assumption of similar dealings. Widows suddenly come into their own legally after their husbands' deaths, were often perceived as manipulating their new status for double-dealing over debts.[27] Ralph Hutchinson,

---

[22] Ibid., 462 (855).   [23] Ibid., 464v (860).   [24] Vives, *Instruction*, 140r–v.

[25] PRO, STAC 5, S6/36 (Symonds v. Parry). Elizabeth presents herself as a woman humbly pleading redress for her 'utter undoing', but her demands are very specific and informed, and this is a case referred to the Star Chamber after it has been already considered at Requests: 'and forasmuchas yo*ur* poore subiect is a very poore woman and not able to *per*sequte at the comen Lawe for the Recovery of the premysses, may it please yo*ur* Highnes to grant yo*ur* Maiesties wrytte of Sub poena to be directed to the said Henry Parry'.

[26] Stretton, *Women Waging Law*, 101–28, 225. The fact that Requests was an equity court, and made it easier for women and poor people to litigate, no doubt made space especially for exploiting the construct of acceptable female roles. But the implications of such models were by no means confined to that court, as the ensuing discussion will indicate.

[27] Ibid., 115. See also PRO Req 1/18, 144–5: William Ponsonby's plea for the stay of the common law suit of debt against him by Elizabeth Stagge, widow and administrator of Edward Stagge's 'goodes and chattel', and the Court's injunction to that effect; and PRO Req 1/17, 130–1: James Buswell's Bill of Complaint against his recently widowed sister-in-law for inequitable dealing with a debt

President of St John's College, Oxford, is in his death-bed in 1606 when he berates his neighbour Lucy Randall for having borrowed money from him privately, without her husband's knowledge, in an arrangement which led to complications involving a third party called Blake. She assures him she has paid it off in kind by paying off 'Blake'; to this Hutchinson replies, 'it is well, but its nought, its nought when women borrow money in their husbands names and make their states worse than they are'.[28] In a Cambridge case, Agnes Stagge confesses that she made a covenant or gift 'in a covert barne', to which her then husband was 'not privie'; neither did he 'in any wise or in any respecte geve . . . his consent thereunto'. She then hid the document 'in a boxe in her bed by hir & in her hands' at a time when she was 'verye sicke', 'fearing least that her husband w*hich* then was . . . should or would in the tyme of her sayd sicknes, come by the writing or Indenture of lease here mentioned and soe make it awaye'.[29] In another Cambridge case from 1620, Mary Ashbie conducts business behind her husband's back: fearing that her second husband may not give her son from her previous marriage a sum of money left for him by her first husband, 'did privately gather, and paye the sayd xx li. . . . without consent or knowledge of the sayd Richard Ashbie'.[30] There was a distinct discomfort about women's knowledge of their husbands' legal affairs, and the possibility of their using it cannily, either during their husbands' lifetime, or as widows. The way they acquired this knowledge was necessarily unverifiable, usually comprising informal communication within a household.[31] Oddly, their

---

that died with the death of his brother, and the Court's agreement to issue an injunction to the widow. The Chancellor's Court Records in the Oxford University Archives also abound in such cases: e.g. OUA, CC Papers, Bodleian, Hyp/A/29 (1605), 48v; Hyp/A/29 (1606), 4r; Hyp/A/34 (1623), 6; Hyp/A/34 (1623), 15–48.

[28] OUA, Chancellor's Court Deposition Book (1606-D), Bodleian, Hyp/B/4, 43–51 (50v). For a historical study of women as economic agents sometimes conducting legally significant business indirectly, see Shepard, 'Meanings of Manhood', Ch. 3, esp. 107–11.

[29] CUL, Comm. Ct., II.3, 91. Alex Shepard directed me to this document in private correspondence.

[30] CUL, V. C. Ct., II.22, 32v–36 (33).

[31] See Stretton, *Women Waging Law*, 114–17. For instances of husbands concealing bills and legal dealings from their wives, to pre-empt precisely this kind of female intervention, see CUL, Comm. Ct. II.4, 235 where Stephen Smith is reported to have wanted to see his debt to Peter Atkinson 'all paid for I have geven my word to Peter' but that he 'would not that [his] wyef should know of yt'. CUL, V. C. Ct. II.30 provides an example of the background – but significant and complicating – role of women in a household: Thomas Woods says he was prevailed upon to write a bill 'by the flattery and persuasion of . . . Edward Overton who '*pro*mised not to take advantage of the sayd bill but only to show his wife & give her satisfaction'; whether or not Overton was telling the truth, the case is suggestive of the possibility of manipulation by women as well as the potential for men to use such perceptions to their own ends. For an excellent general study of later patterns of female litigation on finance and debts, see Muldrew, 'Women, Debt Litigation'.

opponents also accused them of inadequate knowledge of the family's legal and financial business, a disqualifying factor in claiming the right to litigation.

Overall, then, the law had to accommodate women, but still did so from within a patriarchal position severely limiting their legal agency. Conservative resistance and an emergent social and legal recognition of the need for equitable provisions for women came to coexist in the late Elizabethan period. This created a paradox within women's legal position. Excluded from the centre of legal authority, yet subject to law, women managed to circumvent their disadvantages; they used influence and dealt indirectly, or quasi-legally. This earned them the reputation of manipulators and undercover dealers. Evidence about their own activities often eluded the law's categorical procedures, in direct proportion to the degree of their official legal marginalisation.

A larger unease with women's intervention in public matters found a focus in this perception of manoeuvre in law where women's participation gave rise to a cluster of associations. Women were associated with 'bad suits' (*DLC*, IV.i.67) – widows pleading for redress or abusing wills, scolding cases, sexual disputes, cunning indirection. The most female-frequented courts of all were ecclesiastical ('bawdy') courts, so called because of their prerogative on sexual litigation, often involving defamation. Their business included suits of divorce from bed and board, usually involving alleged adultery or cruelty or impotence, and annulment cases.[32] Other cases conspicuously involving women were witchcraft and infanticide trials, where their roles straddled the whole possible range – witnesses, neighbours and the accused.[33] A more specialised role was that of physical examiners, identifying witches by spotting a teat-like protrusion somewhere on their bodies, usually their 'secrets', and determining whether these were marks of childbearing or something less natural. Juries of matrons were also used in cases of disputed pregnancy, in connection with marital or paternity suits, and infanticide, and sometimes to determine accusations of impotence or claims of virginity in annulment cases. This latter was in fact the oldest form of examination by matrons. Here the plea or the allegation of impotence was tested by putting the man in a room with a group of women who would expose their breasts, touch him,

---

[32] Helmholz, *Marriage Litigation*, 89; Pederson, 'Marriage Litigation'.
[33] See PRO, ASSI 45/3/29 where the three key witnesses are female neighbours who saw a male child lying dead in an outhouse near the accused Alice Lewis's home. Compare ASSI 35/39/7, membranes (hereafter, 'm' and 'mm') 14, 79.

and try variously to arouse him.[34] A well-known comic allusion to such tests occurs in Jonson's *Epicœne*. When Morose declares he is 'no man', 'un-abled in nature, by reason of frigidity, to performe the duties . . . of a husband', and a search by physicians is called for, Mistress Otter exclaims, 'No let women search him, madame: we can do it our selves' (V.iv.41–56). Despite the paucity of references to the social practice in the seventeenth century, it had not died out entirely by this period. A celebrated example is the divorce trial between Frances Howard and Robert Earl of Essex who were inspected by a jury of matrons 'to see whether she was a virgin, & whether he was incapable of performing the Duties of the Marriage-Bed'.[35] *To such intimate knowledge men had little access.* Special skills were welcomed: since much hung upon the exact shape of female genitals, midwives were sought out as especially competent. Infanticide actions, even more than witchcraft, and, occasionally, rape cases, involved women above all, and were also notoriously difficult to ascertain.[36] Women could camouflage or invent the fact if need be: testimonies were usually from female neighbours. Infanticide united the threat of peculiarly female unruliness with that of women's expertise, merging associations of women *presented* at law courts and those *employed* by law for their services and skills.[37] Joan Brooker, spinster, wrapped her newborn baby in an apron and suffocated it to death. The jury found her guilty of infanticide, in an inquisition held in Bletchingley in 1580, but she pleaded her belly to escape hanging. A jury of twelve matrons legally appointed to examine her said that the pregnancy was a mere ploy to trick the law.[38] In a 1592 case, Agnes Geary, 'of Gaddesten, spinster', charged with having kicked her child to death, pleaded her belly; the jury of matrons declared, similarly, that this was just a ruse.[39] This continued to be a common occurrence through the first two decades of the seventeenth century. The same trick is known to have been regularly used by female convicts in petty larceny and murder cases.[40] In a 1585 case, five women were examined by a jury of

[34] See Sharpe, 'Women, Witchcraft'.

[35] Salmon, ed., *New Abridgement*, 60. See also the masterful study of the case and the evolving myths in Lindley, *Trials*. As this has been amply researched, I do not address it fully here, as with the Castlehaven trial, in Herrup, *A House in Gross Disorder*.

[36] On midwives' expertise in rape cases, see Shapiro, *Culture of Fact*, 17 and n. 48.

[37] See PRO, ASSI 45/3/29, 133 for a specific account of how the female searchers in this infanticide case were appointed by a warrant from the local Justice of the Peace.

[38] PRO, ASSI 35/23/9, mm. 39 & 62.

[39] Cf. PRO, 30/26/104, m. 24; see also PRO, ASSI 35/1/5, items 17 and 18; ASSI 35/1/5, m. 26; 35/31/7, mm. 9 & 25v; ASSI 35/1/5, m. 26; ASSI 35/32/4, m. 40; ASSI 35/32/4, mm. 8, 39v.

[40] E.g., PRO, ASSI 35/39/7, mm. 34, 21, 82, 41; ASSI 35/18/2, m. 30; ASSI 35/11/1, m. 10; ASSI 35/32/4, m. 17; ASSI 35/32/4, m. 7; ASSI 35/32/4, m. 17; ASSI 35/67/6, m. 140. Bridget Smyth of Southwark,

twelve matrons who proclaimed that all five were pregnant![41] The scenario of seventeen women huddling into an examination room while a largely male judiciary awaited verdict from behind the screen is suggestive.

Thus, the female prerogative embraced not only access to certain legally significant yet 'secret' knowledges, but also the manipulative potential of these knowledges. This necessarily threatened a fundamentally male judiciary, precisely because of its dependence on such skills. It is this sense of women's participation, peripheral yet inaccessible and uncontrollable, that translates itself into fictionalised forms in the drama. Its theatrical expressions can be as symbolic as darkness, masks and bed-tricks, or as direct as deceit and fabrication of evidence.

Finally, being a minority among litigants, women were easily categorised by the overall criterion of femaleness rather than by individual jurisdictions. They had to negotiate a set of recognisable difficulties in handling the law, and were looked upon, or addressed, generically when they took legal initiative, irrespective of their specific suits. Were there common methods by which the legal system dealt with women's legal needs, or by which women across a whole range of classes and jurisdictions used the system's provisions? These questions are more likely to be answered by the historically produced compound of dramatic representations than by the accidentally preserved products of legal documentation. Historical writings on women's place in law are necessarily fragmented and specific. Thus, Laura Gowing makes her inferences from slander litigation in church courts, Tim Stretton from equity suits at Requests, Jim Sharpe from witchcraft trials and assizes, and so on.[42] But drama offers a cumulative and composite notion of women's legal pursuits, accommodating the multiple specificities of individual experience and jurisdictional procedures; an extra-legal vision of what arose nevertheless from their specifically perceived legal or quasi-legal roles.

'spinster', is indicted for grand larceny but remanded without sentence on plea of pregnancy – ASSI 35/66/9, m. 37. It is interesting that marital status is no deterrent in the face of legal process and possible threat of execution: women do not hesitate to resort to feminine means available to them, such as claim of true, or even false, pregnancy. For discussions, see Oldham, 'On Pleading the Belly'; Cockburn, ed., *Calendar*, 121–3. See also Sharpe, *Judicial Punishment*, 41–2; 'Women, Witchcraft', 112.

[41] ASSI 35/28/5, m. 41. The informal practice of using matrons to determine pregnancy continued as late as the late 1630s: see Capp, 'Life, Love and Litigation', esp. 69, on how a maidservant who denied allegations of incontinence and pregnancy, was physically examined by a group of honest women from the neighbourhood assembled by her mistress, and found to be pregnant.

[42] Gowing, *Domestic Dangers*; Stretton, *Women Waging Law*; Sharpe, *Instruments of Darkness* and 'Women, Witchcraft'.

'VILD SUITS' AND 'MAD TRICKS': 'THE DEVIL'S LAW CASE'

In the courtroom scene prefacing the central trial of *Devil's Law Case*, initiated by Leonora, Judge Ariosto exclaims in exasperation to his clerk,

> Are there not whores enough for presentations,
> Overseers, wrong the will o' th' dead,
> Oppression of widows, or young orphans,
> Wicked divorces, or your vicious cause
> Of *plus quam satis*, to content a woman,
> But must you find new stratagems, new pursenets?
> Oh women, as the ballad lives to tell you,
> What will you shortly come to?   (IV.i.23–30)

Later, he denounces Leonora: 'such vild suits/Disgrace our courts' (59–60). Leonora is the title's 'devil', in her unnatural and deceitful legal dealings – 'a cause so odious' (IV.i.21). It is her jealousy that is said to have 'raised the devil up/In the form of a law-case!' (III.iii.190–1). But other women also become involved. Raising issues of marriage law, Act I focuses on Jolenta's pre-contract with Contarino and her later, enforced handfast with Ercole. Women's inherent sexual instinct becomes inseparable from their legal instinct, as her maid Winifred suggests a remedy – she urges Jolenta to sleep with Contarino quickly to render their pre-contract inviolable. This is posited as a legally sounder alternative to the young lovers' '[nobler] wishes' (264) to 'marry' to avoid Ercole's early return:

> To avoid which, get you instantly to bed together;
> Do, and I think no civil lawyer for his fee
> Can give you better counsel.   (250–2)

Winifred is shrewdly aware of the link between law and sex in matters of marriage. Leonora betrays, early on, a certain expediency and irreverence to law (II.iii.158–9) which later manifests itself in an active abuse of it. Meanwhile, we are prepared for witnessing women's legal dealings, directly or indirectly, by Ariosto and Crispiano's dialogue about the 'mad tricks played of late by ladies' (III.i.9):

> Why, they use their lords as if they were their wards;
> . . .
> So silly all their lives of their own estates,
> That when they are sick, and come to make their will,
> They know not precisely what to give away
> From their wives . . .

> . . .
> As you must conceive their game is all i'th' night –
> . . .
> Withal what sway they bear i'th' viceroy's court . . .
>
> (11–22)

Crispiano, in response, vows

> That I will never sit upon the bench more,
> Unless it be to curb the insolencies
> Of these women.   (26–8)

The familiar associations are of concealment, underhand meddling, a power over husbands, impudence and tricks – all threats to domestic hierarchy and the legal system. Also implicit is the connection between specifically legal discomforts with female agency, and the larger context of patriarchal ideas which find a distinctive focus in law.[43]

But Romelio has his own plans, which include passing off his expected child by the young nun Angiolella as Jolenta's by the supposedly dead Ercole, to secure Ercole's inheritance. 'Excellent work/Made for a dumb midwife!' Jolenta replies, touching on the precise awareness enabling her to hatch her quasi-legal counter-plot, to confound Romelio (III.iii.41–2). She now declares that unfortunately for Romelio, she is genuinely pregnant, by her original fiancé, Contarino. Romelio recovers quickly:

> Oh misfortune!
> Your child must then be reputed Ercole's.
>
> (63–4)

Jolenta observes that that would not serve *his* purpose: 'your votary's issue/Must not inherit the land' (64–5). Romelio is 'strangely puzzled' but then speculates:

> Why, suppose that she be brought abed before you,
> And we conceal her issue till the time
> Of your delivery, and then give out
> That you had two at a birth; ha, were't not excellent?
>
> (68–71)

But this approaches female, even midwife, territory. As Jolenta is quick to point out, the lack of resemblance would give a lie to the claim that the babies are twins. Paternity was notoriously a domain where women knew

---

[43] For a complementary reading of 'femininity as challenge' to law in Webster, see Haberman, 'She has that in her belly'. The crucial differences between our positions have been indicated in Ch. 4.

better than men, who could not even access that knowledge, let alone possess it. So Jolenta declares that she had feigned the pregnancy after all (80). For all his dubious attempts at manipulating his sister's sexual life, Romelio cannot ascertain whether she is pregnant, and by whom. He remains powerless to 'open' his 'sister's [case]' – incompetent to look into either her legal 'cause' or her sexual secrets.[44] When she does eventually agree to mother Romelio's child for him, neither Romelio nor we know whether she means it. Implicit in her acquiescence is a power to deceive that is beyond the eye of law or indeed of brothers and others:

> *JOLENTA*: Must I dissemble honesty? You have divers
> Counterfeit honesty . . .
> . . . I must now practise
> The art of a great-bellied woman, and go feign
> Their qualms and swoundings.   (166–70)

Both Leonora and Jolenta have their own plots to outwit Romelio at law. Ercole, too, is kept in ignorance, believing Jolenta's pregnancy to be true, and nobly resolving to accept her as 'Contarino's widow, bequeathed to [him]' (317–18). Women's law-tricks are explicitly associated with plot-making: Leonora's is the master-plot – 'such a plot/As never mother dreamt of', 'my unimitable plot' (349–54, 390). Both senses about women's suits, unnaturalness and uncontrollability, are suggested by the law-clerk Sanitonella's remarks concerning depositions in the pre-trial scene: 'She has that in her belly,/Will dry up your ink' (IV.i.1–2) – suggesting at once a link between women's legal strategies and their sexual knowledge, and how this combination could frustrate the formal sentence and literate procedures of a male court.[45] It is worth recalling the comic treatment of this association in *Epicœne* where the Collegiate ladies are repositories of female knowledge about abortion and contraception. 'And have you those excellent receipts, madam, to keep yourselves from bearing

---

[44] Cf. Ariosto's sexually loaded joke: 'Thus would they jest were they fee'd to open/Their sisters' cases' (IV.ii.221–2). 'Cause' and 'case' were interchangeable words in the legal context, and the sexual pun on a woman's 'case' was equally current – witness Mistress Quickly, whose 'exion is ent'red and [her] case so openly known to the world', in Shakespeare's *2 Henry IV*, II.i.30–1. Compare lawyer Throat's invitation to Francis to 'open [her] case' in *RA*, II.iv.834. On the frequent connection between legal case and female 'case', turning on the misogynistic link between open mouth and open vagina, see Parker, *Literary Fat Ladies*, 106–7.

[45] The specific allusion is to the provision for pleading the belly, or deferring a death sentence until after birth 'lest the issue in her belly should suffer death for the fault of its mother' (King's Bench entry by Robert Maycote, Henrician clerk of the papers of the Court, as quoted by Baker, *Oxford History*, 551–2). This privilege of pregnancy was available to female convicts instead of benefit of clergy which was only open to men. Eventually, the execution was often suspended indefinitely.

children?' Morose asks Haughty. She replies, 'How should we maintain our youth and beauty else? Many births of a woman make her old, as many crops make the earth barren' (IV.iii.51–6).[46]

The trial scene in *Devil's Law Case* (IV.i), set in a mixed jurisdictional space, rapidly resembles a bawdy court as issues of paternity and pregnancy become central, with women entirely taking over the legal event. Leonora is eventually joined by Jolenta and the young nun Angiolella in court. Like Leonora's charge of bastardy against her son Romelio, the other women's claims also hinge on such details as the time-scheme of pregnancy, midwives' complicity, and the possibility of women manipulating physical signs of pregnancy. This latter is precisely what the artfully swollen Jolenta and the genuinely 'great-bellied' Angiolella sit and laugh about as they ponder their womanly misfortunes and remedies. 'Ha, ha, ha! So it's given out', says Jolenta, 'but Ercole's coming to life again has shrunk/And made invisible my great belly' (V.i.14–16). The impressionism of Monticelso's comment on the 'scandal' of female business in court now becomes comprehensible in more concrete detail – various and inter-jurisdictional as these details are.

'SHADOWED IN A VEIL OF STATE': DARKNESS, RIDDLES AND RITUAL

The manipulation of appearances, however, extends beyond the specifically physical or legal into ritualistic self-presentation. Leonora's initial disruption of legal formalities with law-tricks gives over, later, to a mode of performance and anagnoristic mystery uncontainable within the proceedings of the law court. Her entry 'with a black veil over her' provokes the lawyer's instinctive order: 'take off her veil: it seems she is ashamed to look her cause i'th' face' (46–7), thus marking the black mask out to be symbolic. Ariosto says that she *would* be 'kept more dark' (48). Like Paulina in Shakespeare's *The Winter's Tale*, Leonora knows the power of public ritual, re-entering, at the end, 'with two coffins . . . two winding-sheets stuck with flowers', and singing a dirge (s.d., 109). Penitence as a legal trick transmutes to spectacular self-fashioning – the logical obverse of the fact that women at court were repeatedly looked upon, and written about, as spectacles.

Thomas Wright's *Passions of the Mind* claims that 'wise men often, thorow the windowes of the face, behold the secrets of the heart . . . so the

---

[46] *Epicœne* is an obviously relevant play, but I do not consider it in detail as Maus examines the virginity test and its implications in *Inwardness and the Theater*.

hearts of men are manifest vnto the wise' (27). Interestingly enough, Wright emphasises that the 'silent speech pronounced in . . . [the] countenance'

> especially may be obserued in women, whose passions may be easily discouered; for as harlots by the light and wanton motions of their eyes and gestures . . . so honest matrons, by their graue and chast lookes, may soone be discerned . . . The fornication of a woman shall be known by the lifting vp of her eyes . . . (29)

Heywood, in his *Curtaine Lecture*, likewise asks virgins to be 'carefull and cautelous in all their deportments' in similar terms, though in a less technical and more allusive context: 'to be wary in their words, and weighty in their writings, that their countenances bewray no lightnesse, their eyes no loosenesse . . . that their gestures [be] not gross but gracious'.[47] No wonder then that Anne Frankford, the adulterous wife in Heywood's *Woman Killed* is so tormented by the fear that her 'fault' will 'in [her] brow be writ' (vi, 154). No wonder, either, that women in court in the drama of the period seem to be looked upon as a spectacle, their appearance being a sign to read and interpret. In *Arden of Faversham*, a woman's trial for adultery, attended by Franklin, becomes a 'pretty tale to beguile the . . . way' as two men travel together. The play itself is about a contemporary case involving adultery and murder. Arden interjects Franklin's report at the point where he (Franklin) talks of the woman accused of adultery being interrogated by her husband: 'Her answer then? I wonder how she looked . . . ' Franklin's reply is a detailed and carefully observed picture of her gestures and looks at this point in the proceedings:

> First she did cast her eyes down to the earth,
> Watching the drops that fell amain from thence;
> Then softly draws she forth her handkercher,
> And modestly she wipes her tear-stained face;
> Then hemmed she out, to clear her voice should seem,
> And with a majesty addressed herself
> To encounter all their accusations.-[48]

Even this sympathetic portrayal, presumably of a woman perceived as being repentant, is premised on an assumption that women are expressive beings who can be deciphered by discerning eyes – Wright's 'wise men'. In a villainous mode, Iago, that consummate user of scraps of discourses, exploits the established language of female physiognomy in accusing

---

[47] Heywood, *Curtaine Lecture*, 46–7.   [48] *Arden*, ix, 92, 79, 81–7.

Bianca, addressing fellow 'gentlemen' and turning Bianca into a spectacle to be read:

> Behold her well; I pray you, look upon her.
> Do you see, gentlemen? Nay, guiltiness
> Will speak, though tongues were out of use.
> (*Othello*, V.i.108–10)

In this almost post-sceptical play, where scepticism is not so much a philosophy but a construction used by Iago to establish that insides and outsides do not correspond, Iago's main drive has been to persuade the over-integrated Othello that one *cannot* read the mind's construction in the face. The construction of the hidden and the unseeable is not only designed to make Iago himself the very embodiment of opacity, but women too are made the specific focus of hermeneutic frustration. In a casual moment, the women of Venice are said to 'let God see the pranks/ They dare not show their husbands' (III.iii.203–4). That the gods can look into hearts otherwise unreflected in faces is also, of course, a common-place of much Renaissance drama, both the providentialist kind where evidence is a spectacle witnessed as well as organised by God, and plays of intrigue and concealed passions such as Ford's *Broken Heart*, where characters are constantly anxious about being read by the gods even when they escape judgement by men who cannot look into their motives. That Iago should so effortlessly turn the whole thrust of his argument round to suit the need of the moment – the need to prove Bianca whore – is itself suggestive of the susceptibility of physiognomic discourse to Machiavellian manipulation.

As in Anne Sanders's self-presentation as a spectacle in the trial scene of *Warning*, or in Vittoria's flamboyant performance in court in *White Devil*, the women in *Devil's Law Case* pit their own rhetoric against that of legal signs, and against their inevitable legal status as objects of mistrust. Ercole's comments on their 'indirect/Proceedings, shadowed in a veil of state' conflates metaphor with actuality in a play where the women initiating the legal complications work through such devices as veils and material obfuscations (IV.ii.601–2). This tendency reaches its climax in the final scene, where Angiolella and Jolenta enter like a tableau, 'Angiolella veiled, and Jolenta, her face coloured like a Moor' (s.d., V.vi.28). The masque-like entry of the two women needs explication as though it is an emblem. As in the disclosure scene of Shakespeare's *All's Well* (V.iii), the legalistic language here changes into a weird riddle inviting judgement, with a strange verse address from Jolenta:

Like or dislike me, choose you whether:
The down upon the raven's feather,
Is as gentle and as sleek,
As the mole on Venus' cheek.

. . .

Which of us now judge you whiter:
Her whose credit proves the lighter,
Or this black and ebon hue
That, unstained, keeps fresh and true?
For I proclaim't without control,
There's no true beauty, but i'th'soul.

(V.vi.34–49)

This gives moral opposites a visual form, embodying at once the inward and the impossibility of making the inward visible through legal procedure – in effect, flinging a hermeneutic challenge to the assembled court. The opposition between male legal procedures and these ritualistic interjections is ultimately subsumed into what must be identified as the distinct universe of tragicomedy where the judge can only resolve the case by harmonising 'the sentence of the court' with 'these so comical events' (58–62). The legal and symbolic power of women who step into the public sphere, visually compelling and sinister, transcends the pettiness of lawyers and the women's own law-tricks. And opacity and paradox must be accommodated within the stability of legal-speak and material proof, before aesthetic judgement can be concluded. Ritualism itself, meanwhile, emerges as more than the drama's way of translating 'female' legal realities: it is an active response to existent social perceptions, which finds a more formalised vehicle in drama, just as paradox emerges as a literary device which represents rather than merely fictionalises actual paradoxes in legal theory and practice, and in women's relation to these.

'CONTRARIETIES': OF PARADOX, POWER AND POWERLESSNESS

It is time to revisit the final scene of *All's Well*. Structured like a trial, this scene is smugly legalistic until Diana befuddles the assembly with her doublespeak. Significantly, the turning-point, where a potential reunion becomes both a trial and an unexpected recognition, is provided by Diana's plea. This is uttered in the formulaic language of a poor female plaintiff, begging 'for justice', or 'a poor maid is undone' (V.iii.143–4) – a familiar enough strategy in church- or equity courts,[49] *exploiting* available

---

[49] On pleading strategies in the Court of Requests, and women's adoption and refinement of these strategies, see Stretton, *Women Waging Law*, 178–215. On women's strategic use of legal stereotypes

models of poverty or supplication – so 'that man [can] be at woman's command, and yet no hurt done!' (I.iii.92–3). Unable to participate in law-making, women's legal role was solely as subjects; but their active manipulation of their subjecthood makes their position a curious amalgam of exclusion and empowerment. They also become conducive fictional tools for questioning the inconsistencies within law, with its ostensible discourse of positivism and clarity, as well as its aimed and achieved knowledge. Women characters at law come across as the unresolved contradictions, the unstated addendum of law; the frayed margins that cannot be accommodated without stretching the centre's ostensible premises. In a system where the majority of women were *femmes covert*, it is fitting that covertness should characterise their dealings in law. Henry Swinburne, in *Matrimony*, comments suggestively on the semantic link of the word 'nuptiae' with 'nubo', and for its association with covering and making obscure on the one hand, and with the wife's veil on the other:

The woord Nuptiae is deryved of the verbe Nubo which we comonly translate To Marry thoughe properlie and originally yt doe signifie To hyde or couer Like as Nubilo [doth signifie] to obscure or make dark whence also comith Nubes a Clowde and Nubilosus clowdye. How that the verb Nubo which originally signifieth hyde or cover should also signifie to marry is vpon this occasion. In auncient tyme New marryed virgins were accustomed to weare a Vale wherewith they couered theyr heads and shadowed theyr Countenances . . . partly in signe of shamefastnes in asmuche as they had now vundertaken the performance of many secret actions which cannot abyde the lyght but especially in signe of subiection and obedyence . . . {because her Husband is her only head . . . testifyed by ye veil & covering of her head, implied in this word Nuptiae . . .[50]

But the passage also suggests the idea of obscurity that we have seen women being associated with, both as subjects and as manipulators.

The strange combination of vulnerability and privilege is perfectly captured in Helena's position. Having engineered the bed-trick to meet Bertram's condition, Helena claims her rights, proofs in hand: 'This is done./Will you be mine, now you are doubly won?' (V.iii.303–4). Bertram's response suggests bewildered helplessness: 'If she, my liege, can make me know this clearly,/I'll love her dearly, ever, ever dearly'

---

in defamation suits and pension cases respectively, see Gowing, 'Language, Power', and Hudson, 'Negotiating for Blood-money'.

[50] *Matrimony*, 116. Compare Heywood, *Curtaine Lecture*, 103: 'the word nuptiæ is derived from *nubo*, which signifieth to cover'.

(305–6). All the uncertainty surrounding claims of paternity and marriage by visibly pregnant women in church courts weighs on that 'If' – Bertram's last words in this comedy of reunion. Helena's last words, in reply, are equally legalistic: 'If it appear not plain and prove untrue,/ Deadly divorce step between me and you!' (307–8). Bertram is won through duplicity and repossessed through the obscure conflation of two women in the exercise of marriage law. Helena manages to manipulate this double-winning without revealing her role. When she does appear, big with child, her pregnancy, betokening the triumph of her initiative, also evokes associations of the obedient wife whose pleasure lies in being acted upon by her husband. But this is no mere camouflaging of her agency, but indicates her real vulnerability and, oddly, passivity, in the emotional transaction contained in the quasi-legal one. Her utterance, 'Oh my good lord, when I was like this maid,/I found you wondrous kind' (V.iii.309–10), gently reminds us that her active plotting was harnessed to a virtual loss of identity in the sexual act, a self-effacement in the most intimate sphere. Strategy and earnestness, power and powerlessness are inextricably compounded in the bed-trick, as in legal and semi-legal manoeuvres by women who tried to make the best of what was legally available, with the help of whatever means their gender provided. The bed-trick in drama, typically, is premised on darkness and obfuscation; as the Duke in *Measure* says when he instructs Isabella how to engineer the trick: 'the time should have all shadow and silence in it' (III.i.232);[51] Beatrice-Joanna in Middleton and Rowley's *Changeling* 'charg'd [her maid] weep out her request to [Alsemero]/That she might come obscurely to [his] bosom' (IV.ii.120–1) – in reality substituting the maid Diaphanta for herself on the bridal bed so that he does not realise she is no virgin.

Interestingly, even such a patently fictional device as the bed-trick was not unheard of in reality, though its immediate use was not always to turn a *de futuro* contract into matrimony. Apparently, the Earl of Oxford, in 1574, slept with his wife in the belief that she was his mistress, and this by what Francis Osborne calls a '*virtuous deceit*' by his Lady, leading to the

---

[51] Significantly, Heywood concludes his section on the bed-trick in *Curtaine Lecture* with the comment that 'nuptiall faith is seldom violated without revenge' (261). There is a sense in which the bed-tricks in both *AW* and *MfM* are acts of revenge. But Helena is also, as Harriett Walter puts it, 'desperately tentative' – her final 'if' contains both a desperate provisionality and a legalistic fulfilment of necessary conditions which smacks of the exact justice associated with revenge: see Rutter, *Clamorous Voices*, 73–89 (74). But in *MfM*, it becomes even more dubious as the desperation and the avenging justice get split and placed in Mariana and the Duke (and perhaps, to an extent, Isabella) respectively.

birth of a daughter in 1575.[52] Perhaps this was the incident Heywood refers to when he adds a postscript to the story of the 'stratagem' of the bed-trick engineered by a virtuous queen of legend to get children out of her dissolute and neglectful husband:

I need not have travelled so far for an history to the purpose, when our owne kingdome hath afforded the like, betwixt persons of the greatest quality, who by the like sleight practised by the forsaken Ladies, have not been onely a meanes of reconciliation, but of happy propagation and issue.[53]

The best-known alleged use of the ploy, however, was by Frances Howard. During the proceedings for the annulment of her marriage with the Earl of Essex, Frances was physically examined by matrons and midwives to ascertain whether she was a virgin, in a less than logical attempt to establish her husband's impotence.[54] Frances pleaded modesty and asked to be examined veiled. This gesture itself suggests the dialogic relation between fact and fiction, but moreover, generated various reports that Frances had substituted a young girl, 'one Mistris *Fines . . .* at that time too young to be other then *virgo intacta*', as Anthony Weldon writes,[55] and achieving the verdict of virginity through a bed-trick.[56] Whether this report was true is less important here than its underlying assumptions. Frances's veiled entry, whether it was her self-fashioned semiotic, a tool of deceit, or adversaries' anxious fabrication, embodies the conjunction of women's vulnerability before a male judiciary, and the uncontrollable threat they represented when they took up legal procedures. It also recalls the obscuring function of women's presence, somehow disrupting the straight lines of legal method. As Beatrice-Joanna in *The Changeling* keeps Diaphanta waiting for 'an easy trial' of her 'honesty' before letting her take her own place in Alsemero's bed (IV.ii.99–100), the maid wonders nervously, 'She will not search me? Will she?/Like the forewoman of a female jury?' (101–2) – registering at once the currency and associations of the semi-legal procedure of such a search. It is indeed this play that offers the most striking dramatic combination of both bed-trick and virginity test. Female deceit springs from helplessness but takes the form of the inalienability of secret knowledges, giving rise to a general

---

[52] Osborne, *Traditionall Memoryes*, 79 (K8r). There were several alternative versions of this story. For contemporary European examples, see Zacks, *History Laid Bare*, 174–5.

[53] Heywood, *Curtaine Lecture*, 260–1.

[54] See Lindley, *Trials*, 77–122, for a summary of details.

[55] Weldon, *Court and Character*, 80.

[56] Salmon, *New Abridgement*, 60.

distrust of female signs as not only sexual, but often manipulable. Beatrice unlocks her husband's closet to read the book on virginity tests efficiently enough to fake the signs when Alsemero does try her. Is she a victim and a subject, or a cheat and a threat? The bed-trick she resorts to is also an equal and opposite response to the virginity trial set up by her husband pre-emptively, before he has any proof of her deceit. When Burton refers to virginity tests as 'strange absurd trials', he illustrates his point with the story of 'an old bawdy nurse in Aristænetus' who reassured a worried, young non-virgin on the eve of her marriage: 'Fear not, daughter, I'll teach thee a trick to help it.'[57]

It is unsurprising, then, that paradox is something law-givers are deeply uncomfortable with, and women are often shown using, in the drama. From St. German in the sixteenth-century to Geoffrey Gilbert in the eighteenth, legal writers repeatedly specified that inconsistency and contradiction took away a witness's credit in English law.[58] Yet law itself, as we have seen, has made space for these dualities. Drama can address them most freely because of its fictionality, while legal writers rarely can. There are exceptions, of course. Abraham Fraunce, in *Lawier's Logike*, admits that 'contrarieties' are inherent to the human condition, but that law cannot accommodate them: 'opposites are disagreeable arguments . . . So Socrates cannot be father and sonne to the same man: sicke and whole at the same time'.[59] No wonder, then, that when Mariana claims to be neither married, nor a maid, nor a widow, the legal arbiters explode.

The association of women with paradox also works at a specifically linguistic level. Female characters in such plays as *All's Well, Measure* and *Devil's Law Case* adopt an equivocation that challenges the ostensible certitudes of legal discourse. Women were largely excluded from technical legal business as much of this was conducted in Latin, and most was specialised. This reinforced the odd 'subject' position of women, but also empowered literary women characters to speak to the ambivalence of legal signification. Self-division can, of course, be covered by law's own obscurity, also a tool of exclusion. Women thus had only their own distinct brand of darkness to address it with. 'T.E.', whose ostensible

---

[57] Burton, *Anatomy*, III, 284–5. Burton goes on to write that 'some jealous brain was the first founder of them [virginity tests]'. Ambrose Parey's seventeenth-century surgical treatise attests to the general recognition, by that date, that virginity is entirely possible to fake, for women put in 'bladders of fishes, or galles of beasts filled full of blood, and so deceive the ignorant and young lecher, by the fraud and deceit of their evill arts, and in the time of copulation they mixe their sighes with groanes . . . that they may seeme to be virgins': *Works*, Bk 24, 938.
[58] See Shapiro, *Culture of Fact*, 19.   [59] Fraunce, *Lawier's Logike*, 47.

readers are women, writes 'to make this scattered part of Learning, in the great Volumes of the Common-Law-Bookes, and there darkly described, to be . . . more ready, and clearer to the view of the Reader'.[60] Webster's Vittoria defies exactly this exclusivity when she demands to be questioned in English: 'Pray my lord, let him speak his usual tongue./I will make no answer else.' 'Why, you understand Latin', Francisco replies, and she retaliates, 'I do, sir, but amongst this auditory/. . . the half or more/ May be ignorant in't' (*WD*, III.ii.13–17). Her defiance at the same time comments on the obfuscation of legal language – 'I will not have my accusation clouded/In a strange tongue' (18–19). Some audience members might even have recalled the parody of lawyers' language in a play staged only two years before *White Devil* – *Epicœne*, where Otter and Cutbeard, in the guise of canon lawyer and divine, ponderously discuss Morose's legal grounds of divorce till they light on 'manifestam frigidatem'.[61] Such play on audience empathy is more double-edged in *White Devil*. When Vittoria changes her tack to temporarily meet the arbiters on their own terms, she brandishes Latin: '*Casta est quam nemo rogavit*' – chaste is she whom none has solicited (200). Her '[personation]' of masculine virtue is at once a resistance and a subsumption (136). Perhaps it is the curious doubleness about female agency in law that 'T.E.' refers to when he indeterminately remarks on their inventiveness in *Lawes Resolution*:

Women have no voyse in Parliament, they make no lawes, they consent to none, they abrogate none . . . I know no remedy, though some women can shift it well enough. (4)

It is the same sense of strategy again that finds expression in Anthony Benn's distrust of 'the shifts and Importunytes' of the new breed of female litigants whom he sought, like Egerton, to keep out of courts, despite their apparent disadvantage.[62]

Thus, the capacity of female figures to call for a particular methodology has implications for the criteria of historical evidence. This book, on the whole, has argued for salutary caution against an over-generalising model of the drama's critique of law. But there are some spheres of legal experience and corresponding products of the fictional imagination which, in their oblique representation of legality, demand audience in that spirit. Women's presence and role in early modern English law is one such

---

[60] T. E., *Lawes Resolution*, a (Preface).
[61] Jonson, *Epicœne*, V.iii, passim, and 165. *Epicœne* was first performed in 1609 or 1610, and *WD* in 1612.
[62] Quoted in Prest, 'Law and Women's Rights', 182.

domain, acquiring a complex dialectical relation with institutionalised law, and providing a version of the feminised poetic critique that Peter Goodrich identifies in the medieval French troubadour traditions of the courts of love.[63] What Goodrich calls 'the banalisation of the erotic' in critical traditions finds its equivalent in a banalisation of the fictive in historicist reception of plays with exaggeratedly fantastic representations of legal events; significantly, the fictive is usually also implicated in the erotic when it comes to female business. This chapter suggests the reasons why particular 'poetic' modes are chosen to translate legal realities, and what kinds of realities find a conducive expressive medium in such representations, in a culture where courts of love and their alternative framework of judgement were a distant memory, and a largely literary one. It also shows why we, like these challenged but resourceful women litigants, must be prepared 'with windlasses and assays of bias,/By indirections find directions out' (*Hamlet*, II.i.64–5).

It is interesting, too, to reflect on the impact of crafty, prudent, desperate but robust women characters on the drama's treatments of abstract or philosophical notions of legal knowledge or ends. Chapter 1 suggested how self-consciously perfunctory anagnorises help us recognise the precariousness of the knowledge induced by legal signs, when, as in so many of the plays discussed but especially in tragicomedies, trials and recognitions coincide. Legal procedure, after all, has the same structure as anagnoristic plots, proceeding from uncertainty or ignorance to knowledge or disclosure. But the specific 'scandal' surrounding women's use and fashioning of such signs does more than feed into the 'scandal of paralogism'.[64] On the one hand, it highlights the dual nature of legal epistemology itself – like the fictional device of 'recognition', it combines a narratological and human craving for absolute knowledge with a distrust of the cognition offered. Probability itself becomes the twin of 'recognition', mingling gratification with suspicion, belief with resistance. On the other hand, the merely probable is only a step away from the miraculously probable. The real scandal – and the real miracle – is that the sense of possibility in the legal plots twisted by women is based on concrete, ingenious schemes exploiting the nitty-gritty of law and its loopholes. The impostures of sign and identity that the women wield demystify the

---

[63] See Goodrich's inspirationally prejudicial 'Gay Science and the Law'. On the idea of women embodying the passionate, antithetical voice to law in later writing, see Weisberg, *Poethics*, 71; Decicco, *Women and Lawyers*, 31.

[64] Cave, *Recognitions*, 249.

notion of probability, grounding it firmly in the contingent and the practical. Oddly, it is the real emotional imperatives and vulnerabilities driving their enterprise that allow this peculiar combination of contingency and possibility, and make law its agent; indeed they give us that Shakespearean mongrel – the improbable possible – and lend it resilience. In a play like *All's Well* (unlike, say, *Measure*), the critique of the formal satisfactions of law and comedy coexists with an understanding of probability not simply as a failure of certainty but as a necessarily provisional step towards knowledge, and a ground for trust. Amidst the various 'ifs' and 'buts' that haunt the end of this play, we are reminded of the King's tentative acceptance of Helena's improbable promise of medical cure:

> More could I question thee, and more I must,
> Though more to know could not be more to trust:
> From whence thou cam'st, how tended on – but rest
> Unquestioned welcome, and undoubted blessed. (II.i.205–9)

Like a promise, marriage, happy endings to stories, and happiness itself are all, in a sense, absolute and ignorant – like Pascal's wager with God, a leap of faith. Questioning itself has its human limits. Such a perspective is not unrelated to the understanding of probability gradually gaining ground in early modern England, where civil law and legal philosophy were still clinging to an idea of demonstrable certainty, while the common law was moving towards a precedent-based procedure, in which the relatively abstract and technical concept of inherent credibility through specific methods of reasoning combined with the more ordinary notion of likelihood, which was also more akin to possibility.[65] Indeed, it goes halfway towards the position from which, around 1654, Jeremy Taylor calls Augustine a 'good probable doctor', meaning a believable, trustworthy one.[66] Significantly, it is the gendered phenomenon of tactical or indeterminate pregnancy that suggests at once the scandal and the promise of the terrain between fact and fiction – which is the terrain of the theatre, and its understanding of the law. Indeed, it takes us beyond what Lorna Hutson sees as the placing of the burden of error and sexual errancy on women in order for the persuasive Terentian plot in Shakespeare to work its ends legitimately without giving up the structural deployment of

---

[65] See Ch. 4, n. 87, and n. 106; and Serjeantson, 'Testimony and Proof', on how the new scientific emphasis on experiment and 'fact' in the seventeenth century affected the older philosophical hierarchy between inherent proofs and practical-but-inartificial proofs.
[66] Taylor, *Real Presence*, 108.

uncertainty.[67] Helena's pregnancy introduces a sense of unfolding in time that almost embodies the theatre's own relationship to later philosophical formulations of probability. In its dubious yet enabling, forward-looking yet semiotically unstable function, it symbolises the drama's way of articulating 'what the thrush said', of suggesting a way, and a time, to put an end to fretting after knowledge.[68]

Far from being 'unhistorical', then, the fictionality and compositeness of dramatic treatments of law can be precisely what we need to take seriously if we are to recover the experience of law as social action. For dramatic fiction addresses and transmutes legal realities, as well as reflecting on the potential for fiction within law itself. It speaks to, but is distinct from, the shaping forces of what Natalie Zemon Davis calls 'fiction in the archives'.[69] Nor does such a project of reconstructing social experience and perception necessarily need to be based on literary phenomena exclusively. We do not have to 'argue from silence',[70] but find the interface between imaginative constructs and the contradictions of reality, between the silence of texts and the clamour of courtrooms, and indeed between the apparent silence of litigants and the articulacy of dramatic defendants and pleaders.[71] Both theatrical witnesses and real people in court are less silent, and less fantastically opaque, than we might think; but we can only truly understand the meaning of their testimony – and the gaps therein – if we see them in dialogue.

[67] Hutson, *Usurer's Daughter*, 184–223.

[68] Keats, 'What the Thrush said'. In some senses, such pregnancies as Helena's are indeed a physical realisation of Edward Alford's 1610 gloss on the legal concept of the 'negative pregnant' (first formulated in the fifteenth century); this gloss, by applying the metaphor of biological pregnancy to the uncertainty conceived 'in the womb of the future', yet to be 'delivered', added a temporal element of withholding and unfolding to what was originally a synchronic concept of an affirmative element in an otherwise negative plea. What is specially interesting for our purposes is that the affirmative is identified, in Alford's metaphor, with the uncertain. On the 'negative pregnant' and its relation to theatrical pregnancy, and on the context of debate in the House of Commons in which Alford offered his definition, see Wilson, *Theaters of Intention*, 124–9. Time, of course, as Wilson also observes, proverbially delivers the truth. Thus, the metaphor allows access, as Wilson explains, out of pure logic to practice and process – a trajectory often suggested by women characters in their use of law. For an early modern exposition of the 'negative pregnant', see Cowell, *Interpreter*, Yy2v.

[69] Davis, *Fiction in the Archives*.

[70] Shepard, 'Meanings of Manhood' (195, and n. 57), claims, in the context of her study of male sociability in early modern Cambridge, that the 'records are frustratingly mute' when searched for evidence supporting Alan Bray's thesis about the ubiquity and understanding of male homosexual relations in the 'established social institutions of sixteenth- and seventeenth-century England – most pertinently those of the household and the education system'. She comments, ruefully, that 'Bray himself is forced to argue from silence and relies entirely on the literary evidence of satirical verse in referring to homosexual practice in the universities'. See also Bray, *Homosexuality*, 51–3.

[71] A salutary warning against imagining too much drama in real-life courts, or anything much beyond arid paperwork, is offered by Macnair, 'Reading the Evidence'.

Such a dynamic and flexible model of interaction would help us go beyond the stasis of a critical position that stops short at warning against the error of reading literature as history. Tim Stretton takes the latter to be the position of Linda Woodbridge, in *Women and the English Renaissance* (1984), a book he draws on heavily for his literary examples.[72] But to suggest so is to misread Woodbridge.[73] She too is concerned with finding the balance between the two extremes of strict aestheticism and the 'wholesale appropriation of literary materials as documents in the history of popular attitude' (6–7). She is well aware that 'the purely literary approach, like the approach of the social and intellectual historian, has its dangers', but does not claim, as Stretton implies, that literature is merely or purely rhetoric. She does claim, however, that some 'genres' are 'fairer game for social and intellectual history than others' (6). Her chosen genre chosen is the debate on the nature of women – a 'largely literary game' (6). One needs to understand this in context. Woodbridge herself was reacting against a critical tendency to take either anti-feminist invectives or defences of women in literature as real. But it is time to look at genres such as drama, on which critics tend to be drawn to the opposite of what she calls the biographical approach. It is almost too easy to dismiss dramatic representations as 'unreal', just as it seemed too easy in the 1980s to read personal investments into controversialist writing. Stretton is right to assert, in this context, the importance of drama:

The work of dramatists can seem even harder to decipher, *but* the appearance of female litigants in plays at a time when more female litigants than ever before were appearing in court seems to be more than coincidental. (italics mine)[74]

This, however, is a speculative and somewhat defeatist position, which admits the historical importance of a literary phenomenon *in spite of* the fictionality identified by Woodbridge. We now need to examine that fictive component itself as a historically meaningful phenomenon; to decipher the seemingly indecipherable. This is what I hope this chapter has begun to do. The living art of dramatists resides in the middle ground between literal reality and pure invention. That is the ground we need to plough, whether we are engaged in 'gender studies' specifically, or historical and cultural studies in a broader spectrum. In that quest, I believe our diverse efforts remain collaborative and, in a larger sense, unified.

---

[72] See Stretton, *Women Waging Law*, 63.
[73] See Woodbridge, *Women*, esp. Introduction.
[74] Stretton, *Women Waging Law*, 63.

Epilogue: The Hydra head, the labyrinth and the waxen nose: discursive metaphors for law

Having secured a clandestine marriage with Francis, impersonating Constantia, Throat the 'man of law' in Barry's *Ram Alley*, brags that

> The knot is knit, which not the law itself,
> With all its Hydra-heads and strongest nerves
> Is able to disjoin . . .   (1236–8)

The 'Hydra-head' evokes a sense of bewildering, even dangerous, multiplicity which brings us full circle and takes us back to the plurality of marriage laws discussed in Chapter 1, which Swinburne tries to reduce and fix in his treatises. As Justice Tutchin says, 'the laws,/They are so many that men do stand in awe/Of none at all' (*RA*, 1864–6). What he refers to, in a comic key, are the multiple devices at the disposal of law and its users; Swinburne's is a more troubled engagement with the multiple signification of laws that gives rise to the potential multiplicity in their application. Richard Braithwaite, a trenchant critic and satirist of law, is picking up both on the sense of indefinite proliferation and that of manipulability when he writes, around 1630, about the perversity of 'suits of law': 'censuring time and substance in frivolous delays, and multiplicity of orders, which like Hydra's heads, by lopping off or annulling one, gives way to decreeing another'.[1]

In both *Ram Alley* and Swinburne's *Spousals*, the immediate subject is marriage law. As we have seen, the confusion of laws and opinions on the eve of the Reformation created a scenario where any number of the associated formalities coexisting in a reasonable mixture was likely to endow the event of a marriage with a degree of finality at the same time as it left the contract liable to question. But the phenomenon of legal flexibility, and the lack of unitary, stable and unambiguous signifiers in laws, are not confined to one area of litigation or jurisprudence. English common law was a vast forest of memorial tenets and practices, largely

---

[1] Braithwaite, *English Gentleman*, 283.

unwritten; and since so much depended on precedent and its application, the possibilities of interpretation and practice were multitudinous. As the study of women litigants and their use of legal provisions in Chapter 6 reveals, law was eminently capable of being turned around to one's advantage, or to the disadvantage of one's adversary. Indeed, the vision of law that emerges from the drama of the period is one of a peculiarly human and contingent measure, a far cry from the *vera philosophia* or perfect science that humanist jurists would have us believe.[2]

This book has sought, in part, to gesture towards the overlap in the thinking that informed canon, common and Civil law in Renaissance England; much of the debate over legal hermeneutics in Continental jurisprudence and the Romano-canonical tradition is played out at a more pragmatic level in the practice of English law in all its forms. As William Fulbeck, practising lawyer and legal as well as literary writer, put it (provocatively, for 1602), 'the common law cannot be divided from the civil and canon laws any more than the flower from the root and stalk'.[3] Further, because of the unwritten nature of the common law, the importance of Civil law in English legal education, and the paucity of theoretical legal treatises in the late sixteenth and early seventeenth centuries in England, thinking about law has to be traced in philosophical writings in the widest possible sense, and such traditions as Justinian's jurisprudence can only artificially be separated from English legal thinking more generally. The orthodoxy still consisted in positing absolute authority to be the prerogative of law, and certain knowledge its end. Indeed, several major traditions of juristic thought claimed the status of a perfect and self-sufficient science for their discipline.[4] But inevitably, there were other voices, not necessarily legal, articulating the flaws of this position, and suggesting, satirically or constructively, a far more tentative status for law as a 'science' (or indeed 'art').[5]

The threat of multiplicity that we have seen implicit in legal discourse and flamboyantly exploited by the comic crew of *Ram Alley* is also, of course, the threat of uncertainty. Thus, the ever-proliferating possibilities

---

[2] See Kelley, *History, Law and the Human Sciences*, 267–79. On the contested status of jurisprudence as a discipline, and the slowly emergent idea of law as an 'unphilosophical mixture of the necessary and the contingent', see Maclean, *Interpretation*, 20–9.

[3] Fulbeck, *A Parallele*, sig. 25.

[4] See Kelley, *History, Law and the Human Sciences*, 268–9; Turamini, *De Exaequatione*, 170 ff.

[5] See Maclean, *Interpretation*, 22–6, on the debate over whether jurisprudence was an art or a science, and the implications of either definition for the epistemological status of the discipline, studied or practised.

of legal meaning that provide drama with some of its most lively material are exactly what legal writers are wary of. Law, being an entity that necessarily involves application and therefore mediation, has to deal with the problem of interpretation and the associated potential for indeterminacy. This anxiety, so clearly felt by Swinburne, is really as old as Justinian's prohibition of commentary on the *Corpus Juris Civilis* compiled under his auspices:

> We hereby prohibit . . . any other interpretations, or rather perversions, of our laws: lest their verbosity should bring dishonour to our laws by its confusion, as was done by the commentators on the Perpetual Edict, who by extracting new senses from one or another part of this well-made edict, reduced it to a multitude of meanings, causing confusion to arise in nearly all Roman decrees.[6]

The oxymoron of '[reducing]' 'to a multitude of meanings' is telling. If multiple possibilities are a bane, their creation must be a reduction of authority through division. What Swinburne seeks to do with his tool of 'distinction' is precisely a reduction,[7] but here this is a laudable juristic exercise since singleness of meaning is what is needed to guard against what Justinian calls 'perversions' of the assumed truth of legal intention. Nor is Justinian's warning unique. Later jurisprudential treatises such as Stephanus de Federicis' (c.1495), which had at least four sixteenth-century editions, recommended that 'the almost boundless production of volumes might be reduced by . . . good judgement to the smallest possible number'.[8] Whether one considers textual sources of law, or interpretations and commentaries, the emphasis is on checking proliferation and ensuring fixed signification as far as possible. Preservation of legal authority is inseparable from this issue.

Authority was indeed a troubled notion not only in medieval England where heresy brought the problems of theorising authority into focus, but also in the early modern period when many of the debates continued.[9] Like law, it needed to be constantly reasserted as absolute. It applied to various fields by extension, but the Bible and biblical commentary were the principal areas of study where the concept of authority was crucial. What is interesting is that perceptions that were being debated in esoteric

---

[6] *CJC*, 'Digest', 48.10.1.13.

[7] See pp. 23–4 above.

[8] Stephanus, *De Interpretatione*, preface, as quoted in Maclean, *Interpretation*, 55.

[9] On medieval debates around biblical authority in the context of English heresy, see Ghosh, *Wycliffite Heresy*; for a more general account of scholastic engagement with textual authority, see Minnis, *Medieval Theory of Authorship*. On how these debates fed into Reformation ideas in sixteenth-century Europe and England, see Evans, *Problems of Authority*.

terms by theoretical writers also come up in the most unlikely of plays, on a processive, human plane. Let us revisit Barry's satirical play once more, where Throat's assistant Dash ventures a metaphor for the law; 'It is the kingdom's eye, by which she sees/The acts and thoughts of men' (406). The scopic power of law is, of course, amply attested by the drama: witness the invisible eye of the Duke in *Measure for Measure*, standing for the legal authority of the state. The activity of spying, down to peeping in at holes and crannies, is another phenomenon we have witnessed – both in the threatened privacy in adultery plays and in the detailed descriptions of evidence-collecting in depositions. Godly theatre has been seen to define its own notion of the omnipresent eye. Dash's analogy, thus, has obvious aptness. But it is not good enough for 'lawyer' Throat who remonstrates, and pronounces his own dictum on law:

> . . . The kingdom's eye!
> I tell thee, fool, it is the kingdom's nose,
> . . .
> Nor is't of flesh but made merely of wax,
> And 'tis within the power of us lawyers
> To wrest this nose of wax which way we please:
> But if it be, 'tis surely a woman's eye
> That's ever rolling.   (407–14)

By the time Barry was writing, the waxen nose was already a familiar figure, in scholastic thought, for hermeneutic flexibility. It had been first used by Alanus ab Insulis in the twelfth century, in relation to the interpretation and application of classical authorities.[10] In Robert Greene's play *James the Fourth* (1598), a lawyer himself rues 'a wresting power that makes a nose of wax/Of grounded law'; he sees this as the function of a corrupt State but the Divine, in response, suggests that lawyers are themselves responsible for it, additionally ascribing to them the use of 'curious eyes to pry'.[11] Applied satirically to legal practice, as in *Ram Alley*, the image of the malleable nose lacking a stable or unitary position indicates an awareness of the interpretative manipulability of law, and by extension, the fundamental uncertainty of legal signification. The critique of the knowledge brought about by legal evidence in the plays discussed initially is a version of this scepticism about the orthodox position of legal positivism. The radical hierarchy of proofs shown to be

---

[10] Alanus, *De fide catholica*, cols. 305–430.
[11] Greene, *James the Fourth*, V.iv.8–9, 16.

at play in Chapter 4, through a detailed analysis of image-making and pleading with 'colour' in *The White Devil*, is yet another variant on it, if more aesthetically focused. Associated with such a vision is an emergent notion of probability, which plays sometimes offer as a more pragmatic alternative to indubitable knowledge; one that is more in tune with the human condition. Indeed, the epistemological indeterminacy at the end of legal plots provides, at times, a human refuge from the knowledges that characters resist, and struggle to bury or undo, as characters in Henry James's novels do later, in a non-legal framework. Shakespeare's Helena or Portia or indeed Duke Vincentio, are as desperately in need of uncertainty as Millie Theale or Merton Densher or Maggie Verver. Their plays need it, too, to stay precariously, poignantly, poised on the brink between comic resolution and the abyss of terrible cognitions – truths much the same as those for 'pity and dread' of which Maggie buries her eyes, which register them, in her husband's breast, at the end of *The Golden Bowl.*[12] After all, as Alfred says in the final recognition scene of Johann Strauss's opera *Die Fledermaus*, 'Who wouldn't choose happiness over truth?' Such avoidance allows what A. D. Nuttall calls 'a willingness to enter the proffered dream',[13] the world of the possible, or the improbably probable, in Shakespeare's comedies. The dream, however, is also a compromise: by rejecting it at the final moment, Kate Croy emerges from the wings of the dove that sinisterly, deadeningly, 'cover' herself and Merton, along with the truth; she is, in this failure of blindness, saved from the sordid and allowed the inescapable certainty of tragic recognition: 'We shall never be again as we were' (*The Wings of the Dove*).[14] Thus, the relation between knowledge, uncertainty and genre is ever-shifting but ever-germane.

---

[12] Isabella in *MfM* almost belongs with this group, except that she is on the brink between genuine ignorance and blasting knowledge as she acts as the Duke's agent, occupying the elusive space of confusion, which is distinct, however, from the knowing resistance of truths, and conducive to a certain brand of comœdic indeterminacy. Emilia in *Othello* is yet another Shakespearean character who tries to fend off the cost of knowledge, but fails into tragedy. The handkerchief, that petty, 'inartificial', low-level proof, comes back to haunt her intuitive knowledge and establish the case. But what she *knew*, before she spoke, is the zone of mystery – a zone where knowledge is available, but declined – 'I thought so then' (V.ii.191). What Gertrude knew, in *Hamlet*, may just be such another zone.

[13] Nuttall, *New Mimesis*, 81.

[14] Here, my reading of *The Wings of the Dove* differs from Michael Wood's in 'What Henry Knew' (*LRB*, 25, no. 24, 18 Dec. 2003), which in turn mirrors the assumptions underlying Martha Nussbaum's entirely humane and moral reading of Maggie Verver's arrangements in *The Golden Bowl* in *Love's Knowledge*, esp. 53, 125–47 and 214. For Wood, Kate Croy is the master-plotter who wins by dodging knowledge, and Millie the vulnerable dove who loves and dies. My argument about James is not a legal one; but on the 'pervasiveness of legal questions in James's work', and why it has been overlooked in James criticism, see Dennis Flannery, 'Law, Judgement and Revenge'.

But in the early modern plays I have considered, plots of knowledge are also plots of law. This underlines the crucial relation – not necessarily synchronic – between epistemology, legal thinking and literary form in this period. The scepticism about evidence that underlies uncertainty in these plays finds its clearest formulations in English legal treatises of the *late* seventeenth century, by writers such as Matthew Hale and Geoffrey Gilbert. But plays are preoccupied with these ideas from the beginning of the century onwards. The philosophical antecedents to later legal writing, and their relation to the changing practices of common law, thus form a natural next step in the kind of study I have undertaken here. The implicit connection between precedent and probabilistic application of law has been observed by Julian Martin in his work on Francis Bacon's natural philosophy.[15] Bacon, indeed, is a key figure whose contribution to the collective pursuit of truth that became the aim of the Royal Society, as well as to jurisprudential ideas that developed over the century, provides a suggestive framework for understanding the relationship of the literary to the philosophical, scientific and theological traditions of the time. The dramatic treatment of epistemological notions of plausibility and probability can thus be located within the intellectual movements of the period.[16] Such a project would need to be premised on a *longue durée* approach, and involve an in-depth study of common law practices and training.

Epistemology, however, is not simply concerned with the nature of the knowledge sought or obtained, but also the route to it. And this too is something that dramatic treatments of legal processes explore through drama's own anagnoristic plots. For instance, we have seen how this forms the core interest of Heywood's evidentiary preoccupation, as also in the radically different but equally focused engagement with the means of discovery in providentialist texts. A metaphor that straddles the process of knowing and the object of knowledge, and crystallises a significant number of perspectives on law, is the labyrinth, on which I want to dwell briefly, in conclusion. Through this focus, I want to suggest the link of methods and representations of legal enquiry with theories and practices of knowledge in the period, and indicate the way in which literary form in general, and dramatic structure in particular, can throw light on this relation.

---

[15] Martin, *Francis Bacon*, 72–104.

[16] For an excellent starting point for such an enquiry, see Shapiro, *Probability and Certainty*; Hacking, *Emergence* – outdated but still useful; and Franklin, *Science of Conjecture*. But see Serjeantson, 'Testimony and Proof', for useful correctives to Shapiro.

John Day's play *Law-Tricks* (1608), a satire on law and its manipulability, begins with the warning of 'the Booke to the Reader' against interpretation itself, and the 'corrupt translation' that it can involve. Purporting to confine textual meaning to the intention of the author, the text pleads, 'woot read mee, doe: but picke no more out of me, then he that writ put into me'. The 'booke' makes its point against textual semiotics the more explicit by an analogy with physiognomy:

we have a strange secte of vpstart *Phisiognomers*, growne vp amongst vs of late, that will assume out of the depth of their knowings, to calculate a mans intent by the colour of his complexion.[17]

Having set us off with this caveat, Day's book goes on to chart its own dubious course through a series of textual 'signs', the most interesting of which is the spatial metaphor of the labyrinth, used for the architecture of the corrupt lawyer Lurdo's house. The originary labyrinth, built by Daedalus upon the order of King Minos of Crete, housed the strange beast, the Minotaur, at its centre. The Minotaur routinely devoured the youths and maidens sent as tribute from Athens, who were let loose in the maze and never found the exit. When Theseus came to confront the monster and free his country from the tribute, Minos' daughter Ariadne, enamoured of him, gave him the end of a thread which would provide his clue through the labyrinth, help him find the Minotaur and trace his own way back. Lurdo's 'Bawdie house' (854), with its 'backe way', 'priuate doore', 'secret vault', 'sellers', and an underground bed-chamber (638–56), is figured as a labyrinth and specifically associated with Lurdo's proficiency at law-tricks. Through this maze, prince Polymetes and Iulio make their way 'groping and feeling', 'they being unacquainted with the turnings' (945–7), for a supposed rendezvous between the prince and Emilia, who is really his sister but disguised as 'Tristella' and wooed by him. Already ensconced at the heart of the labyrinth is Lurdo himself, also in pursuit of Emilia, his niece but unbeknown to himself. The ostensible goal of the entries into this labyrinthine sanctum is thus, in both cases, potentially unnatural, like the union between the bull and Minos' wife Pasiphae which produced the Minotaur. As the two young men approach, Emilia, the witty manipulator of the situation, hides Lurdo behind the

---

[17] Day, *Law-Tricks*, 'The Booke to the Reader'. For an excellent discussion of legal hermeneutics in the play, also attending to the 'labyrinth', see Collum, '"Sinister Shifts"', 285–311. This article came to my attention too late to actively engage with it. I am grateful to Luke Wilson for making me aware of it.

arras. The arras depicts the 'Poeticall fiction' of Venus kissing Adonis (969–70). As Polymetes and Iulio read this picture, they become suddenly aware of Lurdo's presence – 'the cuckoldly knave Vulcan . . . sneaking behind the brake bush', whom Emilia pretends to pass off as a 'counterfeit' (1029). This is the 'Minotaur' at the end point of this labyrinth, almost a joke on interpretative journeys and flexible meanings. Vulcan, of course, was also the mythological character who trapped Aphrodite in bed with Mars by using a net:[18] reading itself becomes an alluring snare, though Lurdo himself only takes on the 'cuckoldly' ridiculousness of Vulcan, while Vulcan's agency – at once cunning and punitive – is taken on by Emilia. The scene soon becomes a farce of complicity among Emilia, her maid, and the two young men, speculating on the exact relation between Lurdo's 'shadow' and the tapestry, Vulcan and Lurdo, and indeed between the image and the person himself. Meanwhile, Lurdo the law-wielder, stands groaning impotently as though in labour, but unable to move. At his departure, Polymetes tells Emilia that her head is reprieved this once for her wit, 'but beware the next encounter, come Ariadne's clew, will you vnwinde, and light vs through this vault of darkenesse' (1037–40). But *is* there any light at the end? Does this thread lead to any stable truth, or is it just a hermeneutic tease, a 'trick' similar, but superior in its art, to Lurdo's more patent twistings and turnings of the law? Is it about the end at all, or is it about the cleverness of the means? Indeed, what kind of a 'clew' is the play itself, Day's disingenuous 'book', to the nature of textual interpretation, licit and perverse, protesting as it does of never having 'held any irregular course'?

The analogy between law and labyrinth was familiar enough in the period. Not only was Minos traditionally associated with law, having been made judge in Hades, the actual spatial configuration of his maze was often applied to the potential confusions and indeterminacies of the chaotic common law of England. Most famously, John Cowell, in presenting his legal dictionary, laments the 'ancient palace . . . darke and melancholy' that English law is, and its difference from Justinian's sacrosanct legal structure.[19] This latter image is drawn from Justinian himself, who likened the Roman civil law to '*the edifice or structure of a sacred Temple of Justice*', as Bacon points out.[20] Bacon comments ruefully on the 'vastness of volume and a labyrinth of uncertainties' that the memorially accretive common law had become, and urges King James to make it less

[18] Homer, *Odyssey*, Bk. 8, 266–367.   [19] Cowell, *Interpreter*, *3.
[20] Bacon, *Works*, XIV, 361, 'To the King'.

diverse and contradictory, and more uniform.[21] The implicit question as to whether and how certainty of knowledge is attainable acquired a specific focus in discussions of common law. But the labyrinth as an image of error, confusion and incertitude took on additional charge in a culture pervasively preoccupied with epistemological issues in theology, science and philosophy. Calvin wrote that 'each man's mind is like a labyrinth', full of privately forged errors and false semblances.[22] A recognisably negative image, the labyrinth is the space of deceit to which Milton's fallen angels were doomed, 'in wandering mazes lost'.[23] Characters in drama often use it as a figure for moral tangle and stupefaction; witness Anne Frankford in Heywood's *Woman Killed*, drifting helplessly into illicit passion: 'This maze I am in/I fear will prove the labyrinth of sin' (vi, 159–60); or Beatrice-Joanna in *The Changeling*: 'I'm in a labyrinth' (III.iv.71);[24] or her foil the virtuous Isabella who, feigning madness, alludes to the intricate but illicit sexual scheming that constitutes the heart of the play's subplot, when she darkly addresses Antonio, one of the adulterous schemers: 'Stand up, thou son of Cretan Dedalus,/And let us tread the lower labyrinth;/I'll bring thee to the clue' (IV.iii.108–10). Delio's description of Ferdinand in Webster's *Duchess of Malfi* actually implies an analogy between law's snare, spider-web and the Cretan maze: 'the law to him/Is like a foul black cobweb to a spider:/He makes it his dwelling and a prison/To entangle those shall feed him' (I.i.177–80). Thomas Carwell's anti-Protestant tract, *Doctor Lawds Labyrinth*, contrasts the labyrinthine discourse of the Archbishop of Canterbury with 'lightsome monuments' of the 'true religion', such are the 'subterraneous . . . Turnings . . . and tortuous meanders' of Laud's text.[25] In *Instauratio Magnum*, Bacon uses the image to stand for the limits to human understanding, the errors and puzzlements that our quest for truth is heir to:

the universe to the eye of the human understanding is framed like a labyrinth; presenting . . . so many ambiguities of way, such deceitful resemblances of objects and signs, . . . so knotted and entangled. And then the way is still to be made by the uncertain light of the sense . . . while those who offer themselves as guides . . . increase the number of errors and wanderers.[26]

[21] Ibid., XIII, 59–71.
[22] Calvin, *Institutes*, I, 64–5.
[23] Milton, *Paradise Lost*, Bk. II, 561. On Bacon's use of 'labyrinth' as a negative metaphor, see Vickers, *Francis Bacon*, 176–201.
[24] Compare *Volpone*, III.ii.260 – 'lust's labyrinth'.
[25] Carwell, *Labyrinthvs Cantvariensis*, C.
[26] 'Praefatio', *Instauratio Magna, Works*, I, 129; *Works*, IV, 18.

The only deliverance is the 'clue', a 'sure plan', the *Filum Labyrinthi.*[27]

Let us now revisit Swinburne's legal maze – a revealing pointer to the largely overlooked links between the images and metaphors of common and canon laws. The architectural metaphor in *Matrimony* is suggestive. Offering 'a Lanterne in a dark entrie to . . . direct strangers into the chiefest rooms of the house', the treatise ostensibly offers illumination as a legal handbook, but implicitly figures marriage law itself as an obscure textual space.[28] But *Spousals* provides the more explicitly dual analogy. There, Swinburne offers legal 'distinctions' as the 'Thred which Ariadne gave . . . Theseus', to escape out of that dark and 'endless Labyrinth, wherein were so many difficult Turnings and intricate Returnings . . . but one only Out-gate' (*Spousals*, 65–6).[29] Yet the doubleness inherent in the metaphor suggests at the same time that the text of law itself is like a maze which needs to be cut through and made sense of in order to arrive at truth.[30] In either instance, though, the labyrinth is still a space of obscurity which needs to be illuminated by whatever the clue or hermeneutic tool may be. So far, the various associations of the maze are of a piece. Both Swinburne and Bacon grant the possibility of discovering the intention of law, or God, as the case may be, in spite of the bewildering multiplicities of the route.

But curiously enough, the metaphor itself is also potentially self-divided, not just double in its application to law. For when it comes to the path to knowledge rather than the epistemological quarry itself, there is a distinct idea shared by thinkers across the disciplines that difficulty and circuitousness are a function of ethical enquiry, a positive quality of search. There is, indeed, a belief in the value of doubt as a hermeneutic and epistemological tool. The circumlocutory, in this strand of thinking, becomes a positive image. In Donne's *Third Satire*, Truth stands at the top of a cragged hill, and 'hee that will/Reach her, about must, and about must goe'. Swinburne, by explicating legal hermeneutics as the 'thred', puts value on the discourse of law and the demands it makes on the interpreter. Bacon himself explicitly invokes the labyrinth as a necessary path towards truth.[31] It is the way that is 'arduous . . . in the beginning' that 'leads out at last into the open country'.[32] Indeed, he makes a distinction

---

[27] Bacon, *Works*, III, 493–504.   [28] *Matrimony* (Appendix), 115.
[29] For a fuller analysis of this passage, see Ch. 1 above, pp. 23–4.
[30] Quoted on p. 23 above.
[31] Bacon, *Works*, I, 129; IV, 18.
[32] Bacon, 'Proemium', *Instauratio Magna*, *Works*, I, 122; *Works*, IV, 8. The advocated method of knowledge-seeking has a suggestive relation to the Baconian notion of the discovery of the hidden law. On the latter, see Martin, *Francis Bacon*, 79–86.

between two methods of knowledge: a strenuous, rigorous pursuit of truth, which is the legitimate mode, and the other, condemnable desire of knowledge

> upon a natural curiosity and inquisitive appetite; sometimes to entertain their minds with variety and delight . . . as if there were sought in knowledge a couch, wherein to rest a searching and restless spirit.'[33]

The discomfort is the old one, with the pleasure principle, here applied to ways of knowing.

But circuitousness and difficulty can often be the properties of a clever, intricate, ingenious and self-delighting form. And when functioning thus, the labyrinthine can get reassociated with the dubiously pleasurable, and become a trope for the crooked and misleading. Bacon was not unaware of the pleasure afforded by falsehood, the 'natural though corrupt love of the lie itself' ('Of Truth'), and the role of fiction in epistemology.[34] George Herbert, in the distinct context of devotional poetry, suggestively teeters between the two implications of the circuitous aesthetic. His poetry records that process towards discovery which is the hermeneutic field that fallen man must plough before arriving at the place of holiness. Though we are inheritors of a certain illiteracy by virtue of being human – 'Thy word is all, if we could spell'[35] – it is not enough to rest at the passive grace of revelation longed for in the *Jordan* poems. The difficult act of interpretation itself becomes a necessary process, just as signification is a function of the fallen world; why else would God 'anneal in glass [his] story' ('The Windows')? This is in the spirit of Augustine who thought that man needs to travel the path from obscurity to understanding, in proportion to what he has lost through the Fall. The created world is a system of signs in which the Creator is manifest, but these divine metaphors need to be read right. So Herbert's own figurations are as legitimate as our hermeneutic labours are necessary. But Herbert is both writer and reader. As a writer, indirectness often becomes a function of playful intimacy with God, as well as of a text demanding rigorous interpretation. But as reader and devotee, he feels, at the same time, a weariness with the tortuous. There is an intermittent frustration, almost indignation, with the deliberate obscurity in which God clothes himself: witness the

---

[33] Bacon, *Works*, I, 462; III, 294.
[34] Bacon, *Works*, VI, 377; see also Steadman, *The Hill and the Labyrinth*, 3, but also, more generally, 1–16, on the metaphors of hill and labyrinth.
[35] 'The Flower'.

anguished question in 'The Search', wrung from an uncomprehending subject incredulous of the severity, even perversity, of the test God puts him through:

> Where is my God? What hidden place
> Conceals thee still?
> What covert dare eclipse thy face?
> Is it thy will?

So, even as the devotee often takes pleasure in prayer that works and winds its way up, in the 'crooked winding ways' of artifice ('A Wreath'), weaving a chiasmic wreath in the very act of rejecting the way that is not 'straight', there remains a longing for a straight path to knowledge, to truth, to God. In 'The Pearl', the poet knows the ways of learning, honour and of pleasure, just as he knows the price of divine love. And yet,

> Yet through these labyrinths, not my groveling wit,
> But thy silk twist let down from heav'n to me,
> Did both conduct and teach me, how by it
> To climbe to thee.[36]

And if Shakespeare is half-remembering Arachne's spider-web while talking of Ariadne's thread in *Troilus and Cressida*, where Troilus mentions 'Ariachne's broken woof', that would be a swift reminder of how the tremor of a single image, or mingled memory, can capture the closeness between the sinister labyrinth that traps and the *filum labyrinthi* that guides by virtue of its wielder's control over the maze.[37] The 'clue' promised by the virtuous Isabella in *The Changeling* is itself treacherous, albeit as a moral corrective.

What Yeats calls 'the fascination of what's difficult'[38] is precariously poised, in epistemological ventures, between the rigorous and the perverse. When these ventures are enacted in dramatic form, the problem

---

[36] Cf. 'Mattens', where a similar longing is expressed for a light that will reveal both the work and the workman, and thus teach how to 'know' God's love, rather than teasing the mind – 'Then by a sunne-beam I will climbe to thee'.

[37] *Troilus and Cressida*, V.iii.152. The Riverside editors call this 'Shakespeare's error for the name of Arachne, who, according to Ovid . . . was turned into a spider by Pallas'. The New Cambridge editor suggests, more temptingly, that 'though "Ariachne" may be a slip or a spelling invented to fit the metre, it is more likely that Shakespeare conflated Arachne with Ariadne, the Cretan girl whose love for Theseus led her to give him a length of thread to help him find his way out of the labyrinth'. On how half-remembering can lead to a mingling of myths, meanings, and thereby genres, in Shakespeare, see Nuttall, '*A Midsummer Night's Dream*', also brilliantly suggestive of how these little things in Shakespeare are rarely ever accidents.

[38] Yeats, *Selected Poetry*, 66.

becomes multilayered. The scenes of trial presented in early modern play-texts are structures of knowing contained and encoded within plots that themselves seek to proceed from ignorance to knowledge, doubt to certainty. Nor is that all. Renaissance drama abounds in the more specific and intriguing phenomenon of the false trial; numerous instances of characters testing each other, as Edgar does the blind Gloucester on Dover Cliff in *Lear*, or Malcolm does Macduff in *Macbeth*: the 'I did this but to try thee' formula, which raises questions about the motives and means of knowing. There is a peculiar pain often attendant upon these false trials, sometimes a risk, arising out of the very falsity or redundance of the tribulation, and how it acts on the subjecthood of the characters who are put to the test and are not in the know. This is precisely what Sophia chastises her husband and his friend for in Massinger's *The Picture*; this is also what constitutes the perversity of Spinella's trial by her husband in Ford's *The Lady's Trial* – a perversity articulately registered within the play in emotional terms. For such trials are often poised, precariously, 'within a foot/Of th' extreme verge'.[39] The instinct that prompts them is not unrelated to the purely fictive impulse and hard curiosity that Bacon labels as suspect. Romance heroines such as Cariclea in *Aethiopica* are addicted to this habit, driven to tell one intricate lie after another by an almost amoral caprice; Apuleius' adventures also have something of this instinct, a desire for knowledge almost for the sake of it. And plots are spun out of these fictive mazes that delight in themselves and proliferate, intricacy getting detached, in the process, from the ideal of discipline.[40] The ethical as well as human implications of such plots are explored by self-referential theatre precisely through a use of legal structures. Typically, this is a preoccupation of tragicomedy, which is, as a genre, affined to trials, working through tokens and signs to disclose truths of action, relation and identity. But this is a form which has its foundation in the idea of *felix culpa* – 'happier far by affliction made' – and as such, it licenses torment and trial. According to Giambattista Guarini, the Renaissance theorist of tragicomedy, the pain caused by tragicomic plotting is justified by the fact that it is all about the danger, not the

---

[39] Shakespeare, *Lear* F, IV.v.25–6. I have written at greater length about the motif of the false trial in 'False Trials in Shakespeare, Massinger and Ford', *Essays in Criticism* (July 2006), and in '"Within a foot/Of th'extreme verge": the impulse to try in early modern literature', forthcoming in Will Poole and Richard Scholar, eds., *Thinking with Shakespeare: Comparative and Interdisciplinary Essays* (Legenda, 2007).

[40] Interestingly, Carwell specifically associates artifice, intricacy, 'inventive industry' and 'the novel Fancies of . . . Phantastic brains' as he compares the Archbishop to 'Dedalus' (*Doctor Lawd's Labyrinth*, C-Cv).

death (*il pericolo, non la morte*).[41] Yet this is an assurance available to the playwright, and the inscribed artificer, but not to all the characters. The *rassomiglianza del terribile*, on which the form turns, are simulacra only to the plot-maker; to the characters affected, the terror is far from unreal: no wonder that Guarini theorises the 'fictive terror of someone else' as an affect of tragicomedy.[42] By bringing alive the reality of the suffering that the characters undergo, without knowing that all will come right in the end, dramatists draw attention to the emotional cost of ingenious plotting. In foregrounding this cost, tragicomedy becomes a mode actively used to question the relation between literary form and ethics. Herbert's plea to God to 'take these bars, these lengths away' ('The Search'), finds its ethically and formally self-conscious variation in the sense of gratuitousness evoked by the Duke's prolongation of Isabella's ignorance, pain and suspense in *Measure for Measure*, an action aligned with other gratuitous trials in the play – Angelo's being the most glaring instance, also put on by the legal arbiter, the Duke. The questionable legitimacy of such knowing trials becomes even more sharply focused in plots such as that of *Cymbeline*, where the legal idea of 'trying' gets translated into a metaphor, a subtle thing of art, but one that causes real hurt. Iachimo's aesthetic pleasure in the exquisite, evident in the bedroom scene where he collects corporal tokens of Imogen's supposed infidelity with the eye of an art connoisseur, culminates, in the final scene of trial, confession and disclosure, in his zestful, erotic recounting of the act of stealth he repents, which has cost Imogen all her pain. He goes about to expound his story at leisure, in the sensationalist style of an Italianate aria, while an assembly of characters 'stand on fire', breathlessly awaiting disclosures that will change their lives (V.v.168). The potential perversity of this can only be sanctioned by a form that guarantees a happy ending but contains tragic experience – so that the painful can be dwelt on in an artistic way, and between the promise and its delivery there can be infinite and artful delay. So Imogen can wake up and lament, in the most surreally anguished poetry, over what she thinks is her husband's headless body, while the audience titter to see that it is only his gross double, the very Cloten she has scorned to look on (IV.ii.296–332). But we know, as she does not, that her husband is alive. This makes the giggle an uncomfortable one. In such plots, I suggest, the interface between legal and extra-legal engagements with the routes to knowledge and disclosure comes alive. Oftenest, legal

---

[41] Guarini, *Compendium of Tragicomic Poetry*, 504–33 (511).
[42] Guarini, *Il Verato*, 2:259.

structures, and indeed the metaphor of the legal process, are used to examine the larger issue of the ethics of trying and knowing, and of the application of aesthetic form to these processes.

Even entirely comic plots, however, can touch on the discomforts of labyrinthine pursuits. After all, it is Emilia who, in *Law-Tricks*, is the agent behind the diversions and waylayings of the maze scene; though the actual space belongs to Lurdo, its labyrinthine use belongs to the clever artificer, his niece. She is not only teaching the young men and the lecherous old lawyer a lesson, but also having fun doing so! In the later trial-cum-recognition scene, she admits in so many words that she has led her brother 'vp and down the maze of good fellowship' and 'playd Will with the wispe with [him]' (1940–2). The entire exercise, lasting out the span of the play itself, was set up by Emilia to put her 'Brothers humor to the test' and 'to trie what mettle our Genowaies wits are made of' (310–11). But the game has involved a close brush with things perverse such as incest, and is ultimately inseparable from a host of other little mock-trials characters put each other through, which all converge in the official trial scene at the close where the Duke is both the ultimate enquirer after truth, and the judge. This is why the thread or clue upheld by Bacon is not always an innocent tool. In a lighter key, Thomas Churchyard's poem *The Honour of the Lawe* (1596), dedicated to Lord Keeper Egerton, is built around elaborate metaphors for the law, including spatial figures and images of discovery. But it is suspicious of unnecessary circuitousness and aware of its depleting effects:

> Long sutes are like a semstars clue of threed,
> That first was long a spinning of the wheele,
> Long twisting too, to mak it serue the need,
> . . .
> And ouer long a working some men say,
> Yet as the length is long of this same clue,
> So shall you finde an end som kind of way,
> . . .
> But sutes do leaue the sutars all so bare,
> That half vndon world thinks long suters are
> . . .
> Plainness is best, and euer furthest goes,
> Sleight finds a gift, to shuffel cards too long,
> The shortest way vnto the woods who knoes,
> And goes about, shall doe humselfe great wrong.[43]

---

[43] Churchyard, *Honour*, A4–A4v.

Thus, the metaphor of the labyrinth itself turns out to be something of a waxen nose, 'which', according to Alanus, 'means it can be bent into taking on different meanings'.[44] Meanwhile, the use of narrative and plot in drama to enact or interrogate the epistemological sequence of trials emerges as one of the implicit themes of my enquiry.

All this is only to indicate the directions in which this study can be taken forward into the 'open country'. The dialogue intimated here is larger than merely an exchange between court and theatre, drama and law – fascinating as that is in its own right. That particular interaction should be understood in the context of, and in turn be allowed to illuminate, the cross-current of ideas that united the several worlds of philosophy, science, medicine, jurisprudence, imaginative literature and the events of history in the early modern period. But I do not pretend to offer Ariadne's thread; instead, I try to open up this labyrinth of interconnections to the research it invites, and deserves. For places where I have not been able to reach, I find solace in Cymbeline's words: 'This fierce abridgement/Hath to it circumstantial branches which/Distinction should be rich in'.[45]

---

[44] Alanus, *De fide catholica*, col. 333, as translated in Minnis, Scott and Wallace, eds., *Medieval Literary Theory*, 323, n. 49.

[45] *Cymbeline*, V.v.384–6.

Appendix
Mickleton and Spearman, MS. 4,
fos. 115–24: a transcript.

'Of the signification of diverse woordes importing
Matrymonye, and whye yt is <rather> named
matrimonie than Patrymony'

There be divers Latin woordes which albeit at the [nothing els but plane] first
view thei all seame to signifie but one thinge [that is . . . & meanes], Matrimonye
I meane as Matrimonium, Nuptiae, Conjugium, and such Like (a), yet if wee
shall look a little more diligently into their severall Etymologies and originall
foundacions wee shall find each of them to be qualified with some secret vertue
and excellent peculiar property over and besides the generall significacion (b), the
explicacion or unfolding whereof (because yt cannot but bring profitable Light to
our obscure understanding so as therby we may the better perceyve the most
Principall vertues considerable in the thing signified) do the in this discourse as in
every other treatise <ryghtlie> Challenge the formost place (c) [and] <being>
in dede no lesse necessary for begynners than is a Lanterne in a dark entrie to [for
the] direct strangers into the chiefest roomes of the house. First of all therefore to
disclose the [parent] <Ofspring and> Naturall [and originall] foundation of this
woord Matrimonium yt is compounded of two woordes. Viz. Matris Muniam
(e) that is to saye the office or duety of a mother wherein is secretlie delivered
the cause [the cheife and principall end of mariage] <wherefore marrage
was ordeyned> (f) So that it is not a name found by fortune or Coyned by
Chance but after serious premeditation <devised> and <vpon> grave
<considerations> [advisement devised and] delyvered as a most significant
tearme importing <[one of the chiefest endes]> [the very end and scope] <finall
cause> of mariage namelie that the wife may bring forth and become a mother
by procreation of children (e) For therefore especially was matrimonie first
institutid [and ordeyned] of god in paradize that Children may be borne <and
brought up in the feare of god> to replenishe his Church and to fulfill the
number of the elect (H) <[which were] being> predestined before the begyn-
ning of the world by the fre mercy of god in Christe [Jesus] to be saved and to
Lyve in euerlasting blisse amongst the blessed Angells in heaven. (I) frome

whence [Lucifer and other] those other angells which kept not theyre first estate were for theyr pryd {and disobedience throwen down into Hell, and there reteind in everlasting Chaines under darknes (K), for ye repair of which ruine and supply of whose place (as diverse do divine) the Almighty did first create mann & weoman bidding them Encrease & Multiply (m), ordeining and predestinateing so manye of theis earthly creatures to salvation, as on thother part fell from their celestiall seat to condemnacion; if ye Opinion of the Canonists be Canonicall, which nevertheless is much more curious than necessary, and more admirable than warrantizable, for who hath been of God's counsell and who but ye Lord knoweth who are his. But howsoever it be this is true, that matrimony was therefore ordeined that by procreacion of Children the number of ye elect might [?encrease] be accomplished (q)}

116

Neyther shall men marry wives nor wifes be bestowed in mariage but shalbe <whereupon Matrimonie is not vnfithe> called the Seminarie of the Church and common welth (r) but shalbe [as the Angells in heaven (R) with whome they shall dwell for euer. This is the first and principall end of mariage, included in this woord Matrimonie. Ther <And albeit ther> be other endes also of mariage as the avoiding of fornication (s) the mutuall Love and affection wherewith thone ought to enterteyne the other (T) [. . .] besides diverse secondary causes as bewty riches honour frendship and such Civill respectes (v) (wherof more conveniently hereafter). But none of theym are so excellent as is the first cause [of] <included in the woord matrimonie viz.> procreation <of children no not> that [end] of avoyding fornication. (x) the former being instituted in paradise [thother] <[this toher] the other> out of paradise that [former] in the state of mans innocencie this [other] in the state of mans infirmitye [the former as being <an excellent and gloryous [and <an honorable> dignity thother <an honest> no more but a remedy (X) in <case of> mere Folye [Y] This an honest remedy, but that an honorable dignity. (y)

The woord Nuptiae is deryved of the verbe Nubo (z) which we comonly translate To Marry thoughe properlie and originally yt doe signifie To hyde or couer (a) Like as Nubilo [doth signifie] to [make dark] obscure or make dark (b) whence also comith Nubes a Clowde and Nubilosus clowdye (c). How that the verb Nubo which originally signifieth hyde or cover should also signifie to marry is vpon this occasion. In auncient tyme New marryed virgins were accustomed to weare a Vale wherewith they [did] couered theyr heads and shadowed theyr Countenances (d) after the example of Rebecca of whome we read in godes <holie> book that being affianced to Isaack as sone as she sawe him, she couered her selfe with a vale (e), which custome was generally observed of otheres in her race partly in signe of shamefastnes in asmuche as they had now vundertaken the performance of many secret actions which cannot <could not well> abyde the lyght (f) but especially in signe of subiection and obedyence (g) for as god is

Christes head and as christe is mans head so is the husband the wifes head (H) and therefore dothe the woman Cover her owne head {because her Husband is her only head, whose glory shee is, even as he is the image and glory of God, And as her head is covered, because her Husband is her head, so her syrname, for being married shee is now no more to be saluted by that name which she received from her father in whose power shee was before, but by her husbands syrname into whose government shee is transplanted by ye marriage least shee might otherwise seem not to have forsaken her fathers house & family: By this then wee may understand half ye word [Nuptiae] doth not merely signify marriage, but hath a further reach, namely ye duty of ye Wife towards her Husband, testifyed by ye veil & covering of her head, implied in this word Nuptiae, And hence it is, tht ye word Nubo is proper to the weoman as is Duco to ye mann (z), which difference ye Grammarians for ye most part observe with a vigilant eye (m), thereby insinuateing that as it belongeth to ye Husband, as to the head, to guid and govern, so it belongeth to ye weoman as to an inferior member to be governed & to obey.} Coniugium is a metaphoricall woord descending from the verbe Coniugo (n) which Signifyeth to yoke together (o). Like as Jugum signifieth a Yoek wherwith Oxen are Coopled together (p) [so that Coniugium properly strictly vnderstood]. And so Coniugium [therefore] betokenethe

117

the yoke of mariage wherewith the man and the woman are coopled together (r) In which respect also thei be called Coniuges (s) because they be yoked together as it were two oxen to drawe and Lobor in that state of Lyfe whereunto they have betaken theym <selfes vntill by death the yok be disseuered (T) [Causing that is to saye yoke fellowes] ffor the eternal wisdom of god foreseeing that it was not good that man should be alone (v) did provide him a mate (as he had done to other living creatures) to be an helpe vnto him <Like vnto him selfe [Like vnto him self and being] even wooman bone of his bones and fleshe of his fleshe (x) Coopling and ioyning theym together that the [infinite] troubles which <should be Laid vpon theym during theyr lives vpon this earthe> [are laid vpon vs and wherunto we are subiect] might be the more easily borne by the mutuall help and comfort of thone towards the other (y) [Thus is] <So that> marriage <we see is> not vnfitly called <Coniugium] a yoke [which may not be . . . shaken of] [at pleasure]and the marryed coople yokefellows because they are not to shake of this yoke at (the) pleasure but must <whiles they live be content to> endure and beare the same (z) [continually helping and comforting one an other] as well in siknes as in health helping and comforting one an other [as well] <bothe> in the stormie winter of adversitye [as] <and> in the pleasant summer of prosperity which is the third cause wherefore matrimonie was ordeyned.

(a) [Other wise <that is to saye> and certeinly, if mariage were not <a yoke> Coniugium that is] {for although there be no less than a Hundreth comodities belonging to marriage (recited by one tutor yet forasmuch as there be no fewer than two hundreth discomodities waiteing and attending thereupon (recited by Ye same Author (c)) likely it is that diverse upon one dislike or other would quickly be eased of their burthen, but being a yoke, which thing ye word Conjugium import, wee are thereby putt in mind of ye unlawfulness of such Licentious liberty (d)}

There be yet other woordes which besides theyr generall signification of Mariage [import somewhat als] <have some speciall emphasis> not altogether to be neglected as Connubium Contubermium, Maritagium. Wherof the foremost Com*m*ith of the verbe Nubo (e) and therefore what hath been spoken of the woord Nuptiae maye suffice for the vnderstanding of the nature [the record] Connubium. Contubermium hath diverse significations (f). Amongst others by the civill Lawe that which is called <Coniugium> [matrimonie] betwixt theym that be free, that is termed Contubermium betwixt theym tht are bounde (g). So that by the Civill Lawe Contubermium is the mariage of a bond man and a bond woman (H) But by the Common Lawe the Mariage betwixt a bond man and a bond woman is tearmed coniugium aswell as if they were both free (J). Which lawe doth terme those marriages Contubermium & which yt [doth] hath prohibited as unlawfull (k) Maritagium is a word very frequent in the statutes of this Realme (L) and much used of our temporall Lawyers (M) [?..] <and doth rather signifie the right of bestowing one in marriage than> marriage (n). But elsewhere I have not redd it to any remembrance <and yet> The verbe Marito as ani <which is [to marry] to bestowe in marriage is every where extant with? the approvidst Author (o) and thence comes Maritus (p) a husband, and Maritua (q) a wife (thoughe this be as [very] rare as that <comon> [usual].) which names are [not] <neuer> attributed either to the one or to the other vntill they be <fully> bestowed in <perfect mariage <solemnized> and not promised onlie (r). for whiles they be onely affianced they be called spousus or spousa (s)

118

Some in dede ther be which came to say that Maritus is not a simple woord descending frome the verbe Marito but Compounded of Maris & Ritus (T) which signifiethe the duety of a man in respect of his sexe. Howbeit that maritus is Maris Ritus I rather esteeme to be a dallyance with the sound than a sound deryvation. Otherwise seing maritus and Marita flowe both frome one fountayne (V) I cannot see but [if that] [derivation <composition> were mistaken] that Marita should <then> also be [quasi] maris rita which were absurd. I will not say for any to think but even to dreame of any such deduction.) for what more absurde than that a womans name should be deryved frome Mas maris which [importeth] <is proper to> the masculine sexe (X) besides that, there is not any such woorde as rita. And therefore [it is] impossible that Marita should [be maris rita] consist of Maris & rita. (Y) [Marita (if wee will knowe the truth) is nothing else but Maritata, viro marito tradita, gyven or deliuered to a husband.] The accustomed Latin woord for a wife [as (I suppose)] is vxor and not Marita. which woord vxor is as much as vuxor (Z), an Anoynter. for by a superstitious Ceremonie observed at <the Celebration of> marriage amongst the Romans when the bryde was brought home to her husbandes house she did vse to deck and frame the house with garlandes of wollen <yarne> yarle dipt in oyle <for a remedye [for . . . as an inchantement] against wicked spirites, of which ceremonie she had that name <vxor> (a) then which no other name is more vsuall at this daye, thoughe marita be a better name Lesse superstitiouse and more significant for Marita is nothing els but Maritata seu marito tradita (b) that is to saye gyven or delyvered to a husband, of the verbe Marito, as is aforesaid. But whether maritagium Come of the same verbe I cannot saye It seameth rather to be Compoundid ab Agendo Maritum of playing the husband Lyke as Homagium is compoundid ab agendo hominem of playing the man (c). which woord Homagium thoughe yt be not found within the Godye of the Civill Lawe (d) yet is it extant [in diverse places] <within> the text of the Common in diverse places (e). So that as by Homgium is vnderstoode that personall service which is due by the feudall tenant to his landlorde of whome he houldeth <his land> by that kind of tenure even so <I suppose that> by maritagium is vnderstoode that personall duety or service which is due by [theyme] <these persons> which be invested in [that] <the> tenure of wedlock. The bestowing wherof belongith to the Lord of whome any Land is houlden by [knightes service] Escuage that is by knightes services (f).

But wherefore is wedlock called Matrimonie rather than Patrimonie, is not eche thing to receyve denomination of the stronger and [more] woorthier parte (g). And is not the wife the weaker vessel (H), And [is not] the husband [the. . .head] (being the wifes head) the more woorthie parte (I). If thisbe thus; then how comes yt to pass that Matrimonie is so denominated of the weaker and vnwoor-thier parte. The answer is, that it is so denominated of the mother <rather> than of the father partely because the mother is alwaies more certein than the father (k) and truthe is stronger than opinion (L). and partelye

119

because ther is <much> more use of the motheres office in the procreation <[and nourishment]> of children (m) (being the cheife and principall cause wherefore mariage was ordeyned (n)) then of the father ffor vnto the mother (as the text witnesseth (o)) her child is before the birthe onerouse in the birthe dolorouse, and after the birth laboriouse. And Philosophye teacheth us that the child doth participate more of the substance of the mother then of the father (P). [for this] [causes was] Vpon these considerations was wedlock <first> [rather] called matrimonye (q) [and] not patrimonie <masi matrionium - the mothes office>] And forasmuchas yt is the fathers <parte and> dutie to care and provide that this [sic] children <wher with god hath blessed him> may have whereon to lyve when they shalbe taken frome the motheres wing and <growen [when they now shalbe]> past her care [and government] or charge (r) Therefore that <portion [certeyn] or Inheritance> which is left theyme by theyr father for a staye of lyving is no lesse aptly called patrimonies (s) that is to saye her fatheres dutye then is the other called matrimony that is to saye the motheres dutye (T).

The Definicion of Matrimonie with a breif exposicion of the same

Matrimony is defined in this manner, matrimonium est Maris et ffeminae conjunctio individuam vitae consuetudinem continens (a), Matrimony is the coupling together of a Mann & a Wooman comprehending ye inseparable company of life; the excel = lency of which definicion, because some persons cannott so quickly comprehend, & others (perhaps) will not so easily acknowledg, I thought it behoovefull to add this exposicion following as an indifferent remedy both to help the weaknes of ye one and to weaken the unwillingness of ye other It is truely said that Art doth imitate Nature (b), and so very like unto natures handywork is the workmanshipp of Art oftentimes, that being compared together they seem rather to be Twinns of one Mother than the Issue of diverse Seuters, Both which posicions are verified [by Nature & might (being Gods ordinary instrument) doth consist of matter & form (d), so in this action Art showing what shee is (viz. natures diligent scholar) hath com posed this definicion Ex genere et d*ecen*cia (e), ye one resembling ye matter, ye other ye form thereof (f), Nor so content, but as Arachne contented with Pallas (g) the Goddes of arts (H), so in this definicion Art striveing to be equall with nature hath made such an absolute work thereof, describing the essentiall qualities of Matrimony so exactly, that neither the skilfull painter duxis (J), of whom it is reported that by his art he did so lively counterfeit ripe and beautifull grapes that appearing rather naturall than artificiall, the birds came flyeing to them and picked at them, neither yet the famous Parrhasius (more cunning than ye other (k) who had drawn such a perfect picture of a sheet or veil of linnen, that even Zeuxis himself (who contended with Parrhasius) beleiving verily that it had been nothing else but a sheet wherewith Parrhasius had covered his prize, bade take away the sheet that he might see the picture, did more lively, imitate nature in their faculty than nature is imitated or rather matched by Art in this definicion, ffor they did only counterfeit the superficiall shape of a gross & sensible subject, But in this definicion is described the express image of a thing invisible, subject (not to sense but) only to ye force of reason & understanding And yet if wee shall diligently marke ye exposicion following, wee shall rather seem to behold this invisible form with our eyes than comprehend it in our mind.}>>

120V

[Now yf the <comendation of the> Arte of paynting by this [?. . .] endure vntill this day because yt is an imitation of nature describyng the outward forme of suche thinges as be subiect <onelie> to sense how muche more is that art to be comended and admired throughout all ages which teachith to describe not the superficiall forme onely of thinges subiect to sense but the true substance and essentiall forme of thinges invisible or subiect onely to the sense of reason and vnderstanding which thing is evident in this definition wherin Arte hath planely showed what she is that is to say Natures scholar for as Nature doth <frame and> Compose euery thing of matter and forme So <Likewise this artificiall> definition consisting ex genere et *decen*cia thone do the resemble the matter and the other the forme thereof]

120

ffirst of all therefore wheras matrimonie is desyred to be Coniunctio a Coopling or ioyning together By Coniunction in this place is not understood the Joyning together of bodies but of myndes (L), for thus [yt is] wrytith Auncient Ulpian amongst the rules and principles of Lawe. Nuptias non Concubitus sed consensus facit (m), that is, Not bedding but Consent makes marriage. And in an other place it is thus written. Matrimonium quidem non facit Coitus sed voluntas (n). That is, Not Carnall copulation but will makith matrimonie <[And in another]> And in another place *Defloracio virginitatis non facit matrimonium sed pactio conjugalis, The deflowring of virginity doth not make matrimony, but the covenant of Marriage (P), And in another place thus, Sufficit solus secundum leges consensus eorum de quorum consensus et conjunctionibus agitur, qui solus si defuerit Caetera etiam cum ipso coitu celebrata frustrantur(t) etc, Their consent alone is sufficient according to the Lawes, of whose Consent & Conjunction it is entreated, which Consent alone if it be wanting, all the residue celebrated, even with carnall knowledge, are void, besides which and the like authorities(q), wee are informed by evident Examples that perfect matrimony may consist without carnall knowledge, for Joseph & Mary were truely joined together in holy Matrimony, before the birth of Christ (R), and yet as shee was a very wife, so was shee evermore a pure & perfect Virgin (S), likewise the Matrimony instituted and ordeined by Almighty God in Paradise betwixt our first parents Adam & Eve was true and absolute* [and perfect] <matrimonie> in the state of theyre Innocency befor they did knowe eche other carnallye (T). So then we see that by Coniunction in this place is vnderstoode the ioyning together of ther myndes and not of theyr bodies (V).

Some ther be <not withstanding> which doe hould that the word Coniunctio in this place doth Comprehend the coopling together not onely of their myndes but of theyr bodies also (X) because the cheife and principall end of matrimonie is procreation of children and avoyding of fornication (y) which cannot be effected without corporall coniunction wherupon also all suche persons as be impotent in that behalf cannot contract matrimonye (z). Moreover if the definition were to be vnderstoode of [the Coniunction of] consent onely then [one oneli] whereas ther be two kindes of matrimonie Initiation *Legale* & *Ratificatu*m integrum and Consummate] <& consummation (a)> one onely kynd of matrimonie should here be defyned <that is> the begunne matrimony but not the matrimony consummated

121

To three of the authorities whereon the former opinion is grounded - viz. Non concubitus, Non coitus, Non defloracio &c., being all one in effect they make one answer, viz. That ye negative is true, that is to say, Not bedding alone, not carnall copulacion alone, not deflowring alone doth make matrimony (c), But ye affirmative, that is to say, that consent alone doth make matrimony, the former places (say they) do not prove (d); To the last and the like places sufficit solus consensus &c. Consent alone is sufficient &c., It is answered, that ye particle [solus] is exclusive only of the ceremonies & solemnities observed at the celebracion of marriages (e), And to ye examples their answer is that in those cases there was true matrimony (f), but not perfect matrimony (z), or (as they otherwise distinguish) there was matrimony initiate but not consummate (H), And so they conclude that by the word [Conjunctio] is understood a double Conjunction, viz. aswell of the Body as of the mind (I). Others they proceed a stepp further, holding this opinion that the word Conjunctio doth not only comprehend that twofold conjunction of Body & mind, but also contein that community of divine and humane right - we find to be expressed by Modestinus in his old definicion of matrimony extant in the body of the Civill Law (n), And therefore rules this community be conteind under the word Conjunctio, either is this definicion defective, or that superfluous (o). But whether these two <last recited> opynions be true or noe<namelie> whether this Corporall Coniunction and Community of divine and humane right be comprehendid in the woord Coniunctio or implyed in other woordes of the definition <Because it is a matter> of longer and harder discourse (p) than is agreable to an entrance (?) where the Tender myndes of the studiens (?) are to be instructed with simple and easye rudimentes and not to be <ouerloaded or> oppressed with darke and depe misteries (q) I have deferred the execution and determination herof vntill fitter oportunytie be offred Let this Suffice in the meane tyme that althoughe yt be a question whether Corporall Coniunction or that other Communitye be Comprehendid in the woord Coniunctio yet this is without question that the Coniunction of ther myndes [that is to say] consent <(I meane)> is verily ment therby (s). Herupon therefore we may saifely note the thinges <especially> ffirst that suche persons as <either> *cannot consent* for that they be destitute of the vse of Reason and discretion as Children (T), Madfolks (V) [Idiotes (X)] and suche as be ouercome with drink (X) els *doe not consent* for that they be oppressed with feare (y) or seduced by Error mistaking one person for an other (z).

122

one by this definition excludid So that the matrimonie by theym actually contracted is of no moment or effect in Lawe. Secondly that the single consent of thone partie alone is not sufficient to constitute matrimonie (a) for oneles the Consent be mutuall [yt is] Certeinly [that] <it> is no Coniunction that is to say no Coopling together of ther myndes and Consequently no matrimonie (b). Of which necessity of mutuall consent we have alredy spoken sufficiently in the former treatise of Spowsall where also is duly recorded what manner of consent [is necessary] it is which makith matrimonie and by what forme of woords or Signes yt is expressed (c). Thirdly Seing Matrimonie is a Coniunction therefore all impedimentes of what nature soeuer.

Bibliography

PRIMARY SOURCES

MANUSCRIPTS

British Library, MS Additional 12/506.
British Library, MS Egerton 2983.
Bedfordshire Record Office, L28/46.
Cambridge University Library, Commissary Court, II.3, 91.
Cambridge University Library, Commissary Court, II.4, 235.
Cambridge University Library, EDR, E12/9, 1647 file.
Cambridge University Library, EDR, E9/6/5v.
Cambridge University Library, Gg.2.31.
Cambridge University Library, Vice-Chancellor's Court I.3, 109v.
Cambridge University Library, Vice-Chancellor's Court I.3, 109v–121v.
Cambridge University Library, Vice-Chancellor's Court II.22.
Cambridge University Library, Vice-Chancellor's Court II.30, 36.
Cambridge University Library, Vice-Chancellor's Court III.5, items 61,
    63–70, 72.
Canterbury Cathedral Archives, X.10.20.
Canterbury Cathedral Archives, X.10.16.
Canterbury Cathedral Archives, X.10.17.
Canterbury Cathedral Archives, X.10.18.
Canterbury Cathedral Archives, Y.3.15.
Cheshire Record Office, EDC 5 (1634), items 24–5.
Middlesex Guildhall, *Gaol Delivery Register*, Vol. III, 128–37.
Middlesex Guildhall, *Gaol Delivery Roll*, 636/92.
Middlesex Guildhall, *Sessions Roll*, 636/88.
'Fugger Newsletter', Nationalbibliothek, Vienna, MS 8959.
Huntington Library, Ellesmere Papers, EL 34/b/2 fol. 16, 165.
Norfolk and Norwich Record Office, DN/DEP/6.
Norfolk and Norwich Record Office, DN/ACT/4.
Norfolk and Norwich Record Office, DN/ACT/5.
Norfolk and Norwich Record Office, DN/ACT/6, Bk 7B, 303.

Oxford University Archives, Chancellor's Court Deposition Book, Bodleian Library (1606-D), Hyp/b/4.

Oxford University Archives, Chancellor's Court Papers, Bodleian, Hyp/A/29 (1605).

Oxford University Archives, Chancellor's Court Papers, Bodleian, Hyp/A/29 (1606).

Oxford University Archives, Chancellor's Court Papers, Bodleian, Hyp/A/34 (1623).

Oxon Record Office, Quarter Sessions Records, Q3/1687 Mi/14.

Public Record Office, ASSI 35/17/3.

Public Record Office, ASSI 35/39/7.

Public Record Office, ASSI 30/26/104.

Public Record Office, ASSI 35/1/5.

Public Record Office, ASSI 35/11/1.

Public Record Office, ASSI 35/24/3.

Public Record Office, ASSI 35/31/7.

Public Record Office, ASSI 35/34/4.

Public Record Office, ASSI 45/4/1/131.

Public Record Office, ASSI 45/3/29.

Public Record Office Gaol Files. Brecon, 968/13.

Public Record Office, Req 1/19, 618–19.

Public Record Office, Req 2/157/478.

Public Record Office, Req 1/19, 126–8.

Public Record Office, Req 1/17.

Public Record Office, Req 1/18.

Public Record Office, STAC 5, S6/36.

Public Record Office, STAC 8/31/16.

Public Record Office, STAC 8/4/10.

Public Record Office, STAC 8/8/2.

Swinburne, Henry (n.d.), *Of the signification of diverse woordes importing Matrymonye, and whye yt is rather names matrimonie than Patrymony.* Durham University Library, Mickleton and Spearman MS. 4, 115–24.

PRINTED SOURCES

Abraham, Fraunce, *Lawier's Logike, exemplifying the praecepts of Logike by the practise of the common Lawe* (London: T. Gubbin and T. Newman, 1588).

Acts of the Privy Council of England, ed. J. R. Dasent (London: HMSO, 1890–7).

Ad C. Herennium de ratione dicendi, ed. and trans. Harry Caplan (London: Heinemann, 1954).

Adams, Thomas, *The Black Devill or the Apostate; together with The wolfe worrying the lambes; And the spirituall nauigator, bound for the Holy Land: In three sermons* (London: William Jaggard, 1615).

The Works of Tho: Adams. Being the Svmme of his Sermons, Meditations, and other Divine and Morall Discovrses (London: John Grismand, 1630).

Ady, Thomas, *A Candle in the Dark* (London: Tho. Newberry, 1656).

Alanus ab Insulis (Alan of Lille), *De fide catholica*, in *Opera Omnia, Patrologiae Cursus Completus*, ed. J. P. Migne (Paris: J. P. Migne, 1844–64).

The araignment & burning of Margaret Ferne-seede, for the murther of her late husband Anthony Ferne-seede (London: Henry Gaffon, 1608).

Arber, Edward, *A Transcript of the Registers of the Company of Stationers of London, 1554–1640*, 5 vols. (London: privately printed, 1875–94).

Aristotle, *The Rhetoric and Poetics of Aristotle*, trans. W. Rhys Roberts and Ingram Bywater, ed. Friedrich Solmsen (New York: Modern Library, 1954).

  Economics, in J. A. Smith and W. D. Ross, eds., *The Works of Aristotle* (Oxford: Clarendon Press, 1921).

Ascham, Roger, *The Scholemaster*, ed. R. J. Schoeck (Don Mills, Ont: Dent, 1966).

Auden, W. H. *Selected Poems*, ed. Edward Mendelsohn (London: Faber, 1985; first pub. 1979).

Augustine, St, *The City of God*, trans. John Healy (London: J. M. Dent, 1931).

  The Confessions of the Incomparable Doctour S. Augustine, trans. Sir Toby Matthew (London: English College of St Omers, 1620).

  The Soliloquies of St. Augustine, trans. Rose Elizabeth Cleveland (London: Williams & Norgate, 1910), 72–86.

  St. Augustine Against the Academics, trans. John J. O'Meara (London: Longmans, Green & Co., 1950).

Bacon, Francis, *The Works of Francis Bacon*, ed. James Spedding, Robert Leslie Ellis and Douglas Denon Heath, 14 vols. (London: Longmans, 1857–74).

Barnes, Barnaby, *The Devil's Charter* (1607), ed. Jim C. Pogue (New York: Garland, 1980).

Barry, Lording, *Ram Alley*, ed. Peter Corbin and Douglas Sedge (Nottingham: Nottingham Drama Texts, 1981).

Barthes, Roland, *A Lover's Discourse: Fragments*, trans. Richard Howard (London: Cape, 1978).

  The Pleasure of the Text, trans. Richard Miller (Oxford: Blackwell, 1990).

Bateman, Stephen, *A Christall Glasse of Christian Reformation* (London: John Day, 1569).

Beard, Thomas, *The Theatre of Gods judgements: wherein is represented the admirable justice of God against all notorious sinners* (London: Michael Sparke, 1631; 3rd edn; first pub. 1597; 2nd edn 1612).

Beaumont, Francis and Fletcher, John, *The Dramatic Works in the Beaumont and Fletcher Canon*, ed. Fredson Bowers, 8 vols. (Cambridge: Cambridge University Press, 1996).

Beza, Theodore, *Job expounded by Theodore Beza, partly in the manner of a Commentary, partly in manner of a Paraphrase* (Cambridge: J. Legatt, 1589?).

The Book of Common Prayer 1559: The Elizabethan Prayer Book, ed. John E. Booty (Charlottesville, Virginia: Virginia University Press, 1976).

Boys, J., *The Case of Witchcraft at Coggeshall, Essex, in the Year 1699* (London: A. Russell Smith, 1901; first pub. 1699).

Bradford, John, *Godly Meditations vpon the Lordes Prayer, the beleefe, and ten commaundements . . . Whereunto is annexed a defence of the doctrine of gods eternall election and predestination* (London: R. Hall, 1562).

    Two notable Sermons. Made by I. Bradford, the one of repentaunce, and the other of the Lord's Supper (London: John Charlewood and John Wight, 1581).

Braithwait, Richard, *Some Rules and Orders for the Government of the House of an Earl*, Miscellanea Antiqua Anglicana (London: n.p., 1821).

Braithwaite, Richard, *The English Gentleman* (1630).

Brennan, Elizabeth M., John Webster, *The White Devil* (London: Benn, 1966).

The Brideling, Sadling and Ryding, of a rich Churle in Hampshire, by the subtill practise of one Iudeth Philips, a professed cunning woman, or Fortune teller (London: W. Barley, 1595).

Brome, Richard, *The Damoiselle, or, The new ordinary: a comedy* (London: Printed by Richard Marriot; Thomas Dring, 1653).

Browne, Thomas, *Pseudodoxia Epidemica*, ed. Robin Robbins, 2 vols. (Oxford: Clarendon Press, 1981).

Bullen, A. H., *An English Garner: Some Shorter Elizabethan Poems* (Westminster: Archibald Constable and Co. Ltd., 1903).

Bullough, G., ed., *Narrative and Dramatic Sources of Shakespeare*, 8 vols. (London: Routledge & Kegan Paul, 1957–75).

Burn, John S., ed., *The Star Chamber: Notices of the Court and its Proceedings* (London: J. T. Smith, 1870).

Burton, Robert, *The Anatomy of Melancholy*, Everyman's Library, 3 vols. (London: Everyman, 1949).

Butler, Samuel, *Hudibras*, ed. J. Wilders (Oxford: Clarendon Press, 1967).

Calendar of State Papers Domestic, Elizabeth I, 1591–4.

Calendar of State Papers Domestic, James I, 1634–5.

Calvin, Jean (John), *An Admonition against Astrology Iudiciall and other curiosities, that raigne now in the world*, trans. Goddred Gilby (London: publisher unknown, c.1560).

    Defence of the Secret Providence of God (1558), in Henry Cole, trans., *Calvin's Calvinism*, second part (London: Wertheim and Macintosh, 1856).

    Institutes of the Christian Religion, ed. John T. McNeill, 2 vols. (London: S.C.M. Press, 1961).

    John Caluin his Treatise concerning offences, trans. Arthur Golding (London: Seres, 1567).

Carwell, Thomas, *Labyrinthvs Cantvariensis, or Doctor Lawd's Labyrinth. Beeing an Answer to the late Archbishop of Canterbvries Relation of a Conference between himselfe and Mr. Fisher, etc. wherein The true grounds of the roman Catholique Religion are asserted, the principal Controuersies betwixt Catholiques and protestants throughly examined, and the Bishops MEANDRICK windings throughout his whole worke layd open to the publique* view (Paris: John Billaine, 1658).

Chamber, John, *A treatise against judicial astrologie* (London: John Harrison, 1601).

Chapman, George, *The Plays of George Chapman: The Comedies*, ed. Allan Holaday (Urbana: University of Illinois Press, 1970).

Chassanion, Jean, *Histoires mémorables des grans et merveilleux jugemens et punitions de Dieu avenues au monde* (Paris: Jean le Preux, 1586).

Chettle, Henry and Day, John, *The Blind Beggar of Bednal Green* (1659), in W. Bang, ed., *Materialen zur Kunde des älteren Englischen Dramas*, 44 vols., Vol. I (Louvain: Uystpruyst, 1902).

Churchyard, Thomas, *The Honour of the Lawe* (London: William Holme, 1596).

Cicero, *De Oratore*, ed. and trans. E. W. Sutton and H. Rackham, 2 vols. (London: Heinemann, 1942).

Cockburn, J. S., ed., *A Calendar of Assize Records: Home Circuit Indictments. Introduction* (Cambridge: Cambridge University Press, 1985; first pub. 1972).

Coke, Sir Edward, *Fourth Part of the Institutes* (London: W. Lee and D. Pakeman, 1644).

The Twelfth Part of the Reports of Sir Edward Coke, 5th edn, Vol. VII (London: J. Rivington & Sons, 1777).

Consett, Henry, *The Practice of the Spiritual or Ecclesiastical Courts* (London: T. Bassett, 1685).

Cowell, John, *The Interpreter* (Menston: Scolar Press, 1972; first pub. 1607).

Crompton, R., *L'Authoritie et jurisdiction des courts* (London: Caroli Yetsweirti, 1594).

Crosse, Henry, *Vertues Commonwealth* (London: John Newbery, 1603).

Davies, John, *Elegies and Epigrams*, together with Christopher Marlowe, *Ovid's Elegies*, introd. A. J. Smith (Menston: Scolar Press, 1973).

Day, Angel, *English Secretorie, or, Plaine and direct method, for the enditing of all manner of epistles or letters* (London: R. Jones, 1592, 2nd edn; first pub. 1586).

Day, John, *Law-Tricks* (Oxford: Malone Society Reprints, 1950; first pub. 1608).

A detection of damnable driftes practized by three witches arraigned at Chelmsforde in Essex, at the late Assises there holden, which were executed in Aprill London, 1579 (London: Edward White, 1579).

The Devil's Conquest, or a wish obtained: shewing how one lately of Barnsby-street wisht the devil to fetch her . . . and her body was found as black as pitch all over (London: S. Tyus, 1655).

A Discourse Touching the Reformation of the Lawes of England (1542?), in Sidney Anglo, 'An Early Tudor Programme for Plays and Other Demonstrations against the Pope', *Journal of the Warburg and Courtauld Institute*, 20 (1957), 176–9.

Donne, John, *Poetical Works*, ed. Herbert J. C. Grierson (Oxford: Oxford University Press, 1971).

Du Moulin, P., *Elementa Logica* (Leiden: Lugd. Bat, 1598).

Dugdale, William, *Origines Juridicales* (London: F. and T. Warren for the author, 1666).

A True discourse of the practises of Elizabeth Caldwell, Ma: Ieffrey Bownd, Isabell Hall widdow, and George Ferneley, on the person of T. Caldwell, in the

Countie of Chester, to have murdered and poysoned him, with divers others . . . Written by one then present as witnes, theire owne Country-man, Gilbert Dugdale (London: J. Busbie, 1604).

Earle, John, *Microscosmographie* (London: Edward Blount, 1628).

Elyot, Sir Thomas, *The Boke named the Gouernour*, ed. H. H. Croft (London: Kegan Paul, 1883; first pub. 1531).

Erasmus, Desiderius, *The Colloquies of Erasmus*, trans. Craig R. Thompson (Chicago: Chicago University Press, 1965).

On Copia of Words and Ideas, trans. D. B. King and H. D. Rix (Cambridge, Milwaukee: Marquette University Press, 1963).

The Correspondence of Erasmus, trans. R. A. B. Mynors (Toronto: Toronto University Press, 1987).

A Fearefull Example, Shewed vpon a periured person Who . . . being condemned for periurie, in the Honorable Court of Starre Chamber: did there despearately stabbe himselfe (London: T. Nelson, 1591).

Fenner, Dudley, *Certain Learned and Godly Treatises* (Edinburgh: Robert Waldegraue, 1592).

Florio, John, *A Letter written lately from Rome, by an Italian Gentleman, to a freende of his in Lyons in Fraunce* (London: John Charlewood, 1585).

Ford, John, *The Dramatic Works of John Ford*, ed. W. Gifford, 2 vols. (London: John Murray, 1827).

'Tis Pity She's a Whore and Other Plays, ed. Michael Cordner (Oxford: Oxford University Press, 1995).

Fraunce, Abraham, *The Arcadian Rhetorike*, ed. Ethel Seaton (Oxford: Blackwell, 1950).

Lawiers Logike, exemplifying the praecepts of Logike by the practise of the common Lawe (London: T. Gubbin and T. Newman, 1588).

Freud, Sigmund, *On Sexuality*, The Penguin Freud Library, trans. J. Strachey, 24 vols., Vol. VII (Harmondsworth: Penguin, 1953).

Fulbeck, William, *A Parallele or Conference of the Civil Law, the Canon Law and the Common Law of this Realme of England*, 1602).

Fulke, William, *Anti prognosticon: an invective against the vayne and unprofitable predictions of the astrologians as Nostradame. &c.* (London: Henry Sutton, 1560).

Furnivall, Frederick J., ed., *Child-Marriages, Divorces, and Ratifications, &c. in the Diocese of Chester* (London: Kegan Paul, 1897).

Ghosh, Kantik, *The Wycliffite heresy: authority and the interpretation of texts* (Cambridge: Cambridge University Press, 2002).

Gilby, Anthony, *A Pleasaunte dialogue, Betweene a Souldier of Barwicke, and an English Chaplaine* (Middelburg: R. Schilders, 1581).

Golding, Arthur, *A Briefe Discourse* (1573), reprinted as Appendix D in *A Warning for Fair Women*, ed. Charles Dale Cannon (The Hague: Mouton, 1975).

Gomme, A. H., ed., *Jacobean Tragedies* (Oxford: Oxford University Press, 1969).

Goodcole, Henry, *The Adulteresses Funerall day: In flaming, scorching and consuming fire* (London: N. and I. Okes, 1635).

Heavens Speedie hue and cry sent after lust and murther (London: N. and I. Okes, 1635).

The wonderfull discouerie of Elizabeth Sawyer a Witch, late of Edmonton, [her?] conuiction and condemnation and Death . . . Written by Henry Goodcole. Minister of the Word of God, and her continuall Visiter in the Gaole of Newgate (London: William Butler, 1621).

Gosson, Stephen, *Plays Confuted in Five Actions* (London: Thomas Gosson, 1582).

The Schoole of Abuse: containing a pleasant invective against poets, pipers, players, jesters (London: T. Woodcocke, 1579).

Greene, John, *A Refutation of the Apology for Actors* (London: W. White, 1615).

Greene, Robert, *A Disputation Betweene a Hee Conny-Catcher and a Shee Conny Catcher* (1592), facsimile edn (Edinburgh: Edinburgh University Press, 1966).

The Scottish History of James the Fourth, ed. J. A. Lavin (London: Earnest Benn Limited, 1967).

Greene, Thomas, *The History of Friar Bacon and Friar Bungay*, in *English Drama 1580–1642*, ed. C. F. Tucker Brooke and Nathaniel Burton Paradise (Boston: Heath, 1933).

Guarini, Giambattista, *A Compendium of Tragicomic Poetry*, in Allan Gilbert, *Literary Criticism: Plato to Dryden* (Detroit: Wayne State University Press, 1962), 504–33.

Il Verato ovvero difesa di quanto ha scritto M. Giason Denores di quanto ha egli ditto in un suo discorso delle tragicomedie, e delli pastorali (Ferrara, 1588), in *Delle Opere del cavalier Battista Guarini* (Turin: UTET, 1971).

Harington, John, *Orlando Furioso in English Heroical Verse* (London: Richard Field, 1591).

Harleian Miscellany: or, a collection of scarce, curious, and entertaining pamphlets and tracts, as well in manuscript as in print, found in the late Earl of Oxford's Library, 8 vols. (London: T. Osbourne, 1744–53).

Harrison, William, *The Description of England by William Harrison*, ed. Georges Edelen (Ithaca: Cornell University Press, 1968).

Hawarde, John, *Les Reportes del Cases in Camera Stellata 1593 to 1609*, ed. William Baildon (privately printed, 1894).

Heliodorus, *An Aethiopian History*, trans. Thomas Underdowne, ed. W. E. Henley (London: D. Nutt, 1895).

Henslowe, Philip, *Henslowe's Diary*, ed. W. W. Greg, 2 vols. (London: A. H. Bullen, 1904–8).

Heywood, Thomas, *An Apology for Actors*, reprinted with Stephen Gosson, *The School of Abuse* (London: The Shakespeare Society, 1841).

A Curtaine Lecture (London: J. Aston, 1637).

The Generall History of Women, Containing the Lives of the most Holy and Prophane, the most Famous and Infamous in all ages, exactly described not only from Poeticall Fictions, but from the most Ancient, Modern and Admired Historians to our Times (London: WH, 1657).

A Woman Killed With Kindness, ed. R. W. van Fossen (Manchester: Manchester University Press, 1961).

A Woman Killed With Kindness, ed. Brian Scobie (London: Black, 1991, 2nd edn; first pub. 1985).

Holinshed, Raphael, *Chronicles of England, Scotland, and Ireland*, 2nd edn (London: T. Woodcocke, 1587).

Homer, *The Odyssey*, with an English translation by A. T. Murray, 2 vols. (Cambridge, MA: Harvard University Press; London: Heinemann, 1919).

Hondorff, D. Andreas, *Theatrum Historicum Theatrum historicum illustrium exemplorum ad honeste, pie, beateque viuendum mortale genus informantium*; trans. Philip Loncier, 1st pub. 1575 (Frankfurt: Ioannis Bringer, 1616).

Hooker, Richard, *Of the Laws of Ecclesiastical Polity*, ed. P. G. Stanwood (Cambridge, MA: Harvard University Press, 1981).

Hookes, Nicholas, *Amanda: A Sacrifice To an Unknown Goddess* (London: Humphrey Tuckey, 1653).

Howard, Henry, *A Defensative against the poyson of supposed prophesies* (London: I. Charlewood, 1583).

Hypericus, Andreas Gerardus, *Two common places taken out of Andreas Hypericus . . . whereof . . . he sheweth the force that the sonne, the moone and starres have over men*, trans. R.Y. (London: J. Wolfe, 1581).

Jacobs, Joseph, ed., *The Palace of Pleasure: Elizabethan Versions of Italian and French Novels From Boccaccio, Bandello, Cinthio, Straparola, Queen Margaret of Navarre, And Others, Done Into English by William Painter*, 3 vols. (New York: Dover, 1966).

James I, *Daemonologie* (London: Robert Waldegrave, 1603).

Johannes ab Indagine (John De Hayne), *Brief Introductions, both Natural, Pleasant, and Delectable unto the Arte of Ciromancy, or Manuel Divinations, and Physiognomy: with Circumstances upon the Faces of the Signs . . . Whereunto is also Annexed aswell the Artificiall, as Natural Astrologie, with the Nature of the Planets*, trans. Fabian Wither (London: Richard Iugge, 1558).

Jonson, Ben, *Epicœne or The Silent Woman*, ed. R. V. Holdsworth (London: New Mermaids, 1993; first pub. 1979).

The New Inn, ed. Michael Hattaway, The Revels Plays (Manchester: Manchester University Press, 1984).

Staple of News (1626), ed. Devra Rowland Kifer, Regents Renaissance Drama (London: Edward Arnold, 1976).

Volpone or the Fox, ed. David Cook (London: Methuen, 1984; first pub. 1962).

Justinian I, *Corpus Juris Civilis*, ed. Paul Kruger and Theodor Mommsen (Frankfurt am Main: Weidman, 1968–70, 2nd edn; first pub. 1954).

The Digest of Justinian, ed. and trans. Alan Watson, 2 vols. (Philadelphia: University of Pennsylvania Press, 1985).

Keats, John, 'What the Thrush said', in *The Poems* (London: Everyman, 1992), 245.

Kingsmill, Andrew, *A Viewe of Mans Estate* (London: L. Harison and G. Bishop, 1576).

Kyd, Thomas, *The Spanish Tragedy*, ed. J. R. Mulryne (London: New Mermaids, 1989).

Larkin, J. and Hughes, P., eds, *Stuart Royal Proclamations*, 2 vols. (Oxford: Oxford University Press, 1973–83), Vol. I.

Leadam, I. S., ed., *Select Cases in the Court of Requests*, Vol. XII (London: Selden Society, 1898).

London Topographical Society Publication, *The A to Z of Elizabethan London*, compiled by A. Prockter and R. Taylor, no. 122 (London: London Topographical Society, 1979).

The A to Z of Restoration London (the City of London, 1676), introductory notes by Ralph Hyde; index compiled by John Fisher and Roger Cline, no. 145 (London: London Topographical Society, 1992).

Loues Garland or, Posies for Rings, Hand-Kerchers and Gloues (London: J. Spencer, 1624).

MacNeice, Louis, *Collected Poems*, ed. E. R. Dodds (London: Faber, 1979).

Manningham, John, *The Diary of John Manningham of the Middle Temple (1602–3)*, ed. Robert Parker Sorlin (Hanover, NH: University Press of New England, 1976).

Map, Walter, *De Nugis Curialium (Courtiers' Trifles)*, ed. M. R. James, in *Anecdota Oxoniensia* (Oxford: Clarendon Press, 1914).

Massinger, Philip, *The Plays and Poems of Philip Massinger*, ed. Philip Edwards and Colin Gibson, 5 vols., Vol. III (Oxford: Clarendon Press, 1976).

Middleton, Thomas, *Michaelmas Term*, ed. R. Levin (Lincoln: University of Nebraska Press, 1966).

Middleton, Thomas, and Rowley, William, *The Changeling*, ed. N. C. Bawcutt (Manchester: Manchester University Press, 1998).

Milton, John, *The Doctrine and Discipline of Divorce* (1643), in *Complete Prose Works of John Milton*, ed. Ernest Sirluck, Vol. II (New Haven: Yale University Press, 1959), 222–356.

The Poems of John Milton, ed. John Carey and Alastair Fowler (London: Longman, 1968).

Montaigne, Michel de, *Essays*, trans. John Florio, 3 vols. (London: Everyman, 1946).

The Essays of Michel de Montaigne, trans. and ed. M. A. Screech (London: Allen Lane, 1991).

More, Sir Thomas, *A Dialogue concerning Heresies*, ed. Thomas M. C. Lawler, Germain Marc'hadour and Richard C. Marius (New Haven/London: Yale University Press, 1981).

Moryson, Fynes, *Shakespeare's Europe: Unpublished Chapters of Fynes Moryson's Itinerary: Being a Survey of the Condition of Europe at the End of the 16th Century*, introd. Charles Hughes (London: Sherratt and Hughes, 1903).

The most horrible and tragicall murther of John Lord Borough (London: R. Robinson, 1591).

Munday, Anthony, *A Second and Third Blast of Retrait from Plaies and Theatres* (London: H. Denham, 1580).

A View of Sundry examples. Reporting many straunge murthers, sundry persons perjured, signes and tokens of Gods anger towards us (London: William Wright, 1580).

Nashe, Thomas, *The Unfortunate Traveller* in R. B. McKerrow, ed., *The Works of Thomas Nashe*, 5 vols. (Oxford: Blackwell, 1958).

Northbrooke, John, *A Treatise wherein Dicing, Daunving, Vaine Playes or Enterludes . . . are reproued* (London: George Bishop, 1577).

Ogilby, John and Morgan, William, *A large and accurate map of the City of London, 1676* (London: London and Middlesex Archaeological Society, 1895).

Ormerod, Oliver, *The Pictvre of a papist, or a Relation of the damnable heresies, testable qualities, and diabolicall practises of sundry heretickes in former ages* (London: N. Fosbrooke, 1606).

Osborne, Francis, *Traditionall Memoryes on the reign of King James* (London: Thomas Robinson, 1658).

Overbury, Sir Thomas, 'A Fantastique Innes of Court Man', in W. J. Paylor, ed., *The Overburian Characters* (Oxford: Blackwell, 1936).

Parey, Ambrose, *The Works of that famous Chirurgeon, Ambrose Parey, trans. by Thomas Johnson* (London: Thomas Cotes and R. Young, 1634).

Parthenia (London: G. Lowe, 1612).

Parthenia in-Violata (London: J. Pyper, 1624).

Peacham, Henry, *The Garden of Eloquence* (Menston: Scolar Press, 1971).

Pettie, George, *Petite Pallace of Pettie his Pleasure* (London: R. Watkins, 1576).

Plat, Sir Hugh, *Delightes for Ladies* (London: Humfrey Lownes, 1609).

Potts, Thomas, *A Compendious Law Dictionary* (London: T. Ostell, 1803).

A Wonderfvll Discoverie of Witches in the Covntie of Lancaster (London: J. Barnes, 1613).

Prynne, William, *Histriomastix: The Players Scourge, or Actors Tragedie* (London: M. Sparke, 1633).

Pulton, Ferdinand, *De Pace Regis et Regni, viz. A Treatise declaring which be the greatest and generall offences of the Realme* (London: Companie of Stationers, 1610).

Puttenham, George, *The Arte of English Poesie*, ed. Gladys Willcock and Alice Walker (Cambridge: Cambridge University Press, 1970).

Quintilian, *Institutio Oratoria*, ed. and trans. H. E. Butler, 4 vols. (London: Heinemann, 1920–2).

Instutio Oratoria, ed. and trans. Donald A. Russell (Cambridge, MA and London: Harvard University Press, 2001).

Raine, James, ed., *Depositions and Other Ecclesiastical Proceedings from the Courts of Durham*, Vol. XXI (London: Surtees Society, 1845).

Reynolds, John, *The Triumphs of God's Revenge against the Crying and Execrable Sinne of (Willfull and Premeditated) Murther: or His Miraculous discoveries and severe punishments thereof: In thirty severall Tragicall Histories (digested in six Bookes)... Histories, which contain great variety of memorable accidents, Amorous, Morall and Divine, very necessary to refraine, and deterre us from this bloody Sinne, which, in these our dayes, makes so ample, and so lamentable progression* (London: W. Lee, 1635, 4th edn; first pub. 1621).

Rowley, William, Dekker, Thomas and Ford, John &c., *The Witch of Edmonton*, in *Three Jacobean Witchcraft Plays*, ed. Peter Corbin and Douglas Sedge (Manchester: Manchester University Press, 1986).

Ruggles, George, *Ignoramus* (1614), in *Ignoramus: a comedy... with a supplement which... was hitherto wanting/written in Latine by R. Ruggles; and translated into English by R. Codrington* (London: W. Gilbertson, 1662).

Salmon, M., ed., *A New Abridgement and Critical Review of the State Trials and Impeachment for High-Treason; From the Reign of King Richard II* (London: J. & J. Hazard, 1738).

Sampson, W., *The Vow-Breaker. Or the Faire Maide of Clifton*, reprinted in Marie-Hélène Davies, *Reflections of Renaissance England: Life, Thought and Religion Mirrored in Illustrated Pamphlets 1535–1640* (Pennsylvania: Pickwick Publications, 1986).

Sarum Missal, trans. A. H. Pearson (London: Church Printing Company, 1884).

Saxey, Samuel, *A Straunge and Wonderfull Example of the Iudgement of almighty God, shewed vpon two adulterous persons in London, in the parish of S. Brydes, in Fleetestreete, this thirde of Februarie. 1583* (London: H. Jackson, 1583).

Scot, Reginald, *The Discoverie of Witchcraft* (London: W. Brome, 1584).

Shakespeare, William, *The First Folio of Shakespeare: The Norton Facsimile*, prep. Charlton Hinman (New York: W. W. Norton, 1968).

The Riverside Shakespeare, ed. G. Blakemore Evans (Boston: Houghton Mifflin, 1974).

Smith, Thomas, *The Common-Wealth of England, and Manner of Government Thereof* (London: G. Seton, 1601).

St. German, *St. German's Doctor and Student*, ed. T. F. T. Plucknett and J. L. Barton, Vol. 91 (London: Selden Society, 1974).

Stephanus de Federicis, *De Interpretatione Iuris Commentarii IIII iam recens studiosis restituti et a mendis, quantum fieri potuit, repurgati* (Frankfurt, 1535).

Stephen, Henry John, *A Treatise on the Principles of Pleading in Civil Actions* (London: Joseph Butterworth, 1824).

Stow, John, *A Survey of London*, ed. C. L. Kingsford, 2 vols. (Oxford: Clarendon Press, 1908).

Strange Newes of a prodigious Monster, borne in the Towneship of Allington in the Parish of Standish in the countie of Lancaster, the 17 day of Aprill last, 1613 (London: S.M, 1613).

Stubbes, Philip, (a), *Anatomy of the Abuses: Containing A Discouerie, or brief Summarie of such Notable Vices and Corruptions, as now raigne in many*

Christian Countreys of the World: but (especially) in the Countrey of Aligna: Together, with most fearfull Examples of Gods Iudgementes, executed vpon the wicked for the same, as well in ALIGNA of late, as in other places, elsewhere . . . 1584, ed. F. J. Furnivall (London: New Shakespeare Society, 1876–9).

(b) *Anatomy of the Abuses in England in Shakespeare's Youth*, ed. F. J. Furnivall (London: New Shakespeare Society, 1876–9).

Sundrye strange and inhumaine murthers (London: Thomas Scarlet, 1591).

Swinburne, Henry, *A Briefe Treatise of Testaments and Last Willes* (London: John Windet, 1590).

A Treatise of Spousals, or Matrimonial Contracts, ed. Randolph Trumbach (London: Garland, 1985).

Taylor, Jeremy, *The Real Presence and Spiritual of Christ in the Blessed Sacrament Proved Against the Doctrine of Transubstantiation* (1654), in Reginald Heber and Charles Page Eden, eds., *The Whole Works of the Right Reverend Jeremy Taylor* (London, 1847–54), 10 vols., Vol. VI (1850).

T.E., *The Lawes Resolutions of Women's Rights: Or, the Lawes Provision for Women* (London: John More, 1632).

T.M., *Blood for Blood: or Murthers Revenged. Briefly, yet Lively set forth in Thirty Tragical Histories . . . Faithfully digested for the benefit of posterity* (Oxford: John Reynolds, 1661).

Turamini, Alessandro, *De Exaequatione Legatorum et Fidei Commissorum Disputatio Paradoxica* (Naples: Stelliolae, 1593).

T.W., *The Optick Glass of Humors. OR The Touchstone of a golden temperature, or the Philosophers stone to make a golden temper* (London: Martin Clerke, 1607).

Thomas, Thomas, *Dictionarium Linguae et Anglicanae* (London: Richard Boyle, 1587).

The Tragedy of Master Arden of Faversham, ed. M. L. Wine (London: Methuen, 1973).

The Trial of Witches at the Assizes held at Bury St. Edmunds in the County of Suffolk . . . 1664 (London: William Shrewsbery, 1682).

A true and exact relation of the severall informations, examinations and confessions of the late witches arraigned and executed in the county of Essex (London: M.S., 1645).

A True Report of the horrible murther, which was committed in the house of Sir Jerome Bowes, Knight (London: Humphrey Lownes, 1607).

Two Most Unnaturall and Bloodie Murthers (London: V. Simmes, 1605).

Vaughan, William, *The Spirit of Detraction* (London: W. Stansby and T. Snodham, 1611).

Vives, Juan Luis, *A Very Fruteful and Pleasant Boke Callyd the Instruction of a Christen Woman*, trans. Richarde Hyrde (London: Thomas Bertheleti, 1541).

A Warning for Fair Women, ed. Charles Dale Cannon (The Hague: Mouton, 1975).

Webster, John, *The Devil's Law Case*, ed. Elizabeth M. Brennan (London: New Mermaids, 1975).

The Duchess of Malfi, ed. Elizabeth M. Brennan (London: New Mermaids, 1993, revised edn; first pub. 1983).

The Selected Plays of John Webster, ed. J. Dollimore and A. Sinfield (Cambridge: Cambridge University Press, 1983).

The White Devil, ed. John Russell Brown (Manchester: Manchester University Press, 1996).

Webster, John and Overbury, Thomas, *Characters*, in F. L. Lucas, ed., *The Complete Works of John Webster*, 4 vols., Vol. IV (New York: Gordian, 1927).

Weldon, Anthony, *Court and Character of King James* (London: R.I., 1650).

West, William, *Symbolaeography Which may be termed the Art, Description or Image of Instruments, Extraiudicial, as Couenant, Contracts, Obligations, Feffements, Graunts. Wills, &c Or, The paterne of Praesidents. Or the Notarie of the Scrivener* (London: Charles Yetsweirt, 1594; 3rd edn; first pub. 1590).

Whitford, Richard, *A Werke for Householders* (London: Robert Redman, 1537).

Whitney, Isabella, *A Sweet Nosegay, or pleasant Posye containing a hundred and ten Phylosophicall flowers* (London: R. Redman, 1573).

Wilkins, George, *The Miseries of Enforced Marriage* (Oxford: Malone Society Reprints, 1963/4).

Wilson, Thomas, *The Arte of Rhetoricke* (1553), 'The English Experience', no. 206 (New York: Da Capo, 1969).

Wordsworth, Dorothy and William (1967), *Letters of William and Dorothy Wordsworth: The Early Years, 1787–1805*, ed. Ernest de Selincourt, rev. C. L. Shaver (Oxford: Clarendon Press, 1967, 2nd edn; first pub. 1937).

Wright, Thomas, *The Passions of the Minde in Generall* (1604), ed. Thomas O. Sloan (Urbana/London: University of Illinois Press, 1971).

Wright, Thomas, ed., *Queen Elizabeth and her Times: A Series of Original Letters*, 2 vols., Vol. II (London: Henry Colburn, 1838).

Yarrington, Robert, *Two Lamentable Tragedies* (1601), ed. John S. Farmer (London: Tudor Facsimile Texts).

Yeats, W. B., *Selected Poetry*, ed. Timothy Webb (London: Penguin, 1991).

A Yorkshire Tragedy, ed. A. C. Cawley and Barry Gaines (Manchester: Manchester University Press, 1986).

Xenophon, *Memorabilia and Oeconomicus*, trans. E. C. Marchant (London: Heinemann, 1923).

Zepheria (London: Joan Orwin, 1594).

SECONDARY SOURCES

Abbott, L. W., *Law Reporting in England, 1484–1585* (London: Athlone, 1973).

Adams, H. H., *English Domestic or Homiletic Tragedy* (New York: Columbia University Press, 1943).

Aitken, George A., 'John Webster and Thomas Adams', *Academy*, 35 (1889), 133–4.

Altman, Joel, *The Tudor Play of Mind: Rhetorical Inquiry and the Development of Elizabethan Drama* (Berkeley: University of California Press, 1978).

Amussen, Susan Dwyer, *Ordered Society: Gender and Class in Early Modern England* (Oxford: Blackwell, 1988).

Anglo, Sydney, ed., *Chivalry in the Renaissance* (Woodbridge: Boydell, 1990).

Archer, P., *The Queen's Courts* (Harmondsworth: Penguin, 1956).

Ariès, Philippe and Duby, Georges, eds., *A History of Private Life*, 5 vols., Vol. III, *Passions of the Renaissance* (London: Harvard University Press, 1987–91).

Arnold, Morris S., Green, Thomas A., Scully, Sally A. and White, Stephen D., eds., *On the Laws and Customs of England: Essays in Honour of Samuel E. Thorne* (Chapel Hill: University of North Carolina Press, 1981).

Aston, Margaret, *England's Iconoclasts*, Vol. I, *Laws Against Images* (Oxford: Oxford University Press, 1988).

Atkinson, David, 'An Approach to the Main Plot of Thomas Heywood's *A Woman Killed With Kindness*', *English Studies*, 70 (1989), 15–26.

Austin, J. L., *How to Do Things With Words* (Oxford: Oxford University Press, 1992, first pub. 1962).

Avis, P. D. L., 'Moses and the Magistrate: A Study in the Rise of Protestant Legalism', *Journal of Ecclesiastical History*, 26 (1975), 149–72.

Axton, Marie, *The Queen's Two Bodies* (London: Royal Historical Society, 1977).

Baker, J. H., 'Editing the Sources of English Legal History', in *The Common Law Tradition* (London: Hambledon, 2000), 207–22.

'Edward Heath at the Inner Temple, 1629–31', *Inner Temple Yearbook* (1997–8), 75–6.

English Legal Manuscripts, 2 vols. (Zug: Inter Documentation Company, 1975, 1978).

'A History of English Judges' Robes', *Costume*, 12 (1978), 27–39.

An Introduction to English Legal History (London: Butterworth, 1990, 3rd edn; first pub. 1971).

Legal Profession and the Common Law (London: Hambledon, 1986).

'Origins of the "Doctrine" of Consideration, 1535–1585', in *The Legal Profession and the Common Law* (London: Hambledon, 1986).

The Oxford History of the Laws of England, Vol. VI, *1483–1558* (Oxford: Oxford University Press, 2003).

Barish, Jonas, *The Anti-Theatrical Prejudice* (Berkeley: University of California Press, 1981).

Barnes, T. G., 'Star Chamber Litigants and their Counsel, 1596–1641', in J. H. Baker, ed., *Legal Records and the Historian* (London: Royal Historical Society, 1978), 7–40.

Bartlett, Robert, *Trial by Fire and Water: The Medieval Judicial Ordeal* (Oxford: Clarendon Press, 1986).

Barton, Anne, *Ben Jonson, Dramatist* (Cambridge: Cambridge University Press, 1986; first pub. 1984).

Essays, Mainly Shakespearean (Cambridge: Cambridge University Press, 1994).
'"Wrying but a little": Marriage, Law and Sexuality in the Plays of Shakespeare', in *Essays, Mainly Shakespearean* (Cambridge: Cambridge University Press, 1994).
Beckerman, Bernard, *Shakespeare at the Globe* (New York: Macmillan, 1962).
Belsey, Catherine, *Shakespeare and the Loss of Eden: The Construction of Family Values in Early Modern Culture* (Basingstoke: Macmillan, 1999).
Blayney, Peter, *The Bookshops in Paul's Cross Churchyard* (London: Bibliographical Society, 1990).
Bloch, Howard, *Medieval French Literature and Law* (Berkeley: University of California Press, 1977).
Boklund, Gunnar, *The Sources of 'The White Devil'* (Uppsala: Lundquist, 1957).
Bond, Ronald B., '"Dark Deeds Darkly Answered": Thomas Becon's Homily against Whoredom and Adultery, Its Context, and Its Affiliations with Three Shakespearean Plays', *Sixteenth Century Journal*, 16 (1985), 191–205.
Bossy, John, 'The Social History of Confession', *Transactions of the Royal Historical Society*, 5th series, 25 (1975), 21–38.
Bradbrook, M. C., *John Webster Citizen and Dramatist* (London: Weidenfeld and Nicolson, 1980).
Bradbrook, Muriel, *Themes and Conventions in Elizabethan Drama* (Cambridge: Cambridge University Press, 1960).
Bray, Alan, *Homosexuality in Renaissance England* (London: Gay Men's Press, 1982).
Briggs, John C., *Francis Bacon and the Rhetoric of Nature* (London: Harvard University Press, 1989).
Brinkworth, E. R. C., *Shakespeare and the Bawdy Court of Stratford* (London: Phillmore, 1972).
Brooks, C. W., *Pettifoggers and Vipers of the Commonwealth: The 'Lower Branch' of the Legal Profession in Early Modern England* (Cambridge: Cambridge University Press, 1986).
Bryson, Anna, *From Courtesy to Civility: Changing Codes of Conduct in Early Modern England* (Oxford: Oxford University Press, 1998).
'The Rhetoric of Status: Gesture, Demeanour and the Image of the Gentleman in Sixteenth- and Seventeenth-Century England', in Lucy Gent and Nigel Llewellyn, eds., *Renaissance Bodies: The Human Figure in English Culture c.1540–1660* (London: Reaktion, 1990).
Bullen, Paul, 'Lawmakers and Ordinary People in Aristotle', in Leslie G. Rubin, ed., *Justice v. Law in Greek Political Thought* (Lanham, Maryland: Rowman & Littlefield, 1997).
Bury, Shirley, *An Introduction to Rings* (London: HMSO, 1984).
Calhoun, Craig, ed., *Habermas and the Public Sphere* (London: MIT Press, 1992).
Capp, Bernard, *English Almanacs 1500–1800: Astrology and the Popular Press* (Ithaca, NY: Cornell University Press, 1979).
'Life, Love and Litigation: Sileby in the 1630s', *Past & Present*, 182 (February 2004), 55–83.

Carlson, Eric Josef, *Marriage and the English Reformation* (Oxford: Blackwell, 1994).

Cave, Terence, *Recognitions* (Oxford: Oxford University Press, 1988).

Cerasano, Susan, 'Philip Henslowe, Simon Forman and the Theatrical Community of the 1590s', *Shakespeare Quarterly*, 44 (1993), 145–58.

Chitty, Joseph, *A Practical Treatise on Pleading, and on the Parties to Actions, and the Form of Actions*, 2 vols., Vol. I (New York: W. Clarke, 1812).

Cirlot, J. E., *A Dictionary of Symbols*, trans. Jack Sage (London: Routledge & Kegan Paul, 1971).

Clark, Stuart, *Thinking with Demons: The Idea of Witchcraft in Early Modern Europe* (Oxford: Clarendon Press, 1997).

Clarke, M. L., *Classical Education in Britain* (Cambridge: Cambridge University Press, 1959).

Colish, Marcia L., *The Mirror of Language: A Study in the Medieval Theory of Knowledge* (London: Yale University Press, 1968).

Collier, John Payne, *The History of English Dramatic Poetry to the Time of Shakespeare* (London: John Murray, 1831).

Collinson, Patrick, *From Iconoclasm to Iconophobia* (Reading: University of Reading Press, 1986).

Collum, Eric, '"Sinister Shifts" and "Secreat Exceptions": Early Modern Legal Hermeneutics and John Day's *Law-Tricks*', *Explorations in Renaissance Culture*, 28.2 (Winter 2002), 285–11.

Cook, Anne Jennalie, *Making a Match: Courtship in Shakespeare and His Society* (Princeton: Princeton University Press, 1991).

Cooper, J. C., *An Illustrated Encyclopaedia of Traditional Symbols* (London: Thames & Hudson, 1978).

Croft, Pauline, 'Wardship in the Parliament of 1604', *Parliamentary History*, 2 (1983), 39–48.

Cust, Richard, 'News and Politics in Early Seventeenth-Century England', *Past and Present*, 112 (1986), 60–90.

Daston, L., 'Marvelous Facts and Miraculous Evidence in Early Modern Europe', *Critical Inquiry*, 18.119 (1991), 93–124.

Davis, Natalie Zemon, *Fiction in the Archives: Pardon Tales and their Tellers in Sixteenth-Century France* (Stanford: Stanford University Press, 1987).
  The Return of Martin Guerre (Cambridge, Mass.: Harvard University Press, 1983).

Decicco, Lynne Marie, *Women and Lawyers in the Mid-Nineteenth-Century Novel: Uneasy Alliances and Narrative Misrepresentation* (Lewiston: Edwin Mellen Press, 1996).

Dent, R. W., *John Webster's Borrowing* (Berkeley: University of California Press, 1960).

Derrett, J. D. M., 'Henry Swinburne (?1551–1624), Civil Lawyer of York', *Borthwick Papers*, 44 (York, 1973).

Derrida, Jacques, 'The Law of Genre', *Glyph*, 7 (1980), 202–32.

Of Grammatology, trans. Gayatri Chakravorty Spivak (Baltimore: Johns Hopkins University Press, 1974).

Writing and Difference, trans. Alan Bass (London: Routledge & Kegan Paul, 1985, revised edn; first pub. 1978).

Desens, Marliss C., *The Bed-Trick in English Renaissance Drama: Explorations in Gender, Sexuality, and Power* (London: Associated University Press, 1994).

Dibdin, Lewis and Chadwyck Healy, C. E. H., *English Church Law and Divorce* (London: John Murray, 1912).

Dolan, Frances, *Dangerous Familiars: Representations of Domestic Crimes in England, 1550–1700* (London: Cornell University Press, 1994).

Dollimore, Jonathan, *Radical Tragedy* (London: Harvester Wheatsheaf, 1989, 2nd edn; first pub. 1984).

Donaldson, Ian, *Jonson's Magic Houses: Essays in Interpretation* (Oxford: Clarendon Press, 1997).

Doniger, Wendy, *The Bedtrick: Tales of Sex and Masquerade* (Chicago: Chicago University Press, 2000).

Doran, Madeleine, *Endeavours of Art: A Study of Form in Elizabethan Drama* (Madison: University of Wisconsin Press, 1954).

Doyle, Sheila, 'Research Notes: An Uncompleted Work by Henry Swinburne on Matrimony', *Legal History*, 19.2 (1998), 162–72.

Drinker Bowen, Catherine, *The Lion and the Throne: The Life and Times of Sir Edward Coke (1552–1634)* (London: Hamilton, 1957).

Duffy, Eamon, *The Stripping of the Altars: Traditional Religion in England 1400–1580* (New Haven and London: Yale University Press, 1992).

Eden, Kathy, *Poetic and Legal Fiction in the Aristotelian Tradition* (Princeton: Princeton University Press, 1986).

Elias, Norbert, *The Civilizing Process* (Oxford: Blackwell, 1986).

Emmison, F. G., *Elizabethan Life: Morals and the Church Courts: Mainly from Essex Archdiaconal Records* (Chelmsford: Essex Record Office, 1973).

Erickson, Amy Louise, *Women and Property in Early Modern England* (London: Taylor and Francis, 1995; first pub. 1993).

Evans, G. R., *Problems of Authority in the Reformation Debates* (Cambridge: Cambridge University Press, 1992).

Evans, Joan, *English Posies and Posy Rings* (London: Oxford University Press, 1931).

Ewen, C. L'Estrange, *Witchcraft and Demonianism: The Indictment for Witchcraft from the Records of 1373 Assizes Held for the Home Circuit AD 1559–1736* (London: Kegan Paul, 1929).

Fischer, Sandra K., *Econolingua: A Glossary of Coins and Economic Language in Renaissance Drama* (Newark: University of Delaware Press, 1985).

Flannery, Denis, 'Law, Judgement and Revenge in Henry James', *Law and Critique*, 3.1 (1992), 69–97.

Fletcher, Giles, the elder, *The English Works of Giles Fletcher the Elder*, ed. L. E. Berry (Madison: University of Wisconsin Press, 1964).

Foster, F. A., 'Dumb Show in Elizabethan Drama before 1620', *Englische Studien*, 44 (1912), 8–17.

Franklin, James, *The Science of Conjecture: Evidence and Probability before Pascal* (Baltimore: Johns Hopkins University Press, 2001).

Frevert, Ute, *Men of Honour: A Social and Cultural History of the Duel* (Cambridge: Cambridge University Press, 1995).

Friedman, Alice T., *House and Household in Elizabethan England: Wollaton Hall and the Willoughby Family* (Chicago: Chicago University Press, 1989).

Fumerton, Patricia, *Cultural Aesthetics: Renaissance Literature and the Practice of Social Ornament* (Chicago: Chicago University Press, 1991).

Gaskill, Malcolm, 'Attitudes to Crime in Early Modern England', with Special Reference to Witchcraft, Coining and Murder', Ph.D. thesis (Cambridge, 1994).

'Reporting Murder: Fiction in the Archives in Early Modern England', *Social History*, 23 (1998), 1–30.

'Witchcraft and Power in Early Modern England: The Case of Margaret Moore', in Jenny Kermode and Garthine Walker, eds., *Women, Crime and the Courts in Early Modern England* (London: UCL Press, 1994), 125–45.

Gibbons, Brian, ed., *Elizabethan and Jacobean Tragedies* (Tonbridge, Kent: Benn, 1984).

Gillis, John R., *For Better, For Worse: British Marriages from 1600 to the Present* (Oxford: Oxford University Press, 1985).

Gilman, Ernest B., *The Curious Perspective: Literary and Pictorial Wit in the Seventeenth Century* (New Haven and London: Yale University Press, 1978).

Gittings, Clare, *Death, Burial and the Individual in Early Modern England* (London: Croom Helm, 1984).

Giulani, A., 'The Influence of Rhetoric on the Law of Evidence and Pleading', *Juridical Review*, 7 (1962), 216–52.

Gombrich, E. H., *The Image and the Eye: Further Studies in the Psychology of Pictorial Representation* (Oxford: Phaidon, 1982).

Goodrich, Peter, '*Amici curiae*: Lawful Manhood and Other Juristic Performances in Renaissance England', in *Literature, Politics and Law in Renaissance England*, ed. Erica Sheena and Lorna Hutson (Basingstoke: Palgrave Macmillan, 2005), 23–49.

'Gay Science and the Law', in Victorian Kahn and Lorna Hutson, eds., *Rhetoric and Law in Early Modern Europe* (New Haven and London: Yale University Press, 2001).

'Law', in T. Sloane, ed., *Encyclopaedia of Rhetoric* (Oxford: Oxford University Press, 2001).

Legal Discourse: Studies in Linguistics, Rhetoric and Legal Analysis (Basingstoke: Macmillan, 1987).

Oedipus Lex: Psychoanalysis, History, Law (Berkeley: University of California Press, 1995).

Goody, Jack, *Food and Love: A Cultural History of East and West* (London: Verso, 1998).

Gowing, Laura, *Domestic Dangers: Women, Words, and Sex in Early Modern England* (Oxford: Clarendon Press, 1996).

'Language, Power and the Law: Women's Slander Litigation in Early Modern London', in Jenny Kermode and Garthine Walker, eds., *Women, Crime and the Courts* (London: UCL Press, 1994), 26–47.

Greaves, Richard L., *Society and Religion in Elizabethan England* (Minneapolis: University of Minnesota Press, 1981).

Green, Thomas Andrew, *Twelve Good Men and True: The Criminal Trial Jury in England, 1200–1800* (Princeton: Princeton University Press, 1988).

Verdict According to Conscience: Perspectives on the English Criminal Trial Jury, 1200–1800 (Chicago: Chicago University Press, 1985).

Greenblatt, Stephen, *Shakespearean Negotiations: The Circulation of Social Energy in Renaissance England* (Oxford: Clarendon Press, 1990).

Grimm, Harold, *The Reformation Era 1500–1650* (New York: Macmillan, 1954).

Gurr, Andrew, *The Shakespearean Stage, 1574–1642* (Cambridge: Cambridge University Press, 1982, 2nd edn; first pub. 1980).

Guy, John, *The Court of Star Chamber and its Records to the Reign of Elizabeth I* (London: HMSO, 1985).

Haberman, Ina, '"She has that in her belly will dry up your ink": Femininity as Challenge in the "Equitable Drama" of John Webster', in *Lietrature, Politics and Law in Renaissance England* (London: Palgrave Macmillan, 2005).

Habermas, Jürgens, *The Structural Transformation of the Public Sphere: An Inquiry into a Category of Bourgeois Society*, trans. Thomas Burger (Cambridge: Polity, 1992).

Hacking, Ian, *The Emergence of Probability: A Philosophical Study of Early Ideas of Probability, Induction and Statistical Inference* (Cambridge: Cambridge University Press, 1975).

Hair, P., ed., *Before the Bawdy Court: Selections from Church Courts and Other Records Relating to the Correction of Moral Offences in England, Scotland and New England, 1300–1800* (London: Elek, 1972).

Hall, Hubert, 'Some Elizabethan Penances in the Diocese of Ely', *Transactions of the Royal Historical Society*, 3rd series, 1 (1907), 263–77.

Hall, Kim, *Things of Darkness: Economies of Race and Gender in Early Modern England* (Ithaca: Cornell University Press, 1995).

Hanson, Elizabeth, *Discovering the Subject in Renaissance England* (Cambridge: Cambridge University Press, 1998).

Harris, Jonathan Gil and Korda, Natasha, *Staged Properties in Early Modern English Drama* (Cambridge: Cambridge University Press, 2003).

Heinemann, Margot, *Puritanism and the Theatre* (Cambridge: Cambridge University Press, 1980).

Heinzelman, Susan, 'Women's Petty Treason: Feminism, Narrative, and the Law', *Journal of Narrative Technique*, 20 (1990), 89–106.

Heinzelman, Susan and Wiseman, Zipporah, eds., *Representing Women: Law, Literature and Feminism* (London: Duke University Press, 1994).

Helmholz, R. H., *Marriage Litigation in Medieval England* (Cambridge: Cambridge University Press, 1974).

   Roman Canon Law in Reformation England (Cambridge: Cambridge University Press, 2004).

Herrick, Marvin, 'Comic Theory in the Sixteenth-Century', *Illinois Studies in Language and Literature*, 34.1 & 2.

Herrup, Cynthia B., *The Common Peace: Participation and the Criminal Law in Seventeenth-Century England* (Cambridge: Cambridge University Press, 1987).

   A House in Gross Disorder: Sex, Law and the Second Earl of Castlehaven (Oxford: Oxford University Press, 2000).

Hoffer, P. C. and Hull, N. E., *Murdering Mothers: Infanticide in England and New England 1558–1803* (New York: New York University Press, 1981).

Holdsworth, W. S., *A History of English Law*, 17 vols. (London: Metheun, 1922–72).

Holmes, C., 'Women: Witnesses and Witches', *Past and Present*, 140 (1993), 45–78.

Hopf, C., *Martin Bucer and the English Reformation* (Oxford: Blackwell, 1945).

Hosley, Richard, 'The Discovery-Space in Shakespeare's Globe', *Shakespeare Survey*, 12 (1959), 35–46.

Houlbrooke, Ralph, *Church Courts and the People during the English Reformation 1520–1570* (Oxford: Oxford University Press, 1979).

   'The Making of Marriage in Mid-Tudor England: Evidence from the Records of Matrimonial Contract Litigation', *Journal of Family History*, 10 (1985), 339–52.

Hudson, Geoffrey L., 'Negotiating for Blood-money: War Widows and the Courts in Seventeenth-century England', in Jenny Kermode and Garthine Walker, eds., *Women, Crime and the Courts* (London: UCL Press, 1994), 146–69.

Humphreys, S. C., 'The Evolution of Legal Process in Ancient Attica', in E. Gabba, ed., *Tria Corda: Scritti in onore di Arnaldo Momigliano* (Como: New Press, 1983), 229–51.

Hurstfield, Joel, *The Queen's Wards* (London: Longman, 1958).

Hutson, Lorna, 'Rethinking "the Spectacle of the Scaffold": Juridical Epistemologies and English Revenge Tragedy', *Representations* 89 (Winter 2005).

   The Usurer's Daughter: Male Friendship and Fictions of Women in Sixteenth-Century England (London: Routledge, 1994).

Hyams, Paul R., 'Trial by Ordeal: The Key to Proof in the Early Common Law', in M. S. Arnold et al., eds., *On the Laws and Customs of England: Essays in Honour of Samuel E. Thorne* (Chapel Hill: University of North Carolina Press, 1981), 91–126.

Ingram, Martin, *Church Courts, Sex and Marriage in England, 1570–1640* (Cambridge: Cambridge University Press, 1987).

'Spousal Litigation in the English Ecclesiastical Courts, *c.*1350–1640', in R. B. Outhwaite, ed., *Marriage and Society: Studies in the Social History of Marriage* (London: Europa, 1981), 35–57.

Jardine, Lisa, *Francis Bacon: Discovery and the Art of Discourse* (Cambridge: Cambridge University Press, 1974).

Johansson, Bertil, *Law and Lawyers in Elizabethan England as Evidenced in the plays of Ben Jonson and Thomas Middleton* (Stockholm: Almqvist & Wiksell, 1967).

Jones, Emrys, 'The First West-End Comedy', *Proceedings of the British Academy*, 68 (1982), 205–58.

Joseph, Sister Miriam, *Shakespeare's Use of the Arts of Language* (New York: Hafner, 1966, 3rd edn; first pub. 1947).

Kassell, Lauren, 'Simon Forman's Philosophy of Medicine: Medicine, Astrology and Alchemy in London, c.1580–1611', D. Phil thesis (Oxford University, 1997).

Kelley, Donald R., *History, Law and the Human Sciences: Medieval and Renaissance Perspectives* (London: Variorum Reprints, 1984).

'"Second Nature": The Idea of Custom in European Law, Society and Culture', in *The Transmission of Culture in Early Modern Europe*, ed. Anthony Grafton and Anne Blair (Philadelphia: University of Pennsylvania Press, 1990), 31–72.

Kendall, R. T., *Calvin and English Calvinism* (Oxford: Oxford University Press, 1979).

Kermode, Jenny and Walker, Garthine, eds., *Women, Crime and the Courts* (London: UCL Press, 1994).

Kerrigan, John, *Revenge Tragedy: Aeschylus to Armageddon* (Oxford: Oxford University Press, 1997; first pub. 1996).

Kerrigan, John, ed., *Motives of Woe: Shakespeare and 'Female Complaint'* (Oxford: Oxford University Press, 1991).

Kibbey, Anne, *The Interpretation of Material Shapes in Puritanism: A Study of Rhetoric, Prejudice, and Violence* (Cambridge: Cambridge University Press, 1986).

Kiernan, V. G. ed., *The Duel in European History* (Oxford: Oxford University Press, 1988).

Kopperman, Paul E., *Sir Robert Heath 1575–1649: Window on an Age* (London: Royal Historical Society, 1989).

Kunz, George Frederick, *Rings for the Finger* (Philadelphia: J. B. Lippincott, 1917).

Kusukawa, Sachiko, 'Aspectio divinorum operum: Melanchthon and Astrology for Lutheran Medics', in *Medicine and the Reformation*, ed. Ole Grell and A. R. Cunningham (London: Routledge, 1993), 33–56.

'Providence Made Visible: The Creation and Establishment of Lutheran Natural Philosophy', Ph.D. thesis (Cambridge University, 1991).

Langbein, J., *Prosecuting Crime in the Renaissance* (Cambridge, MA: Harvard University Press, 1974).

Lea, Henry C., *Superstition and Force: Essays on The Wager of Law – The Wager of Battle – The Ordeal – Torture* (Philadelphia: H. C. Lee, 1978).

Legal London: an Exhibition in the Great Hall of the Royal Courts of Justice (London: Royal Courts of Justice, 1971).

Lindley, David, 'The Stubbornness of Barnardine: Justice and Mercy in *Measure for Measure*', *Shakespeare Jahrbuch*, 97 (1996), 333–51.

The Trials of Frances Howard: Fact and Fiction at the Court of King James (London: Routledge, 1993).

Llewellyn, Nigel, *The Art of Death: Visual Culture in the English Death Ritual c.1500–c.1800* (London: Reaktion, 1991).

'Honour in Life, Death and in the Memory: Funeral Monuments in Early Modern England', *Transactions of the Royal Historical Society*, 6 (1996), 179–200.

'The Royal Body: Monuments to the Dead, For the Living', in *Renaissance Bodies: The Human Figure in English Culture c.1540–1660*, ed. Lucy Gent and Nigel Llewellyn (London: Reaktion, 1990).

Loomba, Ania, *Gender, Race, Renaissance Drama* (Manchester: Manchester University Press, 1989).

Macdowell, Douglas M., *The Law in Classical Athens* (London: Thames and Hudson, 1978).

Maclean, Ian, *Interpretation and Meaning in the Renaissance* (Cambridge: Cambridge University Press, 1992).

Macnair, Michael, *Law of Proof in Early Modern Equity* (Berlin: Duncker and Humblot, 1999).

'Reading the Evidence: The Use of Depositions and Confessions in Early Modern Criminal Trials and the Self-image of the Common Law', paper delivered at the 'Renaissance Law and Literature' conference, Oxford, 1998.

Marshburn, J. H., *Murder and Witchcraft in England, 1550–1640* (Norman: University of Oklahoma Press, 1971).

Marston, John, *The Selected Plays of John Marston*, ed. Macdonald P. Jackson and Michael Neill (Cambridge: Cambridge University Press, 1986).

Martin, Julian, *Francis Bacon, the State, and the Reform of Natural Philosophy* (Cambridge: Cambridge University Press, 1992).

Martz, Louis L., *The Poetry of Meditation* (New Haven: Yale University Press, 1962).

Maus, Katharine Eisaman, *Inwardness and the Theater in the English Renaissance* (Chicago: Chicago University Press, 1995).

McCabe, Richard A., *Incest, Drama and Nature's Law 1550–1700* (Cambridge: Cambridge University Press, 1993).

McGinn, Donald, *The Admonition Controversy* (New Brunswick: Rutgers University Press, 1949).

McIntyre, Bronwyn, 'Legal Attitudes Towards Women in England, 1550–1750', MA thesis (University of New Brunswick, 1972).

McLelland, Joseph C., *The Visible Words of God: An Exposition of the Sacramental Theology of Peter Martyr Vermigli* (Edinburgh: Oliver and Boyd, 1957).

Megarry, Robert, *Inns Ancient and Modern* (London: Selden Society, 1972).

Mehl, Dieter, *The Elizabethan Dumb Show: The History of a Dramatic Convention* (London: Methuen, 1964).

Mercer, Eric, *English Vernacular Houses: A Study of Traditional Farmhouses and Cottages* (London: HMSO, 1975).

Merton, Charlotte, 'The Women who Served Queen Mary and Queen Elizabeth: Ladies, Gentlewomen and Maids of the Privy Chamber 1553–1603', Ph.D. thesis (Cambridge University, 1992).

Minnis, A. J., *Medieval Theory of Authorship: Scholastic Literary Attitudes in the Later Middle Ages* (London: Scolar Press, 1984).

Minnis, A. J. and Scott, A. B. with Wallace, David, eds., *Medieval Literary Theory and Criticism c.1100–c.1375: The Commentary Tradition* (Oxford: Clarendon Press, 1988).

Mish, Charles C., 'Best Sellers in Seventeenth-Century Fiction', *Papers of the Bibliographical Society of America*, 47 (1953).

Muir, Edward, *Ritual in Early Modern Europe* (Cambridge: Cambridge University Press, 1997).

Mukherji, Subha, '"Lawfull Deede": Consummation, Custom and Law in Shakespeare's *All's Well that Ends Well*', *Shakespeare Survey*, 49 (1996), 181–200; reprinted in Catherine Alexander and Stanley Wells, eds., *Shakespeare and Sexuality* (Cambridge: Cambridge University Press, 2001); reprinted again in Catherine Alexander, ed., *The Cambridge Shakespeare Library* (Cambridge: Cambridge University Press, 2003), 3 vols., Vol. I (*Shakespeare's Times, Texts and Stages*), 270–87.

'"Unmanly Indignities": Adultery, Evidence and Judgement in Heywood's *A Woman Killed with Kindness*', in *Literature, Politics and Law in Renaissance England*, ed. Erica Sheena and Lorna Hutson (Basingstoke: Palgrave Macmillan, 2005).

Muldrew, Craig, 'Women, Debt Litigation and Credit in Early Modern England', paper delivered during Lent Term at the Social and Economic History Seminar, Cambridge University (2000).

The Economy of Obligations: The Culture of Credit and Social Relations in Early Modern England (Basingstoke: Macmillan, 1998).

Nelson, A. H., ed., *Records of Early English Drama*, 2 vols. (Toronto: Toronto University Press, 1989).

Newman, Karen, 'Portia's Ring: Unruly Women and Structures of Exchange in *The Merchant of Venice*', *Shakespeare Quarterly*, 38 (1987), 19–33.

Nussbaum, Martha, *Love's Knowledge: Essays on Philosophy and Literature* (Oxford: Oxford University Press, 1990).

Nuttall, A. D., '*Measure for Measure*: The Bed-trick', in *The Stoic in Love: Selected Essays on Literature and Ideas*' (Savage, Maryland: Barnes & Noble, 1989).

'*Measure for Measure*: Quid Pro Quo', *Shakespeare Studies*, 4 (1968), 231–51.

'*A Midsummer Night's Dream*: Comedy as Apotrope of Myth', *Shakespeare Survey*, 53 (2000), 49–59.

A New Mimesis: Shakespeare and the Representation of Reality (London: Methuen, 1983).

O'Hara, Diana, *Courtship and Constraint: Rethinking the Making of Marriage in Tudor England* (Manchester: Manchester University Press, 2000).

Oldham, J. C., 'On Pleading the Belly: A History of the Jury of Matrons', *Criminal Justice History*, 6 (1985), 1–64.

Orlin, Lena Cowen, '"The Causes and Reasons of All Artificial Things" in the Elizabethan Domestic Environment', *Medieval and Renaissance Drama in England*, 7 (1994), 19–75.

Private Matters and Public Culture in Post-Reformation England (Ithaca: Cornell University Press, 1994).

Owen, Geraint Dyfnallt, *Elizabethan Wales: The Social Scene* (Cardiff: University of Wales Press, 1962).

Parker, Patricia, *Literary Fat Ladies: Rhetoric, Gender, Property* (London: Methuen, 1987).

Partridge, Eric, *Shakespeare's Bawdy* (London: Routledge & Kegan Paul, 1961, 3rd edn; first pub. 1955).

Patey, Douglas, *Probability and Literary Form: Philosophic Theory and Literary Practice in the Augustan Age* (Cambridge: Cambridge University Press, 1984).

Pearn, B. R., 'Dumb-Show in Elizabethan Drama', *Review of Elizabethan Studies*, 2 (1935), 385–405.

Pederson, F., 'Marriage Litigation and the Ecclesiastical Courts of York in the Fourteenth Century', Ph.D. thesis (University of Toronto, 1991).

Peek, Heather and Hall, Catherine P., *The Archives of the University of Cambridge: An Historical Introduction* (Cambridge: Cambridge University Press, 1962).

Platt, Colin, *The Great Rebuildings of Tudor and Stuart England: Revolutions in Architectural Taste* (London: UCL Press, 1994).

Plucknett, T. F., *Early English Legal Literature* (Cambridge: Cambridge University Press, 1958).

Pollock, Linda A., 'Living on the Stage of the World: The Concept of Privacy in Early Modern England', in *Rethinking Social History: English Society 1570–1920 and Its Interpretation*, ed. Adrian Wilson (Manchester: Manchester University Press, 1993), 78–96.

Pollock, William and Maitland, Frederic, *The History of English Law before the time of Edward I*, ed. S. F. C. Milsom, 2 vols. (Cambridge: Cambridge University Press, 1968).

Porter, Martin, 'English Treatises on Physiognomy c.1500–c.1780, D.Phil thesis (Oxford, 1998), published as *Windows of the Soul: Physiognomy in European Culture c.1500–1800* (Oxford: Oxford University Press, 2005).

Posner, Richard, *Law and Literature: A Misunderstood Relation* (Cambridge, MA: Harvard University Press, 1988).

Prest, W. R., *The Inns of Court under Elizabeth I and the Early Stuarts: 1590–1640* (London: Longman, 1972).

'Law and Women's Rights in Early Modern England', *The Seventeenth Century*, 6 (1991), 169–87.

Raymond, Joad, *The Invention of the Newspaper: English Newsbooks 1641–1649* (Oxford: Clarendon Press, 1996).

Reynolds, G. F., *The Staging of Elizabethan Plays at the Red Bull Theatre 1605–1625* (London: Oxford University Press, 1940).

'"Trees" on the Stage of Shakespeare', *Modern Philology*, 5 (1907), 153–68.

Richardson, Catherine, 'Properties of Domestic Life: The Table in *A Woman Killed with Kindness*', in *Staged Properties in Early Modern English Drama*, ed. Jonathan Gil Harris and Natasha Korda (Cambridge: Cambridge University Press, 2002), 129–52.

Roberts, Sasha, '"Let me the curtains draw": The Dramatic and Symbolic Properties of the Bed in Shakespearean Tragedy', in *Staged Properties in Early Modern English Drama*, ed. Jonathan Gil Harris and Natasha Korda (Cambridge: Cambridge University Press, 2002), 153–74.

Robbins, R. H., *The Encyclopaedia of Witchcraft and Demonology* (London: P. Nevill, 1960).

Rollins, H. R., ed., *Old English Ballads 1553–1625* (Cambridge: Cambridge University Press, 1920).

Rushton, Peter, 'The Testaments of Gifts: Marriage Tokens and Disputed Contracts in North-East England, 1560–1630', *Folk Life*, 24 (1985–6), 25–31.

Rutter, Carol, *Clamorous Voices: Shakespeare's Women Today*, ed. Faith Evans (London: Women's Press, 1994, 3rd edn; first pub. 1988).

Sacks, David Harris, 'The Promise and the Contract in Early Modern England: Slade's Case in Perspective', in *Rhetoric & Law in Early Modern Europe*, ed. Victoria Kahn and Lorna Hutson (New Haven and London: Yale University Press, 2001), 28–53.

Sartre, Jean Paul, 'Interview with Kenneth Tynan' (1961), reprinted in *Sartre on Theatre*, ed. Michael Contat and Michel Rybalka, trans. Frank Jellinek (London: Quartet Books, 1976), 121–34.

Schama, Simon, *The Embarrassment of Riches* (New York: Knopf, 1987).

Schochet, Gordon, ed., *Law, Literature, and the Settlement of Regimes: Papers Presented at the Folger Institute Seminar 'Political Thought in the Elizabethan Age, 1558–1603'*, directed by Donald Kelley (Washington, DC: Folger Institute, 1990).

Schramm, Jan-Melissa, *Testimony and Advocacy in Victorian Law, Literature, and Theology* (Cambridge: Cambridge University Press, 2000).

Segalen, Martine, *Love and Power in the Peasant Family* (Chicago: Chicago University Press, 1983).

Serjeantson, R. W., 'Testimony and Proof in Early-Modern England', *Studies in History and Philosophy of Science*, 2 (1999), 195–236.

Shapiro, Barbara, *'Beyond Reasonable Doubt' and 'Probable Cause': Historical Perspectives on the Anglo-American Law of Evidence* (Berkeley: University of California Press, 1991).

'Classical Rhetoric and the English Law of Evidence', in *Rhetoric and Law in Early Modern Europe*, ed. Victorian Kahn and Lorna Hutson (New Haven/London: Yale University Press, 2001), 54–72.

A Culture of Fact; England, 1550–1730 (Ithaca and London: Cornell University Press, 2000).

Probability and Certainty in Seventeenth Century England: A Study of Relationships between Natural Science, Religion, History, Law and Literature (Princeton: Princeton University Press, 1983).

Shapiro, Michael, *Children of the Revels: The Boy Companies of Shakespeare's Time and their Plays* (New York: Columbia University Press, 1977).

Sharpe, J. A., *Defamation and Sexual Slander in Early Modern England: The Church Courts at York*, Borthwick Papers, 58 (York: Borthwick Institute of Historical Research, 1980).

Instruments of Darkness: Witchcraft in England 1550–1750 (London: Hamish Hamilton, 1996).

Judicial Punishment in England (London: Faber, 1990).

'Women, Witchcraft and the Legal Process', in *Women, Crime and the Courts in Early Modern England*, ed. Jenny Kermode and Garthine Walker (London: UCL Press, 1994), 106–24.

Sheehan, M. M., 'The Formation and Stability of Marriage in Fourteenth-Century England: Evidence from an Ely Register', *Medieval Studies*, 33 (1971), 228–63.

Sheen, Erica and Hutson, Lorna, eds., *Literature, Politics and the Law in Renaissance England* (Basingstoke: Palgrave Macmillan, 2005).

Shell, Alison, *Catholicism, Controversy and the English Literary Imagination 1558–1660* (Cambridge: Cambridge University Press, 1999).

Shepard, Alexandra, 'Meanings of Manhood in Early Modern England, with Special Reference to Cambridge, c.1560–1640', Ph.D. thesis (Cambridge University, 1998).

Shoeck, R. J., 'Lawyers and Rhetoric in Sixteenth-Century England', in *Renaissance Eloquence*, ed. James J. Murphy (Berkeley: University of California Press, 1983), 274–91.

'Rhetoric and Law in Sixteenth-Century England', *Studies in Philology*, 50 (1953), 110–27.

Shorter, Edward, *The Making of the Modern Family* (London: Collins, 1976).

Shuger, Debora K., *Sacred Rhetoric: The Christian Grand Style in the English Renaissance* (Princeton: Princeton University Press, 1988).

Sidney, Sir Philip, *An Apology for Poetry*, ed. Geoffrey Shepherd (London: T. Nelson, 1965).

Simpson, A. W. B., *A History of the Common Law of Contract: The Rise of the Action of Assumpsit* (Oxford: Clarendon Press, 1987).

Singer, Irving, *The Nature of Love*, 3 vols., Vols. I and III (Chicago: Chicago University Press, 1987).

Sisson, C. J., *Lost Plays of Shakespeare's Age* (London: F. Cass, 1970, 2nd edn; first pub 1936).

Skinner, Quentin, *Reason and Rhetoric in the Philosophy of Hobbes* (Cambridge: Cambridge University Press, 1996).

Skipp, Victor, *Crisis and Development: An Ecological Case-Study of the Forest of Arden 1570–1674* (Cambridge: Cambridge University Press, 1978).

Slater, Miriam, 'The Weightiest Business: Marriage in an Upper Gentry Family in Seventeenth Century England', *Past & Present*, 72 (1976), 25–54.

Smith, Irwin, *Shakespeare's Globe Playhouse* (New York: Charles Scribner's Sons, 1956).

Sokol, B. J. and Sokol, Mary, *Shakespeare, Law, and Marriage* (Cambridge: Cambridge University Press, 2003).

Sommerville, Johann P., 'The "New Art of Lying": Equivocation, Mental Reservation and Casuistry', in *Conscience and Casuistry in Early Modern Europe*, ed. Edmund Leites (Cambridge: Cambridge University Press), 159–84.

Sonnino, Lee A., *A Handbook to Sixteenth-Century Rhetoric* (London: Routledge & Kegan Paul, 1968).

Steadman, John M., *The Hill and the Labyrinth: Discourse and Certitude in Milton and his Near-Contemporaries* (Berkeley: University of California Press, 1984).

Stephen, Harry L., 'The Trial of Sir Walter Raleigh', *Transactions of the Royal Historical Society*, 4th series, Vol. II (1919), 172–87.

Stephen, James, *A History of the Criminal Laws of England*, 3 vols., Vol. I (London: Macmillan, 1883).

Stewart, Alan, 'The Early Modern Closet Discovered', *Representations*, 50 (Spring 1995), 76–100.

Stone, Julius, *Evidence: Its History and Policies* (Sydney: Butterworths, 1991).

Stone, Lawrence, *The Family, Sex and Marriage in England, 1500–1800* (London: Weidenfeld & Nicolson, 1977).

The Past and the Present (London: Routledge & Kegan Paul, 1981).

Road To Divorce: England 1530–1987 (Oxford: Clarendon Press, 1990).

Stretton, Tim, *Women Waging Law in Elizabethan England* (Cambridge: Cambridge University Press, 1998).

Strong, Roy, *The English Icon* (London: Routledge & Kegan Paul, 1969).

Sugden, E. H., *A Topographical Dictionary to the Works of Shakespeare and His Fellow Dramatists* (Manchester: Manchester University Press, 1925).

Sullivan, Ceri, *Dismembered Rhetoric: English Recusant Writing, 1580–1603* (Madison: University of Wisconsin Press, 1995).

Sutherland, Donald K., 'Legal Reasoning in the Fourteenth Century: The Invention of "Color" in Pleading', in *On the Laws and Customs of England: Essays in Honour of Samuel E. Thorne*, ed. Morris S. Arnold, Thomas A. Green, Sally A. Scully and Stephen D. White (Chapel Hill: University of North Carolina Press, 1981), 182–94.

Tanner, J. R., ed., *The Historical register of Cambridge being a supplement to the Calendar with a record of university offices and honours and distinctions to the year 1910* (Cambridge: Cambridge University Press, 1917).

Tentler, Thomas N., *Sin and Confession on the Eve of the Reformation* (Princeton: Princeton University Press, 1977).

Thomas, Keith, 'Puritans and Adultery: The Act of 1650 Reconsidered', in *Puritans and Revolutionaries: Essays in Seventeenth-Century History Presented to Christopher Hill*, ed. D. Pennington and K. Thomas (Oxford: Clarendon Press, 1978).

Thompson, Stith, *Motif-Index of Folk-Literature*, 6 vols. (Copenhagen: Rosenkilde and Bagger, 1955–8).

Todd, Richard, *The Opacity of Signs: Acts of Interpretation in George Herbert's 'The Temple'* (Columbia: University of Missouri Press, 1986).

Todd, S. C., *The Shape of Athenian Law* (Oxford: Clarendon, 1993).

Todorov, Tzevetan, 'The Origins of Genre', *New Literary History*, 8.1 (Autumn 1976), 159–170.

Tomlinson, Brian Thomas, *A Study of Elizabethan and Jacobean Tragedy* (Cambridge: Cambridge University Press, 1964).

Travitsky, Betty, 'Husband-Murder and Petty Treason in English Renaissance Tragedy', *Renaissance Drama*, 21 (1990), 171–98.

Tucker, E. F. J., *Intruder Into Eden: Representations of the Common Lawyer in English Literature 1350–1750* (Columbia, South Carolina: Camden House, 1984).

Turner, Jane, ed., *The Dictionary of Art* (New York: Grove, 1996).

Underdown, D. E., 'The Taming of the Scold', in *Order and Disorder in Early Modern England*, ed. A. Fletcher and J. Stevenson (Cambridge: Cambridge University Press), 116–36.

Underwood, Malcolm, 'The Structure and Operation of the Oxford Chancellor's Court, from the Sixteenth to the Early Eighteenth Century', *Journal of the Society of Archivists*, 6 (1978), 18–27.

Vance, Eugene, *Mervelous Signals: Poetics and Sign Theory in the Middle Ages* (Lincoln: University of Nebraska Press, 1986).

Vickers, Brian, *Francis Bacon and Renaissance Prose* (Cambridge: Cambridge University Press, 1968).

Vickery, Amanda, *The Gentleman's Daughter: Women's Lives in Georgian England* (New Haven and London: Yale University Press, 1998).

'Golden Age to Separate Spheres? A Review of the Categories and Chronology of English Women's History', *Historical Journal* (1993), 384–414.

Vries, Ad de *Dictionary of Symbols and Imagery* (London: North-Holland, 1974).

Waage, Frederick O., *The White Devil Discover'd: Backgrounds and Foregrounds to Webster's Tragedy* (New York: Peter Lang, 1984).

Wallace, Karl R., *Francis Bacon on Communication & Rhetoric OR: The Art of Applying Reason to Imagination for the Better Moving of the Will* (Chapel Hill: University of North Carolina Press, 1943).

Walsham, Alexandra M., 'Aspects of Providentialism in Early Modern England', Ph.D. thesis (Cambridge University, 1994).

Providence in Early Modern England (Oxford: Oxford University Press, 1999).

Ward, Ian, *Law and Literature: Possibilities and Perspectives* (Cambridge: Cambridge University Press, 1995).

Shakespeare and the Legal Imagination (London: Butterworths, 1999).

Watt, Tessa, *Cheap Print and Popular Piety, 1550–1640* (Cambridge: Cambridge University Press, 1994; first pub. 1991).

Weisberg, Richard, *Poethics: And Other Strategies of Law and Literature* (New York: Columbia University Press, 1992).

Welsh, Alexander, *Strong Representations: Narrative and Circumstantial Evidence in England* (Baltimore: Johns Hopkins University Press, 1992).

White, Paul, 'Calvinist and Puritan Attitudes Towards the Renaissance Stage: A History of Conflict and Controversy', *Explorations in Renaissance Culture*, 14 (1988), 41–56.

Theatre and Reformation: Protestantism, Patronage and Playing in Tudor England (Cambridge: Cambridge University Press, 1993).

White, R. S., *Natural Law in English Renaissance Literature* (Cambridge: Cambridge University Press, 1996).

Wickham, Glynne, *Early English Stages* (London: Routledge & Kegan Paul, 1963).

Williams, E., *Early Holborn and the Legal Quarters of London: A Topographical Survey of the Beginnings of the District Known as Holborn and of the Inns of Court and of Chancery* (London: Sweet & Maxwell, 1927).

Wilson, Luke, *Theaters of Intention: Drama and the Law in Early Modern England* (Stanford: Stanford University Press, 2000).

Woodbridge, Linda, *Women and the English Renaissance: Literature and the Nature of Womankind 1540–1620* (Urbana: University of Illinois Press, 1984).

Wrightson, Keith, *English Society 1580–1680* (London: Hutchinson, 1982).

Zacks, Richard, *History Laid Bare: Love, Sex, and Perversity from the Ancient Etruscans to Warren G. Harding* (London: Michael O'Mara, 1995).

Zeldin, Theodore, *France: 1848–1945*, 2 vols., Vol. II (Oxford: Clarendon Press, 1933).

Index